The Definitive *Golden Girls* Cultural Reference Guide

Matt Browning

LYONS
PRESS

Guilford, Connecticut

An imprint of Globe Pequot, the trade division of
The Rowman & Littlefield Publishing Group, Inc.
4501 Forbes Blvd., Ste. 200
Lanham, MD 20706
www.rowman.com

Distributed by NATIONAL BOOK NETWORK

British Library Cataloguing in Publication Information available

Library of Congress Cataloging-in-Publication Data available

ISBN 978-1-4930-6035-1 (paper : alk. paper)
ISBN 978-1-4930-6337-6 (electronic)

♾™ The paper used in this publication meets the minimum requirements of American National
Standard for Information Sciences—Permanence of Paper for Printed Library Materials, ANSI/
NISO Z39.48-1992.

CONTENTS

Introduction

THEIR FAMILIAR FACES ADORN APPAREL, BOARD GAMES, PLAYING CARDS, coloring books, action figures, cross-stitch patterns, themed restaurants, and cruises—even breakfast cereal. Three decades after its finale, *The Golden Girls* is more popular than ever. The series remains as relevant today as it was during its original run, with new generations of audiences continuing to discover—and fall in love with—those four mature ladies in Miami.

Over the course of seven seasons and 180 episodes, *The Golden Girls* was a consistent Top 10 hit, yielding sixty-eight Emmy nominations, multiple spinoff shows, and millions of, as it turns out, *lifelong* devoted fans, with its biting observations and timeless humor about issues such as dating, sex, marriage, divorce, race, gender equality, gay rights, menopause, elderly care, AIDS, and more. And it is only continuing to gain momentum with new, younger viewers, many of whom weren't even alive when the show aired. Reruns are broadcast daily on multiple cable networks and are accessible through streaming all day, every day. Series star Betty White experienced a career resurgence in more recent years, amassing a universally beloved stature and millions of Twitter followers. With merchandise flooding store shelves and episodes available at the click of a button, it appears that *The Golden Girls* will be around forever.

Despite the timelessness of its humor, however, there is one aspect of *The Golden Girls* that firmly anchors it in its 1980s era, and it isn't Bea Arthur's scrunch boots or Rue McClanahan's shoulder pads. It is the sizable cache of dated references that were topical for the time period—and therefore got sizable laughs from the studio audience—but leave today's viewers, especially those of younger generations, scratching their heads. Every episode is laced with jokes about people, places, brands, and events that have been blurred, or even forgotten, by time.

Why would Gary Hart's campaign manager wear a nightgown? How could Robin Givens return a prizefighter? Was Sophia carrying Steve Garvey's baby? Does Bea Arthur actually look like Fess Parker in heels? So Danny Thomas *isn't* a lesbian? And—more importantly—who are all these people? Online chatter has rumbled for years on message boards and in news articles, with fans attempting to find the answers to such burning questions as "What was *Hee Haw*, and why did it have a cornfield?"

That brings us to this book. Meticulously researched episode by episode, my goal with *The Definitive* Golden Girls *Cultural Reference Guide* was to create an eye-opening, illuminating encyclopedia of "the who, the how, and the ha!" of hundreds of topical jokes. From Joe Isuzu to Socrates, Alan Alda to Shinola, Martha Raye to Madge, and *Ishtar* to *Tattletales*, I hope that you come away from reading this book saying, "Oh, *now* I get it!"

Now, settle in with the first episode, hold this book close, and follow along. It'll be a *Golden Girls* experience like none you've had before.

Or my name isn't Sophia P'Hawkins.

Season One: 1985–1986

In the show's debut season, we descend upon suburban Miami and meet our four heroines, who share their lives, loves, hopes, challenges, and countless cheesecakes as they move through their golden years together. The performances are stellar, the storylines are both timely and timeless, and the jokes are as funny decades later as they were in 1985. And in spite of all of these facts, it is evident from the first episode that much of the humor will rely on topical references, both of the day and of the decades before.

The pilot alone introduces names like Indira Gandhi and Julio Iglesias. Some names and brands require little to no explanation—Dr. Scholl's footwear is still around, and Coke and Abraham Lincoln are ubiquitous. Some wouldn't pack quite the punch as they did in 1985, like Polaroid or even Madonna, yet Chef Boyardee being an insult to a real Italian cook? Still funny.

Recurring themes emerge early on in this season. Burt Reynolds and his dinner theater come up early and often. And the popular-at-the-time *Miami Vice* is milked for humor. There are also plenty of brand names tossed out, mostly medications used to treat the aches and pains of older people.

There are politics, legendary comedians, nearly forgotten cartoons, and plenty more in season one.

Episode 1.1: Pilot

Directed by Jay Sandrich. Written by Susan Harris. Original airdate: September 14, 1985.

Blanche receives a marriage proposal from her new boyfriend, and Dorothy and Rose worry that she's moving too fast. Sophia moves in after Shady Pines burns down.

Reference: Benjamin Moore Paints

> **Dorothy, eyeing Blanche's makeup:** Would you look at this? She has more colors than Benjamin Moore Paints.

Founded in Brooklyn, New York, in 1883 by brothers Benjamin and Robert Moore, Benjamin Moore Paints began with one product before expanding to an entire line of paints. In 2020, the company became the official paint supplier to the Ace Hardware chain.

Reference: MCI

> **Rose:** You can communicate directly from your heart, can't you, Dorothy?
>
> **Dorothy:** Oh, don't ask me. I can't get through to New Jersey with MCI.

MCI is a telecommunications company, originally called Microwave Communications, Inc., founded in 1963.

Reference: The Resurrection

> **Rose:** We were all so lonely, and then by a miracle we found each other.
>
> **Dorothy:** Rose, we both answered an ad to share Blanche's house that we found in the supermarket. It was not the Resurrection. It is hardly a miracle.

The resurrection of Jesus is the Christian belief that God raised Jesus on the third day following his crucifixion, which is considered the most important foundation of the Christian faith and is commemorated by Easter.

Reference: Shotgun wedding

> **Rose:** You had a blowgun wedding?
>
> **Dorothy:** If you live in the Amazon. In Queens, it's called shotgun.

A shotgun wedding is one arranged hastily to avoid the embarrassment of an out-of-wedlock pregnancy, referring to the scenario of the bride's father forcing the groom to marry his daughter with a shotgun.

Reference: Mrs. Gandhi

> **Rose:** My hunches are never wrong. Mrs. Gandhi would be alive today if she had taken my call.

Indira Gandhi (1917–1984) was the first and only female prime minister of India, serving from 1966 to 1977 and again from 1980 until being shot to death by two of her bodyguards in 1984.

Reference: Julio Iglesias

> **Dorothy:** We've tried everything. Golf, the movies, theater tickets. She wouldn't even budge for Julio Iglesias.

Julio Iglesias is a Spanish performer considered one of the most successful European singers ever, with one hundred million record sales to his name.

Episode 1.2: Guess Who's Coming to the Wedding?

Directed by Paul Bogart. Written by Susan Harris. Original airdate: September 21, 1985.

Dorothy's daughter, Kate, arrives with news that she's off to the Bahamas to get married. The girls talk her into having the wedding in Miami, prompting a reunion between Dorothy and her cheating ex-husband, Stan.

Reference: Rand McNally

> **Dorothy:** My daughter is lost. Oh, I'm just terrible at giving directions.
>
> **Blanche:** Dorothy, I gave Kate the directions over the phone.
>
> **Dorothy:** And who are you, Rand McNally?

Rand McNally is a company founded in 1856 that has long been known for making maps.

Reference: Paul McCartney

> **Rose:** Do you think it's serious?
>
> **Dorothy:** Well, they've been together now for six months. It's the longest she's been interested in any man since Paul McCartney.

Paul McCartney is a British singer, songwriter, and musician known for being a member of The Beatles and for a long, successful solo career.

Reference: Harry Belafonte

> **Dorothy:** You are not getting married on an island by a priest wearing clamdiggers and a Harry Belafonte shirt. You are going to get married right here in Miami.

Harry Belafonte is a Jamaican American singer and actor known for such hits as "The Banana Boat Song" (Day-O) and "Jump in the Line," both of which bring to mind images from the film *Beetlejuice* for most of us. Belafonte has enjoyed a long, successful career, including multiple records as well as Grammys, an Emmy, and a Tony. He's also long been a humanitarian and activist.

Reference: Easter in Rotterdam

> **Dorothy:** Your father used to bring me tulips every time we had a fight. Toward the end our place looked like Easter in Rotterdam.

Easter marks the beginning of the tourist season in Rotterdam, a port city in the Dutch province of South Holland. The celebration draws thousands of tourists—and thousands of flowers.

Reference: Dr. Scholl

> **Rose, to Kate's podiatrist fiancé:** Have you ever met Dr. Scholl?

Dr. William Mathias Scholl (1882–1968) was a podiatrist who launched his famous brand of orthopedic foot-care products and shoes in 1906.

Reference: Abraham Lincoln

> **Dorothy:** She was the best Abraham Lincoln the third grade ever saw. When she freed the second grade, there was not a dry eye in the house.

Abraham Lincoln (1809–1865) was the sixteenth president of the United States from 1861 until his assassination in 1865. He served in the role during the American Civil War and the abolishment of slavery.

Reference: Donny Osmond

> **Sophia, upon seeing Stan's toupee:** Who invited Donny Osmond?

Donny Osmond is a singer, actor, TV host, and former teen idol, known as a member of the Osmond Brothers, for a successful solo career, and for his years performing and hosting a variety show—and later, a daytime talk show—with his sister, Marie. In recent years, he's had successful runs on *Dancing with the Stars* and *The Masked Singer*.

Reference: Lent

> **Priest, after eating one of Rose's cheese balls:** Now I know what I'm giving up for Lent.

Lent is the forty-day period before Easter during which many Christians reflect on and celebrate the death and resurrection of Jesus Christ.

Reference: Neil Diamond

> **Sophia:** You want poetry, you listen to Neil Diamond. You want good advice, you listen to your mother.

Singer-songwriter Neil Diamond has sold more than one hundred million albums worldwide. Among his biggest hits are "You Don't Bring Me Flowers," "America," and "Sweet Caroline." Diamond's decades-long career has led to such achievements as being inducted into the Songwriters Hall of Fame and Rock and Roll Hall of Fame, being a Kennedy Center Honors honoree, and receiving a Grammy Lifetime Achievement Award.

EPISODE 1.3: ROSE THE PRUDE

Directed by Jim Drake. Written by Barry Fanaro and Mort Nathan. Original airdate: September 28, 1985.

Rose is reluctant to accept an invitation for a cruise with her new boyfriend, Arnie (played by Harold Gould, who later has a recurring role as Miles Weber). Meanwhile, Dorothy attempts—and fails—to beat Sophia in gin rummy.

Reference: Miami Dolphins

> **Dorothy:** You go out with lots of interesting guys.
>
> **Blanche:** Name one.
>
> **Dorothy:** How about that coach from the Miami Dolphins?

The Dolphins are Miami's professional football team, established in 1965.

References: Willard Scott, *Today*

> **Sophia:** A bunch of us get together and send our pictures in to Willard Scott with a note saying we're a hundred.

Dorothy: Ma, that's ridiculous.

Sophia: You got a better way to get on the *Today* show?

Willard Scott is a television personality, actor, and comedian best known for his work as a weatherman on *Today*, in which he routinely wished centenarians a happy birthday. The long-running morning news and talk show has aired on NBC since 1952.

Reference: The French Quarter

Sophia, finding Rose and Arnie kissing on the front doorstep: Will you take it inside, Rose? This isn't the French Quarter.

The French Quarter is a popular neighborhood in New Orleans, Louisiana, famous for its vibrant nightlife, colorful buildings with cast-iron balconies, jazz clubs, eateries, and tourist draws like Bourbon Street and Jackson Square.

Reference: Coke

Blanche: Is this about Arnie?

Dorothy: No, Blanche, she's upset because they keep changing the taste of Coke.

Coca-Cola is a multinational beverage corporation founded in 1892, originally created by pharmacist John Stith Pemberton in Columbus, Georgia, who advertised it as a medicinal beverage to help treat headaches. The name stemmed from the original formula's two main ingredients, coca leaves and kola nuts. Since those days, Coca-Cola, or Coke for short, has become a household soda brand, expanded worldwide, and added several product lines (e.g., Diet Coke). In 1985, the company attempted to rebrand itself by altering its recipe and relaunching itself with the (unofficial) moniker New Coke. The attempt was considered a colossal failure and, three months later, the original formula was reintroduced and marketed as Coca-Cola Classic.

Reference: Glenn Miller

Rose: Oh, I love Glenn Miller. I met my husband at a Glenn Miller dance. It wasn't really the Glenn Miller Orchestra. It was Dick Singleton and the Singletones.

Glenn Miller (1904–1944) was a big band trombonist, composer, and bandleader from the swing era, known for hits like "In the Mood," "Moonlight

Serenade," and "Pennsylvania 6-5000." He scored sixteen number-one hits in four years. He joined the military in 1942 to entertain troops during World War II, and the aircraft he was in disappeared over the English Channel on December 15, 1944.

Reference: Actifed

> **Arnie:** I need to go into the bathroom, Rose. I hate to go anywhere without my Actifed.

Actifed was an over-the-counter antihistamine and nasal decongestant used to treat cold and allergy symptoms. Launched in 1958, the brand was around for decades but has been discontinued in the United States.

Reference: Chevrolet

> **Arnie:** Molly was my world, and then one day a drunk in a Chevy took my world away.

Chevrolet, known colloquially as Chevy, is an American automobile division of General Motors, founded by Louis Chevrolet and William C. Durant in 1911.

Reference: Charles Boyer

> **Sophia:** You and I had some of our best talks over a game of gin rummy. I don't know why, it just seemed easier for both of us to open up while we were playing cards. Your aunt Jean was the same way. During a pinochle game, she told me that she swam nude in a pool with Charles Boyer.

French actor Charles Boyer (1899–1978) rose to fame in America in the 1930s, with appearances in such films as *The Garden of Allah*, *Love Affair*, and *Gaslight*. His five-decade career resulted in four Best Actor Oscar nominations. He committed suicide by overdose in 1978, two days after his wife's death from cancer.

Reference: Jazzercise

> *Rose mentions Jazzercise while listing the activities aboard a cruise ship.*

Jazzercise is a dance fitness company founded by Judi Sheppard Missett in 1969 that gained momentum in the 1980s and still operates thousands of franchises all over the world.

Reference: O. Henry

> **Blanche:** Most of the boys I dated in college were just for the stories.
>
> **Dorothy:** You must have more stories than O. Henry.

O. Henry (1862–1910) was a celebrated short-story writer known for surprise twist endings. Among his most notable works are "The Gift of the Magi," "The Cop and the Anthem," and "The Duplicity of Hargraves." While the Oh Henry! candy bar has no connection to the writer, the O. Henry Award is a prestigious honor presented annually to exceptional short stories. Probably a more fitting legacy than a chocolate confection.

EPISODE 1.4: TRANSPLANT

Directed by Paul Bogart. Written by Susan Harris. Original airdate: October 5, 1985.

Blanche's sister, Virginia, visits with the news that she is dying from renal failure and needs a kidney transplant.

Reference: Nancy Reagan

> **Blanche:** Oh, I wish I'd gotten a decorator. Nancy Reagan's decorator. That'd kill my sister.

Nancy Reagan (1921–2016) was a former actress who became First Lady of the United States from 1981 to 1989, during the administration of her husband, Ronald Reagan.

Reference: Vaseline

> **Rose:** Sophia, if you hated your sister, would you clean the house?
>
> **Sophia:** I'd put Vaseline on the tips of her walker.

Vaseline is a brand of petroleum jelly–based products introduced in 1872.

Reference: Jack Daniel's

> **Blanche:** One Jack Daniel's and you'd disappear with half the fraternity house.

Jack Daniel's is a brand of Tennessee whiskey founded by its namesake in Lynchburg, Tennessee, in 1875. It's the best-selling American whiskey in the world.

Reference: Poodle skirt

> **Blanche:** All my life you've taken everything that ever meant anything to me.
>
> **Virginia:** What did I take, a couple of cashmere sweaters and a poodle skirt?

Poodle skirts date back to around 1947 but were popularized in the 1950s. The wide swing felt, solid-colored skirt featured an appliquéd design, typically of a poodle.

Reference: Fritos

> **Dorothy:** Ma, could you eat a little more quietly please?
>
> **Sophia:** These are Fritos. You want me to swallow them whole?

Fritos are a brand of corn chips created by Charles Elmer Doolin in 1932 and produced by Frito-Lay since 1959. While original-flavored Fritos have remained the brand's cornerstone, several flavors have been introduced over the years, including Bar-B-Q, Flamin' Hot, and Chili Cheese.

Reference: Pillsbury Doughboy

> **Blanche:** I need both my kidneys. You know what'll happen if I give her one. My ankles will swell, my eyes will puff up. I'll look just like the Pillsbury Doughboy.

The Pillsbury Doughboy is an advertising mascot for the Pillsbury Company, which makes various food products like boxed cake mixes, icing, and canned biscuits and cinnamon rolls. The doughboy actually has a name—Poppin' Fresh—and was first introduced in 1965. In a routine bit, he'd offer a slight "tee hee" when poked in the stomach.

Reference: Ritz Crackers

> **Sophia:** He never calls, he never writes. I only hear from him at Christmas when he sends me a cheddar cheese nativity scene. I'm Catholic. I can't spread a wise man on a Ritz cracker.

Ritz Crackers is a brand of round, buttery snack crackers introduced by Nabisco in 1934.

Reference: Kleenex

> **Blanche:** Are you saying you don't know if you'd give me a kidney?
>
> **Virginia:** No, I don't.
>
> **Blanche:** Well, I'm not surprised. You never even lent me a Kleenex.

Kleenex is a brand of facial tissue, and other paper products, introduced in 1924 that has become so generalized that people often use the brand name to refer to tissues whether or not they're actually Kleenex—kind of like how we call all lip balm ChapStick even though that's also a specific brand.

Reference: Ovaltine

> **Blanche:** That kidney was showroom new. Why, the wildest thing that ever passed through there was Ovaltine.

Ovaltine is a chocolate malted milk drink introduced in 1904.

Reference: Disney World

> **Rose:** Let's drive to Disney World and ride the teacups.
>
> **Dorothy:** Oh, too wild, Rose!

Walt Disney World is a Disney-themed amusement park in Orlando, Florida, first opened in 1971 as a supplement to California's Disneyland theme park.

Reference: Rocky Road

> **Rose:** There's some Rocky Road in the freezer.

Rocky Road is a frozen dairy dessert consisting of chocolate ice cream with nuts and marshmallows mixed into it.

EPISODE 1.5: THE TRIANGLE

Directed by Jim Drake. Written by Winifred Hervey. Original airdate: October 19, 1985.

A rift develops between the girls when Dorothy refuses to believe that her new boyfriend made a pass at Blanche.

Reference: Lena Horne

> **Dorothy:** Your blood pressure is up, you're tired, you have absolutely no color.
>
> **Sophia:** I'm an old, white woman. I'm not supposed to have color. You want color, talk to Lena Horne.

Lena Horne (1917–2010) was a singer, dancer, and actress whose seven-decade career included film, screen, and stage roles, multiple albums, and a string of accolades including four Grammys and a Tony.

References: John Forsythe, *Hamlet*, Burt Reynolds, the Burt Reynolds Dinner Theatre

> **Blanche:** You're just about the most attractive man I've seen in Florida since Mr. John Forsythe performed *Hamlet* at the Burt Reynolds Dinner Theatre.

The six-decade career of celebrated actor John Forsythe (1918–2010) included such films and series as *The Trouble with Harry*, *The Ambassador's Daughter*, *Bachelor Father*, *Charlie's Angels* (as the unseen Charlie), and a long run in the 1980s as Blake Carrington in *Dynasty*. He was also briefly part of NBC's Saturday-night lineup, when he helmed the short-lived sitcom *The Powers That Be*, which costarred Holland Taylor, David Hyde Pierce, and Joseph Gordon-Levitt. The show was sandwiched between *The Golden Girls* and *Empty Nest* in the spring of 1992.

Hamlet is a William Shakespeare tragedy written sometime around 1599 and 1601 about Prince Hamlet, who seeks revenge against his uncle for murdering his father.

Burt Reynolds (1936–2018) was an actor, director, and sex symbol of the 1970s and 1980s, known for such films as *Deliverance*, *Smokey and the Bandit*, *The Cannonball Run*, and *The Best Little Whorehouse in Texas*, among others. He launched a self-titled dinner theater in Jupiter, Florida, in 1979 with a production of *Vanities*, starring Sally Field and Tyne Daly. Throughout its seventeen-year stretch, the venue featured more famous performers than any other in the region, becoming quite the esteemed place to perform. The list of stars to cross the stage is staggering, many already legendary when they appeared and others yet to become famous: Stockard Channing, Eartha Kitt, Farrah Fawcett, Martin Sheen, Sarah Jessica Parker, John Goodman, Annie Potts … I could go on. The name changed to the Burt Reynolds Jupiter

Theatre in 1984. The theater ceased productions in the mid-1990s and, after changing hands here and there, reopened as the Maltz Jupiter Theatre in 2004.

References: Bloomers, Scarlett O'Hara

> **Dorothy:** You keep your bloomers on, Scarlett. He's taking me out tomorrow night.

Bloomers are a divided women's garment for the lower body, named in honor of women's rights activist (and bloomers fan) Amelia Bloomer. Scarlett O'Hara is the fictional protagonist in the 1936 Margaret Mitchell novel and 1939 film *Gone with the Wind*. More on that later.

Reference: Little Richard

> **Blanche:** We were meant for each other. I'm a woman. He's a man.
>
> **Dorothy:** And what am I, Little Richard?

Little Richard (1932–2020) was a pioneering music icon with a flamboyant stage persona, known for hits like "Tutti Frutti," "Long Tall Sally," and "Lucille."

Reference: Sloe gin fizz

> **Blanche:** What would you like?
>
> **Elliot:** Something smooth and sweet with a little kick to it.
>
> **Blanche:** How about a sloe gin fizz?
>
> **Elliot:** You're talking about the drink, and I'm talking about the bartender.

A sloe gin fizz is a cocktail consisting of sloe gin, lemon juice, simple syrup, and club soda.

Reference: Coming-out party

> **Blanche:** I'm just glad little Mai Ling's coming-out party was ruined!
>
> **Dorothy:** Who?

A coming-out party is a social gathering at which a young debutante is formally introduced to society.

Reference: Willie Nelson

Dorothy: Frankly, Rose, I would rather use Willie Nelson's hairbrush.

Willie Nelson is an iconic country music singer and songwriter, known for hits like "On the Road Again," "Pancho and Lefty," and for writing Patsy Cline's hit, "Crazy." He's also well known for his distinctive look, generally consisting of long, occasionally braided hair and bandanas.

Reference: Mama Celeste

Sophia: Rose, one of those girls was me. The other one you probably know as Mama Celeste.

Mama Celeste is a brand of frozen pizza named after Celeste Lizio, who migrated to the United States from Italy in the 1920s and opened a Chicago restaurant in 1932.

Reference: Jerry Vale

Rose: Has anyone ever told you, you look exactly like Jerry Vale?

Jerry Vale (1930–2014) was a singer and actor known for hits like "You Don't Know Me," "Have You Looked into Your Heart," and " 'O Sole Mio."

Reference: Polaroid

Rose: Want to see some Polaroids of me in my tennis skirt?

Polaroid is a company founded in 1937 by Edwin H. Land, best known for its instant film and cameras.

References: Priscilla Presley, Susan Anton

Blanche: The only other woman who could possibly understand what I've been through is Priscilla Presley. And Susan Anton. No, not Susan Anton.

Priscilla Presley is an actress and businesswoman who was married to Elvis Presley from 1967 to 1973 and is known for starring in *The Naked Gun* series of comedy films alongside Leslie Nielsen, who played Blanche's uncle, Lucas, in the series finale of *The Golden Girls*.

Susan Anton is an actress, singer, model, and former Miss California 1969. After appearing in several commercials and variety shows, her career gained momentum in the 1970s, catapulted by a stint as spokesperson for a line of cigars. Film and TV roles followed throughout the 1980s and 1990s, with Anton's personal life—she was linked to the likes of Sylvester Stallone and Dudley Moore—keeping her as much in the limelight as her work.

EPISODE 1.6: ON GOLDEN GIRLS

Directed by Jim Drake. Written by Liz Sage. Original airdate: October 26, 1985. Blanche's grandson, David, visits and proceeds to upend the household with his rebellious behavior. A bit of trivia: David is played by Billy Jacoby, the real-life brother of actor Scott Jacoby, who played Dorothy's son, Michael. The episode's title is a nod to the 1981 film *On Golden Pond*. More on that later.

Reference: Cary Grant

> **Dorothy:** How am I supposed to study for my French final with a fourteen-year-old in the house? It's hard enough with an eighty-year-old.
>
> **Sophia:** Are you referring to me?
>
> **Dorothy:** Of course not, Ma. I'm referring to Cary Grant. He's living in the broom closet.

Considered one of Classic Hollywood's most notable leading men, the debonair Cary Grant's (1904–1986) filmography includes *Madame Butterfly, Bringing Up Baby, His Girl Friday, The Philadelphia Story, Arsenic and Old Lace, To Catch a Thief, North by Northwest,* and *Charade*.

References: *Rambo,* Sylvester Stallone

> **Dorothy:** *Rambo?*
>
> **Rose:** The movie with Sly Stallone.
>
> **Sophia:** I sat through it twice. You'll love it. He sweats like a pig and he doesn't put his shirt on.

Sylvester Stallone is an actor who rose to fame in the 1970s for playing boxer Rocky Balboa in the *Rocky* film series and who also starred as John Rambo, a tough and aggressive Vietnam War veteran who uses violence to solve problems, in the *Rambo* franchise, which launched in 1982 with *First Blood*. The franchise consists of five films over the course of nearly four decades.

Reference: Ernest Borgnine

> **Dorothy:** I do not snore.
>
> **Sophia:** Please. I bet less disgusting noises come out of Ernest Borgnine.

Actor Ernest Borgnine's (1917–2012) six-decade career included roles in such films as *From Here to Eternity* and *Marty*, a four-year run in the sitcom *McHale's Navy*, and voiceover work in *SpongeBob SquarePants*. Borgnine served in the US Navy, won an Oscar and a Golden Globe, and was active up until his death at age ninety-five.

References: The *Niña*, the *Pinta*, and the *Santa Maria*

> **Rose:** You know, David, I went to the Bahamas once.
>
> **David:** Oh yeah? Was it on the *Niña*, the *Pinta*, or the *Santa Maria*?

The *Niña*, the *Pinta*, and the *Santa Maria* were the three ships on which Christopher Columbus and his crew sailed from Spain in 1492.

Reference: *Miami Vice*

> **Blanche:** What time will you be back?
>
> **David:** It's hard to say. It depends on how long the guys from *Miami Vice* want to party.

Miami Vice was a crime-drama television series that ran on NBC from 1984 to 1990 and popularized both series star Don Johnson and the linen and pastel clothes his character wore. Plenty more on this reference later.

Reference: *The Curse of the Cat Woman*

> **Sophia:** You're getting a cold.
>
> **Dorothy:** No, I'm not.
>
> **Sophia:** Yes you are. Tomorrow you'll have a cold.
>
> **Dorothy:** What is this, *The Curse of the Cat Woman*?

This one was tricky, but it is presumably a reference to the 1942 horror film *Cat People*, about a woman who believes she is the descendant of an ancient tribe of cat people, and its 1943 sequel, *The Curse of the Cat People*.

References: Bengay, Vicks VapoRub, Deep Heat, Dramamine

> **Dorothy:** What's that smell?
>
> **Sophia:** I don't smell anything.
>
> **Dorothy:** Are you wearing something?
>
> **Sophia:** A little Bengay on my knees. A little Vicks on my chest. A little Deep Heat on my neck.
>
> **Dorothy:** What are you trying to do, pickle yourself so you'll live to be a hundred?
>
> **Sophia, shortly after as Dorothy tosses and turns in bed:** Keep it up, I'll need a Dramamine.

Bengay is a topical analgesic heat rub for temporary relief of muscle and joint pain that has been easing aches and pains since 1898. The name comes from its French developer, Dr. Jules Bengué, and was sold in the United States as Ben-Gay until 1995, when it was shortened to Bengay. Vicks VapoRub is a mentholated topical ointment first sold in 1905. Deep Heat is an ointment made by the Mentholatum Company, Inc., a company that's been around since the late 1800s. It is used to treat minor aches and pains of muscles and joints by making the skin feel cool, then warm. Lastly, Dramamine is a medication used to treat motion sickness.

Reference: *Long Day's Journey into Night*

> **Rose:** This is like the *Long Day's Journey into Light*.
>
> **Dorothy:** *Night*, Rose.
>
> **Rose:** Night, Dorothy.

Long Day's Journey into Night is a Tony Award–winning 1956 Eugene O'Neill play that takes place on a single day in 1912 in the life of the Tyrone family.

Reference: Jane Goodall

> **Rose:** That's impressive!
>
> **Sophia:** Jane Goodall once taught an ape to rhumba. That's impressive.

Jane Goodall is an English primatologist, anthropologist, and animal activist considered to be the world's foremost expert on chimpanzees. She's best known for her decades-long work with wild chimps.

Repeat Reference: Disney World *(Episode 1.4: Transplant)*

EPISODE 1.7: THE COMPETITION
Directed by Jim Drake. Written by Barry Fanaro and Mort Nathan. Original airdate: November 2, 1985.
The girls participate in a bowling tournament, which brings out Rose's competitive nature. Meanwhile, Sophia wants to visit Sicily with an old boyfriend, but Dorothy isn't sure it's a good idea.

Reference: Tony Bennett

> **Dorothy:** You haven't made this sauce since Uncle Dominic married off that daughter of his. You know, the one who looks like Tony Bennett.

Famed singer Tony Bennett has been on the charts since the 1950s, belting out standards and jazz, big band, and show tunes. With hits like "I Left My Heart in San Francisco" and "Rags to Riches," Bennett rose to fame during the 1950s and 1960s, experienced a bit of a downturn during the rise of the rock era, but has continued to find ways to reintroduce himself to new audiences every decade or so, like an appearance on MTV's *Unplugged* in 1994 and a critically acclaimed 2014 album of duets with none other than Lady Gaga.

Reference: Chef Boyardee

> **Rose:** Oh, Sophia, that smells heavenly. Is it Chef Boyardee?
>
> **Sophia, handing her a knife:** Stick it in my heart, Rose. It'll hurt less.

Chef Boyardee is a brand of boxed or canned Italian food products sold by Conagra Brands. Founded by one-time Plaza Hotel chef and restaurateur Hector Boiardi (1897–1985) in 1938, the brand has been successfully selling canned pastas like ravioli, Beefaroni, and spaghetti, and boxed pizza kits, for decades. Boiardi created the line after customers at his restaurant began asking him to sell his sauce. He anglicized his name so Americans could pronounce it more easily, and launched his first product line—a ready-to-eat spaghetti kit. Boiardi appeared in ads for the brand from the 1940s to the 1960s, and his likeness is still part of the company's logo.

Reference: San Gennaro Festival

> **Dorothy:** It's a shame that he has to go back to Sicily so soon. It would've been nice if the two of you had more time together.
>
> **Sophia:** I'm glad you said that because he wants me to go back with him. Not for good. Just for the San Gennaro Festival. That's where we met sixty-five years ago.

The Feast of San Gennaro is an Italian American festival first celebrated in the United States in 1926 by Italian immigrants in New York City.

Reference: Bruce Springsteen

> **Sophia:** I can't believe you're denying your own mother.
>
> **Rose:** Denying her what?
>
> **Dorothy:** Springsteen tickets, Rose.

Nicknamed "The Boss," Bruce Springsteen is an iconic singer and songwriter whose multi-decade recording career began in the 1970s and includes hits like "Born to Run," "Born in the U.S.A.," "Thunder Road," "Hungry Heart," "Dancing in the Dark," "Glory Days," and many others.

Reference: Viking funeral

> **Rose:** He requested an authentic Viking funeral, and every time they tried to set him and his ship on fire, the Coast Guard kept putting it out.

A popular Hollywood version of a Viking funeral involves the deceased being set adrift on a boat surrounded by his belongings and then a flaming arrow is launched onto the boat, setting it ablaze. That's actually a myth. Some Viking funerals involved a pyre and others involved setting the deceased adrift on a boat, but the two methods weren't actually combined.

Reference: Bocce ball

> **Sophia:** How do you know I'm a good bowler?
>
> **Augie:** Because you were so good at bocce ball.

Bocce is a multiplayer ball game, popular in Europe and among Italian immigrants in the United States, which can be loosely described as tossing a larger ball down a court toward a smaller ball, called a jack, and attempting to get closest to it.

EPISODE 1.8: BREAK-IN
Directed by Paul Bogart. Written by Susan Harris. Original airdate: November 9, 1985.
Traumatized after the house is burglarized, Rose decides to buy a gun. Meanwhile, Blanche obsesses over her stolen jewelry.

Reference: Madonna

> **Rose:** The name Madonna doesn't really fit her.
>
> **Sophia:** "Slut" would be better.

Madonna is a music icon who rose to fame in the 1980s with a string of hit records and a highly sexualized image. A few of her biggest songs are "Like a Virgin," "Material Girl," "Vogue," and "Like a Prayer." Her forays into acting have had as many hits (*A League of Their Own, Evita*) as misses (*Shanghai Surprise, Who's That Girl?*).

Reference: "Do you feel lucky? Well, do you, punk?"

> **Dorothy:** So you have to ask yourself, do you feel lucky? Well, do you, punk?
>
> **Sophia:** Go ahead, make her day.

This bit is a spin on a classic line from the 1971 film *Dirty Harry*, starring Clint Eastwood as the title character, a San Francisco police inspector on the hunt for a serial killer.

Reference: Maalox

> **Rose:** They were probably looking for drugs.
>
> **Dorothy:** We have Maalox and estrogen. How many junkies have gas and hot flashes?

Maalox is a brand of antacid launched in the 1940s, backed by an advertising campaign around the need for the product when having a "Maalox moment."

Reference: Drip-dry

> **Dorothy:** Ma, why in the world would they want your clothes?

Sophia: Who knows? Short girl robber, travels a lot, likes drip-dry.

Drip-dry is a method for drying clothing by hanging it up wet straight out of the wash, instead of putting it into the dryer.

EPISODE 1.9: BLANCHE AND THE YOUNGER MAN

Directed by Jim Drake. Written by James Berg and Stan Zimmerman. Original airdate: November 16, 1985.

Blanche accepts a date with a much younger man from her Jazzercise class. Rose is overprotective of her visiting mother, Alma.

Reference: Bob Hope

> **Rose:** There's nothing wrong with taking a nap. Bob Hope takes naps.
>
> **Sophia:** Unless he's in the bedroom now taking one, I think she'd rather stay here with us.

Comedy legend Bob Hope's (1903–2003) nearly eighty-year career spanned multiple feature films, TV specials, stage appearances, and nineteen Academy Award ceremony hosting gigs. Hope also was widely known for entertaining active military personnel in a series of United Service Organizations (USO) tours between 1941 and 1991. He retired from performing in 1997 and died in 2003 at the age of one hundred.

References: Rexall, Maybelline, Sidney Sheldon, Andy Griffith, Woolworth's, John Cameron Swayze

> **Blanche:** I was working behind the cosmetics counter at the Rexall drugstore. I was stocking the Maybelline display when I heard this booming voice say, "Excuse me, ma'am. Where are the cuticle scissors?" I turned around, and there he was. Our eyes locked, and for one brief moment there was nobody else on Earth but the two of us.
>
> **Dorothy:** Please, Blanche. Sidney Sheldon tells shorter stories.
>
> **Blanche:** I know in my heart if I had just followed my feelings that day at the Rexall drugstore, today I would be Mrs. Andy Griffith. I tell you what, I'm not going to make the same mistake with Dirk that I made with Andy.
>
> **Dorothy:** Didn't she tell us that story before?

Sophia: Yes, but the last time it was Woolworth's, a toenail clipper, and John Cameron Swayze.

Rexall is a chain of drugstores founded in 1903. Maybelline is a popular brand of cosmetics and skin-care products founded by Thomas Lyle Williams in 1915. Sidney Sheldon (1917–2007) was a writer who spent his early career working on Broadway plays, movies, and television before becoming a best-selling romantic suspense novelist whose books have sold more than three hundred million copies worldwide. Beloved actor, producer, and gospel singer Andy Griffith (1926–2012) is best remembered for playing genteel Southern sheriff Andy Taylor on *The Andy Griffith Show* from 1960 to 1968 and lawyer Ben Matlock on *Matlock* from 1986 to 1995. Woolworth's is a retail company considered one of the pioneers of the five-and-dime store, the first of which was opened by Frank Winfield Woolworth in Utica, New York, in 1879. John Cameron Swayze (1906–1995) was a news commentator, game show panelist, and spokesperson for products such as Timex watches.

Reference: Princess phone

Blanche: Got to look good for Dirk. A man his age is used to a trim body with good tone.

Dorothy: Then buy him a Princess phone.

Princess phones were compact telephones designed by Henry Dreyfuss and released in 1959. They were marketed to women and designed for use in the bedroom, with a light-up dial used as a night-light.

Reference: Walt Disney

Blanche: I'm getting younger with each passing day.

Dorothy: Great. When they defrost Walt Disney, he'll have someone to go out with.

Entrepreneur, animator, writer, voice actor, and producer Walt Disney (1901–1966) was an animation pioneer who launched the Walt Disney Company in 1923. As a film producer, Disney holds the most Academy Awards earned by an individual, with twenty-two to his credit. Disney has become a cultural icon as his company continues to grow with each passing decade. A heavy cigarette smoker, he died from lung cancer in 1966. For years, rumors floated around that Disney was cryogenically frozen. In actuality, he was cremated two days after his death.

Reference: Jai alai

> **Rose:** Where's Mother?
>
> **Sophia:** She was feeling lucky, so she wanted to try her hand at jai alai.
>
> **Dorothy:** Why didn't you go with her?
>
> **Sophia:** I'm too short to play jai alai.

Jai alai is a sport dating back to the fourteenth century involving a ball bounced off a wall using a handheld wicker device.

References: Peter Pan, *Mommie Dearest*, Josephine the Plumber

> **Dorothy:** Blanche thinks she's Peter Pan, and Rose is turning into *Mommie Dearest*.
>
> **Sophia:** That's nothing. You think you're Josephine the Plumber.

Peter Pan is a fictional character, created by novelist and playwright J. M. Barrie, who first appeared in *The Little White Bird* in 1902. Peter Pan is known as a mischievous boy who can fly and never grows up, spending his never-ending youth on the island of Neverland, leading the Lost Boys and battling Captain Hook. The character has become a cultural icon, bolstered by a 1953 animated Disney film, famous stage productions, and multiple incarnations.

Mommie Dearest is the 1981 biographical film depicting the abuse and manipulation suffered by Christina Crawford, the adopted daughter of actress Joan Crawford. It's based on Christina Crawford's 1978 autobiography of the same name. Thanks in part to the over-the-top performance by actress Faye Dunaway as Joan Crawford, the film has achieved cult-classic status.

Josephine the Plumber was the spokes-character for Comet cleanser, portrayed by actress Jane Withers in a series of television commercials in the 1960s and 1970s.

Reference: Macrobiotics

> **Blanche:** Isn't this a lovely place? It's one of my favorite restaurants.
>
> **Dirk:** I'm into macrobiotics myself.

Macrobiotics is a plant-based diet that attempts to balance the yin and yang of food.

Reference: *Pumping Iron*

> **Blanche:** Read any good books lately?
>
> **Dirk:** *Pumping Iron.* I saw the movie, too, but I don't think it did the book justice.

Pumping Iron is a 1977 docudrama film about the world of professional body-building, focusing largely on the 1975 Mr. Universe and Mr. Olympia competitions. It was inspired by the book of the same name by George Butler and Charles Gaines. Bodybuilders Arnold Schwarzenegger and Lou Ferrigno feature prominently.

Reference: Betty Crocker

> **Blanche:** My date with Dirk was a disaster. He was looking for a mother, not a lover. It was humiliating.
>
> **Rose:** I think it's sweet.
>
> **Blanche:** You would, Betty Crocker.

Brace yourself: Betty Crocker is not a real person. The well-known brand name of food and kitchen products, cookbooks, and recipes was created by the Washburn-Crosby Company in 1921, which eventually became General Mills. While there have been several depictions of Ms. Crocker over the years—in order to provide a personalized response to customer questions, both on-screen and in printed advertisements—alas, she is fiction. The name "Betty" was chosen because it was viewed as an all-American name. Betty White fans would agree.

Repeat References: Jazzercise *(Episode 1.3: Rose the Prude)* and Jack Daniel's *(Episode 1.4: Transplant)*

EPISODE 1.10: THE HEART ATTACK
Directed by Jim Drake. Written by Susan Harris. Original airdate: November 23, 1985.
The girls fear that Sophia is having a heart attack, and the paramedics are stalled by a terrible storm.

Reference: Princess Diana

> **Dorothy:** Ma, you don't look good.
>
> **Sophia:** I'm short and I'm old. What did you expect, Princess Di?

Diana, Princess of Wales (1961–1997), became the first wife of Britain's Prince Charles, the heir apparent to the British throne, in 1981. She was the mother of Prince William and Prince Harry. She and Charles divorced in 1996, and Princess Diana died in a car wreck while fleeing from paparazzi in 1997. A popular and iconic figure across the globe, Princess Diana was known for her activism and for her style.

Reference: Luciano Pavarotti

> **Dorothy:** Why do you think you're having a heart attack?
>
> **Sophia:** I'm eighty years old. I've got Pavarotti sitting on my chest. Odds are it's a heart attack.

Luciano Pavarotti (1935–2007) was an Italian opera singer known as one of the Three Tenors. He was also a rather large fellow.

Reference: Arlington National Cemetery

> **Blanche:** I want a fancy funeral. I want a big parade with a rider-less horse. And then I want to lie in state and then be buried in Arlington Cemetery.
>
> **Rose:** Why Arlington Cemetery?
>
> **Blanche:** Because it's full of men.

The Arlington National Cemetery is a US military cemetery located in Arlington, Virginia, near Washington, DC. Controlled by the US Army, the cemetery was created during the Civil War. One of the most visited parts of the cemetery is the Tomb of the Unknown Solider, a monument dedicated to the remains of unidentified service personnel.

Reference: Heckle and Jeckle

> **Sophia, to Blanche and Rose:** And you two, Heckle and Jeckle, thank you for letting me live here. It was some treat.

Heckle and Jeckle were a pair of animated anthropomorphic talking magpies, created by Paul Terry, who appeared in various cartoons and animated series beginning in 1946. The characters proved popular and were licensed for merchandise and comic books over the decades.

Reference: Saks

> **Sophia:** I saw the golden light, and some angels in white robes with harps. I thought I was at Saks at Christmas.

Saks is a chain of luxury department stores, with its flagship located on Fifth Avenue in New York City.

Reference: Milk Duds

> **Blanche:** Oh, and the Milk Duds. Remember, you had those two boxes of Milk Duds.
>
> **Dr. Harris:** Milk Duds?
>
> **Sophia:** They're delicious, I love them. The trouble is they take out my dentures.

Milk Duds are a brand of candy created in 1928 by Hoffman and Company, consisting of a little ball of chocolate-coated caramel. The brand is now owned and manufactured by the Hershey Food Corporation.

Reference: The English Channel

> **Sophia:** It's incredible. You think you're dying, you feel death enter your body. A doctor comes, he says you're fine, you're ready to swim the English Channel.

The English Channel is an arm of the Atlantic Ocean separating southern England from northern France. Considered the busiest shipping area in the world, it is about 350 miles long and, at its widest, 150 miles wide.

Episode 1.11: Stan's Return

Directed by Jim Drake. Written by Kathy Speer and Terry Grossman. Original airdate: November 30, 1985.
Stan shows up with the announcement that his new wife, Chrissy, has left him. The girls debate where to spend their vacation.

Reference: Brooke Shields

> **Sophia:** Brooke Shields takes her mother everywhere.

Brooke Shields is an actress and model known for such works as *Pretty Baby*, *The Blue Lagoon*, *Endless Love*, and the sitcom *Suddenly Susan*.

Reference: Camp Snoopy

> **Stan:** Chrissy left me for a younger man.
>
> **Dorothy:** Younger than Chrissy? Where did she meet him, Camp Snoopy?

Camp Snoopy is a *Peanuts*-themed area for kids at various amusement parks in the Cedar Fair Entertainment Company family of parks, named after the comic strip's character Snoopy, a beagle. It debuted at the Knott's Berry Farm amusement park in 1983 and is still active. You'll also find Camp Snoopy sections at Cedar Point in Ohio and Carowinds in North Carolina, while several other locations have been rebranded as Planet Snoopy. The rides are mostly *Peanuts* themed, of course, with names like Charlie Brown's Kite Flyer, Linus Launcher, and Pig Pen's Mud Buggies.

Reference: The Fontainebleau

> **Stan:** I can take you to dinner. How about that little seafood place near The Fontainebleau where we were on our honeymoon?

The Fontainebleau is a luxury hotel in Miami Beach, opened in 1954.

Reference: Frank Sinatra

> **Blanche, on New York City:** The people are rude. The streets are full of criminals. Everything's overpriced. I don't know why Frank Sinatra sings about it.

Frank Sinatra (1915–1998), nicknamed "Ol' Blue Eyes," was an iconic singer and actor who remains one of the best-selling artists of all time. Many of his songs have become classics.

Reference: Cinderella

> **Sophia:** Not only am I not allowed to go, I'm not allowed to talk about it. This is the same deal Cinderella had with her stepsisters.

The protagonist in a folktale (which later became a classic animated Disney film among countless other incarnations), Cinderella is a young woman living a rather glum existence at the behest of her wicked stepmother and stepsisters, who make her do a relentless amount of chores while they run around being generally terrible. She eventually transforms into a ball gown– and glass slipper–wearing beauty who wins the prince in the end. The name has since become synonymous with one who rises from obscurity to great ranks after overcoming adversity.

Reference: Barbara Billingsley

> **Rose:** I've always wanted to go to Hollywood. When I was a young girl, I used to dream about becoming a movie star. Mr. Mason, who owned the corner drugstore, said I was a young Barbara Billingsley.

Actress Barbara Billingsley (1915–2010) is best known for her role as June Cleaver, the doting mother of Beaver Cleaver in the classic sitcom *Leave It to Beaver*, which ran from 1957 to 1963. Of course, many also recall her appearance as a jive-speaking passenger in the 1980 comedy *Airplane!* but it's June Cleaver for which Billingsley is synonymous. She reprised the role in the sequel series *The New Leave It to Beaver*, an early example of the more recent string of TV reboots, which aired for several years in the 1980s, and she also had a cameo in the 1997 film version of *Leave It to Beaver*. Billingsley also has a connection to the *Golden Girls* extended universe. She appeared on an episode of spinoff series *Empty Nest*, as the retired former nurse of Dr. Harry Weston.

Reference: Lucille Ball

> **Dorothy:** I'm sorry but I am not going to spend my vacation sitting in a tour bus looking at houses that may or may not belong to Lucille Ball.

Comedy icon Lucille Ball (1911–1989) was the producer and star of a string of television shows bearing her name: the iconic *I Love Lucy*, *The Lucy Show*, *Here's Lucy*, and *Life with Lucy*. While only the last of those shows was a flop, it's *I Love Lucy* that catapulted the fiery redhead into superstardom and has made her a household name ever since. Prior to that, she'd appeared in radio, onstage, and in multiple B-movies, but it was her pioneering work in television that defined her. Throughout her six-decade career, Ball racked up numerous accolades, married twice (most notably to Desi Arnaz), and had two children, both of whom went into show business themselves.

Reference: Mr. Wizard

> **Rose:** I don't understand how a thermos keeps things both hot and cold.

Dorothy: Neither do I, but I'll tell you, if ever I sleep with Mr. Wizard I'll find out.

Mr. Wizard was the alter ego of Don Herbert (1917–2007), who hosted the children's educational programs *Watch Mr. Wizard* from the 1950s to the 1970s and *Mr. Wizard's World* in the 1980s.

Reference: The Rose Parade

Stan: Don't leave on my account.

Dorothy: They have to. They're hitching up the house to the car and entering it in the Rose Parade.

The Rose Parade is an annual parade first held in 1890 that marks the start of the Rose Bowl Game.

Reference: Harry S. Truman

Stan: I can't believe how expensive roses got since the last time I sent them to you.

Dorothy: Yeah, well, everything's gotten more expensive since Truman left office.

Harry S. Truman (1884–1972) was president of the United States from 1945 to 1953. He implemented the Marshall Plan to rebuild the Western Europe economy and established NATO.

Reference: USO

Rose: When Charlie went off to war, I went to work with our local USO club.

Founded in 1941, the United Service Organizations, Inc. (USO) is a non-profit charitable corporation that provides entertainment such as musicians, actors, and comedians to members of the armed forces and their families.

Episode 1.12: The Custody Battle

Directed by Terry Hughes. Written by Winifred Hervey. Original airdate: December 7, 1985.

Dorothy's wealthy sister Gloria visits and invites Sophia to live with her in California. Blanche auditions for a part in a community theater production of *Macbeth*.

References: Lady Macbeth, William Shakespeare, *Macbeth*

> **Dorothy:** Where are you going?
>
> **Blanche:** Out to dinner with Jason, the director of our community theater. He's considering me for the role of Lady Macbeth in Mr. William Shakespeare's masterpiece, *Macbeth*.

Lady Macbeth is a prominent character who goads her husband into killing the king in Shakespeare's *Macbeth*. William Shakespeare (1564–1616) was an English playwright, poet, and actor who many consider the world's greatest dramatist. *Macbeth* is a Shakespeare tragedy first performed in 1606, about the psychological effects of political ambition, focusing on the title character, who murders the king and takes the throne for himself.

Reference: Jane Pauley

> **Rose:** Maybe he can explain to me how the three-way bulb works. I've always wondered about that.
>
> **Dorothy:** I've always wondered about the same thing, Rose. That and what Jane Pauley looks like standing up.

Jane Pauley is a journalist known for hosting gigs on NBC's *Today*, *Dateline NBC*, and *CBS Sunday Morning*. In other words, she's spent a lot of years sitting at a news desk.

Reference: Ditty bag

> **Rose:** Why don't you just kiss and make up?
>
> **Sophia:** Why don't you just blow it out your ditty bag?

A ditty bag is a bag for carrying odds and ends, used especially by sailors. It was originally called a ditto bag because sailors would carry two of everything in it.

References: Elizabeth Arden, Captain Hook

> **Gloria:** It's a gift certificate for a complete makeover at Elizabeth Arden.
>
> **Sophia:** Maybe now you can get a date.
>
> **Dorothy:** Please, Ma. I am not calling Captain Hook.

Elizabeth Arden is a major fragrance, cosmetic, and skin-care line founded in 1910 by, you guessed it, Elizabeth Arden. Arden died in 1966, and today, Elizabeth Arden, Inc., is a subsidiary of Revlon.

The fictional pirate, Captain James Hook—known for having a hook for a hand, obviously—is the arch nemesis of Peter Pan, the boy who wouldn't grow up. The character was created by J. M. Barrie for his 1904 play, *Peter Pan*, and has been portrayed in literature, stage, screen, and television productions, both live-action and animated, ever since. Among the most notable portrayals of the character is the animated version in the 1953 Disney film *Peter Pan* and the 1991 live-action version in the film *Hook*, where he is portrayed by Dustin Hoffman.

Reference: Michael Landon

> **Rose:** After Daddy hung the star at the very top of the tree, we'd all join hands and pray, and then Daddy would tell us a story and tuck us into our feather beds . . .
>
> **Dorothy:** Who was your father, Rose, Michael Landon?

Michael Landon (1936–1991) was a beloved actor known for playing Little Joe Cartwright in *Bonanza*, Charles Ingalls in *Little House on the Prairie* (the role this joke references), and Jonathan Smith in *Highway to Heaven*. He is second only to Lucille Ball for the most covers of *TV Guide*.

Reference: Bert Convy

> **Gloria:** I have a huge house with servants and an ocean view. And Bert Convy shops in my grocery store.
>
> **Dorothy:** Bert Convy? Let's leave now.

Actor and singer Bert Convy (1933–1991) is best remembered for hosting and being a panelist on a series of successful game shows in the 1960s, 1970s, and 1980s, including *Tattletales*, *Super Password*, and *Win, Lose or Draw*. Convy died of cancer in 1991 at the age of fifty-seven.

Reference: Mallomars

> **Blanche:** Girls, please. Will one of you just say something so I can become hysterical, eat a box of Mallomars, and get it over with?

Mallomars are a Nabisco-brand cookie introduced in 1913, consisting of a graham-cracker circle topped with marshmallow and coated with dark chocolate.

Reference: Mary Poppins

> **Rose:** Well, what about us? Who's going to keep after us, make us linguine, and tell us stories about Sicily?
>
> **Dorothy:** I don't know, Rose. Maybe Mary Poppins has an Italian cousin.

Mary Poppins is a beloved 1964 Disney musical film starring Julie Andrews and Dick Van Dyke as the magical titular nanny and her handyman friend, based on the P. L. Travers book series of the same name.

Repeat Reference: Willard Scott *(Episode 1.3: Rose the Prude)*

EPISODE 1.13: A LITTLE ROMANCE
Directed by Terry Hughes. Written by Barry Fanaro and Mort Nathan. Original airdate: December 14, 1985.
Rose is hesitant to tell the girls that she's dating a little person.

Reference: Super Bowl

> **Blanche:** For six consecutive hours I was on my back while dozens of eligible men pressed their lips to mine and breathed air into my limp little body.
>
> **Dorothy:** So what? You did the same thing at McSorley's Bar Super Bowl weekend.

The Super Bowl is an annual championship game of the National Football League, first played in 1967.

References: Cheryl Tiegs, Sears

> **Blanche:** To the untrained eye, that polyester could almost pass for silk.
>
> **Rose:** It is silk.
>
> **Blanche:** Oh sure, Rose, and Cheryl Tiegs really buys her clothes at Sears.

Often described as the first American supermodel, Cheryl Tiegs is best known for appearing on the covers of such publications as the *Sports Illustrated*

Swimsuit Issue and *Time*. Sears is a department store chain founded by Richard Warren Sears and Alvah Curtis Roebuck in 1893. In the early 1980s, Tiegs released a clothing line available exclusively at Sears and appeared in an ad campaign to promote it.

Reference: Boston Celtics

> **Jonathan:** Don't get me wrong. I would love to know what it feels like to be the center on the Boston Celtics, but all in all I'm pretty happy with who I am.

A professional basketball team founded in 1946, the Boston Celtics were one of the NBA's original eight teams. Over the years, the Celtics have been home to such greats as Bill Russell, Paul Pierce, and (during *The Golden Girls* era) Larry Bird.

Reference: Gandhi

> **Dorothy:** And to think that the two of you were almost kept apart because Benjamin was Black.
>
> **Blanche:** Black? Benjamin wasn't Black. He was from New Jersey. I went to my senior prom with a Yankee!
>
> **Dorothy:** A Yankee? That is incredible. And to think, they made a movie about that deadbeat Gandhi while there's a story like this that hasn't been told.

Mahatma Gandhi (1869–1948) was an Indian lawyer, politician, and activist known for his nonviolent philosophy of passive resistance. He led India's nonviolent independence movement against British rule. He was assassinated in 1948 at the age of seventy-eight. His life was made into a 1982 biographical film aptly titled *Gandhi*.

Reference: Ford Falcon

> **Blanche:** That color you dye your hair? Honey, that hasn't existed since they discontinued the Ford Falcon.

The Ford Falcon was a six-passenger compact car produced by Ford from 1959 to 1970.

Reference: Jeane Dixon

> **Mr. Lindstrom:** No one can predict the future.

Blanche: Not necessarily true, Daddy Lindstrom. For, Rose, you see, one of your wedding guests is none other than famed psychic Jeane Dixon.

Psychic Jeane Dixon (1904–1997) rose to fame with a syndicated newspaper astrology column, some well-publicized predictions, and a string of hit books.

References: Senator Edward Kennedy, Jackie O.

Rose: Could you tell me what the future holds?

Jeane: Sure. In January, Brooke Shields and Lady Di will star together in a Broadway musical comedy. Senator Edward Kennedy will once again run for—

Rose: No, what the future holds for me and Jonathan.

Jeane: Rose, I'm not getting a clear picture on that. However, I do know that Jackie O. will tie the knot again . . .

Edward "Ted" Kennedy (1932–2009) was a lawyer and Democratic politician who served as a US senator from Massachusetts from 1962 until his death in 2009. He was the brother of President John F. Kennedy. Jackie Onassis (1929–1994) was a journalist and fashion icon who became the First Lady of the United States from 1961 to 1963, as wife of President Kennedy. After Kennedy's assassination, she married shipping magnate Aristotle Onassis and worked as a book editor in New York.

Repeat References: Brooke Shields *(Episode 1.11: Stan's Return)*, Princess Diana of Wales *(Episode 1.10: The Heart Attack)*

EPISODE 1.14: THAT WAS NO LADY
Directed by Jim Drake. Written by Liz Sage. Original airdate: December 21, 1985.
Dorothy is devastated when she discovers that her new boyfriend is married. Rose buys Blanche's car.

Reference: Jesse Owens

Rose, reading a trivia card: Who was known as the world's fastest human being?

Sophia: Dominic Tanzi.

Rose: It says Jesse Owens here.

Sophia: Trust me, it was Dominic Tanzi. He got four women pregnant in one night.

Jesse Owens (1913–1980) was a track-and-field athlete and four-time gold medalist in the 1936 Olympics.

Reference: World Trade Center

Blanche: Honey, you've been hit by the thunderbolt. Love at first sight. It happened to me once.

Sophia: Once? You've been hit by more lightning than the World Trade Center.

The World Trade Center was originally a complex of seven buildings in New York City, first opened in 1973. It was destroyed in 2001 in the September 11 terrorist attacks that struck the Center's most notable buildings, the Twin Towers.

Reference: Godzilla

Dorothy: You can't hide anything in the daytime. At night I could be Godzilla, you'd still be thrilled.

A fictional character and pop culture icon from a series of Japanese films beginning with 1954's *Godzilla*, Godzilla is a giant prehistoric, nuclear radiation–powered creature that emerges from the sea to wreak havoc all over the city.

Reference: Disneyland

Rose, to a Japanese man: I'm so glad you got your own Disneyland.

The first theme park built by the Walt Disney Company, Disneyland opened in Anaheim, California, in 1955. A Tokyo version opened in 1983, the first such park to be built outside the United States.

Reference: Phyllis George

Rose: Are you depressed about Glen?

Dorothy: No, I'm depressed because Phyllis George left the *Morning News*.

After being crowned Miss America 1971, Phyllis George (1949–2020) worked as a sportscaster, actress, and journalist. She worked on *The NFL*

Today in the 1970s and early 1980s, and coanchored the *CBS Morning News* briefly in 1985. She was First Lady of Kentucky while married to Governor John Y. Brown Jr.

References: Debbie Reynolds, Eddie Fisher, Elizabeth Taylor, Richard Burton, Martin and Lewis, Rowan and Martin

> **Rose:** That's the same attitude that broke up Debbie and Eddie, Eddie and Liz, Liz and Dick, Martin and Lewis, Rowan and Martin.

Debbie Reynolds (1932–2016) was a beloved actress and singer whose seven-decade career included such classics as *Singin' in the Rain*, *The Affairs of Dobie Gillis*, *Susan Slept Here*, and *The Unsinkable Molly Brown*, among many others. She also appeared on *The Golden Girls* as Truby, Dorothy's potential replacement roommate, in season six's "There Goes the Bride." Singer and actor Eddie Fisher (1928–2010) was quite popular in the 1950s, with records selling in the millions, his own TV show, and a widely reported split from his first wife, Reynolds, to marry her best friend, Elizabeth Taylor. He was the father of four children, including Carrie Fisher.

Elizabeth Taylor (1932–2011) was an actress known for such films as *National Velvet*, *A Place in the Sun*, *Suddenly, Last Summer*, and *Cleopatra*. She's also well known for her personal life, which included eight marriages to seven men. Two of those marriages were to actor Richard Burton (1925–1984), who rose to fame as quite the notable Shakespearean actor in the 1950s and 1960s and appeared in a string of successful films, including *The Spy Who Came In from the Cold*, *Who's Afraid of Virginia Woolf?*, and *Anne of a Thousand Days*.

Martin and Lewis were a comedy duo consisting of singer Dean Martin (1917–1995) and comedian Jerry Lewis (1926–2017), who performed in nightclubs, radio, television, and films. They split contentiously in 1956 and both went on to successful solo careers. Martin became known as "The King of Cool," with hits like "That's Amore," "Everybody Loves Somebody," and "Memories Are Made of This." Lewis, meanwhile, was known as "The King of Comedy" and went on to a successful career in comedic films. For decades, he hosted an annual Labor Day telethon in support of muscular dystrophy.

Finally, Rowan and Martin were a comedy duo consisting of Dan Rowan (1922–1987) and Dick Martin (1922–2008), who hosted *Rowan & Martin's Laugh-In*, a sketch comedy show which ran from 1968 to 1973.

Reference: Spanish Inquisition

> **Dorothy:** What is this, the Spanish Inquisition?

The Tribunal of the Holy Office of the Inquisition was established in 1478, with the goal of rooting out and punishing heresy among those who converted from Judaism and Islam to Catholicism. It was particularly infamous for the severity of its torture and persecution of Jews and Muslims. It was disbanded in 1834.

Reference: Sodom and Gomorrah

> **Dorothy:** We didn't drive to Sodom and Gomorrah, Rose.

Sodom and Gomorrah were a pair of biblical cities from the Book of Genesis that were destroyed by fire and brimstone for the sinful ways of their inhabitants.

Reference: Don Shula

> **Blanche:** Never check in as Mr. and Mrs. Smith. Always check in as Mr. and Mrs. Don Shula. That way you always get a complimentary fruit basket and a bottle of champagne.

Don Shula (1930–2020) was a professional football coach and player known for his longtime stint as head coach of the Miami Dolphins. He is the winningest coach in NFL history.

Reference: The Amazing Kreskin

> **Sophia:** So you started up with your married man again.
> **Dorothy:** How did you know?
> **Sophia:** I'm the Amazing Kreskin.

Kreskin is a mentalist who rose to fame as an entertainer in the 1970s. He hosted the syndicated series *The Amazing World of Kreskin* throughout the decade, and has appeared regularly on *The Tonight Show*, *Late Night with David Letterman*, *The Howard Stern Show*, and *Late Night with Jimmy Fallon*.

Reference: "Purple Rain"

> *Sophia is listening to a Walkman and singing the song.*

Purple Rain is a 1984 film and accompanying soundtrack album and song by Prince. The film, a rock musical drama and Prince's acting debut, received mixed to average reviews, while the accompanying album was a massive success. It spent twenty-four consecutive weeks atop the *Billboard 200* chart and spawned hits like the title track, "When Doves Cry," and "Let's Go Crazy."

Reference: Martha and the Vandellas

> **Blanche:** It's a piece of junk. It's the noisiest thing to come out of Detroit since Martha and the Vandellas.

Martha and the Vandellas was an all-female singing group formed in Detroit who rose to fame with Motown during the 1960s. Led by Martha Reeves, the group's hits included "Heat Wave," "Dancing in the Street," and "Come and Get These Memories."

EPISODE 1.15: IN A BED OF ROSE'S
Directed by Terry Hughes. Written by Susan Harris. Original airdate: January 11, 1986.
Rose's new boyfriend, Al, dies in her bed—a repeat of what happened with her late husband, Charlie.

Reference: Buying the farm

> **Sophia:** He bought the farm.
> **Rose:** What farm?
> **Dorothy:** Rose, he's dead.

There are plenty of unsubstantiated theories regarding the origin of the phrase "buy the farm," such as some dating back to World War II involving the death of US soldiers, whose insurance was sufficient for their families to settle the mortgage back home. Regardless of its true origins, to buy the farm simply means to die.

References: Herb Alpert and the Tijuana Brass, Doritos

> **Blanche, sharing how she found out her husband died:** . . . put me on hold with that music while you wait. I sat there at two in the morning listening to Herb Alpert and the Tijuana Brass . . . Puts me on hold and then eats Doritos while he tells me my life is over.

Band leader and trumpeter Alpert and his Tijuana Brass charted a slew of albums and songs throughout the 1960s, racking up multiple platinum and gold records, Grammy Awards, and other accolades. Alpert disbanded the original lineup at the end of that decade, and embarked on a solo career while still forming various incarnations of the Tijuana Brass over the following decades. He also cofounded A&M Records with Jerry Moss, their initials forming the name. Alpert released the solo record "Over the Rainbow" in 2019.

Doritos is a brand of flavored tortilla chips from the Frito-Lay company that debuted in 1966. Toasted Corn was the first flavor, followed in 1967 by Taco. The popular Nacho Cheese flavor, arguably the brand's flagship flavor, didn't appear until 1972.

References: *Dallas, Dynasty, Falcon Crest, Knots Landing*

Blanche: Not me. Last night on *Dallas*, or *Dynasty*, or *Falcon's Landing*, or one of those. They're all the same.

Four prime-time soap operas that were indeed fairly similar. One of the biggest drama series of the 1980s, *Dallas* ran from 1978 to 1991 on CBS, revolving around the Ewing family, wealthy Texas oil tycoons. The ensemble cast included Larry Hagman, Barbara Bel Geddes, Patrick Duffy, Victoria Principal, and several others over the years. A famous storyline involved the shooting of popular character J. R. Ewing (Hagman), leading to the timeless phrase, "Who shot J. R.?" *Knots Landing*, a spinoff of *Dallas*, ran on CBS from 1979 to 1993. It was set in a fictitious Los Angeles suburb and initially centered on the lives of four married couples living on the Seaview Circle cul-de-sac.

Dynasty aired on ABC from 1981 to 1989 and revolved around the wealthy Carrington family in Denver, Colorado. John Forsythe played oil magnate Blake Carrington, Linda Evans his doting new wife, Krystle, and Joan Collins his conniving ex, Alexis. The series was conceived to compete with *Dallas*. After ending its nine-season run in 1989, a two-part reunion miniseries aired in 1991 and a reboot with a new cast debuted on The CW Network in 2017.

Another CBS entry into the prime-time soap world was *Falcon Crest*, which ran from 1981 to 1990. This one revolved around the feuding factions of the Gioberti/Channing family of Falcon Crest Winery. The show starred Jane Wyman, Robert Foxworth, David Selby, Susan Sullivan, Lorenzo Lamas, and plenty of others. It was set in the fictional Tuscany Valley of California, modeled after the state's winery-filled Napa Valley.

Reference: Avon

> **Mrs. Beatty:** I'll save you some time. I don't wear Avon, I have a mop, and I'm still paying for an encyclopedia that my son used just once to look up *sexual genitalia—female.*

Avon is a company specializing in beauty, personal care, and household products. Founded in 1886 by David H. McConnell, and adopting the Avon name in 1939, the company grew over the years to be one of the world's most well-known names in beauty products.

EPISODE 1.16: THE TRUTH WILL OUT
Directed by Terry Hughes. Written by Susan Beavers. Original airdate: January 18, 1986.
Rose's daughter, Kirsten, visits to review her mother's will and becomes furious when she discovers that Rose has apparently dwindled away her father's estate.

Reference: Rice Krispies

> **Rose:** It's my special maple syrup, honey, brown sugar, molasses, Rice Krispies log.
>
> **Dorothy:** How practical. A snack you can panel your den with.

Rice Krispies is a breakfast cereal introduced by the Kellogg Company in 1927, consisting of crisped rice that makes "snap, crackle, and pop" sounds when milk is added, which has served as the brand's marketing angle for decades.

Reference: Dickies

> **Blanche:** His wife was found at the bottom of their private lake clutching his dickie in her hand.

A dickie is a piece of apparel dating back to the nineteenth century, essentially a mock turtleneck worn under clothing that gives the appearance of wearing a full turtleneck underneath when in actuality it's just the collar.

Reference: "The Lady Is a Tramp"

> **Sophia:** She dated Frank Sinatra. You know the song "The Lady Is a Tramp"? It used to be "Teresa Is a Tramp." They had to change it for legal reasons.

"The Lady Is a Tramp" is a song written for the 1937 Rodgers and Hart musical *Babes in Arms* but turned into a popular standard once recorded by the likes of Frank Sinatra, Ella Fitzgerald, Bing Crosby, and Tony Bennett and Lady Gaga.

References: The Astrodome, Wedgwood china, AT&T

> **Blanche:** I'd love to put some surprises in my will, like leaving a small remembrance to each of the men who has brought some special joy or pleasure to my life.
>
> **Dorothy:** And where would they read that will, Blanche, the Astrodome?
>
> **Blanche:** Or maybe I'd just do something like, to my sister Virginia, I hereby bequeath my diamond brooch, my collection of Wedgwood china, and all my stock in AT&T.
>
> **Dorothy:** You have stock in AT&T?
>
> **Blanche:** I don't have any of those things, but for one brief moment, Virginia would think she'd hit the jackpot.

The Astrodome is the world's first domed sports stadium—and a pretty big place. Located in Houston, Texas, construction on the Astrodome began in 1962. The stadium opened in 1965 and has served as home to the city's professional baseball, football, and basketball teams. It was also the first major venue to use artificial turf, which came to be known as AstroTurf. Wedgwood is a brand of fine china, porcelain, and luxury accessories founded in 1759 by Josiah Wedgwood. AT&T is the world's largest telecommunications company. It's been around since 1885, when it began as the Bell Telephone Company, founded by none other than Alexander Graham Bell, who is credited with inventing the first practical telephone.

Reference: Oreos

> **Dorothy:** Blanche, you caught me one night sneaking out of the kitchen naked with an Oreo in my mouth. We have no secrets.

The best-selling brand of cookie in the United States, Oreos are sandwich cookies consisting of—in the original version—two chocolate wafer cookies with a sweet crème filling. They were first introduced in 1912 and have expanded to include multiple flavors and varieties, including Double Stuf Oreos with twice the crème.

References: Blue Angel Squadron, the National Anthem

> **Announcer:** Please join us when we return to the air at six a.m. We now conclude our broadcast day with the Blue Angel Squadron accompanied by our National Anthem.

The Blue Angels is a flight demonstration squadron formed in 1946 by the US Navy that performs aerial displays. The National Anthem of the United States is the patriotic musical composition "The Star-Spangled Banner," with lyrics by Francis Scott Key and music by John Stafford Smith. It was adopted as the National Anthem in 1931.

Reference: Miss Piggy

> **Rose:** We're in the middle of a makeup lesson.
>
> **Sophia:** I hope the kid can help you. You wear more rouge than Miss Piggy.

A fictional character created by Jim Henson, Miss Piggy first appeared on *The Muppet Show* in 1976 and has become a pop culture icon, known for her diva-like behavior and on-again, off-again relationship with Kermit the Frog.

Reference: Space Mountain

> **Sophia:** I can't sleep. All night long, tossing and turning. I'd get more rest on Space Mountain.

Space Mountain is a space-themed indoor roller coaster located at various Disney Parks locations. The original was opened in 1975 at Walt Disney World in Florida.

Reference: Fudgsicle

> **Sophia:** It's like having two size-nine Fudgsicles pressed up against my butt.

Fudgsicles are a brand of frozen chocolate dairy desserts on a stick.

References: Barbie, Poligrip

> **Dorothy:** My mother is trying to help her put Barbie's hair back on with Poligrip.

Simply *the* fashion doll of the twentieth century, Barbie first graced toy shelves in 1959 and is still going strong today. Mattel, the toymaker, has sold over a billion Barbie dolls, not to mention Barbie's friends, family, accessories, and additional product lines like games, cartoons, music, and so on. The line was invented by Ruth Handler, who noticed her daughter, Barbara, assigning adult roles to her paper dolls, which at the time were regularly created as infants. Using her daughter's name for the doll, and eventually her son's name for Barbie's male counterpart, Ken, the dolls took off, and Barbie soon became a cultural icon.

Poligrip is a brand of denture adhesive.

Repeat References: Frank Sinatra *(Episode 1.11: Stan's Return)*, Bruce Springsteen *(Episode 1.7: The Competition)*

EPISODE 1.17: NICE AND EASY
Directed by Terry Hughes. Written by Stuart Silverman. Original airdate February 1, 1986.
Blanche discovers that her visiting niece, Lucy, is more promiscuous than she. Dorothy and Rose disagree over how to deal with a mouse in the kitchen.

Reference: Windex

> **Blanche:** Terrific little figure. Gorgeous hair. Perfect skin. Just like looking in a mirror.
>
> **Sophia:** Get some Windex!

Windex is a brand of glass cleaner invented in 1933.

Reference: O. J. Simpson

> **Dorothy:** He's back. I saw him running across my dresser.
>
> **Rose:** Who's back?
>
> **Dorothy:** O. J. Simpson, Rose.

O. J. Simpson is a former professional football player and actor who played for the Buffalo Bills and the San Francisco 49ers before starring in *The Naked*

Gun series of comedy films. He's best remembered, however, for being tried for the murders of his former wife and her friend in the mid-1990s. He was acquitted after a lengthy and much-publicized trial, only to be arrested in 2007 on felony robbery and kidnapping charges. He was convicted the following year and granted parole in 2017.

Reference: Dogpatch

> **Dorothy:** That should give them something to talk about back in Dogpatch.

Dogpatch was the fictional setting of Al Capp's comic strip *Li'l Abner*, which depicted a clan of hillbillies who lived in the middle of nowhere and were quite averse to progress. The strip ran from 1934 to 1977.

Reference: Purple Heart

> **Rose:** Emmett received three Purple Hearts, all for head wounds.

The Purple Heart is a US military decoration awarded in the name of the president to those wounded or killed in service. It was first awarded in 1932.

Reference: *Our Town*

> **Dorothy:** Rose, are you telling a story or performing *Our Town*?

Our Town is a 1938 Pulitzer Prize–winning Thornton Wilder play about the day-to-day lives of the citizens of a small American town.

Reference: The Rockettes

> **Blanche:** For two months, I was a Rockette under an assumed name.

The Rockettes are a precision dance company founded in 1925 who have performed at Radio City Music Hall in New York City since 1932.

Reference: Crockett and Tubbs

> **Ed:** I know a lot of people prefer Sonny Crockett on the show, but me, I'm strictly a Tubbs man.

Sonny Crockett and Rico Tubbs were the pastel-clad, sockless detectives portrayed by Don Johnson and Philip Michael Thomas, respectively, on NBC's *Miami Vice* from 1984 to 1990. Colin Farrell and Jamie Foxx portrayed the characters in a 2006 film adaptation.

Reference: Don Johnson

> **Ed:** Tuesday night I'm getting together with a couple buddies. We're going through Don Johnson's trash!

After rising to fame as Detective James "Sonny" Crockett on *Miami Vice*, Johnson followed it up with a five-year run on another police drama, *Nash Bridges*, in the 1990s. That show costarred Cheech Marin, who was part of the cast of *The Golden Girls* spinoff series, *The Golden Palace*. He's been a Hollywood fixture for decades, recently costarring in the NBC sitcom *Kenan*.

Repeat References: *Miami Vice (Episode 1.6: On Golden Girls)*, Disneyland (*Episode 1.14: That Was No Lady*)

EPISODE 1.18: THE OPERATION
Directed by Terry Hughes. Written by Winifred Hervey. Original airdate: February 8, 1986.
Dorothy aggravates an old injury while practicing for a tap-dancing recital and winds up in the hospital.

Reference: Pat Sajak

> **Sophia:** We stake out a bench, knock a few sherries back, and discuss what we think the clouds look like. One afternoon I thought I saw Pat Sajak riding sidesaddle on a dolphin.

Pat Sajak is a television personality best known for his long stint as host of the game show *Wheel of Fortune* since 1981. He also briefly hosted a late-night talk show on CBS from 1989 to 1990.

References: Elvis Presley, Graceland

> **Dorothy:** This toothless old wino who claimed he was Elvis kept hounding me for bus fare to Graceland.

Elvis Presley (1935–1977) was an iconic singer and actor known as the "King of Rock and Roll," whose many hits include "Don't Be Cruel," "Love Me Tender," "Heartbreak Hotel," "Burning Love," "Jailhouse Rock," and many others. Graceland is a mansion in Memphis, Tennessee, once owned by Presley (and owned by his daughter, Lisa Marie, since his 1977 death). It is a massively popular tourist attraction since it was opened as a museum in 1972. It's reportedly the second-most-visited house in the United States, after the

White House. Hundreds of thousands of visitors flock to the property each year to see things like the famed Jungle Room, Presley's cars and planes, and the famed singer's grave.

Reference: The friendly skies

> **Dorothy:** You met a handsome pilot. He invited you into the cockpit. Of course, you said yes, as you usually do in these stories. The two of you made passionate love, and now you cannot get enough of the friendly skies.

"Fly the friendly skies" was a famous slogan of United Airlines introduced in 1965.

References: Shirley Temple, Mary Janes

> **Blanche:** There were thirteen little girls up there with our little Shirley Temple curls, our little starched-white pinafores, and our little Mary Jane shoes, and then they opened the curtain, the music started, and twelve little girls started to dance. And one little girl wet her pants.

Shirley Temple (1928–2014) was a popular child actress in the 1930s, known for her cherub face and ringlet curls. As an adult, she was named US ambassador to Ghana and Czechoslovakia. Mary Janes are low-cut shoes with a closed toe and a strap across the inset. They're sometimes called "doll shoes."

Reference: "Singin' in the Rain"

> **Rose:** If you end up in a puddle tonight, well, you'd just better break into "Singin' in the Rain."

"Singin' in the Rain" is the title song to the 1952 movie-musical of the same name, starring Gene Kelly, Donald O'Connor, and Debbie Reynolds as performers transitioning from silent films to "talkies."

Reference: The Lone Ranger

> **Sophia:** She's not the Lone Ranger. She'll be back. I sent her to the cafeteria to get me a sandwich.

The Lone Ranger was a fictional masked Texas Ranger of radio, television, and film, who first appeared in 1933.

Episode 1.19: Second Motherhood

Directed by Gary Shimokawa. Written by Christopher Lloyd. Original airdate: February 15, 1986.

Blanche accepts the marriage proposal from her wealthy boyfriend but has second thoughts when realizing her new family would come with two small children. Dorothy and Rose attempt to repair a broken toilet.

Reference: The Ty-D-Bol Man

> **Dorothy:** Call the Ty-D-Bol Man. He'll jump in his boat and spread the news.

The Ty-D-Bol Man was a nautical spokes-character for Ty-D-Bol toilet cleaner, who piloted a boat inside a toilet tank in a series of commercials from the 1960s to the 1980s.

Reference: Girl Scouts

> **Sophia:** Was that a plumber?
>
> **Dorothy:** No, Ma, no. It was a little girl selling Girl Scout toilets.

The Girl Scouts is a youth organization for girls founded in 1912 by Juliette Gordon Low and known for their annual cookie sale—and occasional door-to-door toilet sale.

Reference: The pyramids

> **Rose:** If the Egyptians built the pyramids, now we can move this toilet.
>
> **Dorothy:** Fine, get me twenty thousand Hebrews, and I'll have it out of here in no time.

The pyramids are ancient masonry structures located in Egypt, built as tombs for the country's pharaohs. There are more than a hundred pyramids located in Egypt, but the most famous are those found in Giza. The Great Pyramid of Giza is one of the Seven Wonders of the Ancient World.

Reference: Texaco

> **Dorothy:** I'm ready to throw in the wrench and start using the Texaco station down the street.

Texaco is an oil subsidiary of the Chevron Corporation, founded in 1902.

Reference: Fats Domino

> **Rose:** Little Richard was in Bermuda?
>
> **Dorothy:** Yes, Rose. He was burying Fats Domino in the sand.

Fats Domino (1928–2017) was a singer and musician considered to be a pioneer of rock-and-roll music. His seven-decade career included hits like "Ain't That a Shame" and "Blueberry Hill."

Repeat References: Ovaltine *(Episode 1.4: Transplant)*, Little Richard *(Episode 1.5: The Triangle)*

EPISODE 1.20: ADULT EDUCATION
Directed by Jack Shea. Written by James Berg and Stan Zimmerman. Original airdate: February 22, 1986.
Blanche takes a college course to get a promotion at the museum and receives an unwanted proposition from her professor. Dorothy attempts to purchase tickets to a Frank Sinatra concert.

Reference: Don King

> **Sophia:** The last time I was late, Ronald gave me the broken hairdryer. I came out looking like Don King.

Don King is a controversial former boxing promoter, known for promoting such classic events as the Rumble in the Jungle (George Foreman vs. Muhammad Ali, 1974) and the Thrilla in Manila (Ali vs. Joe Frazier, 1975)—and also, for his tall, wild hair.

Reference: NBC

> **Rose:** My best friend in St. Olaf has a nephew who is a page at NBC in Hollywood.

The National Broadcasting Company is a major television and radio network founded in 1926. It was home to *The Golden Girls*.

Reference: Barbara Walters

> **Dorothy:** I had a slight speech impediment. It's different for kids these days. They have Barbara Walters to look up to.

Barbara Walters is a broadcast journalist known for her work on *Today*, the *ABC Evening News*, *20/20*, and *The View*.

Reference: Jell-O

> **Sophia:** I hate Jell-O. If God wanted peaches suspended in midair, he would've filled them with helium.

Jell-O is a brand of fruit-flavored gelatin desserts and puddings. The original line, the gelatin dessert, was invented in 1897 by Pearle Bixby Wait and his wife, May.

Reference: Feen-A-Mint

> **Rose:** Did all that stuff come out of your purse?
> **Sophia:** No, Rose. I'm also cleaning out my ears. That's where the Feen-A-Mint and the rain bonnet came from.

Feen-A-Mint is an over-the-counter oral laxative.

Reference: Soda jerk

> **Rose:** He worked at Lars Erikson's drugstore and tackle shop. He was a soda jerk.

A soda jerk was an employee, typically a young man, who operated the soda fountain at a drugstore lunch counter.

Reference: Tina Sinatra

> **Sophia:** I called Frank. I told you I had connections.
> **Rose:** You know Frank Sinatra?
> **Sophia:** No, Frank Garavicci, from the fish market. He's always been good to me. Never a bad piece of cod. He knows Frank.
> **Blanche:** Sinatra?
> **Sophia:** No, Frank Tortoni, the dry cleaner. Tina's third cousin once removed.
> **Dorothy:** Tina Tortoni?
> **Sophia:** Tina Sinatra!

Tina Sinatra is a producer, agent, former actor, and the daughter of iconic singer Frank Sinatra.

Repeat References: Frank Sinatra *(Episode 1.11: Stan's Return)*, Bob Hope *(Episode 1.9: Blanche and the Younger Man)*

EPISODE 1.21: THE FLU
Directed by Terry Hughes. Written by James Berg and Stan Zimmerman. Original airdate: March 1, 1986.
Blanche, Dorothy, and Rose each come down with the flu days ahead of an important charity banquet.

References: Listerine, Scope

> **Rose:** I have a fever and my throat is sore and my stomach is upset, and I keep having this recurring dream where I am being chased by a giant Listerine bottle. And when I open my mouth to scream, all I can do is gargle.
>
> **Dr. Richmond:** Are you experiencing the same symptoms?
>
> **Dorothy:** Yes, except in my dream, I'm chased by a bottle of Scope.

Listerine and Scope are brands of mouthwash introduced in 1914 and 1966, respectively.

Reference: Michael DeBakey

> **Rose:** My mother always used to sing to us and make us gingerbread men.
>
> **Dorothy:** Really, Rose? I think Michael DeBakey does that before surgery.

Dr. Michael DeBakey (1908–2008) was a prominent cardiovascular surgeon and a pioneer in surgical procedures to treat cardiovascular defects and diseases.

Reference: Hot toddy

> **Dorothy:** How can you be so disgustingly cheerful?
>
> **Rose:** It's my folk medicine book. It has the most wonderful hot toddy recipe. Here, taste.
>
> **Dorothy, tasting the drink:** Rose, this stuff should have an octane rating.

A hot toddy is a drink made from a brown liquor, such as whiskey, mixed with hot water, honey, and lemon juice, commonly used to soothe a cough and cold.

Reference: *Another World*

> **Dorothy:** You watched it yesterday.
>
> **Blanche:** That's exactly why I have to watch it today, Dorothy, to find out what happens. That's why they always say, "Stay tuned for the continuing story of *Another World*."

Another World was a daytime soap opera that ran on NBC from 1964 to 1999. The show became the first soap opera to discuss abortion in 1964, launched two spinoff series, and had a Top 5 theme song in the Crystal Gayle–Gary Morris duet "(You Take Me Away to) Another World." Ratings began to erode in the 1990s and a mid-decade attempt to revamp the show toward a more youthful audience faltered. Its last episode aired in June 1999.

Reference: NyQuil

> **Rose:** You lost the premeasured cup off of my NyQuil.

NyQuil is an over-the-counter nighttime cold medicine manufactured by Vicks.

References: Sucrets, Smith Brothers

> **Harold:** Sucret?
>
> **Rose:** No, thank you. I'm still sucking on a Smith Brothers.

Sucrets and Smith Brothers are brands of over-the-counter throat lozenges.

References: The *New York Times*, Norman Mailer

> **Blanche:** Tommy's a writer. According to the *New York Times*, he is the most exciting new novelist to come along since Norman Mailer.

The *New York Times* is an influential daily newspaper founded by Henry Jarvis Raymond and George Jones (not the singer) in 1851. Norman Mailer (1923–2007) was a writer and actor who authored eleven best-selling books, including *The Naked and the Dead*, *Armies of the Night*, and *The Executioner's Song*.

Repeat References: Cary Grant *(Episode 1.6: On Golden Girls)*, Girl Scouts *(Episode 1.19: Second Motherhood)*, Vicks VapoRub *(Episode 1.6: On Golden Girls)*, Don Johnson *(Episode 1.17: Nice and Easy)*, Miami Vice *(Episode 1.6: On Golden Girls)*

EPISODE 1.22: JOB HUNTING

Directed by Paul Bogart. Written by Kathy Speer and Terry Grossman. Original airdate: March 8, 1986.

After losing her job, Rose has trouble finding new employment because of her age. Dorothy prepares for a date with an old high school friend.

Reference: "Kentucky Babe"

> *Blanche is singing the song while preparing food.*

"Kentucky Babe" is an 1896 tune written by Richard Henry Buck and Adam Geibel.

Reference: Dan Rather

> **Sophia:** We're out of pepperoni.
>
> **Dorothy:** Did you call Dan Rather?

Dan Rather is a journalist and author known for anchoring the *CBS Evening News* from 1981 to 2005.

Reference: Kennedy Space Center

> **Rose:** They closed the center.
>
> **Blanche:** Not your grief counseling center.
>
> **Dorothy:** No, the Kennedy Space Center.

The Kennedy Space Center is the Cape Canaveral, Florida, NASA location opened in 1962 and used as the primary launch site for spaceflight.

Reference: *Newsweek*

> **Milton:** I'm learning to get in touch with my emotions.
>
> **Dorothy:** Tell me, will it take long? You're reading my *Newsweek*.

Newsweek is a weekly newsmagazine founded in 1933.

Reference: *The Young and the Restless*

> **Sophia:** If you have to go out tomorrow, ask those crybabies not to call during *The Young and the Restless*.

The Young and the Restless is a daytime soap opera created by William J. Bell and Lee Phillip Bell that has aired on CBS since 1973.

Reference: Jeep Wagoneer

> **Rose:** Mrs. Montez found her cat. I bet she's happy, too!
>
> **Sophia:** Not exactly. She found it under a Jeep Wagoneer.

The Jeep Wagoneer was a sport utility vehicle manufactured by Jeep from 1963 to 1993.

Reference: Buddy Ebsen

> **Dorothy:** If I don't get at least six hours' sleep, I look like Buddy Ebsen.

Actor and dancer Buddy Ebsen's (1908–2003) seven-decade career included the roles of Jed Clampett in the sitcom *The Beverly Hillbillies* (1962–1971) and the titular role in the detective drama *Barnaby Jones* (1973–1980). He was also originally cast to play the Tin Man in the 1939 musical version of *The Wizard of Oz*, but the aluminum dust used in the makeup for the character made him seriously ill, and he was replaced by Jack Haley.

Reference: Mary Lou Retton

> **Blanche:** Let's face it, Rose. You're not exactly Mary Lou Retton.

Olympic gymnast Mary Lou Retton won the all-around gold medal at the 1984 Summer Olympics, the first woman to do so. The win propelled her to stardom, and she was named the *Sports Illustrated* "Sportswoman of the Year," landed on the box of Wheaties cereal, and became the brand's first official spokeswoman.

References: Judge Crater, Jimmy Hoffa

> **Rose:** You'll never guess what I found!
>
> **Dorothy:** Judge Crater?
>
> **Rose, later:** Oh, you'll never guess what I found!
>
> **Dorothy:** Jimmy Hoffa?

Two well-known missing persons. New York State Supreme Court Justice Joseph Force Crater vanished in 1930 amid political scandal. He was last seen getting into a cab after leaving a Manhattan restaurant and became one of the most mysterious missing persons cases of the twentieth century. Despite his disappearance receiving massive publicity, he was never found. The case was officially closed forty years later.

Jimmy Hoffa was a labor union leader and president of the International Brotherhood of Teamsters from 1957 to 1971. He became involved in organized crime, was convicted in 1964 of jury tampering and other charges, and was imprisoned in 1967, serving four years. An attempt to regain leadership in 1975 met with Mafia opposition, and Hoffa disappeared on July 30 of that year. Believed to have been murdered by the Mafia, his remains were never found, and he was declared dead in 1982.

Reference: Pinch an inch

> **Milton:** Men of our generation like a little meat on their women. Maybe you don't want to pinch an inch, but I do.

This line references a popular ad campaign in the 1980s for the breakfast cereal Special K, which suggested that if you could pinch more than an inch of your love handles, you'd better lose some weight—by eating cereal.

Reference: Buster Crabbe

> **Dorothy:** Barry Glick is gay.
>
> **Sophia:** I knew he was gay. I could tell by the way he used to worship Buster Crabbe.

A two-time Olympic swimmer, Buster Crabbe (1908–1983) won a bronze medal in 1929 and a gold medal in 1932 before launching a successful acting career on film and television. Among his notable roles were comic-strip heroes Tarzan, Flash Gordon, and Buck Rogers. When the roles began to dry up in the 1950s and 1960s, he embarked on a career as a businessman and stockbroker but never totally stopped acting.

Reference: Mel's Diner

> **Dorothy:** She's working at the Fountain Rock. It's not Mel's Diner.

Mel's Diner was the fictional setting for the sitcom *Alice*, which ran on CBS from 1976 to 1985. The show starred Linda Lavin, Vic Tayback (as Mel), and Polly Holliday, who also played Rose's sister, Lily, on *The Golden Girls*.

Repeat Reference: Scarlett O'Hara *(Episode 1.5: The Triangle)*

EPISODE 1.23: BLIND AMBITIONS
Directed by Terry Hughes. Written by Bob Colleary. Original airdate: March 29, 1986.
Rose receives a visit from her sister, Lily, who has recently lost her eyesight. The girls plan a garage sale to raise funds for a new television.

Reference: X-15

> **Dorothy:** Blanche's bed is next to the X-15 at the Space and Aviation Museum.

The X-15 was a hypersonic rocket-powered aircraft used by the US Air Force and NASA from 1959 to 1968.

Reference: *St. Elsewhere*

> **Lily:** You couldn't drag me out of this house tonight. *St. Elsewhere* is on. It's my favorite program. I never miss it.

St. Elsewhere was a medical drama series that aired on NBC from 1982 to 1988, focusing on a group of teaching doctors at a Boston hospital. Its series finale ranks among television's most memorable. In the final scene, the exterior of the hospital is revealed to actually be a replica inside of a snow globe belonging to the autistic son of one of the show's characters, suggesting that the events of the entire series existed only in the boy's imagination.

References: Benson, Miss Ellie

> **Sophia:** With our crummy TV, we get two channels at once. For a while there I thought Benson was having an affair with Miss Ellie.

Benson DuBois was the title character of the sitcom *Benson*, which ran from 1979 to 1986, and was a spinoff of the Susan Harris–created sitcom *Soap*, which debuted in 1977. On *Soap*, the character Benson, played by Robert Guillaume, was the wisecracking butler to the wacky, rich Tate family. The breakout character was popular enough to get his own series, in which Benson lands the gig of head of household affairs for a widowed governor.

Benson works his way up the career ladder over the course of the show's seven seasons, eventually running for the governor spot himself against his former employer.

Miss Ellie was a fictional character from the CBS television series *Dallas*, portrayed by Barbara Bel Geddes.

Reference: *The Cosby Show*

> **Sophia:** And what am I supposed to do while every other old lady on the block is watching *Cosby*?
>
> **Dorothy:** Well, you can sit in the new driveway and hope that an amusing Black family drops by.

One of the biggest sitcoms of the 1980s, *The Cosby Show* ran for eight seasons on NBC, from 1984 to 1992, and starred Bill Cosby and Phylicia Rashad as Cliff and Clair Huxtable, an upper-middle-class Black family raising their children in Brooklyn. The show was a consistent number-one hit and spent all eight of its seasons in the Top 20. It also made breakout stars of the actors playing the Huxtable children, including Lisa Bonet, who helmed the first season of the spinoff series, *A Different World*. Despite being credited with paving the way for the expansion of more Black-led television series, the legacy of *The Cosby Show* has been tainted by Cosby's 2018 conviction for sexual assault.

Reference: Ann-Margret

> **Dorothy:** Her hair is falling out. Her clothes are all worn. She smells of mothballs.
>
> **Sophia:** I may not be Ann-Margret, but I'm still your mother.

Ann-Margret is an actress, singer, and dancer known for her roles in such films as *Bye Bye Birdie*, *Carnal Knowledge*, and *Grumpy Old Men*. Once billed as the "female Elvis," Ann-Margret was romantically linked to the legend while they filmed *Viva Las Vegas*. Her varied career spans several films, television roles, albums, and a slew of accolades. Working steadily for five decades, her recent roles include appearances on *Ray Donovan* and *The Kominsky Method*.

References: Woodstock, Richie Havens, Bob Dylan

> **Blanche:** I remember wearing this outfit the night George took me to Woodstock. Oh, what a night. I will never forget it. Listening to the music of Mr. Richie Havens and Mr. Bob Dylan and then making love in the mud.
>
> **Rose:** You went to Woodstock?
>
> **Blanche:** Well, actually it was the movie, but afterwards we did go home and make love in the mud.

Woodstock was a famous music festival held over three days on a New York dairy farm in the summer of 1969. Thirty-two acts performed, including Richie Havens, Joan Baez, the Grateful Dead, Janis Joplin, The Who, The Band, Jimi Hendrix, and others—but, despite this line, not Bob Dylan. Billed as "3 Days of Peace & Music," it is considered a pivotal point in music history and a defining moment for the counterculture generation. A documentary film about the festival was released in 1970. Richie Havens (1941–2013) rose to fame after being the opening act at Woodstock and released a string of records over the following decades, dabbled in acting, and worked in environmental activism. Bob Dylan's illustrious, five-decade career began with his debut 1962 album and has included such iconic songs as "Blowin' in the Wind," "The Times They Are a-Changin'," "Like a Rolling Stone," and countless other hits. He has recorded some of the most influential records in folk and rock-and-roll history, including *Highway 61 Revisited*, *Blonde on Blonde*, and *Blood on the Tracks*. In 2016, Dylan was awarded the Nobel Prize in Literature for his songwriting.

Reference: Gidget

> **Sophia:** Who invited Gidget to the garage sale?

Gidget began as a character in the 1957 novel *Gidget, the Little Girl with Big Ideas* by Frederick Kohner, about a teenage girl and her Malibu surfing pals. Several book sequels followed, as did films (the first of which starred Sandra Dee in the title role) and, perhaps most notably, the 1965 television series starring a young Sally Field.

Reference: Neiman Marcus

> **Dorothy:** Ma, that's no way to sell things.

Sophia: Hey, go to Neiman Marcus sometime, see if they treat you any better.

Neiman Marcus is a chain of luxury department stores founded in 1907 by Carrie Marcus Neiman, Herbert Marcus, and Abraham Lincoln Neiman.

Reference: Dr. Pepper

Blanche: I will have you know the day I bought these salt and pepper shakers at the Graceland gift shop, I thought I saw the King himself walk by, eating a giant chili cheeseburger and drinking a thirty-six-ounce Dr. Pepper.

Dr. Pepper is a carbonated soft drink created in the 1880s by pharmacist Charles Alderton in Waco, Texas, and now a worldwide brand. Interestingly, Dr. Pepper precedes Coca-Cola by a year.

Reference: Bobby Hull

Dorothy: This isn't an ordinary hockey stick. Bobby Hull used this. This is a piece of history.

Bobby Hull is a former Canadian hockey player whose twenty-three-year career in the National Hockey League and World Hockey Association included stints with the Chicago Black Hawks, Winnipeg Jets, and Hartford Whalers. Regarded as one of the greatest players of all time, Hull's hockey sticks have been rumored to fetch as much as $1,100 at Miami garage sales.

Reference: Shirley MacLaine

Dorothy: Get out of here. You've come back more times than Shirley MacLaine.

Enduring actress Shirley MacLaine's multi-decade career has spanned several hits (*Some Came Running*, *The Apartment*, *Steel Magnolias*, and the Oscar-winning *Terms of Endearment*) and also a lot of duds—making those comebacks all the sweeter.

Repeat References: Elvis Presley and Graceland *(Episode 1.18: The Operation)*

EPISODE 1.24: BIG DADDY

Directed by Terry Hughes. Written by Barry Fanaro and Mort Nathan. Original airdate: May 3, 1986.

Blanche's father, Big Daddy, visits with the announcement that he's sold the family home and has become a country music singer. The girls battle a cranky neighbor over a fallen tree on the lanai.

References: Mint julep, "Cotton Fields (The Cotton Song)"

> **Blanche:** The ladies would retire to the shade of an old magnolia to sip mint juleps and exchange prize-winning pecan pie recipes.
>
> **Dorothy:** Tell me, Blanche, would the farmhands suddenly break into a chorus of "Them Old Cotton Fields Back Home"?

A mint julep is a cocktail consisting of bourbon, sugar, water, ice, and fresh mint. "Cotton Fields (The Cotton Song)" is a 1940 song written by Huddie Ledbetter, aka Lead Belly, and popularized through covers by such acts as The Beach Boys and Creedence Clearwater Revival.

References: Baltimore Colts, New York Jets

> **Sophia:** Ridiculous? The curse works, believe me. I've used it before.
>
> **Dorothy:** Oh, when?
>
> **Sophia:** Baltimore Colts, New York Jets, 1969. Draw your own conclusion.

The Colts was Baltimore's professional football team for three decades, from 1953 to 1983, before they galloped off in the middle of the night to Indianapolis. The Jets is a New York–based professional football team founded in 1959. The two teams squared off in Super Bowl III on January 12, 1969, the first game to bear the official Super Bowl trademark. The eighteen-point underdog Jets defeated the champion Colts sixteen to seven in what is considered one of the greatest upsets in the history of sports.

Reference: Denny's

> **Blanche:** Ladies, how do I look?
>
> **Sophia:** Like the night hostess at Denny's.

Denny's is a chain of diner-style eateries with over 1,700 locations in countries throughout the world. It originally opened as a California coffee shop under the name Danny's Donuts in 1953. The name Denny's officially took hold in 1961, franchising took off in 1963, and by the 1980s, Denny's restaurants were popping up like crazy.

Reference: The Mason–Dixon Line

> **Big Daddy:** Looking at you takes my breath away. Hair as shiny as the dew on a field of sunflowers, eyes that sparkle bluer than the Mississippi, and the prettiest smile on either side of the Mason–Dixon Line.

The Mason–Dixon Line is a demarcation line that was surveyed in the 1760s by Charles Mason and Jeremiah Dixon to resolve a border dispute, and informally became the border between the Northern and Southern states during the Civil War. It forms part of the borders of Delaware, Maryland, Pennsylvania, and West Virginia.

Reference: Dinah Shore

> **Big Daddy:** Has anyone ever told you, you are the spitting image of Ms. Dinah Shore?

Dinah Shore (1916–1994) was a singer, actress, and television personality who charted a string of hits during the big band era of the 1940s and 1950s. She moved toward acting after that period of time and, in the 1970s, hosted a couple of popular talk/variety shows.

Reference: *Gone with the Wind*

> **Rose:** This is so much fun! It's like being in *Gone with the Wind*.

A 1939 epic film based on the 1936 novel of the same name by Margaret Mitchell, *Gone with the Wind* is an American Civil War and Reconstruction-era epic about strong-willed Scarlett O'Hara and her suitor Rhett Butler. Vivien Leigh and Clark Gable portrayed the pair in the film, which won a slew of Academy Awards, including Best Picture, and has been considered one of the greatest films of all time. It's also one of the most controversial, with its depiction of racist stereotypes and glorification of slavery.

Reference: Hank Williams

> **Big Daddy:** I know I'm no Hank Williams yet.

Hank Williams (1923–1953) was an influential country music singer and songwriter known for such hits as "Move It on Over," "Lovesick Blues," "Your Cheatin' Heart," "Hey, Good Lookin'," and "I'm So Lonesome I Could Cry."

References: White wine spritzer, Volvo

> **Rose:** Are these all real cowboys?
>
> **Dorothy:** Of course, Rose. You can tell because they wear cowboy hats and drink white wine spritzers and drive Volvos.

A white wine spritzer is a cocktail made by mixing white wine with club soda. Volvo is a Swedish automobile manufacturer founded in 1927.

Reference: The Beatles

> **Big Daddy:** I never should've tried that Beatles medley.

The Beatles were an English rock band formed in Liverpool in 1960, consisting of John Lennon, Paul McCartney, Ringo Starr, and George Harrison. Often regarded as the most influential band in music history, not to mention the best-selling band of all time, what is there to say about The Beatles that will do them justice in a few short sentences? Oh well. After conquering the world over the course of a decade, and releasing thirteen studio albums, the band broke up in 1970, with each member going on to varying degrees of solo success. Lennon was assassinated in 1980, and Harrison died from lung cancer in 2001. McCartney and Starr remain active today.

EPISODE 1.25: THE WAY WE MET
Directed by Terry Hughes. Written by Kathy Speer, Terry Grossman, Winifred Hervey, Mort Nathan, and Barry Fanaro. Original airdate: May 10, 1986.
Unable to sleep after watching the movie *Psycho*, the girls reminisce about how they came to live together.

Reference: Mariachi band

> **Dorothy:** Next time I walk into a dark room in the middle of the night, I'll send a mariachi band ahead of me.

Mariachi is a genre of Mexican music dating back to the eighteenth century, typically consisting of violins, trumpets, a guitar, and other instruments.

References: *Psycho*, Roxy Theatre

> **Dorothy:** We never should've watched *Psycho*. For twenty-five years I have avoided that picture, even when Stan invited me to the Roxy instead of over to his mother's for dinner. And it turns out my instincts

were right. Norman Bates is scarier than my mother-in-law and a much better dresser.

Psycho is a 1960 psychological horror film produced and directed by Alfred Hitchcock, and starring Janet Leigh as a woman on the run for embezzling and Anthony Perkins as the shy (and psychopathic) motel proprietor—Norman Bates—who becomes enamored with her. The film spawned several sequels and a 1998 remake starring Vince Vaughn. The Roxy Theatre was a movie theater located just off Times Square in New York City that opened in 1927 and closed in March 1960. Funnily enough, *Psycho* wasn't released until June of that year.

Reference: *Goldilocks and the Three Bears*

> **Blanche:** I never should've watched it either. It always upsets me, especially that shower scene. Why, it's the reason I prefer never to shower alone.
>
> **Dorothy:** Sure, Blanche, and *Goldilocks and the Three Bears* is why you prefer never to sleep alone.

Goldilocks and the Three Bears is a fairy tale dating to the nineteenth century about a little girl who wanders into the home of three bears while they are away and proceeds to make herself welcome. Actually, the original version involved an older woman and three male bears. The story evolved to the more-iconic version of a young Goldilocks and a family of bears—Papa, Mama, and Baby Bear.

Reference: The Archduke Ferdinand

> **Blanche:** You didn't get dumped?
>
> **Rose:** Well, actually I did, by my landlord. He threw me out of my apartment. But I couldn't sleep with his best friend. He's over eighty years old and thinks he's the Archduke Ferdinand.

The Archduke Ferdinand (1863–1914) was the presumptive heir to the throne of Austria-Hungary following the deaths of a couple of the gentlemen in line in front of him, one by suicide and the other by typhoid fever. He had the audacity to marry a lady of lower class—such a scandal!—and eventually renounced his rights to the throne. He was later named inspector-general of the Austro-Hungarian armed forces and then, in 1914, he and his wife were assassinated. That event, among others, contributed to the start of World War I.

References: Mister Rogers, Dale Evans

> **Rose:** It's been such a lovely day. Mr. Sunshine really gave us one of his biggest and brightest smiles. I feel like putting my arms around Mother Nature and giving her a big kiss. Hi, you must be Dorothy.
>
> **Dorothy:** And you must be Mrs. Rogers.
>
> **Rose:** No, but we have a Mrs. Rogers at the grief center, and there's a Mrs. Rogers lives across the street. And then of course there's Dale Evans, the most famous Mrs. Rogers of them all.

This joke is a play on Fred Rogers (1928–2003), a beloved host of the long-running children's television program *Mister Rogers' Neighborhood*, which ran from 1968 to 2001. Actress and singer Dale Evans (1912–2001) was married to singing cowboy Roy Rogers from 1947 until his death in 1998.

Reference: "Kumbaya"

> **Rose:** If there's ever a night where you can't sleep, I'll come to your room and sing "Kumbaya."

"Kumbaya" is a spiritual of disputed origins believed to have ties to enslaved West Africans. It has become a popular kids' campfire song after gaining popularity in the folk revival of the 1950s and 1960s.

References: Dairy Queen, Blizzard

> **Rose:** We'd better hurry because the strawberry Blizzard special at the Dairy Queen only lasts until five.

Dairy Queen is a quick-service restaurant specializing in frozen treats made from soft-serve ice cream, as well as fast-food items like hamburgers and hot dogs. The first Dairy Queen opened in Joliet, Illinois, in 1940. The place took off quickly, with 1,600 servings being dished out within the first two hours of opening its doors. Its popularity hasn't faded. Thousands of Dairy Queens are operating today in countries all over the world. One of the restaurant's most popular offerings is the Blizzard, made from mixing ice cream with ingredients like fruit or candy bar pieces.

References: Bette Midler, Grammys

> **Blanche:** It was at that moment I realized my bosoms had the power to make music.
>
> **Dorothy:** Didn't Bette Midler win a special Grammy for that?

Introduced in 1959, the Grammys are the annual awards presented by the Recording Academy to recognize musical achievement. Bette Midler is a singer and actress known for hits like "The Rose," "Wind beneath My Wings," and "From a Distance," and films such as *Beaches*, *Ruthless People*, *Hocus Pocus*, and *The First Wives Club*. She's received four Golden Globes, three Grammys, three Emmys, and a Tony over her multi-decade career.

Reference: Cold Duck

> **Blanche:** If you ever have a date with a man who's a little sluggish, a tin of [smoked oysters], a bottle of Cold Duck, you'll be prying him off the wall.

Cold Duck is a sparkling wine created in 1937 by Harold Borgman of Pontchartrain Wine Cellars in Detroit. It was originally a mixture of champagne and sparkling burgundy poured into a hollow-stem wineglass. The recipe now varies and multiple companies have produced a beverage under the Cold Duck name.

References: *Globe*, *Tatler*, *Midnight Star*, *Enquirer*, *People*

> **Blanche, picking out magazines:** I almost forgot, I need a *Globe* and a *Tatler* and a *Midnight Star* and an *Enquirer*, and I guess maybe one serious newsmagazine so we know what's going on in the world. One *People*.

These are all supermarket tabloid magazines, although *People* does rely on actual celebrity interviews and human interest content, as opposed to the typical tabloid fodder. The reference to *Midnight Star* isn't entirely correct. The actual name of the magazine is simply *Star*, while *Globe* was indeed once known as *Midnight Globe*.

Reference: *The Price Is Right*

> **Rose:** That Windex isn't on sale this week. The regular price is a dollar ninety-nine.

Dorothy: Rose, why don't you save it for *The Price Is Right*.

The Price Is Right is a long-running, beloved television game show created by Bob Stewart, Mark Goodson, and Bill Todman, which debuted in 1972 and features contestants competing to win cash and prizes by guessing the price of merchandise. Bob Barker hosted the show until his retirement in 2007, when actor and comedian Drew Carey took over.

Reference: Raisin Bran

Blanche: All right, who put the Raisin Bran in the refrigerator?

Raisin Bran is a breakfast cereal consisting of raisins and bran flakes, first marketed by the Skinner Manufacturing Company in 1926. While several companies sell a version of the cereal, Kellogg's Raisin Bran is probably the most recognized.

Reference: SeaWorld

Rose: A herring circus. Sort of like SeaWorld, only smaller. Much, much smaller.

SeaWorld is an Orlando, Florida, theme park first opened in 1964, specializing in marine mammals.

Repeat References: Jerry Lewis *(Episode 1.14: That Was No Lady)*, Windex *(Episode 1.17: Nice and Easy)*, Mary Poppins *(Episode 1.12: The Custody Battle)*, Rice Krispies and Oreos *(Episode 1.16: The Truth Will Out)*

Season Two: 1986–1987

Season Two is a nearly perfect season of television, beginning with the powerful "End of the Curse" and only faltering (if massively so) with the season-ending backdoor pilot episode for the thankfully later-reimagined spinoff series, *Empty Nest*.

The style of humor, firmly established last season, continues unaltered this year: relevant storylines, brilliant performances, and writing loaded with references to people, places, events, and popular brands of the day. There's history (the Bay of Pigs and the Yalta Conference), plenty more Burt Reynolds jokes, nods to the news of the day (Hands Across America, Pat Robertson), and an indictment of John Derek's love life.

Episode 2.1: End of the Curse

Directed by Terry Hughes. Written by Susan Harris. Original airdate: September 27, 1986.

Blanche is devastated to discover she's in the early stages of menopause. Dorothy and Rose try their hands at mink breeding.

Reference: Spanish fly

> **Dorothy:** They need an aphrodisiac.
>
> **Rose:** An African what?
>
> **Dorothy:** An aphrodisiac. It's a substance that makes you feel sexy.
>
> **Rose:** Really? Like what?
>
> **Dorothy:** Like Spanish fly.

Spanish fly is a green beetle that secretes terpenoid cantharidin, a substance that was once used as an aphrodisiac.

Reference: Columbo

> **Dorothy, to Blanche's bedroom door:** Blanche?

Rose: She's in there.

Dorothy: Really, Columbo?

Columbo is a fictional Los Angeles homicide detective portrayed by Peter Falk in the TV series *Columbo*, beginning in the late 1960s through the late 1970s and in various television movies up until 2003.

References: University of Minnesota, Harvard

Rose: And then we can send him to the University of Minnesota.

Dorothy: Minnesota? Are you crazy, Rose? This kid is going to Harvard.

The University of Minnesota system consists of five campuses spread throughout Minnesota. The largest campus, in the Twin Cities, is the oldest and largest and was established in 1851. Harvard University is a private Ivy League university in Cambridge, Massachusetts, established in 1636. It's the oldest institution of higher learning in the United States, as well as one of the most prestigious.

Reference: Wolfie's

Blanche: I don't know why you all have to be here with me. I'm fine by myself.

Sophia: I'm here because you're having lunch at Wolfie's after.

The original Wolfie's was a famed Miami Beach deli owned by Wilfred Cohen and known for its overstuffed sandwiches. It closed in 2002.

Reference: Joan Collins

Blanche: Look at Mr. Cary Grant. He can have any woman he wants, and he's in his eighties. You just show me a woman in her fifties who can do that, and don't tell me Joan Collins. That woman belongs in a wax museum.

Dame Joan Collins is an English actress, author, and columnist known for playing vengeful, scheming Alexis Carrington in the long-running series *Dynasty*. In addition to that career-defining role, Collins has a lengthy filmography; she's written several columns, novels, and lifestyle books; has been active in charity work; and, more recently, had a role on *American Horror Story*.

Reference: Danielle Steel

> **Blanche:** The only reason I'm sticking around is to read Danielle Steel's next book.

Danielle Steel is a well-known romance novelist who has written well over one hundred novels and is one of the best-selling fiction authors of all time.

Reference: Yasser Arafat

> **Sophia:** You grow a beard, Dorothy. Believe me. I woke up one morning, I looked like Arafat.

Yasser Arafat (1929–2004) was a Palestinian political leader and chairman of the Palestine Liberation Organization from 1969 to 2004 and president of the Palestinian National Authority from 1994 to 2004. Most Palestinians view Arafat as a hero, while most Israelis considered him a terrorist. In fact, the Israeli government tried for years to assassinate Arafat. He died in 2004, his cause of death in dispute, with theories ranging from AIDS-related illnesses to radioactive poisoning.

Reference: BMW

> **Blanche:** I never had PMS.
> **Rose:** Neither did I, but I had a BMW.

Bayerische Motoren Werke AG—more reasonably known as BMW—is a German line of luxury automobiles, founded in 1916.

Reference: *Guinness Book of Records*

> **Sophia:** I had a cousin once didn't get her period for twenty years, then at seventy-two she got pregnant.
> **Dorothy:** Ma, that never happened.
> **Sophia:** Yes, it did.
> **Dorothy:** Oh, come on. Then it must be in the *Guinness Book of Records*.

An annual reference book of world records chronicling human achievements and natural extremes, *The Guinness Book of Records* was created in the UK in the early 1950s.

Repeat References: Neiman Marcus *(Episode 1.23: Blind Ambition)*, Cary Grant *(Episode 1.6: On Golden Girls)*

Episode 2.2: Ladies of the Evening

Directed by Terry Hughes. Written by Barry Fanaro and Mort Nathan. Original airdate: October 4, 1986.

References: Tonto, *Evita*

> **Sophia:** Oh no, not this time. I'm tired of being the Tonto of the group.
>
> **Blanche:** Sophia, I tried to get another ticket and I couldn't.
>
> **Sophia:** Then this time we'll have to draw cards. I missed out on *Evita*.

Tonto was a fictional Native American character who was a companion to the Lone Ranger in various radio and television series. The character first appeared in 1933.

Evita is an Andrew Lloyd Webber musical, based on the life of Argentine political leader Eva Perón, which debuted on the West End and Broadway in the late 1970s and has starred the likes of Elaine Paige and Patti LuPone in the title role. A 1996 film version starred Madonna. Despite rumors, the role was never played by Ruth Buzzi at the Burt Reynolds Dinner Theatre.

References: Oscars, *Deliverance*, *Starting Over*, Sir Laurence Olivier, *The Cannonball Run*

> **Blanche:** Mr. Burt Reynolds is one of our finest living actors. Why, he should've won the Oscar for *Deliverance*, not to mention *Starting Over*. That Academy's just jealous. You put Sir Laurence Olivier in *Cannonball Run*, see what he can do.

The Oscars, also known as the Academy Awards, are given out annually by the Academy of Motion Picture Arts and Sciences for artistic and technical merit in the film industry. They were first awarded in 1929.

Deliverance is a 1972 thriller starring Burt Reynolds, Jon Voight, and Ned Beatty that follows a group of Atlanta businessmen deep into the Georgia wilderness, where they run afoul of backwoods mountain men. The critically acclaimed film is noted for its "Dueling Banjos" musical scene and the notorious male rape scene, which included the infamous "squeal like a pig" line. The film was nominated for three Academy Awards, although Reynolds's performance was not among them.

Starting Over is a 1979 comedy film based on the Dan Wakefield novel of the same name, starring Reynolds, Jill Clayburgh, and Candice Bergen as a divorcé, his new girlfriend, and his ex-wife, respectively. Both Clayburgh and Bergen were nominated for Oscars.

Sir Laurence Olivier (1907–1989) was a renowned British actor known for a variety of stage, film, and television roles, including *Wuthering Heights*, *Rebecca*, *Hamlet*, *Long Day's Journey into Night*, *Cat on a Hot Tin Roof*, and *Brideshead Revisited*, among many others. Among his many accolades were four Oscars, five Emmys, and knighthood. *The Cannonball Run* is a 1981 comedy film about a cross-country car race starring Reynolds, Roger Moore, Dom DeLuise, and Farrah Fawcett. The film was a box office hit and spawned two sequels.

Reference: Richard Nixon

Dorothy: Blanche, you and Nixon?

Blanche: Nixon? Yuck. No. I can't even picture Nixon naked.

Republican Richard Nixon (1913–1994) was president of the United States from 1969 to 1974, when he resigned from office amid the Watergate scandal, in which members of his administration were caught breaking into Democratic Party headquarters at the Watergate complex in 1972. It revealed several other illegal activities in which the administration was involved.

References: Dom DeLuise, Loni Anderson, Charles Nelson Reilly

Rose: You won't believe who's going to be there. Dom DeLuise.

Dorothy/Blanche: Wow!

Rose: Loni Anderson.

Dorothy/Blanche: Wow!

Rose: Charles Nelson Reilly.

Silence.

Rose: Charles Nelson Reilly.

Dorothy: Wow, who else?

Actor, voiceover artist, and chef Dom DeLuise (1933–2009) rose to fame in the 1970s as a frequent guest on variety shows and through his work in the films of Mel Brooks and Gene Wilder. He also did a string of performances with his friend Burt Reynolds, such as *The Cannonball Run*, *Cannonball Run II*, *Smokey and the Bandit II*, and *The Best Little Whorehouse in Texas*. He also hosted a revival of *Candid Camera* in the early 1990s. Loni Anderson became as well known for her personal life as her acting career after rising to fame as radio station receptionist Jennifer Marlowe in *WKRP in Cincinnati*, which ran from 1978 to 1982 and won her three Golden Globe awards. While her acting career had varying levels of success post-*WKRP*, it was Anderson's marriage to Burt Reynolds in 1988 that kept her in the media limelight through their six-year relationship. They divorced in 1994. Anderson, meanwhile, found herself in *The Golden Girls* extended universe in 1993, when she was brought in to helm the *Empty Nest* spinoff series *Nurses*, which failed to find a solid footing in its first two seasons amid a variety of cast changes. Anderson's character, Casey MacAfee, became administrator of Community Medical Center and flirted with *Empty Nest*'s Dr. Harry Weston. Charles Nelson Reilly (1931–2007) was an actor, comedian, and director known for a variety of roles and appearances, including regular appearances on *The Tonight Show Starring Johnny Carson* and as a panelist on *Match Game*.

References: Publishers Clearing House, Ed McMahon

> **Rose, on the phone:** What? I'm one of the winners of the Publishers Clearing House? Ed McMahon wants to see me right away? I should leave my Burt Reynolds ticket on the dresser before I go?
>
> **Dorothy:** Ma, get off the phone!

Publishers Clearing House is a direct marketing company founded in 1953 that markets magazine subscriptions and merchandise but is best known for its sweepstakes cash prize. Ed McMahon (1923–2009) was a beloved announcer, game show host, and second banana to Johnny Carson on *The Tonight Show* from 1962 to 1992. Among his many hosting gigs were *Who Do You Trust?*, *Star Search*, and *TV's Bloopers & Practical Jokes*. He was also the presenter of the sweepstakes prizes for the American Family Publishers company—not, surprisingly enough, Publishers Clearing House. The two companies were actually competitors and were often mistaken for one another, like in this joke.

Reference: Ethel Merman

> **Rose:** I'll fall in with a bad crowd whose leader looks like Ethel Merman.

Ethel Merman (1908–1984) was a Tony and Grammy Award–winning actress and singer with a distinctively powerful voice, known for roles in musical theater and film. Among her many works were *Anything Goes*, *Annie Get Your Gun*, *Gypsy*, *Hello, Dolly!*, and *It's a Mad, Mad, Mad, Mad World*.

Reference: Attica

> **Dorothy:** Listen, you punk. If you want to fight with someone, you're going to have to fight with me. But I warn you, I did time in Attica.
>
> **Hooker #3:** Attica's a men's prison.
>
> **Dorothy:** I know. I was there a year before they found out.

Attica Correctional Facility is a maximum-security prison located in Attica, New York. The facility was built in the 1930s and has housed many of the most dangerous criminals around. A 1971 riot at the prison resulted in forty-three deaths. Notable inmates over the years have included David Berkowitz, Mark David Chapman, and Joel Rifkin.

References: Butterfly McQueen, Olivia de Havilland

> **Rose:** I wanted to be Butter Queen.
>
> **Blanche:** Oh, yeah. What an actress. She was so good in *Gone with the Wind*. I wanted to be Ms. Olivia de Havilland myself.

The joke here references actress Butterfly McQueen (1911–1995), who played Prissy in *Gone with the Wind*. She was unable to attend the film's premiere because it was held at a segregated theater. Her role in the film got her typecast as a maid for several years. She won a Daytime Emmy in 1980 for her appearance in an *ABC Afterschool Special*. The decades-long career of actress Olivia de Havilland (1916–2020) included roles in such films as *The Snake Pit*, *To Each His Own*, *The Heiress*, and *Gone with the Wind*. She died in 2020 at the age of 104.

Reference: Jerry Reed

> **Sophia:** I think that was just about the time I was nibbling a giant shrimp out of Jerry Reed's hand.

Jerry Reed (1937–2008) was a country music singer, songwriter, and actor who costarred with Burt Reynolds in *Smokey and the Bandit* and was known for such hits as "Guitar Man," "When You're Hot, You're Hot," "East Bound and Down," "The Bird," and "She Got the Goldmine (I Got the Shaft)."

Repeat References: Burt Reynolds and John Forsythe *(Episode 1.5: The Triangle)*, Neiman Marcus *(Episode 1.23: Blind Ambitions)*, Gone with the Wind *(Episode 1.24: Big Daddy)*, Cinderella *(Episode 1.11: Stan's Return)*

EPISODE 2.3: TAKE HIM, HE'S MINE
Directed by Terry Hughes. Written by Kathy Speer and Terry Grossman. Original airdate: October 11, 1986.
Blanche spends the evening with Stan as a favor to Dorothy, but Dorothy becomes jealous when the two continue to see one another. Rose and Sophia team up to sell sandwiches at a construction site.

References: The Commodores, Lionel Richie

Sophia: She's got a date with Jeffrey, the commodore.

Rose: He's a commodore? In the Navy?

Dorothy: No, Rose. The singing group. He's the one in the middle, used to be on the end until Lionel Richie left.

The Commodores are an American funk and soul band most popular in the 1970s and early 1980s, when Lionel Richie was a co–lead singer. Hit singles included "Easy," "Three Times a Lady," and "Brick House," among others. Richie left to pursue a solo career in 1982, and other members came and went over the years. Still active today, the Commodores have sold over seventy million albums worldwide. Lionel Richie, meanwhile, is a Grammy Award–winning singer and musician who launched a successful solo career after leaving the group, with hits like "Hello," "All Night Long," "Say You, Say Me," "Dancing on the Ceiling," and the "We Are the World" collaboration with Michael Jackson and others. More recently, he's served as a judge on *American Idol*.

Reference: *Barnaby Jones*

Stan: I don't know what I might do.

Dorothy: Oh, I do. You'll watch an old *Barnaby Jones*, eat a half-gallon of rum raisin, throw up, and fall asleep in your kimono.

Barnaby Jones is a 1970s detective series starring Buddy Ebsen and Lee Meriwether as a Los Angeles–based father and daughter-in-law running a private investigation firm. The show ran on CBS from 1973 to 1980.

Reference: Chanel No. 5

> **Dorothy:** I will give you outright, *outright*, my practically full bottle of Chanel No. 5.

An iconic fragrance for women, Chanel No. 5—despite its name—was the first perfume launched by Coco Chanel in 1921, not the fifth. The reference to five stems from a particular affinity Chanel had for the number.

Reference: *Treasure Island*

> **Rose:** The minute I heard you were dating a sailor, I said to myself there'll be nothing but heartaches. Those swabbies drift into port, park their ditties on your doorstep, show you some tricks they learned in the Orient, and then it's "Avast, me hearties!" and they shove off with a serpent tattoo and your heart as souvenirs.
>
> **Dorothy:** You've been reading *Treasure Island* again, Rose.

Treasure Island is an 1883 adventure novel by Robert Louis Stevenson, about an innkeeper's young son who becomes embroiled in a treasure hunt with a group of pirates led by Long John Silver.

References: Jamie Farr, *The Caine Mutiny Court-Martial*

> **Blanche:** I'd be out of my mind to pass up the chance to see Mr. Jamie Farr in *The Caine Mutiny Court-Martial*.

Actor/comedian Jamie Farr is best known for playing cross-dressing Corporal Maxwell Q. Klinger on the TV series *M*A*S*H*. Klinger's penchant for dresses stemmed from his desire to be proven crazy and therefore discharged. Interesting tactic. *The Caine Mutiny Court-Martial* is a two-act courtroom drama play written by Herman Wouk, based on his 1951 novel, *The Caine Mutiny*. The play centers around the court-martial of the mutiny aboard the navy warship USS *Caine*.

References: Bess Truman, *Pinocchio*, Jiminy Cricket

> **Dorothy:** I thought you were Blanche.

Sophia: Once I thought I was Bess Truman but then they switched me to twenty milligrams a day.

Rose: I had a cousin who thought he was Jiminy Cricket. Of course, that was at the height of the *Pinocchio* craze, and everyone at the bank went along with it.

Dorothy: And I wondered how the two of you got together to start a business.

Bess Truman (1885–1982) was the wife of President Harry S. Truman and First Lady of the United States from 1945 to 1953. Pinocchio is a fictional character originating in *The Adventures of Pinocchio*, an 1883 children's novel by Carlo Collodi, about an animated marionette and his father, a woodcarver named Geppetto. Among the characters Pinocchio meets on his adventures is an advice-giving talking cricket. The book was made into a 1940 animated Disney film—arguably more beloved than the book—and, in that version, the cricket was named Jiminy Cricket, a dapper little insect who carries a top hat and umbrella and serves as Pinocchio's de facto conscience.

References: Suzanne Somers, *The Tonight Show*

Dorothy: You're wearing your toupee to bed. That means one of two things. Either there's a woman in your bed or Suzanne Somers is on *The Tonight Show*.

Actress, self-help author, and businesswoman Suzanne Somers is best known for her roles on the sitcoms *Three's Company* and *Step by Step*, as well as for being spokeswoman for the ThighMaster exercise machine. *The Tonight Show* is a long-running NBC late-night talk show that debuted in 1954. Hosts have included Steve Allen, Jack Paar, Johnny Carson, Jay Leno, Conan O'Brien, and Jimmy Fallon.

Repeat References: Burt Reynolds Dinner Theatre *(Episode 1.5: The Triangle)*, Kleenex *(Episode 1.4: Transplant)*, jai alai *(Episode 1.9 Blanche and the Younger Man)*

Episode 2.4: It's a Miserable Life
Directed by Terry Hughes. Written by Barry Fanaro and Mort Nathan. Original airdate: November 1, 1986.
The girls battle their crotchety neighbor, Frieda Claxton, in an attempt to save a historic oak tree on her property.

Reference: *Nancy Drew*

> **Rose:** One summer, I worked up enough nerve to check out the latest *Nancy Drew* mystery.

The *Nancy Drew* mystery book series for young readers was created by publisher Edward Stratemeyer and features a fictional female sleuth who was conceived as a girls' counterpart to the popular *Hardy Boys* book series.

References: Winston Churchill, Yalta Conference

> **Rose:** Mr. Minky always said books belong in a library.
>
> **Dorothy:** Really, Rose? I always thought Churchill said that at Yalta.

Sir Winston Churchill (1874–1965) was a British statesman, army officer, and writer who served as prime minister of the United Kingdom from 1940 to 1945, during which he led the country to victory in World War II, and from 1951 to 1955, when Queen Elizabeth II ascended to the throne. Churchill died at the age of ninety and remains one of the most significant political figures of the twentieth century. Actor John Lithgow won an Emmy in 2017 for his portrayal of Churchill in the Netflix series *The Crown*. The Yalta Conference was the post–World War II meeting between leaders from the United States, the United Kingdom, and the Soviet Union to discuss the reorganization of Germany and Europe.

References: *National Velvet*, *The Godfather*

> **Sophia:** He woke up the next morning sharing a pillow with National Velvet.

National Velvet is a 1944 horse-racing film, based on the 1935 novel by Enid Bagnold, starring Mickey Rooney and Elizabeth Taylor. The joke here is a nod to *The Godfather*, a 1972 film directed by Francis Ford Coppola and based on the 1969 novel by Mario Puzo. The film centers around a New York Mafia family and features a stellar ensemble cast, including Marlon Brando, Al Pacino, and Diane Keaton. In one classic payback scene, a man wakes up to find the severed head of his beloved horse next to him in bed.

Reference: *The Exorcist*

> **Sophia:** If she spits up pea soup and her head spins around, we're in big trouble.

This line refers to a scene from *The Exorcist*, a 1973 supernatural horror film based on the 1971 novel by William Peter Blatty, about the demonic possession of a twelve-year-old girl. Ellen Burstyn, Max von Sydow, Lee J. Cobb, and Linda Blair starred in the critically acclaimed film, which has since been elevated to classic status.

Reference: Menudo

> **Ed:** It is the consensus of the committee that the promoter's petition for the outdoor Menudo concert be denied.

Menudo was a successful Puerto Rican–based, Latino boy band formed in 1977 that had various members over the years, including Ricky Martin, who was part of the group from 1984 to 1989. The group disbanded in 2009.

Reference: "Why Do Fools Fall in Love?"

> **Rose:** Why do people die, Dorothy?
>
> **Dorothy:** Rose, please, I don't even know why fools fall in love.

The joke here is a nod to "Why Do Fools Fall in Love?," a 1956 song by the rock-and-roll group Frankie Lymon & the Teenagers.

Reference: Vanna White

> **Blanche:** At that moment, I vowed to make that town pay for valuing my personality over my perfect body.
>
> **Dorothy:** I hear that Vanna White has the same problem.

Vanna White is a television personality known for serving as hostess on the game show *Wheel of Fortune* since 1982. Her 1987 autobiography, *Vanna Speaks!*, became a bestseller.

Reference: Superman

> **Mr. Pfeiffer, showing the girls a casket:** It's also lead-lined.
>
> **Dorothy:** We're not burying Superman. How much?

Superman, created by Jerry Siegel and Joe Shuster, is a fictional superhero from the DC Comics company. The character first appeared in 1938 and has become a cultural icon, appearing in comics, cartoons, merchandise, series, and movies. Among the most notable screen versions of the character was the series of successful films in the 1970s and 1980s in which Christopher Reeve played the title role.

Reference: *TV Guide*

> **Sophia:** Not Thursday. Hell no.
>
> **Mr. Pfeiffer:** Sorry, forgot. *The Cosby Show.* How about Friday?
>
> **Sophia:** Do you have a *TV Guide* we could check?

TV Guide is a magazine featuring television program listings, television-related news and celebrity interviews, film reviews, and crossword puzzles. It was created as a New York–based publication in 1948 and went national in 1953.

Reference: Tommy Lasorda

> **Sophia:** Two men on. The bottom of the ninth. And that baciagaloop Lasorda has him bunt.

Tommy Lasorda (1927–2021) was a Major League Baseball player, coach, and manager known for his two-decade stint managing the Los Angeles Dodgers from 1976 to 1996.

References: Alka-Seltzer, *Richard III*

> **Sophia:** My kingdom for an Alka-Seltzer.

Alka-Seltzer is an effervescent antacid that's been treating acid indigestion since 1931. The product's various advertising efforts bolstered its pop culture cred. (Remember "Plop, plop, fizz, fizz"?) The joke is a nod to a famous line from William Shakespeare's *Richard III*, in which the king cries out, "A horse! A horse! My kingdom for a horse!" after his horse is killed in battle.

Repeat References: Girl Scouts *(Episode 1.19: Second Motherhood)*, *The Cosby Show (Episode 1.23 Blind Ambition)*

Episode 2.5: Isn't It Romantic?
Directed by Terry Hughes. Written by Jeffrey Duteil. Original airdate: November 8, 1986.
Dorothy's lesbian friend, Jean, visits and develops a crush on Rose.

Reference: Steven Spielberg

> **Dorothy:** Hi, Ma. What are you watching?
>
> **Sophia:** It's one of those Steven Spielberger movies.

Steven Spielberg is a famed film director who has risen to icon status with films like *Jaws, Raiders of the Lost Ark, E.T. the Extra-Terrestrial, Jurassic Park,* and many others.

Reference: *Seven Brides for Seven Brothers*

> **Sophia:** The last time you brought back *Seven Brides for Seven Brothers.* Do you know how disappointed I was to find out it's a musical?

Seven Brides for Seven Brothers is a 1954 Oscar-winning musical starring Howard Keel and Jane Powell. The title pretty much summarizes the plot.

References: *Love Story, Terms of Endearment*

> **Rose:** We saw *Love Story* and *Terms of Endearment.* It was the Cry Me a River Matinee at the Rialto.

A pair of tear-jerker classics. *Love Story* is a 1970 romantic drama film, based on the Erich Segal novel of the same name, starring Ali MacGraw and Ryan O'Neal. *Terms of Endearment* is an Academy Award–winning 1983 drama starring Shirley MacLaine, Debra Winger, Jack Nicholson, and Danny DeVito, which covers the thirty-year relationship between a woman and her daughter.

Reference: Little Miss Muffet

> **Dorothy:** Ma, come on. It's not funny.
>
> **Sophia:** The hell it's not. Jean in love with Little Miss Muffet? Come on.

Little Miss Muffet is a character in an English nursery rhyme dating back to the early nineteenth century who was a big fan of cottage cheese—but spiders, not so much.

Reference: Danny Thomas

> **Blanche:** What's so funny?
>
> **Sophia:** For starters, Jean is a lesbian.

Blanche: What's funny about that?

Sophia: You aren't surprised?

Blanche: Of course not. I mean, I've never known any personally, but isn't Danny Thomas one?

Dorothy: Not Lebanese, Blanche. Lesbian.

Danny Thomas (1912–1991) was a famous comedian, singer, actor, producer, and philanthropist whose career spanned five decades. First appearing on radio and in clubs in the 1930s, followed by films in the 1940s, Thomas rose to national fame when he created and starred in one of the longest-running, most successful sitcoms of the 1950s and 1960s, *Make Room for Daddy* (later called *The Danny Thomas Show*), which ran from 1953 to 1964. He later worked as a producer on such classics as *The Dick Van Dyke Show*, *The Andy Griffith Show*, and *That Girl*, which starred his daughter, actress and activist Marlo Thomas. Despite a successful television career, Thomas's most enduring legacy is for his philanthropic work. In 1962, he founded St. Jude's Children's Research Hospital, a pediatric treatment and research facility in Memphis, Tennessee, focused on children's catastrophic diseases, particularly cancer. Thomas's son, Tony, was an executive producer on *The Golden Girls* and its spinoff series, *Empty Nest*. In his final on-screen role, Thomas appeared in an episode of *Empty Nest* as the aging mentor of the show's central character, Dr. Harry Weston. The episode garnered Thomas an Emmy nomination. He died of heart failure days after the episode aired.

EPISODE 2.6: BIG DADDY'S LITTLE LADY

Directed by David Steinberg. Written by Russell Marcus. Original airdate: November 15, 1986.

Blanche's father, Big Daddy, arrives with the news that he's getting married to a younger woman. Dorothy and Rose team up for a songwriting contest.

Reference: Howard Johnson

Dorothy: You're getting dates out of the obituaries? That's sick.

Sophia: It is not sick, it's practical. Life is for the living. Maria's loss is my date for the 2-for-1 special at the Howard Johnson's.

Howard Johnson is a chain of restaurants founded by Howard Deering Johnson in 1920, and also a chain of hotels and motels founded in 1954. The restaurant chain was at one time the largest in the United States in the 1960s and 1970s but has dwindled down to one remaining restaurant today. Meanwhile, the hotel chain is now part of Wyndham Hotels and Resorts.

Reference: A&P

> **Rose:** Dorothy, this is unbelievable. Look at this.
>
> **Dorothy, reading headlines:** Heart surgeon turns out to be produce manager at the A&P.

The Great Atlantic & Pacific Tea Company—or A&P, as it was more widely known—was a grocery store chain that was, at one time, the largest in the country. It was founded by George Gilman and was in operation from 1859 until 2015, when it closed its doors after years of decreased sales and financial difficulties.

References: Rodgers and Hammerstein, Simon and Garfunkel, Shari Lewis and Lamb Chop

> **Dorothy:** We could be the next Rodgers and Hammerstein. The next Simon and Garfunkel. The next—
>
> **Rose:** Shari Lewis and Lamp Chop!
>
> **Dorothy:** I don't know if I can get my hand that far up your dress.

Rodgers and Hammerstein was a creative duo consisting of composer Richard Rodgers (1902–1979) and lyricist Oscar Hammerstein II (1895–1960), whose string of hit musicals included *Oklahoma!*, *Carousel*, *South Pacific*, *The King and I*, and *The Sound of Music*. Simon and Garfunkel was a folk-rock duo consisting of Paul Simon and Art Garfunkel, who were wildly successful in the 1960s with hits like "The Sound of Silence," "Mrs. Robinson," and "Bridge over Troubled Water." Shari Lewis (1933–1998) was a beloved ventriloquist and puppeteer, and Lamb Chop, her most well-known sock-puppet companion. The pair first appeared on *Captain Kangaroo* in the 1950s, and they were a children's show mainstay until Lewis's death in 1998.

Reference: Sophia Loren

> **Big Daddy:** Do my eyes deceive me or do I see Sophia Petrillo standing before me? Or did you all get Sophia Loren as a new roommate?

Sophia Loren is an Oscar-winning Italian actress of the Classic Hollywood era, known for roles in *Two Women, Marriage Italian Style, A Special Day,* and *Grumpier Old Men.*

Reference: *Ruthless People*

> **Sophia:** Great news. Teresa Lombardi passed away.
>
> **Dorothy:** Ma, what's so great about that?
>
> **Sophia:** Her husband Freddy, he has nothing to do, and neither one of us has seen *Ruthless People.*

Ruthless People is a 1986 comedy film starring Danny DeVito and Bette Midler, about a couple who kidnap their ex-boss's wife for ransom, unaware that he's happy she's gone.

Reference: Burl Ives

> **Blanche:** She's no better than a tick on a slow-movin' hound dog.
>
> **Dorothy:** Why is everyone around here talking like Burl Ives?

Burl Ives (1909–1995) was a beloved singer and Oscar-winning actor of stage, screen, and radio, known for roles in films like *Cat on a Hot Tin Roof* and *The Big Country.* He's also widely remembered as the voice of Sam the Snowman in the 1964 special *Rudolph the Red-Nosed Reindeer,* a holiday classic.

Reference: Tang

> **Dorothy:** We're blocked.
>
> **Sophia:** I've been having good luck with Tang, immediately followed by a granola bar.

Tang is an artificially flavored drink mix introduced in 1957 and popularized in the 1960s when NASA astronauts began bringing it on space-flight missions. The most common flavor is orange, but several additional flavors have been introduced over the years.

References: John Derek, Ursula Andress, Linda Evans, Bo Derek

> **Dorothy:** You see older men with younger women all the time. It's very common. Look at John Derek and Ursula Andress, John Derek and Linda Evans, John Derek and Bo Derek. You know, maybe it's not so common. Maybe it's just one guy who gets around a lot.

Actor, director, and producer John Derek (1926–1998) appeared in such films as *Knock on Any Door, All the King's Men,* and *Rogues of Sherwood Forest* during his decades-long career, but he is also largely remembered for his marriage to actress Bo Derek, who rose to fame after her role in the 1979 film *10,* in which her cornrow-sporting character was portrayed as the ideal woman (i.e., "a 10") by the film's protagonist, played by Dudley Moore. It proved to be Derek's breakthrough role and positioned her as a sex symbol. Ursula Andress is a Swiss actress and model known for playing Honey Ryder in the first James Bond film. Arriving in Hollywood in the 1950s, she dated the likes of James Dean and Dennis Hopper before beginning an affair with John Derek, who was at the time a married father of two. They eventually married in 1957 and divorced in 1966. Andress hit a career peak in the 1960s and continued to work to varying degrees of success over the following three decades before roles dried up in the 1990s. Actress Linda Evans is known primarily for her roles on the TV shows *The Big Valley* (1965–1969) and, perhaps most widely, *Dynasty* (1981–1989).

Reference: *Petticoat Junction*

> **Blanche:** Ollie and Mollie? Must we take yet another trip to *Petticoat Junction?*

Petticoat Junction was a sitcom that aired on CBS from 1963 to 1970, set at the rural Shady Rest Hotel and centering around the widowed owner, her lazy uncle, and her three daughters.

References: The Great Depression, Milano cookies

> **Rose:** For five extra dollars, she'd buff more than your nails.
> **Blanche:** Five dollars?
> **Dorothy:** It was during the Depression.
> **Sophia:** Hey, in Italy, for five dollars you got a woman, a manicure, a cappuccino, and a box of Milano cookies to take home to your wife.

The Great Depression was a worldwide economic depression—a sustained downturn in economic activity—that began in the United States in 1929 and lasted through most of the 1930s. It was the longest and most widespread depression of the twentieth century. Milano cookies are sandwich cookies from Pepperidge Farm consisting of a thin layer of chocolate between two biscuit cookies.

Reference: Tom Cruise

> **Blanche:** Sophia, people in their seventies and eighties can have great sex.
>
> **Sophia:** Yeah, with people in *their* seventies and eighties. Put me in a bedroom with Tom Cruise and you'd be peeling me off the ceiling.

Actor Tom Cruise rose to superstardom in the 1980s in films such as *Risky Business*, *Top Gun*, and *Rain Man* and has maintained a successful film career ever since, with hits including *A Few Good Men*, *The Firm*, *Interview with the Vampire*, *Jerry Maguire*, and a series of *Mission: Impossible* movies. Despite continued box office success, he's drawn criticism in more recent years as a vocal advocate for the Church of Scientology.

Reference: Anita Bryant

> **Dorothy:** They told us to get out of the way when they took the winner's picture with Anita Bryant.

A singer with a few hits to her name during the 1950s and 1960s, Anita Bryant became better known in the 1970s as an outspoken opponent of gay rights.

Repeat Reference: *Gone with the Wind (Episode 1.24: Big Daddy)*

EPISODE 2.7: FAMILY AFFAIR
Directed by Terry Hughes. Written by Winifred Hervey. Original airdate: November 22, 1986.
Rose's daughter, Bridget, and Dorothy's son, Michael, visit at the same time and end up sharing a bed. Blanche injures herself at an exercise class.

Reference: *Norma Rae*

> **Sophia:** Michael stands up for his principles.
>
> **Dorothy:** He's the Norma Rae of the music business.

Norma Rae is a 1979 drama film starring Sally Field as a North Carolina factory worker who becomes involved in trade union activities. It was based on the true story of Crystal Lee Sutton. Field won an Academy Award for the role.

Reference: Triscuits

> **Rose:** Where are the little wooden shoes I carved out of cheese?
>
> **Dorothy:** My mother spread them on the tiny windmill you built out of Triscuits.

Triscuit is a brand of snack crackers introduced by Nabisco in the early 1900s. The original version is a square, baked, whole-wheat wafer.

Reference: Julie Newmar

> **Sophia:** What did the doctor say?
>
> **Blanche:** After commenting that I am the most spectacular specimen of the female anatomy he has seen since Ms. Julie Newmar, he said I have a back problem.

Julie Newmar is a Tony Award–winning actress known for a variety of roles, including *The Marriage-Go-Round, Ziegfeld Follies, Damn Yankees!,* and Catwoman in the original *Batman* television series in the 1960s.

Reference: *The Journey of Natty Gann*

> **Dorothy:** Here's ten dollars. Go take your grandmother to see *The Journey of Natty Gann.*

The Journey of Natty Gann is a 1985 Walt Disney Pictures family film starring John Cusack and Lainie Kazan, about a young girl during the Great Depression who travels across the country in search of her father.

References: Julie Andrews, "If I Had a Hammer"

> **Rose:** Guess what?
>
> **Dorothy:** Julie Andrews showed up, you all fed deer from your hand, and sang "If I Had a Hammer."

Dame Julie Andrews is an English actress, singer, and writer known for her roles in *Mary Poppins, The Sound of Music,* and *The Princess Diaries.* Younger fans may also recognize her voice work in hits like the *Shrek* and *Despicable Me* franchises. With a career spanning decades, Andrews has turned up just about everywhere in stage, screen, and film. She's racked up an Oscar, multiple Emmys, Grammys, and Golden Globes.

"If I Had a Hammer" is a folk song written in 1949 by Pete Seeger and Lee Hays and recorded by artists such as The Weavers, Peter, Paul, and Mary, and Trini Lopez.

Reference: Chita Rivera

> **Sophia:** For fifty years, I had the body of Chita Rivera. One morning I woke up, my butt looking like the neck of a bulldog.

Chita Rivera is a Tony Award–winning actress, dancer, and singer known for her various stage roles, including playing Anita in *West Side Story*. She was awarded the Presidential Medal of Freedom in 2009.

Reference: *The Katzenjammer Kids*

> **Dorothy:** Are the kids back from their date yet?
>
> **Rose:** Our kids?
>
> **Dorothy:** No, Rose, *The Katzenjammer Kids*.

The Katzenjammer Kids is a comic strip created by Rudolph Dirks in 1897 about the shenanigans of a pair of prankster brothers. The strip was drawn by various artists over the decades before concluding in 2006. It is still distributed in reprint form.

Reference: Corvette

> **Blanche:** My body feels like a Corvette up on blocks with its engine racing, the wheels just spinning and spinning with nowhere to go.

The Corvette is a two-door, two-passenger sports car manufactured by Chevrolet since 1953.

Reference: Raggedy Andy

> **Rose:** I've never seen Bridget in bed with a man before, except Raggedy Andy.

Raggedy Andy is a character created by Johnny Gruelle as the brother of his other creation, Raggedy Ann. The characters are rag dolls with red yarn for hair. Raggedy Ann first appeared as a doll in 1915 and in a children's book, *Raggedy Ann Stories*, in 1918. Raggedy Andy first appeared in its sequel, *Raggedy Andy Stories*, in 1920.

Reference: Alan Thicke

> **Dorothy:** I can't believe Alan Thicke has a hit series, but that doesn't mean it isn't so.

Alan Thicke (1947–2016) was an actor, songwriter, and host best known for playing Dr. Jason Seaver in the 1980s sitcom *Growing Pains*. He also hosted various game or talk shows, including a short-lived late-night show called *Thicke of the Night* in 1983, and cowrote several TV show theme songs, including those for *Diff'rent Strokes* and *The Facts of Life*.

Reference: Henry Kissinger

> **Rose:** He doesn't even have a job.
>
> **Blanche:** Well, neither does Henry Kissinger really, but he's still very highly regarded.

Henry Kissinger is a controversial politician and diplomat who served as the US secretary of state and national security advisor during the administrations of Richard Nixon and Gerald Ford.

Reference: Marcus Allen

> **Dorothy:** Rose, face it. Your daughter moves faster than Marcus Allen.

Marcus Allen is an accomplished former NFL football player known for being the first player in the league to gain more than 10,000 rushing yards and 5,000 receiving yards during his career, which spanned fifteen years between the Los Angeles Raiders and the Kansas City Chiefs.

Reference: Crockett and Tubbs

> **Blanche:** I guess you're still upset with me about last night, aren't you?
>
> **Dorothy:** No, I'm upset because Crockett and Tubbs are wearing darker colors.

Another *Miami Vice* reference. Sonny Crockett and Rico Tubbs were the pastel-clad, sockless detectives portrayed by Don Johnson and Philip Michael Thomas, respectively, in NBC's *Miami Vice* from 1984 to 1990. Colin Farrell and Jamie Foxx portrayed the characters in a 2006 film adaptation.

References: Henry Mancini, *The Pink Panther*

> **Blanche:** I sent the kids to the symphony to hear Mr. Henry Mancini's tribute to *The Pink Panther*. I didn't expect them to come back here and jump into bed.

Henry Mancini (1924–1994) was a composer and musician who won four Academy Awards, a Golden Globe, and twenty Grammys, and is considered one of the greatest composers in film history. *The Pink Panther* is a British-American franchise created by Maurice Richlin and Blake Edwards, which began as a series of comedy-mystery films featuring inept French detective Inspector Jacques Clouseau, played by Peter Sellers. The first film, titled simply *The Pink Panther*, was released in 1963 and derived its name from the valuable pink diamond at the center of the movie's plot. The opening credits also introduced an animated pink panther that came to be more widely representative of the franchise and was even spun off into its own animated series and line of merchandise. Sellers appeared in six films before his death in 1980; others filled in, to less success; and Steve Martin revived the role in a pair of films in 2006 and 2009.

References: Spock, Dr. Spock

> **Sophia:** Who are you, Mr. Spock?
>
> **Rose:** I think you mean Dr. Spock, Sophia.
>
> **Sophia:** They're both real smart, and they've got big ears, so don't get technical, okay?

Spock is a fictional, pointy-eared character in the *Star Trek* franchise, originally played by Leonard Nimoy, who was half human and half Vulcan. Dr. Benjamin Spock (1903–1998) was a pediatrician who wrote *Baby and Child Care*, one of the best-selling parenting books in history.

Episode 2.8: Vacation
Directed by Terry Hughes. Written by Winifred Hervey. Original airdate: November 29, 1986.
Dorothy, Blanche, and Rose set off on a Caribbean vacation while Sophia woos their Japanese gardener.

Reference: Pepto-Bismol

> **Rose:** Did you remember to bring Pepto-Bismol?

Pepto-Bismol is an antacid elixir used to treat nausea, heartburn, indigestion, upset stomach, and diarrhea. It's known for its bright pink color.

Reference: Lawn-Boy

> **Sophia:** Driving your Lawn-Boy was so exciting.

Lawn-Boy is a brand of lawn mowers first introduced in the 1930s.

Reference: Mai tai

> **Dorothy:** If I put cracked ice and an umbrella on your head, you'd be a mai tai.

A mai tai is cocktail made from rum, curaçao, orgeat syrup, and lime juice.

Reference: Grandma Moses

> **Rick:** You think we're happy having to gargle next to Grandma Moses and the Mosettes?

Anna Mary Robertson Moses (1860–1961), better known as Grandma Moses, was a folk artist who began painting scenes of rural life at the age of seventy-eight.

Reference: "I'd Like to Teach the World to Sing (in Perfect Harmony)"

> *Rose leads the song after she and the girls are rescued following a shipwreck.*

"I'd Like to Teach the World to Sing (in Perfect Harmony)" is a pop song that originated as a jingle for the groundbreaking 1971 "Hilltop" commercial for Coca-Cola. It was originally recorded by The Hillside Singers and, once the commercial gained momentum, both The Hillside Singers and The New Seekers recorded full-length singles, dropping the soda reference.

Reference: The Hyatt Regency

> **Dwayne:** You're right, there is a waterfall, and it empties into a pool in the lobby of the Hyatt Regency.

Hyatt is multinational hotel, resort, and vacation property corporation founded in 1957 by Hyatt Robert von Dehn and Jack Dyer Crouch.

Repeat References: Gidget *(Episode 1.23: Blind Ambitions)*, Dramamine *(Episode 1.6: On Golden Girls)*, Tang *(Episode 2.6: Big Daddy's Little Lady)*, Great Depression *(Episode 2.6: Big Daddy's Little Lady)*, Girl Scouts *(Episode*

1.19: Second Motherhood), Sidney Sheldon *(Episode 1.9: Blanche and the Younger Man)*

EPISODE 2.9: JOUST BETWEEN FRIENDS

Directed by Terry Hughes. Written by Scott Spencer Gordon. Original airdate: December 6, 1986.

Blanche gets Dorothy a job at the museum and becomes jealous when their boss seems to favor Dorothy.

Reference: The Vatican

> **Mr. Allen:** Obviously Blanche thinks very highly of you.
>
> **Dorothy:** Yes, she's dropping off my résumé at the Vatican this afternoon.

The Vatican is an independent city-state in Rome, Italy, and home of the Holy See, the governing body of the Catholic Church.

Reference: Giacomo Puccini

> **Sophia:** So we sing a little Puccini, stretch out on the couch, and take a nap together.

Giacomo Puccini (1858–1924) was a famed Italian opera composer whose notable works include *La Bohème* and *Madama Butterfly*.

Reference: Fotomat

> **Blanche:** As long as you're here, would you like a tour?
>
> **Sophia:** No thanks. If I want to look at pictures I go to Fotomat.

A defunct chain of photo-developing drive-through kiosks usually located in shopping center parking lots, Fotomat was founded by Preston Fleet in the 1960s. The first kiosk opened in Point Loma, California, in 1965 and, by its early-1980s peak, there were more than four thousand throughout the country. Changing times and company buyouts resulted in an eventual move into online territory, but even that dried up in 2009.

Reference: Paul Gauguin

> **Mr. Allen:** I'd love for you to see my most-prized acquisition—a magnificent pair of Gauguins.

Sophia: What are you, a pervert? I was married for forty-five years, I never even saw my husband's Gauguins!

Not to be confused with a certain part of the male anatomy, Paul Gauguin (1848–1903) was a nineteenth-century French post-Impressionist artist.

Reference: Di-Gel

Dorothy: Ma, give me a break. The Di-Gel's on the bottom shelf.

Di-Gel is an over-the-counter medication used to treat heartburn and acid indigestion.

Reference: Sandra Day O'Connor

Blanche: I'm the one who's been wearing low-cut blouses and picking up pencils off the floor. I'm the one he always gropes at the annual Christmas party.

Dorothy: And they picked Sandra Day O'Connor over you.

Justice Sandra Day O'Connor was the first woman to serve on the US Supreme Court, which she did from 1981 until her retirement in 2006.

EPISODE 2.10: LOVE, ROSE

Directed by Terry Hughes. Written by Kathy Speer and Terry Grossman. Original airdate: December 13, 1986.

Rose puts an ad in the personals column and, when no one responds, Dorothy and Blanche invent a suitor.

References: Bay of Pigs, David Horowitz, David Hartman

Sophia: I could only find one person who could speak English, and he tried to blame me personally for the Bay of Pigs.

Rose: So how'd you get home?

Sophia: I took the bus the other way. That's when I also noticed that they changed the name of the number ten bus to the number seven. I'm going to write David Horowitz.

Rose: Sophia, I think you got on the wrong bus.

Sophia: Maybe I did, but I'm going to write Horowitz anyway. I want someone to arrest David Hartman's dentist.

The Bay of Pigs invasion was a failed landing operation attempt in April 1961 by Cuban exiles opposing Fidel Castro's Cuban Revolution. Directed by the US government, the invasion was considered a US foreign policy failure and furthered the divide between the United States and Cuba. Geographically, the Bay of Pigs is located along Cuba's southern coast.

David Horowitz is a conservative activist, outspoken opponent of liberal politics, and writer who founded the David Horowitz Freedom Center, edited *FrontPage Magazine*, and directed Discover the Networks, a website that tracks the political Left.

While starting his career as an actor in the 1960s, including a turn in the original Broadway production of *Hello, Dolly!*, David Hartman, who didn't have the best-looking teeth, is better known as a journalist who served as the first host of ABC's *Good Morning America* from 1975 to 1987, as well as the host of documentaries on Discovery Channel, History, and PBS.

Reference: The Dance of the Seven Veils

Sophia: Rose, I need to borrow a silk scarf tonight.

Rose: You have a date?

Sophia: No, I'm doing the Dance of the Seven Veils and I'm one short.

The Dance of the Seven Veils refers to the dance performed by Salome in the New Testament of the Bible at the birthday celebration of her stepfather, Herod Antipas, who had John the Baptist beheaded at her request. The biblical story does not name the dance. That dates to a translation from Oscar Wilde's 1891 play *Salome*.

Reference: Café Vienna

Blanche: I'm going to have to give that mailman another talking-to.

Dorothy: This time, you may want to try something a little more forceful than asking him in for a Café Vienna and a warm bath.

Café Vienna was one of the original flavors of the General Foods International Coffee line of instant coffee drinks, sold in little tin cans beginning in the 1970s. The line gained momentum in the 1970s and 1980s, with its ad campaign marketing it as the height of sophistication—at least as far as instant coffee goes. The brand changed names and packaging over the years and is now a Maxwell House line.

Reference: Uncle Sam

> **Rose:** I haven't been this depressed since I was rejected by Uncle Sam.
>
> **Blanche:** Well, honey, if he was your uncle it wasn't meant to be.

Uncle Sam is the national personification of the US government that allegedly came into use during the War of 1812 and has become an iconic symbol of American patriotism. He is depicted as an older, white-bearded and -goateed white man in a top hat and tailcoat, decked out in red, white, and blue.

References: Korean War, WAC

> **Rose:** It was during the Korean conflict. I was rejected as a WAC. I failed the inkblot test.

The Korean War was fought from 1950 to 1953, between North Korea and the US–backed South Korea. WAC, meanwhile, stands for Women's Army Corps, a women's branch of the US Army that was created in 1942 and disbanded in 1978 when the army fully integrated.

Reference: Buick Riviera

> **Blanche:** He's reasonably good-looking, he drives a new Buick Riviera, and I heard he just opened a third dry-cleaning store in Boca Raton.

The Riviera was an automobile from the luxury Buick line manufactured from 1963 to 1999, except for a short hiatus in 1994.

Reference: Bouffant hairstyle

> **Blanche:** Jackie and I go way back together, before bouffant.

A bouffant is a type of hairstyle where the hair is raised high on the head like a big, round helmet. It became popular in the early 1960s.

References: Bert Parks, Hands Across America

> **Rose:** We both requested to stand next to Bert Parks in Hands Across America.

Bert Parks (1914–1992) was an actor and singer best known for hosting the Miss America pageant from 1955 to 1979. Hands Across America was a fund-raising event held on May 25, 1986, in which more than five million people held hands for fifteen minutes in an attempt to form a continuous human chain across the continental United States. While virtually impossible to realistically create an unbroken chain all across the nation, the event was considered successful after raising $15 million for various local charities fighting hunger and homelessness. The event was conceived by music manager Ken Kragen as part of USA for Africa, the music supergroup that recorded the hit charity single "We Are the World."

References: Isaac Newton, Ted Koppel, Howdy Doody

> **Dorothy:** Isaac Newton was the first name that came to mind?
>
> **Blanche:** Actually, Ted Koppel was the first name that came to mind, but he looks like Howdy Doody's illegitimate son.

Isaac Newton (1642–1727) was a mathematician, physicist, and astronomer who was an influential figure in the Scientific Revolution. He is known for having invented calculus, developing the three laws of motion that formed the basic principles of physics, and formulating the theory of gravity. Ted Koppel is a well-known broadcast journalist who anchored ABC's *Nightline* from 1980 until 2005. Howdy Doody was the freckle-faced marionette and namesake of the *Howdy Doody* children's television program created and produced by E. Roger Muir. It ran on NBC from 1947 to 1960 and featured Western frontier and circus themes. The character was created by entertainer Buffalo Bob Smith, who starred alongside the puppet clad in cowboy garb.

Reference: Lord Byron

> **Dorothy:** He doesn't write poems, Blanche, *we* write poems. Actually, Lord Byron writes poems, we just copy them onto loose-leaf paper.

George Gordon Byron (1788–1824) was an English poet and politician who was one of the leaders of the Romantic era, the well-known artistic and literary movement begun in the late eighteenth century. He's regarded as one of the greatest English poets ever.

Reference: Metamucil

> **Sophia:** Dorothy, I've got a big problem.
>
> **Dorothy:** The Metamucil's in the top cabinet.

Metamucil is a fiber supplement.

Reference: Smudge pot

> **Rose:** He's going to be the smudge pot supervisor of the first domed orange grove in Canada.

A smudge pot is an oil-burning heater, typically with a round base and a chimney coming out of the top, which is used to prevent frost on fruit trees in orchards.

Reference: *The Yellow Pages*

> **Rose:** Blanche, you make it sound like I found him in *The Yellow Pages*. It's not like I don't know him.

The Yellow Pages is a telephone directory first issued in 1966, featuring businesses organized by category instead of alphabetical by name.

Repeat References: *People (Episode 1.25: The Way We Met)*, The Archduke Ferdinand *(Episode 1.25: The Way We Met)*, Deliverance *(Episode 2.2: Ladies of the Evening)*

EPISODE 2.11: 'TWAS THE NIGHTMARE BEFORE CHRISTMAS
Directed by Terry Hughes. Written by Barry Fanaro and Mort Nathan. Original airdate: December 20, 1986.
After exchanging homemade gifts, the girls head out on holiday travel, only to end up seeking refuge from a storm in an all-night diner on Christmas Eve.

References: Burdines, Ralph Lauren

> **Dorothy:** The Three Wise Men in the nativity scene at Burdines were wearing Ralph Lauren ski parkas.

Burdines was a popular department store chain headquartered in Miami. The first store appeared at the end of the nineteenth century, when William M. Burdine teamed up with Henry Payne. Payne hit the road after about a year, but Burdine brought in his son and kept on going. A corporate merger in the 1950s expanded locations, and as other corporate mergers happened in the ensuing decades (at one time there were Burdines-Macy's stores), the Burdines name was dropped altogether in 2004. Ralph Lauren is the fashion designer behind the multibillion-dollar luxury products of the Ralph Lauren Corporation.

Reference: Fidel Castro

> **Sophia:** Who was that?
>
> **Blanche:** He's a Santa Claus.
>
> **Sophia:** You're kidding. I thought it was Fidel Castro.

Politician and revolutionary Fidel Castro (1926–2016) served as prime minister and president of Cuba from 1959 to 2008 and, during his tenure, the Republic of Cuba became a one-party communist state. Quite the controversial figure, Castro was heralded by his supporters as a socialist hero and considered by his detractors as a dictatorial tyrant.

Reference: Ebenezer Scrooge

> **Sophia:** Don't tell me. Tell Scrooge.

Ebenezer Scrooge was the classic crotchety protagonist in Charles Dickens's 1843 holiday novella *A Christmas Carol* (more on that in a moment), and the name has become synonymous with anyone who fits the character's description.

Reference: Jordan Marsh

> **Sophia:** You know what she took back? A set of pearl earrings.
>
> **Dorothy:** The ones I fell in love with at Jordan Marsh?

Jordan Marsh was a former department store chain founded by Eben Dyer Jordan and Benjamin L. Marsh in 1841. The brand was retired in the mid-1990s, with most of its stores converting to Macy's.

Reference: Rockefeller Center

> **Dorothy:** Unless it's Christmas in New York. A light snow falling over Fifth Avenue. The ice skaters at Rockefeller Center. Santas on every street corner.

Rockefeller Center is a complex built in the 1930s, made up of multiple buildings covering twenty-two acres in Midtown Manhattan, New York City.

References: "The First Noel," *A Christmas Carol*

> **Rose, after singing a verse of "The First Noel":** Did I ever tell you about the time one Christmas we tried to launch a production of *A Christmas Carol* with an all-chicken cast?

"The First Noel" is a classic traditional Christmas carol dating back to sometime in the early nineteenth century. *A Christmas Carol* is an 1843 holiday novella by Charles Dickens in which a crotchety old miser named Ebenezer Scrooge is visited by the ghost of a former business partner and three spirits—Christmases Past, Present, and Yet to Come—in an attempt to soften his mean ways before it's too late. The story has become a holiday classic, adapted countless times for film, screen, and stage by the likes of everyone from Jim Carrey to The Muppets.

Reference: *Howard the Duck*

> **Rose:** This man is still very down about his financial situation. He was one of the principal backers of *Howard the Duck*.

Howard the Duck is a 1986 science-fiction comedy film based on the Marvel comic book of the same name about an anthropomorphic alien duck who lands on Earth. Produced by George Lucas and starring Lea Thompson, Jeffrey Jones, and Tim Robbins, the film was a critical and commercial bomb upon release and is considered one of the worst films ever made.

Reference: "Silent Night"

> **Santa Claus:** Does everybody know "Silent Night"?
>
> **Meyer:** Know it? I wrote it.

"Silent Night" is a popular Christmas carol written in 1818 in Austria by Franz Xaver Gruber and Joseph Mohr. It's been recorded countless times over the years by everyone from Bing Crosby to Stevie Nicks.

References: *Charlie's Angels*, Cheryl Ladd

> **Dorothy:** Blanche, what do we look like, *Charlie's Angels*?
>
> **Blanche:** I have been told I bear a striking resemblance to Ms. Cheryl Ladd, although my bosoms are perkier.
>
> **Dorothy:** Not even if you were hanging upside down on a trapeze.

An ABC crime-drama series, *Charlie's Angels* ran from 1976 to 1981 and followed the adventures of a revolving trio of crime-fighting female detectives, who accepted their assignments from an unseen boss, the titular Charlie. John Forsythe voiced Charlie, while Kate Jackson, Farrah Fawcett, and Jaclyn Smith were the original trio of Angels. Fawcett and Jackson eventually left, and Cheryl Ladd, Shelley Hack, and Tanya Roberts later stepped in. The show developed a following by emphasizing the sex appeal of the stars and had a long list of notable guests throughout its run. *Charlie's Angels* has lived on for decades in syndication and various reboot attempts, as well as a pair of successful films in the early 2000s starring Cameron Diaz, Drew Barrymore, and Lucy Liu. Actress Elizabeth Banks wrote and directed a new film version released in 2019, starring Kristen Stewart, Naomi Scott, and Ella Balinska. It received mixed reviews and fared poorly at the box office. Ladd is an actress and author best known for her work on the show and for a string of made-for-TV movies in the ensuing years.

References: Potsie, *Happy Days*

> **Santa Claus:** Did you know that that guy who wrote "Silent Night" was also the original choice for Potsie on *Happy Days*?

Happy Days is a popular sitcom that ran on ABC from 1974 to 1984, set in the 1950s American Midwest. The show, created by Garry Marshall, followed the Cunningham family and starred Ron Howard, Tom Bosley, Marion Ross, and—in a career-defining breakout role—Henry Winkler as Arthur "Fonzie" Fonzarelli. Warren "Potsie" Weber was a supporting character and friend of Howard's character, Richie Cunningham, and was played by actor Anson Williams.

Reference: The Mayo Clinic

> **Meyer:** I'm Dr. Rooney from the Mayo Clinic. I'd like to fill you in on the particulars of this man's case.

The Mayo Clinic is a prestigious nonprofit academic medical center founded by the Mayo family of Rochester, Minnesota, in 1864, which draws patients from around the globe.

Reference: Knott's Berry Farm

> **Rose:** I'd like a mug of hot apple cider with a cinnamon stick.

Albert: Lady, does this look like Knott's Berry Farm?

Knott's Berry Farm is a theme park in Buena Park, California, first opened in 1920 as a roadside berry stand operated by Walter Knott. The property grew with more and more attractions until becoming a full-fledged amusement park.

Reference: *The Waltons*

> **Dorothy:** Merry Christmas, Rose. Merry Christmas, Blanche.
>
> **Rose:** Merry Christmas, Dorothy. Merry Christmas, Blanche.
>
> **Blanche:** Merry Christmas, Rose ...
>
> **Sophia:** What the hell is this, *The Waltons*?

The Waltons is a drama series that ran on CBS from 1972 to 1981, about a family living in rural Virginia during the Great Depression and World War II. The large cast included Richard Thomas, Ralph Waite, and Michael Learned. Episodes routinely ended with an exterior shot of the darkened family house at night, with various characters wishing one another a good night.

Reference: "Surfin' Safari"

> *Rose accidentally selects this song on the jukebox when searching for a Christmas carol.*

"Surfin' Safari" is a hit song (and title of an album) by The Beach Boys, released in 1962.

Repeat Reference: Neiman Marcus *(Episode 1.23: Blind Ambitions)*

EPISODE 2.12: THE SISTERS
Directed by Terry Hughes. Written by Christopher Lloyd. Original airdate: January 3, 1987.
Dorothy attempts to surprise Sophia for her birthday by flying her estranged sister, Angela, to Miami, unaware that the two have been feuding for decades.

Reference: Monty Hall

> **Dorothy:** Ma, you want better presents, adopt Monty Hall.

Monty Hall (1921–2017) was a television host and producer best known for hosting the long-running game show *Let's Make a Deal*.

Reference: Beethoven

> **Dorothy:** I couldn't accept your favorite album, *Hans Klebnermeyer Yodels Beethoven*.

Ludwig van Beethoven (1770–1827) was a German composer and pianist whose classical music is among the most admired and performed to this day.

Reference: The Statue of Liberty

> **Angela:** There I was on the boat alone, watching Lady Liberty grow smaller in the distance, when suddenly I heard a voice from the vicinity of my knees.

The Statue of Liberty is a torch-bearing colossal sculpture of Libertas, the Roman goddess of liberty, that was gifted to the United States from France in the late nineteenth century. It is located on Liberty Island in New York Harbor and stands 151 feet tall.

Reference: Mighty Mouse

> **Dorothy:** You win. You always win.
>
> **Sophia:** I know. Me and Mighty Mouse.

Mighty Mouse is an animated anthropomorphic superhero mouse who debuted in 1942 and has starred in multiple theatrical shorts, cartoon shows, and comic books. You may remember his classic "Here I Come to Save the Day!" theme song.

Reference: Gina Lollobrigida

> **Sophia:** Angela?
>
> **Angela:** No, Gina Lollobrigida.

Gina Lollobrigida is an Italian actress of the 1950s and 1960s who starred in films such as *Beat the Devil*, *Trapeze*, and *The Hunchback of Notre Dame*. She launched a second career as a photojournalist in the 1970s.

Reference: DC-3

> **Blanche:** She looked like a DC-3 coming in for a landing.

The Douglas DC-3 is a propeller-driven airliner introduced in 1936.

Reference: Bromo-Seltzer

> **Sophia:** I go upstairs for a Bromo-Seltzer when suddenly Salvador grabs me from behind and begins passionately kissing me.

Originally manufactured in cobalt-blue bottles by Emerson Drug Company of Baltimore, Maryland, Bromo-Seltzer was an antacid pain reliever first produced in 1888. Taking its name from a component of its original formula, sodium bromide, the product was discontinued in 1975 when it was discovered that prolonged use of bromide was detrimental to one's health. It reappeared in the 1990s using a different formula.

Reference: Judas

> **Sophia:** If you didn't come in here to apologize, why don't you leave?
>
> **Angela:** Why should I apologize?
>
> **Sophia:** I'll tell you why. Because you're nothing but a backstabbing Judas in sensible shoes.

Judas Iscariot was one of the Twelve Apostles of Jesus Christ, notorious for betraying Jesus by revealing his whereabouts in exchange for silver. The betrayal led to Jesus's arrest, trial, and execution.

Repeat References: Dairy Queen *(Episode 1.25: The Way We Met)*, Pepto-Bismol *(Episode 2.8: Vacation)*, Jerry Vale *(Episode 1.5: The Triangle)*

EPISODE 2.13: THE STAN WHO CAME TO DINNER
Directed by Terry Hughes. Written by Kathy Speer and Terry Grossman. Original airdate: January 10, 1987.
Stan stays with the girls while recuperating from surgery.

Reference: Stevie Wonder

> **Stan:** Not everybody knows this isn't real.
>
> **Dorothy:** Please, Stevie Wonder could tell it's a rug.

Stevie Wonder is a singer, songwriter, and musician, blind since shortly after his birth, who has won a record twenty-five Grammys, an Oscar, and the Presidential Medal of Freedom.

References: Merv Griffin, *The Crucible*

> **Dorothy:** We have tickets to see Merv Griffin in *The Crucible*. I'll risk it.

Sometimes called (at least by Dorothy) the most beloved man in America and the "Anti-Trump," Merv Griffin (1925–2007) was a TV show and media mogul who hosted his own talk show, *The Merv Griffin Show*, from 1965 to 1986 and created the enduringly popular game shows *Jeopardy!* and *Wheel of Fortune*.

Reference: Timex

> **Sophia:** I have a recurring dream. John Cameron Swayze straps a Timex to my chin and tosses me across an icy pond.

Timex is an enduring brand of wristwatches that was originally founded in 1854 as the Waterbury Clock Company.

Reference: Sammy Davis Jr.

> **Stan:** Babe, don't worry. I'm a survivor. Everything's cool. The cat who's gonna cut me is primo.
>
> **Dorothy:** I said pull yourself together, not talk like Sammy Davis Jr.

Nicknamed "Mister Show Business," singer, actor, and dancer Sammy Davis Jr. (1925–1990) has been regarded as one of the greatest entertainers to ever grace a stage. He began performing in vaudeville at the ripe old age of three and rose to fame as an adult in the 1950s, hosted his own variety TV show in the 1960s, and had what some call his signature hit song, "The Candy Man," in the 1970s.

Reference: Mount Olympus

> **Dorothy:** I'm sitting at home with two screaming kids, praying you'll sell enough chain link to put food on the table, and you're off planting your flag on Mount Olympus.

Mount Olympus is the highest mountain in Greece and is notable in Greek mythology as being the home of the gods.

Reference: Best Western

> **Rose:** When the last piece is gone, that's when the bride and groom leave to start their wedding night, which takes place in a tent—or a Best Western.

Best Western is a hotel chain founded in 1946 with more than 4,500 locations worldwide.

Reference: Strawberry Quik

> **Dorothy:** I went to three different stores, but I finally found the stuff you asked for to make you go to sleep.
>
> **Stan:** Oh wow, Strawberry Quik. You are the best, babe!

Quik was originally a chocolate-flavored drink mix launched by Nestlé in 1948. Additional flavors eventually followed, with a strawberry version released in 1960. In 1999, the brand became officially known worldwide as Nesquik.

Reference: Magic Johnson

> **Dorothy:** You feeling better, Magic?
>
> **Stan:** Dorothy, Dorothy. I know this sounds insane. But I thought that a little physical activity would help me snap this setback. I was wrong, you were right. I should just rest. Could you help me back into bed?

Earvin "Magic" Johnson is a retired former athlete who spent his NBA career playing for the Los Angeles Lakers. He stands six feet, nine inches tall.

Repeat References: Grandma Moses *(Episode 2.8: Vacation)*, John Cameron Swayze *(Episode 1.9: Blanche and the Younger Man)*, Wolfie's *(Episode 2.1: End of the Curse)*, The Vatican *(Episode 2.9: Joust Between Friends)*, Jazzercise *(Episode 1.3: Rose the Prude)*, Peter Pan *(Episode 1.9: Blanche and the Younger Man)*

Episode 2.14: The Actor

Directed by Terry Hughes. Written by Barry Fanaro and Mort Nathan. Original airdate: January 17, 1987.

The girls are smitten with an attractive actor who is in town for a community theater production. Sophia gets a job at a fast-food restaurant.

Reference: *Dennis the Menace*

Sophia: Who do I look like, Dennis the Menace?

Dennis the Menace is a daily syndicated newspaper comic strip created by Hank Ketcham. It debuted in 1951 and continues today under the direction of the former assistants and son of Ketcham, who died in 2001. The character proved popular and has been adapted into other media, including both live-action and animated television shows and several feature films. The strip centers around adorable but rambunctious young Dennis Mitchell, who lives with his parents in a suburban neighborhood. Dennis's misadventures include frequent run-ins with cantankerous neighbor Mr. Wilson.

Reference: Morley Safer

Sophia: Yeah right, and Morley Safer just happened to wander in there by mistake.

Morley Safer (1931–2016) was a broadcast journalist best known for his decades-long stint on the CBS newsmagazine television series *60 Minutes*.

References: Meryl Streep, *The Diary of Anne Frank*

Dorothy: You say that every year, and every year we end up with Miami's answer to Meryl Streep, Phyllis Hammerow. She stinks.

Rose: Oh, I thought she was terrific last year in *The Diary of Anne Frank*.

Considered by many to be the best actress of her generation, Meryl Streep has won three Academy Awards and eight Golden Globes. Among her many noted films are *Kramer vs. Kramer*, *Sophie's Choice*, *The Iron Lady*, *The Bridges of Madison County*, and *The Devil Wears Prada*.

The Diary of Anne Frank is a 1955 play written by Frances Goodrich and Albert Hackett, adapted into a 1959 film, and based on the writings of Anne Frank, a young Jewish girl who spent two years hiding with her family in an attic during the Nazi occupation of the Netherlands during World War II. The family was discovered and apprehended in 1944, and Frank died of typhus in a concentration camp the following year. The diary was discovered by Miep Gies, who hid the family in the attic, and was given to Frank's father—the family's only known survivor—after the war ended. The diary was first published in 1947 as *The Diary of a Young Girl* and has since been printed in more than sixty languages.

Reference: Häagen-Dazs

Rose: I hate to admit it, but he melts my Häagen-Dazs.

Häagen-Dazs is a premium ice-cream brand launched in New York in 1960 with three flavors: vanilla, chocolate, and coffee. It has since expanded into a variety of other flavors and frozen treats, as well as retail stores with franchises in countries all over the world.

Reference: Strait of Magellan

Rose: Is that a Captain Jack's Seafood Shanty uniform you're wearing?

Sophia: No, Rose, I'm off to discover the Straits of Magellan.

The Strait of Magellan is a sea route in southern Chile that separates mainland South America and Tierra del Fuego and is considered the most important passage between the Atlantic and Pacific oceans.

Reference: Vasco da Gama

Sophia: You're embarrassed by your own mother?

Dorothy: When she's dressed like Vasco da Gama, yes.

Vasco da Gama (c. 1460s–1524) was a Portuguese explorer from back in the late fifteenth, early sixteenth centuries who was the first seafaring European to reach India. He contracted malaria on one of his many voyages and died.

References: Linda Ronstadt, *The Pirates of Penzance*

Patrick: And you are?

Sophia: Linda Ronstadt. I'm doing *The Pirates of Penzance* across town.

Linda Ronstadt is a multiple Grammy Award–winning singer known for hits like "Blue Bayou," "You're No Good," "Don't Know Much," and many others. She retired from performing in 2011. *The Pirates of Penzance* is an 1879 comic opera by Arthur Sullivan and W. S. Gilbert, about a young apprentice and a band of tenderhearted pirates.

Reference: Hervé Villechaize

Patrick: There are no small theaters, no small parts, only small actors.

Rose: Like Hervé Villechaize.

Hervé Villechaize (1943–1993) was an actor known for the 1974 James Bond film *The Man with the Golden Gun* and for his role as Tattoo in the television series *Fantasy Island*. Born with dwarfism, Villechaize stood at three feet, eleven inches.

Repeat References: *People (Episode 1.25: The Way We Met)*, Judas *(Episode 2.12: The Sisters)*

EPISODE 2.15: BEFORE AND AFTER
Directed by Terry Hughes. Written by Bob Rosenfarb. Original airdate: January 24, 1987.
A health setback causes Rose to rethink her life and move out of the house.

Reference: Cream of Wheat

Sophia: You can't eat Cream of Wheat because it's too spicy.

A brand of breakfast porridge mix similar to grits but smoother, Cream of Wheat was invented in 1893 and is still sold today. And it certainly isn't spicy.

Reference: Canasta

Sophia: My canasta club gives this hospital's Jell-O three stars.

Canasta is a card game of the rummy variety commonly played by two teams of two, who try to deplete the cards in their hand by making melds of cards of the same rank. The game was devised by Segundo Santos and Alberto Serrato of Uruguay in 1939. It hit the United States in the late 1940s and gained popularity throughout the 1950s.

Reference: *Fantasia*

Dorothy: Remember that New Year's Eve when you had the three margaritas? You thought you were an animated broom in *Fantasia*.

Fantasia is a 1940 animated film from Disney consisting of a series of segments set to pieces of classical music.

References: Grand Central Station, Hare Krishna

Rose: It was an enormous train station—like Grand Central, only cleaner, and without Hare Krishnas asking for money.

Grand Central Station is a commuter rail terminal in New York City and one of the busiest train stations in North America. The International Society for Krishna Consciousness, or simply the Hare Krishnas, is a religious organization founded in 1966 and based on Hindu scripture.

References: Life, shredded wheat

> **Sophia:** I ate Life once. Not a bad cereal. When we run out of shredded wheat, let's give it a try again.

Life is a breakfast cereal introduced in 1961 by the Quaker Oats Company. Shredded wheat is also a type of breakfast cereal consisting of little pillow-shaped biscuits of whole wheat that dates back to 1890, when Henry Perky first invented it. Kellogg's obtained a patent on the product in 1915 that eventually led to a lawsuit in the 1930s, in which the court ruled that "shredded wheat" is a generic term and not trademarkable.

References: Liberace, Don Rickles, Mitzi Gaynor

> **Sophia:** He says celebrities stop by there all the time. In one day, he saw Dean Martin, Liberace, Don Rickles, and Mitzi Gaynor.

Liberace (1919–1987) was a flamboyant singer, actor, and pianist whose stage presence and busy schedule of touring and Las Vegas residencies earned him the nickname "Mr. Showmanship." Don Rickles (1926–2017) was a stand-up comedian and actor known for his particular brand of insult comedy. Actress and singer Mitzi Gaynor appeared in a string of successful films in the 1950s and 1960s, many of which are considered classics, including *There's No Business Like Show Business*, *South Pacific*, and *Anything Goes*.

References: Valium, Life Savers

> **Stephanie:** Do you have a Valium?
>
> **Rose:** No, but I do have a tangerine Life Saver.

Valium is a prescription anxiety medication. Life Savers are little ring-shaped hard and soft candies introduced in 1912, with fruit and mint flavors.

Reference: Tallulah Bankhead

> **Blanche:** I cannot believe it is Saturday night and I, Blanche Devereaux, the most witty, stunning, criminally sensuous woman to come out of the South since Ms. Tallulah Bankhead, do not have a date.

A gay icon of stage and screen, Tallulah Bankhead (1902–1968) was as well-known for antics in her personal life as for her tremendous skill as a performer. While largely a stage actress, her most notable film role was in Alfred Hitchcock's *Lifeboat*. Away from the stage, she was a vocally liberal Democrat, bisexual, and she struggled with alcoholism, drug addiction, and a smoking habit.

Reference: "I Left My Heart in San Francisco"

> **Blanche:** He may have left his heart in San Francisco, but he left his shorts on my radiator.

"I Left My Heart in San Francisco" is a song that was written in 1953 by George Cory and Douglass Cross and became the signature song of Tony Bennett when it was released in 1962.

Repeat References: Jell-O *(Episode 1.20: Adult Education)*, Shirley MacLaine *(Episode 1.23: Blind Ambitions)*, Tony Bennett *(Episode 1.7: The Competition)*, Dean Martin *(Episode 1.14: That Was No Lady)*

Episode 2.16: And Then There Was One

Directed by Terry Hughes. Written by Russell Marcus. Original airdate: January 31, 1987.

The girls worry that a baby left in their care has been abandoned. Sophia prepares to compete in a walkathon.

Reference: Mother Teresa

> **Dorothy:** Who eats linguine with clam sauce for breakfast?
>
> **Sophia:** Mother Teresa. It's a recipe from her new workout book.

Mother Teresa (1910–1997) was a Nobel Peace Prize–winning Roman Catholic nun and missionary known for her charitable work.

Reference: The Ford Foundation

> **Rose:** I love charities. In fact, I helped establish The Henry Fjord Foundation.
>
> **Dorothy:** The Fjord Foundation?
>
> **Blanche:** Yes, Dorothy, you know that's the man who built the Fjord Fjalcon.

A classic St. Olaf play on words with the Ford Foundation, a private foundation created in 1936 by Edsel Ford and Henry Ford, with the mission of advancing human welfare.

Reference: Mr. Potato Head

> **Rose:** It's a variation on an old idea. Homemade Mr. Potato Heads.

Mr. Potato Head is a children's toy introduced in 1952, consisting of a plastic potato that can be decorated with various facial features and body parts.

Reference: Ben Gazzara

> **Rose:** She needs to hear a feminine voice.
>
> **Dorothy:** And what was I doing, my Ben Gazzara impersonation?

Actor Ben Gazzara's (1930–2012) nearly six-decade career spanned film, stage, and screen, including roles in *Anatomy of a Murder*, *Run for Your Life*, *Voyage of the Damned*, *Road House*, *The Big Lebowski*, *The Thomas Crown Affair*, and an Emmy Award–winning turn in *Hysterical Blindness*.

Reference: Wendy's

> **Sophia:** I hit the wall.
>
> **Dorothy:** Oh, Ma, you ran out of steam.
>
> **Sophia:** No, I actually hit a wall. They put up a new Wendy's on Collins Avenue.

Wendy's is a fast-food restaurant chain founded by Dave Thomas in 1969 and named after his daughter. The chain is known for its "old-fashioned" square hamburgers, salty fries, and the popular Frosty frozen dairy dessert.

Reference: *Sports Illustrated*

> **Sophia:** If that's *Sports Illustrated*, tell them to call back tomorrow.

Sports Illustrated is a popular sports magazine first published in 1954.

Reference: *Family Circle*

> **Rose:** Where else can you get beef jerky and *Family Circle* this time of night?

A magazine typically found at supermarket checkout stands that focused on home and women's topics, *Family Circle* was published monthly from 1932 until it ceased production in December 2019.

Reference: Yoo-hoo

> **Rose:** What's an ooh-hoo?
>
> **Dorothy:** It's a chocolate soft drink.

Yoo-hoo is a brand of chocolate soft drink developed in 1928.

Reference: Yellowstone Park

> **Dorothy:** I'm sure it'd be a lot easier for us after all we've been through.
>
> **Rose:** What've we been through?
>
> **Dorothy:** Yellowstone Park, Rose.

Yellowstone Park is a National Park located in parts of Wyoming, Montana, and Idaho, known for beautiful views, wildlife, and the Old Faithful geyser.

Reference: Sean Penn

> **Sophia:** The paparazzi! Now I know why Sean Penn gets so ticked off.

Sean Penn is an Academy Award–winning actor known for such films as *Taps, Fast Times at Ridgemont High, At Close Range, Carlito's Way, Mystic River*, and *Milk*. His 1985 marriage to Madonna, which occurred six months after they met, made the couple tabloid fodder and led to several violent interactions with members of the press, one of which landed Penn in jail on assault charges. He and Madonna divorced in 1989.

Reference: Gimlet

> **Sophia:** Triplets? I thought you said your wife had gimlets.

A gimlet is a cocktail consisting of gin and lime juice.

Reference: The Olympics

> **Sophia:** Seoul, Korea, 1988. The Olympics. I'd like to be there competing for the USA.

The Olympics is a series of international sporting events featuring summer and winter sports competitions between thousands of athletes from around the world competing for medals. They're held every four years, with summer and winter events alternating every two years in the four-year period. In 1988, the Summer Olympics were held between September and October in Seoul, South Korea.

Repeat References: Sammy Davis Jr. *(Episode 1.13: The Stan Who Came to Dinner)*, Texaco *(Episode 1.19: Second Motherhood)*, Ford Falcon *(Episode 1.13: A Little Romance)*

EPISODE 2.17: BEDTIME STORY
Directed by Terry Hughes. Written by Kathy Sper, Terry Grossman, Mort Nathan, and Barry Fanaro. Original airdate: February 7, 1987.
While discussing sleeping arrangements for visiting relatives, the girls reminisce about unusual places they've had to sleep in the past.

Reference: Beetle Bailey

Sophia: What do I look like, Beetle Bailey?

Beetle Bailey is the title character of a comic strip created by Mort Walker that debuted in 1950 and is still running daily today. Private Bailey, who is depicted with a helmet or hat covering his eyes, is a shiftless, lazy US Army private always facing the scorn of superior officer Sergeant Snorkel.

Reference: "Sunrise, Sunset"

Rose: He's going to be in town for the fourteenth annual Hog Expo.

Dorothy: Is it the fourteenth annual already? It seems like just yesterday it was the twelfth annual. Sunrise, sunset . . . sunrise, sunset.

"Sunrise, Sunset" is a 1964 song by Jerry Bock and Sheldon Harnick from the musical *Fiddler on the Roof.*

Reference: Dick Cavett

Dorothy: You talk in your sleep.

Sophia: And let's face it, you're no Dick Cavett awake.

Television personality, columnist, comedian, actor, and talk show host Dick Cavett was a regular broadcasting presence for decades. He gained momentum behind the scenes at *The Tonight Show* in the 1960s, as writer and talent coordinator, and has hosted various incarnations of his own talk show since 1968.

Reference: Lean Cuisine

> **Dorothy:** Turn up the heat.
>
> **Sophia:** It's already on nine. On ten you could cook a Lean Cuisine.

Lean Cuisine is a brand of lower-calorie, lower-fat, frozen dinners introduced by the Nestlé company in 1981.

Reference: The Three Stooges

> **Dorothy:** Goodnight, Ma. Goodnight, Moe. Goodnight, Larry.

This joke references The Three Stooges, a comedy team active from 1922 to 1970, known for a series of short-subject films. The original stooges were Moe Howard, Larry Fine, and Curly Howard. While Moe and Larry were mainstays, other third stooges over the years were Shemp Howard, Joe Besser, and "Curly" Joe DeRita.

Reference: Pat Robertson

> **Dorothy:** God wouldn't mind if you skipped a night. He's very busy these days. Most of his free time is spent talking to Pat Robertson.

Pat Robertson is an evangelist and political commentator who advocates for conservative Christianity and hosts *The 700 Club*, a Christian newsmagazine show. During the time of this episode, he had announced his intent to seek the Republican nomination for president of the United States.

Reference: *Star Search*

> **Rose:** There's some things I don't understand. Like poverty, and the spokesmodel category on *Star Search*.

Star Search is a television talent show that aired from 1983 to 1995, hosted by Ed McMahon, which featured contestants competing in such categories as male and female singer, dance, spokesmodel, and comedy.

References: Christie Brinkley, Billy Joel, Wilford Brimley

> **Blanche:** I am contouring my eyebrows. I use Ms. Christie Brinkley as a guide because we have exactly the same bone structure. I just hope she

doesn't let herself go to pot after that baby comes. I don't want that big-eyed husband of hers coming after me.

Rose: I never do much with my eyebrows.

Blanche: That's why, from the nose up, you look like Wilford Brimley.

Model and actress Christie Brinkley gained worldwide fame as a *Sports Illustrated* swimsuit model in the late 1970s, began an acting career with a turn as the girl in the Ferrari in *National Lampoon's Vacation*, and spent twenty-five years as the face of CoverGirl cosmetics. She married "big-eyed" rock star Billy Joel in 1985, and the pair divorced in 1994. Various other acting roles and professional pursuits have kept her busy ever since. Joel, meanwhile, is a music legend who rose to fame in the 1970s and is known for hits like "Piano Man," "You May Be Right," "Uptown Girl," "We Didn't Start the Fire," and many others. His expansive discography has made him one of the best-selling musical artists of all time. Wilford Brimley (1934–2020) had an acting career spanning five decades, appearing in such films and television shows as *The Waltons*, *The China Syndrome*, *Our House*, *Cocoon*, and *The Firm*. Despite an impressive filmography, it's perhaps his commercial work for which Brimley is most remembered. He was a spokesperson for Quaker Oats and appeared in a series of ads for Liberty Medical about diabetes, which he famously pronounced "diabeetus."

Reference: Dr. Art Ulene

Sophia: I saw Dr. Art Ulene explain it on the *Today* show with a plastic mop.

Dr. Art Ulene is a physician who served as the medical expert on NBC's *Today* for two decades.

References: Opie, Aunt Bea

Dorothy: Please say hello to Opie and Aunt Bea for me when you see them.

Opie and Aunt Bea are fictional characters from *The Andy Griffith Show*, a popular sitcom that ran from 1960 to 1968 and, in addition to making household names of the likes of Griffith and Don Knotts, also launched the career of a then-very-young Ron Howard, who played Opie. Set in the fictional town of Mayberry, North Carolina, which has become all but synonymous with the quintessential American small town where everybody knows everybody, the show centered around widowed sheriff Andy Taylor (Griffith), who lived with his son and wise old Aunt Bea (Frances Bavier) while maintaining order on the dusty streets of Mayberry with the help of bumbling deputy Barney Fife (Knotts). In a *Golden Girls* connection, the show got its start as an episode of *The Danny Thomas Show*, which starred the father of *The Golden Girls* producer Tony Thomas.

Reference: *The Twilight Zone*

> **Blanche:** This is like *The Twilight Zone*. Somehow we got on a train that ended up inside Rose's mind.

The Twilight Zone is a science-fiction anthology television series created by Rod Serling that originally ran from 1959 to 1964 and evolved into a media franchise that included various series revivals, films, radio programs, and merchandise. The most recent version of the series, developed in part by actor and filmmaker Jordan Peele, debuted in 2019 and ran for two seasons on the CBS All Access streaming platform, which was rebranded Paramount+ in 2021.

Reference: *Kama Sutra*

> **Dorothy:** *The Kama Sutra* had to publish a supplement because of you.

The *Kama Sutra* is an ancient Indian Sanskrit text all about sexuality and eroticism, often considered to be a manual on sex positions.

Reference: Holiday Inn

> **Blanche:** What do you say we all chip in and put them up at the Holiday Inn?

Holiday Inn is an international hotel chain founded in 1952.

Repeat Reference: *Today (Episode 1.3: Rose the Prude)*

EPISODE 2.18: FORGIVE ME, FATHER
Directed by Terry Hughes. Written by Kathy Speer and Terry Grossman. Original airdate: February 14, 1987.
Dorothy woos an attractive colleague, unaware that he's a priest.

Reference: Joan Rivers

> **Rose:** What does he do? Pulls alongside, shouts obscenities that would make Joan Rivers blush, then speeds off down the street.

Joan Rivers (1933–2014) was a foul-mouthed comedian, actress, and host who rose to prominence as a stand-up comedian on *The Tonight Show* in the 1960s. She was the first woman to host a late-night talk show when she began hosting *The Late Show with Joan Rivers* in 1986. She also hosted a daytime talk show, appeared in various films and series, including *Hollywood Squares*, and in later years became known for her comedic red-carpet award-show interviews and fashion commentary alongside her daughter, Melissa.

Reference: Kareem Abdul-Jabbar

> **Sophia:** I can't find my lucky handkerchief. . . . I'm trying to get my kit together for a major bingo game, and it's not here. There's no way I can play without it. It's like Kareem without his goggles.

Kareem Abdul-Jabbar, born Ferdinand Lewis Alcindor Jr., in 1947, is one of the greatest professional basketball players to ever take the court. Throughout his twenty-season career, he racked up accolade after accolade—and point after point. When he retired in 1989, at age forty-two, he led the NBA in points scored and games played. Since then, he's worked as an actor, coach, and author and has competed on *Dancing with the Stars*. Standing at a whopping seven-foot-two, Abdul-Jabbar's dancing shortcomings knocked him out of the running fairly early. For comparison, Estelle Getty was four-foot-eleven. In 2016, President Barack Obama awarded Abdul-Jabbar the Presidential Medal of Freedom, the nation's highest civilian honor.

Reference: Concertina

> **Sophia:** They mean good health, have a nice day, and would you like to squeeze my concertina?

A concertina is a musical instrument similar to an accordion, dating back to the nineteenth century.

Reference: Jane Fonda

> **Sophia:** If you do it your way, you'd better use Jane Fonda's body. Otherwise, it'll just be the four of us for dinner.

Actress and activist Jane Fonda is known for a successful career spanning stage and screen, with films like *Barefoot in the Park*, *Barbarella*, *The China Syndrome*, and *9 to 5*. She was an outspoken activist against the Vietnam War, taking a controversial approach that led to the nickname "Hanoi Jane" and her being basically blacklisted for a time. She began producing a successful series of home-workout videos in the 1980s, retired for a while in the 1990s, and launched a major comeback in more recent years with hit films like *The Butler* and *Book Club* and a multi-season run on the hit Netflix comedy *Grace and Frankie* with longtime friend Lily Tomlin.

Reference: Eric Sevareid

> **Blanche:** With her complexion, those yellow garden lights make Dorothy look like Eric Sevareid.

Eric Sevareid (1912–1992) was an author and journalist for CBS News from 1939 to 1977.

Reference: Cupid

> **Blanche:** With a little help from us, I think she could fire Cupid's arrow into the tushie of love.

Cupid is the god of desire, erotic love, attraction, and affection in classical mythology, often portrayed as the son of the love goddess Venus and the war god Mars. There have been many depictions of Cupid as a winged, diaper-wearing baby who shoots heart-shaped arrows.

Reference: *Hell Town*

> **Rose:** I'm so sorry *Hell Town* was canceled.

Hell Town was a short-lived NBC drama that ran from September to December 1985, featuring Robert Blake as a Catholic priest in a crime-ridden Los Angeles neighborhood.

Reference: Nehru jacket

> **Dorothy:** Please tell me that's a Nehru jacket.

A Nehru jacket is a hip-length tailored coat modeled after the garment worn by Jawaharlal Nehru, the prime minister of India from 1947 to 1964.

Reference: *Solid Gold*

> **Frank:** You look lovely tonight.
> **Dorothy:** I look like the mother of a *Solid Gold* dancer.

Solid Gold was a musical television series that ran from 1980 to 1988 that featured a group of professional (and flashily dressed) dancers who would perform choreographed numbers to popular songs.

References: La-Z-Boy

> **Blanche:** He was a fabric salesman. We never made love again after that, but he did cover my La-Z-Boy for free.

La-Z-Boy is a Michigan-based furniture company founded in 1927 and known for comfortable recliners.

Reference: Hugh Downs

> **Sophia:** I told Father Donatelli I'm going to ask Hugh Downs to investigate.

Renowned broadcaster, host, news anchor, and author Hugh Downs (1921–2020) held the Guinness World Record for years for having the most hours on commercial network television. Among the notable posts during his multi-decade career were serving as sidekick for *The Tonight Show Starring Jack Paar*, cohosting the *Today* show, hosting the *Concentration* game show, and anchoring ABC's *20/20* program from 1978 to 1999.

References: *The Dating Game*, the Pope

> **Dorothy:** I was a contestant on *The Dating Game*, and I won. I went around the corner to meet the bachelor who picked me, and it was the Pope.

The Dating Game was a game show that ran in its original incarnation on ABC from 1965 to 1973 and in various subsequent versions up until the turn of the century. Jim Lange hosted the original version that would typically have a bachelorette toss questions to three bachelors whom she couldn't see and, based on their responses, choose one for a date.

The Pope serves as bishop of Rome as well as the chief pastor of the Catholic Church and resides in the Apostolic Palace in the Vatican City in Rome, Italy.

Reference: Pam Dawber

> **Dorothy:** The first really wonderful guy I've met in a long time, and he turns out to have a more serious involvement.

Rose: With whom?

Dorothy: Pam Dawber!

Actress Pam Dawber rose to fame costarring alongside Robin Williams on the TV series *Mork & Mindy* from 1978 to 1982 and played the titular Sam in the sitcom *My Sister Sam* from 1986 to 1988. She was a TV-movie mainstay through the 1990s and has done the occasional guest spot since then. She's involved in charity work and is married to actor Mark Harmon.

Reference: Duke and Duchess of Windsor

> **Blanche:** You take the religious aspect out of this, and it's really quite romantic. A man giving up everything for the woman he loves. Kind of like the story of the Duke and Duchess of Windsor.

The Duke of Windsor was the title given to former British king Edward VIII (1894–1972) after he abdicated the throne in 1936 to marry American divorcée Wallis Simpson (1896–1986) who, when the marriage happened, assumed the title of Duchess.

Repeat Reference: Best Western *(Episode 2.13: The Stan Who Came to Dinner)*

EPISODE 2.19: LONG DAY'S JOURNEY INTO MARINARA
Directed by Terry Hughes. Written by Barry Fanaro and Mort Nathan. Original airdate: February 21, 1987.
Sophia's sister Angela moves to Miami—and into the girls' house. Rose cares for a piano-playing chicken.

Reference: Tom Brokaw

> **Blanche:** I was fantasizing what Tom Brokaw looks like naked.

Broadcast journalist and author Tom Brokaw was the anchor and managing editor of *NBC Nightly News* from 1982 to 2004 and is the only person to have hosted all three major NBC News shows: the *Today* show and *Meet the Press* in addition to the evening news. He was considered one of the "Big Three" US anchors during his tenure at *NBC Nightly News*, along with his competitors at ABC and CBS, Peter Jennings and Dan Rather, respectively. He retired from the anchor desk in late 2004 and has continued to serve as a special correspondent for NBC.

Reference: Milton Berle

> **Blanche:** Isn't she the woman who thought Milton Berle was sending her secret messages through her dentures?

The career of comedian and actor Milton Berle (1908–2002), aka Uncle Miltie, spanned more than eighty years. From silent films and stage roles to radio to television and movies, he did it all. He became an American household name as host of the *Texaco Star Theater* on NBC in the late 1940s, becoming known—in addition to the affectionate aforementioned nickname—as Mr. Television. With a filmography spanning the bulk of the twentieth century, Berle was active up until 2000.

Reference: *Bye Bye Birdie*

> **Rose:** Maybe I can convince the Count to give us some live entertainment with dessert. Will there be any requests?
>
> **Blanche:** How about *Bye Bye Birdie*?

Bye Bye Birdie is a Tony Award–winning 1960 Broadway musical inspired by the popularity of Elvis Presley (or, in the case of the play, the fictional Conrad Birdie) and his draft notice into the army. Dick Van Dyke, Chita Rivera, and Dick Gautier starred in the original production, while the likes of Doris Roberts, Gina Gershon, and John Stamos have appeared in various revivals over the decades.

Reference: Count Basie

> **Rose:** This is not a farm chicken. Count Bessie is a showbiz chicken!

The chicken's name is a play on William James "Count" Basie (1904–1984), a jazz pianist, bandleader, and composer who formed the Count Basie Orchestra in the 1930s and led the group for nearly fifty years.

Reference: Benny Goodman

> **Dorothy:** I wonder who that could be.
>
> **Blanche:** Maybe it's the Count's clarinet player, Henny Goodman.

This one is a play on the "King of Swing," Benny Goodman (1909–1986), a jazz clarinetist and bandleader who led one of the most popular groups in the 1930s.

References: Porcelana, the Temptations

> **Sophia:** She used up my entire bottle of Porcelana. Look at these liver spots. I've got more brown skin than the Temptations.

Porcelana is a skin-lightening cream. The Temptations are a popular singing group that rose to fame with Motown Records in the 1960s, with hits like "Cloud Nine," "My Girl," "Ain't Too Proud to Beg," and "I Wish It Would Rain."

Reference: Doc Severinsen

> **Blanche:** Count Bessie was a chicken. It's not as if Angela had fried up Doc Severinsen.

Doc Severinsen is a jazz trumpeter who led the band for *The Tonight Show Starring Johnny Carson*.

Reference: Preparation H

> **Angela:** May your shampoo get mixed up with your Preparation H and shrink your head to the size of a mushroom!

Preparation H is a medication used to shrink hemorrhoids.

Reference: Benihana

> **Rose:** Who stabbed Sophia?
>
> **Dorothy:** The chef at Benihana, Rose.

Benihana is a Florida-headquartered chain of Japanese cuisine restaurants with more than seventy locations in multiple countries. The chain began in New York City in 1964, when twenty-five-year-old Hiroaki "Rocky" Aoki started the business using $10,000 he earned from driving an ice-cream truck in Harlem. Benihana helped popularize the format of chefs preparing food on teppanyaki grills while surrounded by diners, using a touch of theatrics and impressive knife skills.

References: Peter Marshall, *The Love Boat*, the Landers sisters

> **Rose:** Peter Marshall played this microbiologist on *The Love Boat*, and he was conducting sinister experiments on the Landers sisters.

Peter Marshall is a television personality and actor who, in addition to a lengthy filmography, is known for hosting *The Hollywood Squares* from 1966 to 1981. *The Love Boat* is a long-running ABC series set aboard a luxury cruise ship, the SS *Pacific Princess*, with storylines revolving around the captain and crew, as well as various passengers played by famous guest stars. The show aired from 1977 to 1987, along with various subsequent specials and a late-1990s reboot. The original show starred Gavin MacLeod, Bernie Kopell, and Ted Lange. Audrey and Judy Landers are singing and acting siblings. Audrey is best known for her work in *Dallas* and *A Chorus Line* in the 1980s. Judy's filmography includes roles in *Happy Days, Charlie's Angels, Murder, She Wrote*, and plenty of other 1970s and 1980s mainstays. The sisters appeared together on the cover of *Playboy* in 1983 and often collaborated with one another on projects.

Reference: *Wheel of Fortune*

> **Sophia:** I'm going over there to kill her. I'll be back in time for *Wheel of Fortune.*

Wheel of Fortune is a long-running game show created by Merv Griffin that debuted in 1975 and features contestants competing to solve word puzzles, with cash and prizes determined by spinning a giant carnival wheel. It is hosted by Pat Sajak and Vanna White.

Reference: Conan the Barbarian

> **Angela:** You think I know how to kill a live chicken? What do I look like, Conan the Barbarian?

Conan the Barbarian is a fictional hero created by Robert E. Howard in 1932. The character originated in pulp magazines and has since been adapted to books, comics, TV shows, games, and films, such as the 1982 epic starring Arnold Schwarzenegger in the title role.

Repeat References: Tom Cruise *(Episode 2.6: Big Daddy's Little Lady)*, Morley Safer *(Episode 2.14: The Actor)*, Poligrip *(Episode 1.16: The Truth Will Out)*, bocce ball *(Episode 1.7: The Competition)*

EPISODE 2.20: WHOSE FACE IS THIS, ANYWAY?
Directed by Terry Hughes. Written by Winifred Hervey. Original airdate: February 28, 1987.

When a college sorority reunion doesn't go according to plan, Blanche decides to get extensive plastic surgery. Rose makes a video for her college course.

Reference: Fess Parker

> **Sophia:** Dorothy's always been a little camera-shy. You'd be too if you looked like Fess Parker in heels.

Fess Parker (1924–2010) was an actor best known for playing the title roles in *Davy Crockett*, a 1954 Disney miniseries, and *Daniel Boone*, which ran on NBC from 1964 to 1970.

Reference: It's a Small World

> **Dorothy:** Why are you dressed like someone who's just escaped from It's a Small World?

It's a Small World is a water-based boat ride at the various Walt Disney parks. The attraction was originally to be called Children of the World, but the ride's theme song, "It's a Small World (After All)," written by Robert B. and Richard M. Sherman in the 1960s, was so well liked by Walt Disney that he renamed the ride after it.

Reference: Joe Pepitone

> **Dorothy:** Who do you see when you look at me, Blanche? Joe Pepitone?

Joe Pepitone is a former Major League Baseball player who played with such teams as the New York Yankees, Houston Astros, Chicago Cubs, and Atlanta Braves.

Reference: Ajax

> **Sophia:** Tea stains my dentures. Last night I had to soak them in Ajax.

Ajax is a brand of household cleaning products that's been around since the 1940s. Powdered Ajax cleaner was one of the first major brands produced by the Colgate-Palmolive Company, marketed as "stronger than dirt," a nod to the Greek hero Ajax the Great, who was as strong and courageous as they come. The brand expanded its product line and rose to its peak in the 1960s and 1970s. While still easily found in the United States, the line has shrunk to only dishwashing liquid and that trusted powdered cleaner.

Reference: Play-Doh

> **Sophia:** You think I was born with white hair and a butt like Play-Doh?

Play-Doh is a modeling compound for kids to make arts and crafts projects, first manufactured in Cincinnati in the 1930s as a wallpaper cleaner, and then reworked and rebranded in the mid-1950s.

Reference: Fabergé eggs

> **Dorothy:** They would fight over who got to keep the footprints you left in the mud?
>
> **Sophia:** It was a poor village, Dorothy. What did you want them to collect? Fabergé eggs?

A Fabergé egg is a jeweled egg created in St. Petersburg, Russia, by the House of Fabergé between 1885 and 1917. Fifty-seven of a supposed sixty-nine eggs survive today.

Reference: Shelley Hack

> **Dorothy:** It would be better with Shelley Hack, Rose. Just turn it on.

Actress and model Shelley Hack is best known as the face of Revlon's Charlie perfume throughout the mid-1970s and early 1980s, and as one of *Charlie's Angels*.

Reference: Carol Burnett

> **Blanche:** I want to get Linda Evans's eyes and Lena Horne's cheek-bones and Cheryl Tiegs's nose and Carol Burnett's chin.

A comedy legend, Carol Burnett's multi-decade career dates back to the 1950s, when she had a Tony Award–nominated role in *Once Upon a Mattress* on Broadway. A few years later she scored her first Emmy for *The Garry Moore Show*. But it was her eleven-year run at the helm of her own variety series, *The Carol Burnett Show*, that made Burnett a household name. The series ran from 1967 to 1978 and produced multiple famous sketches and characters, including Thelma Harper (Vicki Lawrence) and her insufferable daughter, Eunice (Burnett). The sketch led to the series *Mama's Family*, which starred both Betty White and Rue McClanahan during its early seasons. Burnett, meanwhile, has never stopped working. In 2005, she received the Presidential

Medal of Freedom, and in 2019, she was the first recipient of the Carol Burnett Award at the Golden Globes.

Reference: Gavin MacLeod

> **Sophia:** Why is everyone looking at a picture of Gavin MacLeod?

Gavin MacLeod (1931–2021) was an actor best known for roles in *McHale's Navy*, *The Mary Tyler Moore Show*, and *The Love Boat*.

Reference: John Madden

> **Rose:** This is my hair's natural color.
>
> **Sophia:** Yeah, and John Madden is a finicky eater.

John Madden is a former football coach who won a Super Bowl as head coach with the Oakland Raiders. Following his coaching career, he became a popular commentator for NFL games and also lent his name to the Madden NFL video-game series.

Reference: Stepin Fetchit

> **Rose:** They became the internationally known Scandinavian dance team of Step and Fetchik.

This is a play on Stepin Fetchit (1902–1985), a vaudeville comedian and actor who was born Lincoln Theodore Monroe Andrew Perry. Going by the persona Stepin Fetchit, he is considered to be the first Black actor to receive a feature screen credit and to launch a successful film career, earning a million dollars. Among his films are *In Old Kentucky*, *Show Boat*, and *A Tough Winter*.

Reference: Vidal Sassoon

> **Rose:** The town would've gone under if Oslo's most famous hairstylist, Vidal Sassbogadotter, hadn't relocated his shop in St. Olaf because of our more favorable tax laws.

A play on Vidal Sassoon (1928–2012), a British hairstylist and businessman known for his chain of hairstyling salons and hair-treatment products.

Reference: Miss Marple

> **Sophia:** Excuse me, Miss Marple. I'm new at this.

Miss Marple is a famed fictional amateur detective created by Agatha Christie and appearing in multiple novels, short stories, films, and television series.

Repeat References: Scarlett O'Hara *(Episode 1.5: The Triangle)*, Mama Celeste *(Episode 1.5: The Triangle)*, Chef Boyardee *(Episode 1.7: The Competition)*, Cheryl Tiegs *(Episode 1.13: A Little Romance)*, Linda Evans *(Episode 2.6: Big Daddy's Little Lady)*, Lena Horne *(Episode 1.5: The Triangle)*, Art Garfunkel *(Episode 2.6: Big Daddy's Little Lady)*, Miami Dolphins *(Episode 1.3: Rose the Prude)*, NBC *(Episode 1.20: Adult Education)*

EPISODE 2.21: DOROTHY'S PRIZED PUPIL
Directed by Terry Hughes. Written by Christopher Lloyd. Original airdate: March 14, 1987.
Dorothy inadvertently gets the student she is tutoring deported. Rose agrees to become Blanche's personal servant after losing her pair of valuable earrings.

References: *Father Knows Best,* Jane Wyatt, Jane Wyman, Nancy Davis, *All About Eve,* Bette Davis, Joan Crawford, *Highway Patrol,* Broderick Crawford, Walter Mondale

> **Sophia:** The president is in town, so a bunch of us are going to his hotel to see his wife. I just loved her in *Father Knows Best.*
>
> **Rose:** Sophia, you're a little confused, honey. That was Jane Wyatt. The president was married to Jane Wyman.
>
> **Sophia:** That old crow from *Falcon Crest?*
>
> **Rose:** That doesn't matter, they're not married anymore. Now he's married to Nancy Davis.
>
> **Sophia:** From *All About Eve?*
>
> **Rose:** That's Bette Davis.
>
> **Sophia:** The one who beat her kids with wire hangers?
>
> **Rose:** No, that was Joan Crawford.
>
> **Sophia:** The fat cop from *Highway Patrol?*
>
> **Rose:** That was Broderick Crawford.
>
> **Sophia:** The president was married to Broderick Crawford? And Mondale still lost? What an idiot.

Father Knows Best is a sitcom that began as a radio show in 1949, before transitioning to television in 1954. It focused on the Andersons, a middle-class Midwestern family. The show ran for six seasons on TV and was canceled in 1960. Jane Wyatt (1910–2006) was one of the stars of the show. Jane Wyman (1917–2007) was an actress who won the Academy Award for the film *Johnny Belinda* and who was married to future president Ronald Reagan from 1940 to 1948. Nancy Davis is indeed the maiden name of Nancy Reagan.

All About Eve is a 1950 drama film starring Bette Davis (1908–1989) as aging Broadway star Margo Channing, and Anne Baxter as Eve Harrington, the adoring young fan with an ulterior motive: her own desire to be a Broadway star. The film racked up fourteen Oscar nominations and won six, including Best Picture. Regarded as one of the greatest actresses in history, Bette Davis was known for a range of roles spanning historical, contemporary, horror, suspense, comedy, and romantic dramas. Davis is one of the most Academy Award–nominated actors ever, with ten nods for Best Actress to her name. She won twice. Davis was known for, among other things, her piercing deep blue eyes, which inspired the 1981 Kim Carnes hit song "Bette Davis Eyes." With a six-decade career and a filmography of classic films, actress Joan Crawford (190?–1977) is considered one of Classic Hollywood's greatest, and most controversial, stars. Among her most notable films are *Mildred Pierce*, *Possessed*, *Sudden Fear*, and *Whatever Happened to Baby Jane?*, which paired her with longtime rival and feuding partner Davis.

Highway Patrol is a syndicated crime-drama TV series that aired from 1955 to 1959 and starred Broderick Crawford (1911–1986), an actor often cast as the tough guy and who is most remembered for his Oscar-winning turn in *All the King's Men* in 1949, in addition to *Highway Patrol*.

Walter Mondale is a former Minnesota senator who served as vice president of the United States from 1977 to 1981, during the Carter administration. He was the Democratic Party's presidential nominee in the 1984 election but lost to Ronald Reagan in a landslide.

Reference: Civil War

> **Blanche:** I never intended to keep those earrings my entire life, like my mama did, and my grandmama, and my great-grandmama, who fashioned those earrings from the Civil War bullets that killed Great-Granddaddy.

The American Civil War was fought from 1861 to 1865 when the Northern states loyal to the Union battled the Southern Confederate States, primarily as a result of the long-standing controversy surrounding the enslavement of Black people. The Confederacy advocated for states' rights to uphold slavery. Thankfully, they lost.

Reference: Arnold Schwarzenegger

> **Dorothy:** Some people come here and they stay. You're looking at one: Arnold Schwarzenegger. He became an American citizen, started a whole new career, married a Kennedy. Right now he happens to be tearing off another guy's arm and hitting him with it, but you do see my point.

Arnold Schwarzenegger is a former bodybuilder, actor, and politician who served as governor of California from 2003 to 2011. He's well-known for his roles in films like *Conan the Barbarian*, *The Terminator*, *Predator*, *Total Recall*, *Twins*, and *Kindergarten Cop*. He was married from 1986 to 2017 to journalist Maria Shriver, whose mother Eunice was the sister of President John F. Kennedy.

Repeat References: *Falcon Crest (Episode 1.15: In a Bed of Rose's)*, Nancy Reagan and Jack Daniel's *(Episode 1.4: Transplant)*, Julio Iglesias *(Episode 1.1: Pilot)*

EPISODE 2.22: DIAMOND IN THE ROUGH

Directed by Terry Hughes. Written by Jan Fischer and William Weidner. Original airdate: March 21, 1987.

Blanche begins dating a handsome caterer but hesitates to make a commitment.

References: Baked Alaska, Mars bars

> **Rose:** I did learn that Baked Alaska can actually be cooked locally.
>
> **Dorothy:** Rose, I have an even bigger scoop for you. Mars bars are made right here on Earth.

Baked Alaska is a dome-shaped dessert that, despite its geographically centered name, can indeed be made in Miami. The dish consists of ice cream (any flavor will do, but Neapolitan is common) surrounded by sponge cake, and covered in meringue. Once the sponge cake has been layered around the ice cream and covered in the meringue, the whole thing is popped into the oven and "baked" just long enough to brown. Mars bars are candy bars dating back to 1932 and made right here on Earth. An original English version consisted of caramel and nougat coated in milk chocolate, while the American version included toasted almonds. The American version was discontinued in 2002.

Reference: Popeye

Jake: Isn't this romantic?

Blanche: Oh yes, it certainly is. If you happen to be Popeye.

Popeye is a fictional muscular sailor created by Elzie Crisler Segar in the *Thimble Theatre* comic strip in 1929, who loves spinach and often battles with the brutish Bluto for the affections of Olive Oyl. Since his debut, Popeye has appeared in comics, animated cartoons, and even a live-action 1980 film starring Robin Williams as the title character.

Reference: Huey Lewis and the News

Mr. Hinkley: And now for my next number, I'd like to play something by one of my favorites, and I hope one of yours: Huey Lewis and the News!

Huey Lewis and the News is a pop-rock band that rose to fame in the 1980s with hits like "The Power of Love," "I Want a New Drug," "The Heart of Rock & Roll," and others.

Reference: "Hey, Look Me Over"

Mr. Hinkley: I hold up two lit sparklers with my hands, and I play "Hey, Look Me Over" with my feet!

"Hey, Look Me Over" is a 1960 tune written by Cy Coleman and Carolyn Leigh for the Broadway musical *Wildcat*, originally performed and sung by actress Lucille Ball in her only Broadway appearance.

Reference: Andy Granatelli

Jake: I stopped to help a lady who was stranded on the side of the road, and I ended up fixing her transmission.

Blanche: Aren't there people who do that for a living?

Rose: Andy Granatelli does. Although he doesn't actually fix them himself. I guess he doesn't want to get his trench coat dirty.

Andy Granatelli (1923–2013) was a businessman, CEO of the STP motor oil company, and prominent figure in the world of automobile racing beginning in the 1960s. He is believed to have attended every Indianapolis 500 race from 1945 until 2012. He appeared in a series of STP commercials wearing a trench coat.

Reference: Charlton Heston, J. C. Penney

Rose: Suddenly, Charlton Heston walks in dressed like Moses, and he tries to part the dessert table. When that doesn't work, he rounds up all the guests and leads them to the lingerie department at the nearest J. C. Penney's.

Charlton Heston (1923–2008) was an actor and political activist who appeared in nearly one hundred films over his six-decade career, including career-defining roles such as Moses in *The Ten Commandments* in 1956, an Oscar-winning turn in *Ben-Hur* in 1959, and *Planet of the Apes* in 1968. He served as president of the National Rifle Association for several years, announced that he'd been diagnosed with Alzheimer's disease in 2002, and received the Presidential Medal of Freedom in 2003. J. C. Penney is a department store chain founded in 1902 by James Cash Penney.

Reference: Prince

Sophia: I wasn't paying close attention but, from what I could make of it, she's going to sleep with that little Black guy, Prince.

Prince (1958–2016) was an iconic pop singer, songwriter, musician, and actor who rose to fame in the 1980s with hits like "Purple Rain," "Little Red Corvette," "Kiss," and "1999."

Reference: *Hindenburg* disaster

Dorothy: You'll have to excuse my mother. She was a witness to the *Hindenburg* disaster.

The *Hindenburg* was a German passenger airship that departed from Frankfurt, Germany, and headed toward the United States, carrying ninety-seven passengers. On May 6, 1937, as it attempted to dock at Naval Air Station Lakehurst in Manchester Township, New Jersey, the *Hindenburg* caught fire and was destroyed. Thirty-five people died. The disaster was well documented through newsreel coverage, including a famous broadcast by Chicago journalist Herbert Morrison, whose emotional reaction to the disaster included the oft-quoted phrase, "Oh, the humanity!"

Repeat Reference: Susan Anton *(Episode 1.5: The Triangle)*

EPISODE 2.23: SON-IN-LAW DEAREST
Directed by Terry Hughes. Written by Patt Shea and Harriet Weiss. Original airdate: March 28, 1987.
Dorothy's daughter Kate reveals that her husband has been having an affair. Blanche and Rose stay up all night to watch an *I Love Lucy* marathon.

References: *I Love Lucy*, Desi Arnaz

> **Blanche:** Rose, there's an *I Love Lucy* marathon on tonight. You want to stay up and watch it with me?
>
> **Rose:** That sounds great. Who's in it?
>
> **Blanche:** Who's in it? Lucille Ball and Desi Arnaz, the Ricardos, the Mertzes.

Considered a classic television sitcom, *I Love Lucy* aired on CBS from 1951 to 1957 and starred real-life husband and wife Lucille Ball and Desi Arnaz (1917–1986) as Lucy and Ricky Ricardo, a middle-class housewife and her Cuban bandleader husband, often accompanied by their friends and neighbors, Fred and Ethel Mertz. After the original run ended, a modified version continued with a series of one-hour specials from 1957 to 1960.

Reference: Buffalo nickel

> **Rose:** Charlie was a wonderful man, but he could squeeze a nickel 'til the buffalo pooped.

Buffalo nickels were five-cent coins struck by the US Mint from 1913 to 1938, featuring an American bison on one side and the profile of a Native American on the other.

Reference: Tina Turner

> **Rose:** I am a natural blonde!
>
> **Dorothy:** Right, Rose. You and Tina Turner.

Tina Turner is a singer known as "The Queen of Rock 'n' Roll," who rose to fame in the 1960s alongside then-husband Ike as part of the Ike & Tina Turner Revue, with hits like "A Fool in Love," "River Deep—Mountain High," and "Proud Mary." She then launched a highly successful solo career in the 1980s, with hits like "Private Dancer," "Let's Stay Together," and "What's Love Got to Do with It."

Reference: Ted Danson

> **Dorothy:** With that new toupee, I thought you were Ted Danson.

Actor Ted Danson rose to fame playing former baseball player turned barkeep Sam Malone on the long-running TV series *Cheers* in the 1980s, which led to film roles throughout the decade like the popular *Three Men and a Baby* and *Three Men and a Little Lady* movies. When *Cheers* ended in 1993, Danson continued to work steadily and remains a TV mainstay to this day. His filmography includes such shows as *Ink*, *Becker*, *Bored to Death*, and *The Good Place*.

References: Bertrand Russell, Nipsey Russell

> **Sophia:** A brave front is the first step back. I think Bertrand Russell said that. Or was it Nipsey Russell? I get them confused. They're both so witty.

Bertrand Russell (1872–1970) was a British philosopher, writer, and social critic who won the Nobel Prize in Literature in 1950. Nipsey Russell (1918–2005) was a comedian, dancer, and actor known for playing the Tin Man in *The Wiz* and for his many appearances on game shows from the 1960s to the 1990s, like *Match Game*, *Password*, *Hollywood Squares*, and others.

References: Gloria Steinem, Betty Friedan, Marlo Thomas

> **Dennis:** Where'd she go?
>
> **Blanche:** To meet with Gloria Steinem and Betty Friedan and Marlo Thomas. They're going to drink white wine spritzers and try to figure out how to fry your wandering male behind.

Gloria Steinem is a journalist and activist who became a well-known leader and spokesperson for the feminist movement in the 1960s and 1970s. Betty Friedan (1921–2006) was a feminist writer and activist who penned the 1963 book *The Feminist Mystique* and was cofounder and first president of the National Organization for Women. Marlo Thomas is an actress, activist, and philanthropist known for starring in the sitcom *That Girl* from 1966 to 1971 and for her recurring role as Rachel Green's mother on *Friends*. In 1973, she joined Steinem and others to found the Ms. Foundation for Women, and has worked for years with St. Jude Children's Research Hospital, founded by her father, Danny Thomas. She received the Presidential Medal of Freedom in 2014.

Reference: Cesar Romero

> **Sophia:** I was in the middle of a dream where I was held captive on a desert island by Cesar Romero in a loincloth.

Cesar Romero (1907–1994) was an actor and singer whose multi-decade career included roles in *The Thin Man*, *The Little Princess*, and the original *Ocean's 11*. He is perhaps best remembered for his role as The Joker in the 1960s live-action *Batman* series. He also guest-starred on *The Golden Girls* in the season six episode, "Girls Just Wanna Have Fun . . .Before They Die."

Repeat References: Lucille Ball *(Episode 1.11: Stan's Return)*, the Amazing Kreskin *(Episode 1.14: That Was No Lady)*, white wine spritzer *(Episode 1.24: Big Daddy)*

EPISODE 2.24: TO CATCH A NEIGHBOR

Directed by Terry Hughes. Written by Russell Marcus. Original airdate: May 2, 1987.
A pair of undercover policemen conduct a stakeout in the girls' house in hopes of catching their jewel-thief neighbors.

Reference: "Getting to Know You"

> **Rose:** Cousin Dat would play "Getting to Know You" through the hole in his windpipe.

"Getting to Know You" is a song from the 1951 musical *The King and I* by Rodgers and Hammerstein. Gertrude Lawrence performed it in the show's original Broadway production, while artists such as Bing Crosby, Della Reese, James Taylor, and Julie Andrews have recorded it over the years.

Reference: Whoopi Goldberg

> **Dorothy:** You'll have to excuse my mother. She's a little upset. She just found out she has the same hairdresser as Whoopi Goldberg.

Actress, comedian, and TV host Whoopi Goldberg is one of few entertainers to win the prestigious EGOT—an Emmy, Grammy, Oscar, and Tony. Among her most notable movies are *The Color Purple*, *Ghost*, and the *Sister Act* films. In 2007, she began a stint as cohost and moderator of the daytime talk show *The View*.

Reference: *Dick Tracy*

> **Dorothy:** I don't believe this. Hey, Dick Tracy!
> **Al:** What's your problem now?

Dick Tracy is a comic strip launched in 1931 by Chester Gould about detective Dick Tracy, who uses forensic science, gadgetry, and old-fashioned wits to catch criminals. The strip was immediately popular, with a line of merchandise soon following and, in 1990, a live-action film starring Warren Beatty in the title role.

Reference: Jeno's Pizza Rolls

> **Dorothy:** They steal jewels, not Jeno's Pizza Rolls.

Jeno's Pizza Rolls are a frozen food product invented by Jeno Paulucci in 1951, consisting of a bite-sized breaded pocket stuffed with typical pizza toppings like sauce, cheese, and pepperoni. The product was rebranded Totino's Pizza Rolls in 1993.

Reference: Oliver North

> **Sophia:** "Should I go on this mission?" is out of my area of expertise. Who do you think I am, Oliver North?

Oliver North is a retired US Marine Corps lieutenant colonel who was involved in the Iran-Contra scandal of the 1980s, in which members of the Reagan administration secretly facilitated the illegal sale of weapons to the Khomeini government of Iran and planned to use the proceeds to fund the Contras, an anti-communist rebel group whose aim was to overthrow the government of Nicaragua.

Reference: *In Cold Blood*

> **Rose:** There's a great movie on TV.
>
> **Blanche:** What is it?
>
> **Rose:** *In Cold Blood.* It's about this innocent family that's brutally murdered . . .

In Cold Blood is a 1966 true-crime novel by Truman Capote that details the 1959 murders of the Clutter family in Holcomb, Kansas. The book is considered a pioneer in narrative nonfiction, was nominated for the Nobel Prize, and was adapted into a critically acclaimed 1967 film starring Robert Blake and John Forsythe.

Reference: *Bewitched*

> **Sophia:** You're looking at a woman who lived through two World Wars, fifteen vendettas, four major operations, and two Darrins on *Bewitched*.

A sitcom that ran on ABC from 1964 to 1972, *Bewitched* was about a witch named Samantha, played by Elizabeth Montgomery, who married an ordinary man, Darrin (played first by Dick York and then eventually by Dick Sargent). Despite Samantha's best attempts at being a normal suburban housewife, her magical powers always seemed to surface when she found herself in a jam with neighbors or Darrin's boss and clients.

Reference: Danno

> **Sophia:** Let's roll, Danno!

This is a spin on the catchphrase, "Book 'em, Danno!" from the CBS police procedural series *Hawaii Five-0*, which ran from 1968 to 1980. It starred Jack Lord as detective Steve McGarrett, who would often end episodes by saying the popular line to his colleague, Danny "Danno" Williams, played by James MacArthur. A reboot of the show aired from 2010 to 2020 with Alex O'Loughlin and Scott Caan in the McGarrett and Williams roles.

Repeat References: Princess Diana *(Episode 1.10: The Heart Attack)*, Barnaby Jones *(Episode 2.3: Take Him, He's Mine)*, Tommy Lasorda *(Episode 2.4: It's a Miserable Life)*

Episode 2.25: A Piece of Cake

Directed by Terry Hughes. Written by Kathy Speer, Terry Grossman, Mort Nathan, and Barry Fanaro. Original airdate: May 9, 1987.
The girls reminisce about past birthday celebrations while preparing a surprise party for a friend.

Reference: *Gunsmoke*

> **Sophia:** The woman is eighty-eight. She still tries to find *Gunsmoke* on Sunday nights.

Gunsmoke is a long-running radio and TV Western drama series taking place in Dodge City, Kansas, during the settlement of the American West, centering around Marshal Matt Dillon. The radio series ran from 1952 to 1961 with William Conrad in the Dillon role, and on television from 1955 to 1975 with James Arness as Dillon.

Reference: Nikita Khrushchev

> **Sophia:** That's not a wart. It's a beauty mark.
>
> **Sal:** On Sophia Loren it's a beauty mark. On you and Khrushchev, it's a wart.

Nikita Khrushchev (1894–1971) was a Soviet politician who served as first secretary of the Communist Party of the Ukraine from 1947 to 1949, chairman of the Council of Ministers of the Soviet Union from 1958 to 1964, and first secretary of the Communist Party of the Soviet Union from 1953 to 1964. He was responsible for the de-Stalinization of the Soviet Union.

Reference: *Your Show of Shows*

> **Dorothy:** Ma, you're forty-eight.
>
> **Sophia:** That's what I thought until last night, during *Your Show of Shows*, when he hands me some papers he found in the hall closet. He tells me they made a mistake on my birth certificate when I came into this country, and I'm actually fifty.

Your Show of Shows was a live variety show that aired on NBC from 1950 to 1954, starring Sid Caesar and Imogene Coca.

Reference: Ralph Edwards

> **Sophia:** Enough already. Ralph Edwards makes less of a fuss over people.

Radio and TV host Ralph Edwards (1913–2005) is best remembered for hosting the shows *Truth or Consequences* and *This Is Your Life* in the 1940s and 1950s.

Reference: Krystle Carrington

> **Sophia:** What's a lanai?
> **Dorothy:** The porch!
> **Sophia:** Excuse me, Krystle Carrington.

Krystle Carrington is a fictional character from the TV show *Dynasty*, portrayed by Linda Evans, who won a Golden Globe for the role. Evans played the role through most of the show's nine-season run, from 1981 to 1989, but left early in the last season. She reprised the role in a 1991 miniseries, and a version of the character was also part of the 2017 reboot.

Reference: Frances Farmer

> **Dorothy:** Ma, there's no party. Maybe I should take you home now.
> **Sophia:** What am I, Frances Farmer? I know what I saw. There's a party out there.

Frances Farmer (1913–1970) was an actress more notorious for sensationalized accounts of her personal life than for her filmography. She dealt with mental health struggles and spent time involuntarily committed to psychiatric hospitals after being diagnosed with paranoid schizophrenia in the 1940s. Her work includes roles in films such as *Ebb Tide*, *World Premiere*, *Among the Living*, and *The Party Crashers*. Her life has been the subject of multiple films, books, and songs.

Reference: Trader Vic's

> **Sophia:** Stick an umbrella in it and serve it with straws. Everyone will think they're at Trader Vic's.

Trader Vic's is a restaurant and tiki bar chain founded in 1934 by Victor Jules Bergeron Jr.

Repeat References: Sophia Loren and the Great Depression *(Episode 2.6: Big Daddy's Little Lady)*

EPISODE 2.26: EMPTY NESTS

Directed by Jay Sandrich. Written by Susan Harris. Original airdate: May 16, 1987.

The girls' neighbor, Renee, laments her loneliness because her husband works long hours and her children have moved out. This is the original backdoor pilot for the spinoff series *Empty Nest*, which was retooled and recast before going on air a year later.

Reference: Empty nest syndrome

> **Rose:** It's the empty nest syndrome. When I had it, I didn't know what it was. I was just very depressed. By the time I figured out what it was, I was going to tell Charlie, but he died that night.

The empty nest syndrome, while not a clinical diagnosis, is a phenomenon in which parents feel sadness and loss after all of their children have moved out of the house. It is, obviously, the concept driving this backdoor pilot episode, written by Susan Harris, who was experiencing empty nest syndrome herself at the time. It is widely considered the worst episode of *The Golden Girls* by fans.

Reference: Israeli–Palestinian conflict

> **Renee:** At two in the morning, waiting for George to come home, I called a radio talk show. I gave them the solution to the crisis in the Middle East.
> **Rose:** Giving the Palestinians Greenland?
> **Renee:** You heard it?

This refers to the ongoing Israeli–Palestinian conflict in the Middle East, which dates back to the mid-twentieth century and continues today. Its main phase was between 1964 and 1993. In a nutshell, it's a conflict between the Jewish Zionist project and the Palestinian nationalist project, who lay claim to the same territory.

Reference: St. Francis of Assisi

Sophia: Don't you think St. Francis of Assisi's wife had a similar problem? Don't you think she said, "Frank, enough donkeys"?

St. Francis of Assisi (1181–1226) was an Italian Catholic friar and philosopher known as the patron saint of animals and the environment.

Reference: Vaudeville

Sophia: This is great. It's better than vaudeville!

Vaudeville is a theatrical genre of variety entertainment popular mainly in the early twentieth century, featuring various specialty acts like burlesque comedy, songs, and dancing.

Reference: Taster's Choice

Renee: I saw it on a coffee commercial. I think Taster's Choice.

Taster's Choice is a freeze-dried coffee brand introduced by Nestlé in 1966.

Reference: *A Nightmare on Elm Street 4: The Dream Master*

Renee: What are you seeing?

Blanche: *Nightmare on Elm Street 4.*

Rose: Do you have to see 1, 2, and 3 to appreciate it?

Dorothy: No, Rose. It stands alone.

A Nightmare on Elm Street 4: The Dream Master is a 1988 horror film in the *Elm Street* series, which featured Robert Englund as Freddy Krueger.

Reference: Weight Watchers

Dorothy: You were never rejected?

Blanche: Well, once, but just once.

Jenny: By who?

Blanche: Weight Watchers, for being too thin.

Weight Watchers is a weight-loss program and commercial diet based on a point system, meal replacements, and counseling, originally conceived by Jean Nidetch in the 1960s.

Reference: Perrier

> **Oliver:** You're out of Perrier, George.

Perrier is a French brand of sparkling mineral water known for its distinctive green bottle. It's named in honor of Dr. Louis Perrier, who bought the spring from which the water is sourced in 1898.

Repeat Reference: Shirley MacLaine *(Episode 1.23: Blind Ambitions)*

Season Three: 1987–1988

A PHRASE TO DESCRIBE THE THIRD SEASON MIGHT BE, "IF IT AIN'T BROKE, don't fix it." Again, the writing this season puts the girls into a series of hard-hitting storylines, like the struggles of Alzheimer's disease, and also throws in some farce, like having them raise a pig in the house or jetting off to Hollywood to appear on a game show.

The number of topical references is on par with the previous two seasons, while there are some classic exchanges peppered throughout that were specific to the era: Sophia's curse on Shelley Long, getting drunk while watching *My Sister Sam*, and Michael Jackson's travels with Bubbles the Chimp, to name a few.

Politics plays a heavy role in episodes like "Letter to Gorbachev," while Valerie Harper's firing from her own self-titled sitcom is mined for chuckles. And, ripped from the headlines of the day, we're introduced to Jim and Tammy Faye Bakker.

EPISODE 3.1: OLD FRIENDS

Directed by Terry Hughes. Written by Kathy Speer and Terry Grossman. Original airdate: September 19, 1987.

Sophia befriends an old man at the boardwalk who begins exhibiting symptoms of Alzheimer's disease. Blanche accidentally gives away Rose's cherished teddy bear to a little girl who refuses to give it back.

Reference: Dodge City

> **Sophia:** Why didn't you just buy the one that says "Marshal, Dodge City."

Dodge City is a town in Kansas famous for its history as a frontier town of the Old West, often associated with the exploits of famed gambler and lawman Wyatt Earp.

Reference: Ocean Spray

> **Sophia:** Or is it Ocean Spray? No, that's a cranberry juice.

Ocean Spray is an agricultural cooperative headquartered in Massachusetts, known for its brand of cranberry juices and fruit products.

Reference: Alvin and the Chipmunks

> **Rose:** Alvin from the boardwalk?
>
> **Sophia:** No, Rose, Alvin from the Chipmunks.

Alvin and the Chipmunks are an animated band of singing chipmunks, brothers Alvin, Simon, and Theodore. Created by singer-songwriter Ross Bagdasarian Sr. for a novelty record in 1958, they've been around in one incarnation or another ever since. Bagdasarian went by the stage name David Seville, and an animated "Dave Seville" became the Chipmunks' adoptive father and manager. With novelty hits like "Witch Doctor" and "The Chipmunk Song (Christmas Don't Be Late)," the characters were a success, and have enjoyed decades of cartoon shows, movies, and records. Younger audiences are likely most familiar with the live-action / computer-animated film series that launched in 2007 and has spawned a series of sequels.

Reference: Clams casino

> **Sophia:** Here they could dive for clams casino. What's your point?

Clams casino is a dish consisting of clams served on the half-shell with breadcrumbs and bacon.

Reference: Schwinn

> **Daisy:** In Sunshine Cadets, we learn you have to pay for your mistakes. This one's going to cost you a ten-speed Schwinn.

Schwinn is a well-known brand of bicycles founded by Ignaz Schwinn in 1895.

Repeat Reference: The Amazing Kreskin *(Episode 1.14: That Was No Lady)*

EPISODE 3.2: ONE FOR THE MONEY

Directed by Terry Hughes. Written by Kathy Speer, Terry Grossman, Barry Fanaro, Mort Nathan, and Winifred Hervey Stallworth. Original airdate: September 26, 1987.

The girls recall past attempts to earn extra money, including opening a catering business and entering a dance marathon.

Reference: Two Guys from Italy

> **Sophia:** Why do you think there are only two guys from Italy?

Two Guys from Italy is an Italian restaurant chain established in the 1970s.

Reference: Jehovah's Witnesses

> **Blanche:** Who on earth could that be at three o'clock in the morning?
>
> **Dorothy:** Maybe it's a Jehovah's Witness with a caffeine problem?

Jehovah's Witnesses are a Christian denomination dating back to the 1870s, with beliefs that differ from mainstream Christianity. They're best known for their tactic of preaching and distributing literature door-to-door.

References: *M*A*S*H*, *Hotel*, Donna Rice

> **Sophia:** I want to make sure I don't miss that final episode of *M*A*S*H* I've been hearing so much about.
>
> **Blanche:** Sophia, honey, that show hasn't been on the air in years.
>
> **Sophia:** Is *Hotel* still on?
>
> **Blanche:** Yes.
>
> **Sophia:** *Hotel* is still on but *M*A*S*H* isn't? How gullible do you think I am? Do I look like Donna Rice?

M*A*S*H was a long-running CBS sitcom that aired from 1972 to 1983 and starred Alan Alda, Loretta Swit, and others. The show followed a team of doctors and staff in a Mobile Army Surgical Hospital (hence, the acronym) during the Korean War. The show was adapted from a 1970 feature film of the same name, which was itself adapted from Richard Hooker's 1968 novel. The series was one of the highest-rated in history, with its finale watched by 125 million viewers. *Hotel* is a prime-time soap opera that aired on ABC from 1983 to 1988, based on the 1965 Arthur Hailey novel and produced by Aaron Spelling. The show centered around the goings-on at a fictional elegant San Francisco hotel and starred Anne Baxter, James Brolin, and Connie Sellecca.

Donna Rice was accused of having an affair with Senator Gary Hart in 1987 while Hart was seeking the Democratic nomination for president. The scandal contributed to the end of Hart's campaign, and Rice went on to become president of the nonprofit organization Enough Is Enough, whose stated purpose is to make the Internet safe for children.

References: Noël Coward, Canarsie

> **Sophia:** Lucky me. I'm married to the Noël Coward of Canarsie.

Sir Noël Coward (1899–1973) was an English playwright, composer, director, and actor with a distinct personal style that *Time* magazine once called a combination of cheek and chic, pose and poise. He published more than fifty plays, including *Hay Fever*, *Private Lives*, and *Blithe Spirit*, and composed hundreds of songs, screenplays, poetry, and short stories, among other works. Canarsie is a neighborhood in Brooklyn.

Reference: Swanson TV Dinners

> **Dorothy:** Ma, TV is not a fad. Otherwise, Swanson would've called those Radio Dinners.

TV Dinners were a brand of frozen dinners featuring oven-ready meals in compartmentalized aluminum trays, introduced by the Swanson company in 1953 during the boom of the television industry. They were marketed as TV dinners to encourage customers to eat them on a tray in the living room while watching television.

References: *Person to Person, Make Room for Daddy*

> **Sophia:** You can come over here and watch *Person to Person* with me, and maybe once a week the whole family can come over and watch that new show, *Make Room for Daddy*.

Person to Person is a television interview show that originally ran from 1953 to 1961, with a brief attempted revival in 2012. It was originally hosted by Edward R. Murrow. *Make Room for Daddy* was the original title of the sitcom *The Danny Thomas Show*, which ran on ABC from 1953 to 1957 and on CBS from 1957 to 1964. Thomas played a comedian and nightclub entertainer attempting to balance career and family. Thomas was the father of *The Golden Girls* producer Tony Thomas.

Reference: Errol Flynn

> **Sophia:** I look at him, I see Errol Flynn.

One of the biggest stars of the Golden Age of Hollywood, Errol Flynn (1909–1959) appeared in a string of successful films in the 1930s and 1940s, such as *The Adventures of Robin Hood*, *Captain Blood*, and *Dodge City*.

Reference: Mamie Eisenhower

> **Blanche:** These things can be a little strenuous for a woman of your years.
>
> **Dorothy:** Who am I, Mamie Eisenhower?

Mamie Eisenhower (1896–1979) was the wife of President Dwight D. Eisenhower and First Lady of the United States from 1953 to 1961.

Reference: Battle of Iwo Jima

> **Announcer:** He outran enemy fire at Iwo Jima, but phlebitis is the enemy he couldn't outrun tonight.

The Battle of Iwo Jima was a major World War II battle in which the US Marines and Navy captured the island of Iwo Jima from the Imperial Japanese Army.

Reference: Paul Newman

> **Sophia:** Just picture my face on this jar filled with my tomato sauce. We could put Paul Newman out of business.

Paul Newman (1925–2008) was an Academy Award–winning actor, director, race-car driver, and entrepreneur known for roles in *The Hustler*, *Cool Hand Luke*, *Butch Cassidy and the Sundance Kid*, *The Sting*, and other films. He won several championship auto races, was active in charity work, and launched a line of food products called Newman's Own in the early 1980s, known for salad dressing, pasta sauces, and other items. Profits from the company are donated to charity.

Repeat References: Perrier *(Episode 2.26: Empty Nests)*, *New York Times* *(Episode 1.21: The Flu)*, Judas *(Episode 2.12: The Sisters)*

Episode 3.3: Bringing Up Baby

Directed by Terry Hughes. Written by Barry Fanaro and Mort Nathan. Original airdate: October 3, 1987.
Rose's uncle dies and leaves her his baby to raise, but she soon discovers the baby is actually a pig. Meanwhile, Sophia loses her eyeglasses.

Reference: PBS

> **Dorothy:** Been watching PBS again, Rose?

The Public Broadcasting Service is a public broadcaster and television distributor of educational programming, founded in 1970.

Reference: Buick

> **Sophia:** Dorothy, who the hell parked a Buick in my bedroom?

The Buick Motor Company was first incorporated by owner David Buick in 1903 in Detroit, Michigan, and, for much of its existence, has been marketed as a line of premium automobiles. Its parent company is General Motors.

Reference: New York Yankees

> **Dorothy:** We'll all wear Yankee caps and scratch our behinds after every beer.

The Yankees are a New York–based professional baseball team established in 1901.

Reference: Buddy Holly

> **Sophia, trying on her new glasses:** These are black. I look like Buddy Holly.

Buddy Holly (1936–1959) was a bespectacled singer, songwriter, and musician considered a pioneering figure in 1950s rock and roll, known for such hits as "Peggy Sue," "That'll Be the Day," and "Not Fade Away." Holly died in a plane crash in 1959 alongside Ritchie Valens and The Big Bopper in what became known as "The Day the Music Died." He was twenty-two.

References: James Dean, Jimmy Dean

> **Rose:** In a lot of ways, he reminds me of Jimmy Dean.
> **Dorothy:** The actor or the sausage?

Let's cover both. Actor James Dean (1931–1955) became an icon of teen-age disillusionment for his roles in the classic 1950s films *Rebel Without a Cause*, *East of Eden*, and *Giant*. Jimmy Dean Foods, meanwhile, is a company founded in 1969 by country music singer Jimmy Dean (1928–2010), known for making breakfast sausage.

Reference: Johnny Carson

> **Sophia:** Twenty-five grand in ten seconds? Now I know how Johnny Carson feels.

A television icon, comedian, writer, and producer, Johnny Carson (1925–2005) is best remembered as the long-running host of *The Tonight Show*, from 1962 to 1992. After thirty years at the helm, he retired in 1992, the same year he was awarded the Presidential Medal of Freedom.

Reference: EF Hutton

> **Dorothy:** The money never even crossed my mind.
> **Sophia:** Oh yeah? Then what were you doing with these EF Hutton brochures?

At one time the second-largest stock brokerage firm in the United States, EF Hutton was founded in San Francisco in 1904 by Edward Francis Hutton and his brother, Franklyn. Various troubles and mergers and name changes ensued over the years and the company suspended operations in 2019.

Reference: Sizzlean

> **Sophia:** When I looked in on Baby this morning, he was a half-hour away from Sizzlean.

Sizzlean is a cured-meat product popular in the 1970s and 1980s that was marketed as an alternative to bacon.

Reference: Baby Doc

> **Dorothy:** How is Baby, Doc?
> **Sophia:** I read in *Newsweek* they ran him out of Haiti.

"Baby Doc" was the nickname of Haitian president Jean-Claude Duvalier (1951–2014), who served in the role from 1971—when he took over at age nineteen from his father, who died in office—until he was overthrown in 1986.

Thousands were killed or tortured, and thousands more fled Haiti during his term in office. Uprisings against him broke out in 1985, and he went into exile in France. He returned to the country twenty-five years later and was promptly arrested on corruption charges. The nickname stemmed from that of his physician father, who had been called "Papa Doc," innocently enough, by his patients, well before his own dictatorial rule as president began.

Reference: Mercedes-Benz

> **Dorothy:** Blanche, that's a Mercedes.
>
> **Blanche:** I know. Don't you just love it? It's ours!

Mercedes-Benz is a German luxury automobile manufacturer founded in 1926.

Repeat References: Spock *(Episode 2.7: Family Affair)*, Newsweek *(Episode 1.22: Job Hunting)*

EPISODE 3.4: THE HOUSEKEEPER

Directed by Terry Hughes. Written by Winifred Hervey Stallworth. Original airdate: October 17, 1987.

Strange things begin happening after the girls fire their mysterious housekeeper, leading them to believe they've been cursed.

Reference: Abe Vigoda

> **Sophia:** She's got a husband. He doesn't care that she looks like Abe Vigoda. Why should I?

Abe Vigoda (1921–2016) was an actor best known for his roles in the film *The Godfather* and the TV series *Barney Miller* and *Fish*. He also appeared in the 2010 Snickers commercial that also featured Betty White.

References: San Quentin, Johnny Cash

> **Midge:** San Quentin. Fifteen years I spent in that stinking hole. I saw violence. I saw despair. I saw Johnny Cash eight times.

San Quentin State Prison is a California prison for men that opened in 1852. A music icon, Johnny Cash (1932–2003) is considered one of the greatest performers not only in his primary genre, country, but in all of music. Beyond singing and songwriting, Cash was an actor, television host, and author whose crossover appeal landed him in the Country Music, Rock and Roll, and Gospel Music Halls of Fame. Among his most famous songs are "I Walk the Line," "Folsom Prison Blues," "Ring of Fire," and "A Boy Named Sue." He released nearly one hundred albums (studio, live, and compilations) over his decades-long career and received the Grammy Lifetime Achievement Award in 1999. He was known as the "Man in Black" for his penchant for wearing black clothing.

Reference: Pine-Sol

Dorothy: I think Marguerite has been inhaling too much Pine-Sol.

Pine-Sol is a line of cleaning products that was originally based on pine oil and was introduced by Clorox in 1929.

Reference: Sandy Duncan

Rose: Blanche is dating Norman, you're sleeping better than you have in years, and Sandy Duncan is finally back on TV!

Actress Sandy Duncan rose to fame in the 1970s for a string of stage, film, and television roles. She is perhaps best remembered for her Tony Award–nominated role in the 1979 Broadway revival of *Peter Pan*, in which she played the title role, and for taking over from Valerie Harper in the sitcom *The Hogan Family* after Harper was fired. Duncan joined the show in 1987 as the sister-in-law of Harper's character, who was killed off by producers. The series ended in 1991. Since then, Duncan has appeared in some screen roles but has worked mostly in theater.

References: Mustard gas, Fourth of July

Rose: When we were studying World War I, she told us mustard gas was something you got from eating too many hot dogs. That's why to this day in St. Olaf, everybody celebrates the Fourth of July with a thin omelet on a bun.

Mustard gas is a substance that was used in chemical warfare because of its ability to cause blisters on the skin and in the lungs. It was first used in World War I by the Germans against British and Canadian soldiers. The name derives from the fact that it can have an odor similar to mustard. The Fourth of July is a federal American holiday celebrating the Declaration of Independence.

References: *Give 'Em Hell, Harry!*, Father Mulcahy

> **Blanche:** I think Norman is finally going to invite me to the premiere of *Give 'Em Hell, Harry!* starring Mr. Father Mulcahy from *M*A*S*H*.

Give 'Em Hell, Harry! is a 1975 play and film written by Samuel Gallu about former president Harry S. Truman. Father Mulcahy is a fictional Catholic priest in the novel, movie, and television series *M*A*S*H*. The character was played by René Auberjonois in the film and William Christopher in the series.

Reference: Gene Shalit

> **Dorothy:** She's a little upset. She just found out Gene Shalit wants his hair to look that way.

Gene Shalit was the film and book critic with wild hair and an oversized handlebar mustache who reviewed works on the *Today* show from 1973 to 2010.

Reference: *The Facts of Life*

> **Blanche:** I just want you to know that Tootie is my favorite on *The Facts of Life*.

One of the longest-running sitcoms of the 1980s, *The Facts of Life* ran on NBC from 1979 to 1988 and even sparked two made-for-TV movies. It began as a spinoff of *Diff'rent Strokes*, focusing on housekeeper Edna Garrett, who became housemother to a group of girls at a posh New York private school. Her primary charges were snobby Blair (Lisa Whelchel), precocious Tootie (Kim Fields), wisecracking Natalie (Mindy Cohn), and streetwise Jo (Nancy McKeon). During its later seasons, the show was part of NBC's Saturday-night lineup along with *The Golden Girls*.

References: Velveeta, B.B. King

> **Rose:** I feel like crawling under the covers and eating Velveeta right out of the box.
>
> **Dorothy:** I hear B.B. King does that when he's tired of singing the blues.

Velveeta is a brand of processed cheese product, similar in taste to American cheese, invented in 1918. B.B. King (1925–2015) was a famous blues musician, songwriter, and record producer widely considered an R&B legend and known for playing his signature guitar, Lucille. His multi-decade career included several Grammy wins and induction into the Rock and Roll Hall of Fame.

Reference: Orange Bowl

Black Crow: This isn't the Orange Bowl, is it?

The Orange Bowl is an annual college football game played in Miami, one of the top bowl games for the NCAA Division I Football Bowl Subdivision. It was first played in 1935.

Reference: Keds

Rose: One year during the Depression, I just got a block of coal, which I carved into a pair of high-top Keds.

Keds is a brand of canvas shoes with rubber soles, founded in 1916.

Reference: Miss Black America

Sophia: What is this, the Miss Black America contest?

The Miss Black America contest is a beauty contest for young African American women dating back to 1968.

Reference: The Supremes

Sophia: So what are we celebrating? Did The Supremes get back together?

The Supremes were a singing group originally consisting of Diana Ross, Florence Ballard, Mary Wilson, and Betty McGlown, who rose to fame with Motown Records in the 1960s. Among their many hits were "Where Did Our Love Go," "Baby Love," "Come See About Me," and "Stop! In the Name of Love."

Reference: Gumby

Sophia: Hey, take it easy. I'm not Gumby!

A green humanoid character created and modeled by Art Clokey, Gumby has become a well-known example of the stop-motion clay animation style and a cultural icon, spawning TV shows, a film, and merchandise since his debut in the early 1950s.

References: Shelley Long, *Cheers*

> **Sophia:** Do you really think Shelley Long was tired of playing in *Cheers?* Wrong, baby. *I* was tired of *her.*

Cheers was one of the most successful series of the 1980s, airing on NBC for eleven seasons, from 1982 to 1993, racking up a record 117 Emmy nominations (and 28 wins), and spawning the equally long-running series *Frasier.* Set in a Boston bar, the series starred Ted Danson and Shelley Long in a classic "will they, won't they" pairing and made household names out of supporting players like Rhea Perlman, Kelsey Grammer, and George "Norm!" Wendt. Long left midway through the series to pursue film projects but arguably never reached the same heights as in the Diane role. More recently, she had a recurring role as DeDe Pritchett on the ABC series *Modern Family.*

Reference: William Conrad

> **Rose:** I haven't felt this dumb since I found out William Conrad wasn't one guy in a jacket and another guy in a pair of pants.

Actor William Conrad (1920–1994) enjoyed a five-decade career in radio, TV, and film and was even a World War II fighter pilot. He is perhaps best remembered for his roles as private detective Frank Cannon in the TV series *Cannon* from 1971 to 1976 and district attorney J. L. "Fatman" McCabe in *Jake and the Fatman* from 1987 to 1992.

Repeat References: Donna Rice *(Episode 3.2: One for the Money)*, People *(Episode 1.25: The Way We Met)*, Ovaltine *(Episode 1.4: Transplant)*, M*A*S*H *(Episode 3.2: One for the Money)*, the Great Depression *(Episode 2.6: Big Daddy's Little Lady)*, Chanel No. 5 *(Episode 2.3: Take Him, He's Mine)*

EPISODE 3.5: NOTHING TO FEAR BUT FEAR ITSELF

Directed by Terry Hughes. Written by Christopher Lloyd. Original airdate: October 24, 1987.

Dorothy and Blanche help Rose confront her fear of public speaking when she's asked to give the eulogy at her great-aunt's funeral. Sophia enters a cooking competition.

Reference: Jay Leno

> **Sophia:** Just because you have the chin doesn't mean you're Jay Leno.

Jay Leno is a prominent-chinned comedian who, after years doing stand-up, became host of NBC's *The Tonight Show* in 1992, after the retirement of Johnny Carson. Leno hosted the show until 2009.

Reference: *Jeopardy!*

> **Dorothy:** Rose, I take it that no member of your family was ever a returning champion on *Jeopardy!*

Jeopardy! is a popular quiz competition game show created by Merv Griffin in 1964. The original daytime run was hosted by Art Fleming and lasted until 1975 on NBC, with a couple other versions carrying it through 1979. A new daily syndicated version debuted in 1984 with Alex Trebek as host. With the beloved host's death in 2020 after nearly four decades of hosting, the show began its next chapter with a series of guest hosts.

Reference: Jascha Heifetz

> **Dorothy:** Ma, are you going to tell a story?
>
> **Sophia:** Please. Does Heifetz rosin a bow?

Jascha Heifetz (1901–1987) was a violin virtuoso who many believe was the greatest violinist of all time.

Reference: Joe Frazier

> **Blanche:** You were afraid of something? A big old strong, strappin' thing like you?
>
> **Dorothy:** Who am I, Joe Frazier?

"Smokin' Joe" Frazier (1944–2011) was a popular professional boxer active from 1965 to 1981. He was the heavyweight champion from 1970 to 1973, won an amateur gold medal at the 1964 Summer Olympics, and was the first boxer to beat Muhammad Ali.

Reference: Mel Gibson

> **Blanche:** You don't have to succumb to any dream, unless it involves meeting Mel Gibson at an oyster bar.

Mel Gibson is an actor and filmmaker best known for a string of action movies in the 1980s, including the successful *Mad Max* and *Lethal Weapon* series, as well as *Braveheart* and *The Passion of the Christ*.

Reference: The Four Tops

> **Rose:** Uncle Gunther just hums a lot. If he has something important to say, he spells it out in salt. Unless he's quoting a song by the Four Tops, then he spells it out in pepper.

The Four Tops is a vocal quartet from Detroit who helped define the Motown sound of the 1960s. They rose to fame with hits like "I Can't Help Myself (Sugar Pie Honey Bunch)" and "Reach Out (I'll Be There)." The group kept its original lineup—Levi Stubbs, Duke Fakir, Obie Benson, and Lawrence Payton—from 1953 until Payton's death in 1997. Additional lineup changes occurred over the years, with Fakir being the only surviving member of the original group.

Reference: Dennis Hopper

> **Dorothy:** Right now she is doubled over with cramps, crying out with pain, and making the most spectacular comeback since Dennis Hopper.

Dennis Hopper (1936–2010) was a prominent actor and filmmaker whose decades-long career included appearances in such films as *Rebel Without a Cause* (1955), *Apocalypse Now* (1979), and *Speed* (1994); writing and directing films like *Easy Rider* (1969); and successful forays into photography, painting, and sculpting. Despite steadily appearing on film, by the early 1980s Hopper's drug use and erratic behavior caused his career to suffer, and he entered rehab in 1983. In late 1986, he returned with a critically acclaimed, award-winning role in *Blue Velvet*, followed quickly by an Oscar-nominated turn in *Hoosiers*, essentially reviving his career.

Reference: *My Sister Sam*

> **Sophia:** I always drink wine during cooking contests and *My Sister Sam*.

My Sister Sam is a sitcom that aired on CBS from 1986 to 1988, starring Pam Dawber as freelance photographer Sam Russell, and Rebecca Schaeffer as her teenage sister, Patti. The show centered around the sisters' relationship, with Sam serving as Patti's guardian following the death of their parents. The show was canceled in 1988 and, a year later, Schaeffer was shot and killed by an obsessed fan at her Los Angeles apartment. The show's surviving cast members reunited to film a public service announcement for the Center to Prevent Handgun Violence in Schaeffer's honor, and Dawber has remained a staunch advocate for gun control.

Reference: The Copacabana

Stewardess: Take a seat, lady. This isn't the Copacabana.

The Copacabana is an iconic New York City nightclub that has existed in several locations since it opened in 1940. A popular setting for several classic films, the club hosted a variety of well-known entertainers over the years, including Danny Thomas, Dean Martin, and Jerry Lewis. It's also immortalized in the popular Barry Manilow song that bears its name. The Copacabana closed its doors in 2020, during the COVID-19 pandemic, with plans to reopen in yet another location once the pandemic ended.

Reference: Mr. Clean

Rose: They were all former Mr. Cleans on their way to a reunion in the Bahamas.

Mr. Clean is a brand of all-purpose cleaner made by Procter & Gamble, its accompanying mascot depicted as a tan, muscular, bald man.

Reference: Al Capone

Dorothy: Isn't she the one who brags about being Al Capone's piano teacher?

Also known as Scarface, Al Capone (1899–1947) was a notorious gangster who gained notoriety during Prohibition as boss of the Chicago Mafia. At one point dubbed Public Enemy No. 1, Capone was prosecuted by federal authorities in 1931 for tax evasion and sentenced to eleven years in prison. His health began to deteriorate while incarcerated, and he was released in 1939 after serving nearly eight years. In 1986, Geraldo Rivera hosted a live TV special centered on opening a secret vault in Chicago's Lexington Hotel that had been owned by Capone. Thirty million viewers watched as the vault was opened to reveal nothing but debris.

EPISODE 3.6: LETTER TO GORBACHEV

Directed by Terry Hughes. Written by Barry Fanaro and Mort Nathan. Original airdate: October 31, 1987.

Rose's letter to Mikhail Gorbachev about nuclear disarmament draws international attention. Sophia attempts to perfect a talent show act.

References: Bubbles the Chimp, Michael Jackson

> **Dorothy:** Just yesterday, her biggest concern was whether Bubbles the Chimp was traveling with Michael Jackson against his will.

The self-proclaimed "King of Pop," Michael Jackson (1958–2009) rose to fame as a member of the Jackson 5 alongside his brothers in the 1960s. But it was his solo career in the 1980s that catapulted him to international superstardom and made him one of the most significant entertainers in music history, with hits like "Thriller," "Beat It," "Billie Jean," "Bad," and others. In addition to his notable musical contributions, however, Jackson was also embroiled in consistent controversy throughout his adult life, with his odd behavior, a changing appearance, marriage to Lisa Marie Presley, and accusations of child sexual abuse. He died of cardiac arrest in 2009 of an overdose of propofol in what ended up being ruled a homicide. His personal physician, Conrad Murray, was convicted of involuntary manslaughter and served two years in prison. Bubbles the Chimp was a chimpanzee kept as a pet by Jackson during the 1980s. Bubbles frequently traveled with him while on tour, when not sleeping in a crib in Jackson's bedroom at his famed Neverland Ranch. Bubbles eventually outgrew the crib—and his life as a domesticated pet—and was moved to a Florida animal sanctuary in 2005.

Reference: Cleopatra

> **Rose:** What does this picture look like to you?
>
> **Blanche:** Me sitting on a throne dressed as Cleopatra, watching while two naked men wrestle to see who gets to make love to me.

Cleopatra (69–30 BC) served as queen of the Ptolemaic Kingdom of Egypt from 51 BC to 30 BC. Her legacy lives on through countless works of art, literature, sculpture, song, and screen, including the 1963 film *Cleopatra*, in which Elizabeth Taylor played the titular role.

Reference: Valerie Harper

> **Sophia:** One minute you're about to entertain the masses. The next, you're back on a foot covering a corn pad. Now you know how Valerie Harper feels.

Actress Valerie Harper (1939–2019) began her long career on Broadway in the 1950s but rose to fame in the Emmy Award–winning role of Rhoda Morgenstern on *The Mary Tyler Moore Show* in 1970, a character she successfully spun off into her own series, *Rhoda*, in 1974. She returned to series television in 1986 as the lead in *Valerie*. A salary dispute led to her firing in 1987, and the show continued by killing off Harper's character and bringing in Sandy Duncan to helm what was rebranded as *Valerie's Family*, then *The Hogan Family*. Harper sued the production company and received $1.4 million and a portion of the show's profits. She continued to work steadily afterwards and battled cancer in her later years.

Reference: Ronald Reagan, Mikhail Gorbachev

> **Blanche:** How are you going to fix this nuclear war thing? By writing a letter to President Reagan?
>
> **Rose:** Well, now that would be pretty stupid, wouldn't it, Blanche? Reagan's only responsible for half the problem. I'd have to write to Gorbachev, too.

Ronald Reagan (1911–2004) was a former actor and conservative Republican who served as president of the United States from 1981 to 1989. Mikhail Gorbachev is a Russian politician who served as general secretary of the Communist Party of the Soviet Union during most of the run of *The Golden Girls*. He also served as president of the Soviet Union from 1990 to 1991, until he resigned and the Soviet Union dissolved. Physically, Gorbachev has long been characterized by the prominent port-wine stain birthmark on his forehead.

Reference: MTV

> **Nancy:** This is boring. I want to watch MTV!

MTV is a cable network launched in 1981 that originally aired a twenty-four-hour cycle of music videos, forever changing the face of music. Over the decades, the network increasingly lessened its focus on music and has become better known as a vehicle for youth-targeted reality shows.

Reference: Imogene Coca

> **Blanche:** I am still in my child-bearing years.
>
> **Dorothy:** Sure, Blanche. You and Imogene Coca.

Rubber-faced actress Imogene Coca (1908–2001) got her start in vaudeville as a child acrobat and worked toward a serious career in music and dance. She gained fame in her forties as a celebrated comedian with a string of successful series and TV gigs, most notably on *Your Show of Shows* alongside Sid Caesar. She received multiple Emmy nominations, including one at the age of eighty for a guest spot on *Moonlighting* in 1988. She won the Emmy for Best Actress in 1951. Her body of work expanded beyond television with successful stage and screen work, including a memorable role in 1983's *National Lampoon's Vacation*.

Reference: *Poltergeist*

> **Blanche:** They're back!
>
> **Dorothy:** Now I know how the family in *Poltergeist* felt.

Poltergeist is a 1982 horror film written by Steven Spielberg and starring JoBeth Williams and Craig T. Nelson as the parents of a family whose home is invaded by ghosts who abduct their young daughter, Carol Anne. After her first encounter with the evil spirits, Carol Anne announces, "They're here," which became a sort of catchphrase for the film. A 1986 sequel's tagline was "They're back," which has become even more commonly associated with the films. A third film in the franchise came out in 1988.

References: The lost city of Atlantis, Bobby Vinton

> **Dorothy:** Why would he want to meet the same woman who once said, "If the city of Atlantis is lost, how can Bobby Vinton appear there twice a year?"

The so-called lost city of Atlantis is a fictional island dating back to the works of Plato in 360 BC, who created it as an antagonistic empire to ancient Athens. At the end of Plato's tale, Atlantis falls out of favor with the gods and sinks into the Atlantic Ocean, never to be seen again. Well, sort of. The concept of a lost city of Atlantis, which came to be viewed as a utopia full of ancient wisdom, has persisted in pop culture. It's been the subject of literature, film, music, art—and in comics, as the place where Aquaman lives. Bobby Vinton, meanwhile, performed in Atlantic City. The singer was considered a teen idol in his early days and is known for hits like "Blue Velvet," "There! I've Said It Again," and "Mr. Lonely."

Reference: Ke-mo sah-bee

Dorothy: Ke-mo sah-bee, I think the world is in heap big trouble.

Ke-mo sah-bee is a term of endearment said by the character Tonto in the TV and radio program *The Lone Ranger*.

Reference: Edwin Newman

Edwin Newman: Good evening, I'm Edwin Newman. The eyes of the entire world were on Moscow today as Rose Nylund continued her mission of peace.

Edwin Newman (1919–2010) was a newscaster and journalist known for his two-decade career with NBC News.

Reference: *Doctor Zhivago*

Rose: I want you to know *Doctor Zhivago* is my favorite movie of all time!

Doctor Zhivago is an epic 1965 film based on the 1957 Boris Pasternak novel of the same name. It takes place in Russia and stars Omar Sharif as Yuri Zhivago, a doctor whose life is upturned by the Russian Revolution and the Russian Civil War of the 1910s and 1920s. Released to mixed reviews, some of whom balked at its three-plus-hour length, the film is now considered a classic of cinema.

Reference: Communism

Blanche, singing "Happy Birthday" to Gorbachev: Happy birthday, Mr. Number One Communist . . .

Communism is a political and economic system intent on creating a classless society, in which the means of production are owned and controlled by the public instead of by individuals. So all property is public, and people work and are given things by the government based on their needs. Communist ideology was developed by Karl Marx, positioned as the opposite of a capitalist ideology. A prominent example of a communist society was the Soviet Union, which collapsed in 1991.

References: Medicare, Blue Cross Blue Shield, "Thanks for the Memory"

> **Sophia, singing to the tune of "Thanks for the Memory":** Thanks for the Medicare. For Blue Cross and Blue Shield. For a hip that finally healed . . .

Medicare is a national health insurance program founded in 1966 under the Social Security Administration, providing insurance for those ages sixty-five and older. Blue Cross Blue Shield is a company providing health insurance to more than one hundred million Americans. It was formed in 1982 by the merger of, you guessed it, Blue Cross and Blue Shield, companies that had existed individually since the 1920s and 1930s, respectively. "Thanks for the Memory" is an Academy Award–winning song written by Ralph Rainger and Leo Robin for the Bob Hope film *The Big Broadcast of 1938*.

Reference: Levi's

> **Dorothy:** Was there anything we can get you? Coffee, tea, pair of Levi's?

Levi's is a brand of American-made denim jeans and other clothing founded in 1853 by German immigrant Levi Strauss.

Reference: *Rocky IV*

> **Dorothy:** *Rocky IV* had a profound effect on you, didn't it, Blanche?

Rocky IV is the fourth film in the *Rocky* franchise, in which Rocky goes up against a Soviet boxer to avenge his friend Apollo Creed's death.

Reference: Jerry Falwell

> **Rose:** Can you believe it, Dorothy?
>
> **Dorothy:** No, but then again, I can't believe that God wanted Jerry Falwell to go down that waterslide in a cheap suit.

Jerry Falwell (1933–2007) was a conservative Southern Baptist pastor and televangelist who founded what is now the Liberty Christian Academy and Liberty University, both in Lynchburg, Virginia; the Thomas Road Baptist Church, also in Lynchburg; and cofounded the Moral Majority, a conservative, right-wing political organization. In 1987, he promised to ride down a fifty-three-foot "Killer Typhoon" waterslide if his followers met a fund-raising goal for his ministry, which they did.

Repeat References: *The Cosby Show (Episode 1.23: Blind Ambitions)*, Coca-Cola *(Episode 1.3: Rose the Prude)*

EPISODE 3.7: STRANGE BEDFELLOWS

Directed by Terry Hughes. Written by Christopher Lloyd. Original airdate: November 7, 1987.

The girls campaign for city councilman Gil Kessler, who claims to be having an affair with Blanche in order to bolster his image.

Reference: *ALF*

> **Dorothy:** Ma, you promised you'd stay in your room until the meeting was over.
>
> **Sophia:** Who am I, ALF?

ALF was a sitcom that ran on NBC from 1986 to 1990, about an Alien Life Form (hence, the acronym) who crash-landed from planet Melmac into the garage of the suburban Tanner family, led by curmudgeonly Willie Tanner, played by Max Wright. Episodes centered around ALF's attempts to adjust to life on Earth and the family's attempts to keep him hidden from friends and neighbors, and from eating their cat. And, well, that's about it. The character became hugely popular, spawning a line of merchandise and a Saturday-morning cartoon show.

References: Thomas Dewey, Melvil Dewey, the Dewey Decimal System

> **Rose:** I haven't had this much fun since I worked on the Dewey campaign.
>
> **Dorothy:** Rose, you worked for Thomas Dewey?
>
> **Rose:** No, Melvil Dewey, the founder of the Dewey Decimal System.

Lawyer and politician Thomas Dewey (1902–1971) served as governor of New York from 1943 to 1954 and attempted runs for president of the United States a couple of times as the Republican nominee but never succeeded. His loss to Harry S. Truman in the 1948 election was one of the greatest upsets in election history. A pioneering librarian and educator, Melvil Dewey

(1851–1931) invented the Dewey Decimal System of library classification in 1876, a system still widely used today, and was a founder and former president of the American Library Association (ALA), who later named its top honor after him: the Melvil Dewey Medal. His landmark work, however, hasn't overshadowed controversy. Dewey has a cited history of racism, anti-Semitism, and sexual harassment, which eventually led the ALA to rename that honor the ALA Medal of Excellence in 2020.

Reference: Agatha Christie

> **Dorothy:** It's like having Agatha Christie right here in our kitchen.

Sometimes called the "Queen of Crime," English writer Agatha Christie (1890–1976) is the best-selling novelist of all time, authoring more than sixty detective novels and fourteen short-story collections. Christie's books, including classics like *Murder on the Orient Express* and *And Then There Were None*, have sold over two billion copies. Her books and characters, including Inspector Hercule Poirot and Miss Marple, have been adapted to film and television countless times.

References: Desenex, Benito Mussolini

> **Sophia:** It's the peak of the wine season and all our grape stompers are ravaged by an outbreak of athlete's foot. Soon the chianti has a green hue and tastes like Desenex. They call in Sicily's foremost podiatrist, Bruno Bonfiglio. He's the one who prescribed arch supports for Mussolini.

Desenex is a topical medication used to treat fungal infections like ringworm, athlete's foot, and jock itch. Benito Mussolini (1883–1945) was an Italian dictator who founded the National Fascist Party and served as prime minister of Italy from 1922 to 1943. He was executed in 1945.

Reference: *Eight Is Enough*

> **Rose:** It took me two years to learn everybody's name on *Eight Is Enough*.

Eight Is Enough is a sitcom that ran on ABC from 1977 to 1981, based on the book of the same name by newspaper columnist Tom Braden, the real-life father of eight children. The show starred Dick Van Patten as Tom Bradford, a columnist for the fictional *Sacramento Register*.

Reference: *60 Minutes*

Blanche: People lie on television, Dorothy. They do it on *60 Minutes* all the time.

The CBS weekly newsmagazine *60 Minutes* debuted in 1968.

References: Jim Bakker, Tammy Faye Bakker, *Nightline*

Blanche: Now, did that sound like a liar?

Dorothy: No, it sounded like Jim and Tammy Faye on *Nightline!*

Jim Bakker is a televangelist, entrepreneur, and convicted felon. Bakker rose to fame alongside then-wife Tammy Faye (1942–2007) as hosts of *The PTL Club*, a Christian talk show of sorts, which ran from 1974 to 1987. The show welcomed everyone from religious leaders to the stars of the day, like Mr. T. The Bakkers lived a lavish lifestyle eventually undone by scandal. Bakker resigned over an alleged hush-money cover-up involving Jessica Hahn, the church secretary who accused him of rape. Then accounting fraud charges led to conviction and divorce from Tammy Faye. He was sentenced in 1989 to forty-five years in prison, which was reduced in 1992 to eight years. In 1994, he was paroled, eventually remarried, and returned to evangelism.

Tammy Faye, meanwhile, became as well known for her campy persona as for her evangelical work, what with her lavish style, eccentric personality, and penchant for heavy—very heavy—makeup, which she applied, according to Sophia, with a butter knife. She also drew the ire of many conservatives with her liberal views on homosexuality and her support for AIDS patients. She even embraced the label of gay icon and appeared at Pride events in the 1990s. Despite standing by her husband during the downfall of their empire and his subsequent fraud conviction, she eventually filed for divorce in 1992 and got remarried to property developer Roe Messner the following year. Messner, who'd known and been involved with the Bakkers for years, was himself convicted of bankruptcy fraud charges in 1996 and served twenty-seven months. Tammy Faye indeed stood by her man that time. Meanwhile, she continued with a series of books and TV appearances; briefly hosted a talk show with actor Jim J. Bullock; and appeared on a season of the VH1 series *The Surreal Life*, alongside porn star Ron Jeremy and rapper Vanilla Ice. After an eleven-year battle with cancer, she died in 2007.

Nightline is a half-hour news program on ABC that debuted in 1980.

Reference: Roger Ebert

Dorothy: Horizontal stripes make you look like Roger Ebert.

Roger Ebert (1942–2013) was film critic for the *Chicago Sun-Times* from 1967 until his death in 2013 and, in 1975, was the first critic to win the Pulitzer Prize for Criticism. He gained additional popularity in the 1970s when he began cohosting a film-reviewing TV program—first for PBS, followed by various syndicated versions—alongside *Chicago Tribune* critic Gene Siskel. The pair became known for the gimmick of giving either a thumbs-up or thumbs-down to whatever movie they were reviewing. When Siskel died in 1999, Ebert continued the show with Richard Roeper. A cancer diagnosis in 2002 eventually led to the removal of his lower jaw, leaving him disfigured and unable to speak normally. He continued to write reviews, however, until his death.

Reference: Silly Putty

Rose: What are they made of?
Dorothy: Silly Putty, Rose!

Silly Putty is a silicone plastic clay toy for children.

Reference: *The Facts of Life Goes to Australia*

Dorothy: It's been a terrible night and I'm very upset.
Rose: You mean because Gil dropped out of the election and Blanche hates us?
Dorothy: No, Rose. I'm upset because they haven't re-run *The Facts of Life Goes to Australia*.

Actually titled *The Facts of Life Down Under*, this 1986 made-for-TV movie transplanted the characters from *The Facts of Life* from New York to Australia at the height of the *Crocodile Dundee* craze of the mid-1980s. Despite the fact that they were well out of high school at the time, somehow the show's four principal girls (along with new cast member Cloris Leachman, who had replaced former lead Charlotte Rae) were picked to represent their alma mater, Eastland Academy, at a sister school in Australia. So off they went, and hijinks ensued.

Repeat References: The Pope *(Episode 2.18: Forgive Me, Father)*, Attica *(Episode 2.2: Ladies of the Evening)*, Dr. Scholl *(Episode 1.2: Guess Who's Coming to the Wedding?)*, People *(Episode 1.25: The Way We Met)*

Episode 3.8: Brotherly Love
Directed by Terry Hughes. Written by Jeffrey Ferro and Fredric Weiss. Original airdate: November 14, 1987.
Dorothy begins dating Stan's visiting brother, Ted. Rose battles insomnia.

Reference: Johnny Bench

> **Sophia:** This from a woman who wears more padding on her chest than Johnny Bench.

Johnny Bench is former professional baseball player who played as catcher for the Cincinnati Reds from 1967 to 1983. He was inducted into the Baseball Hall of Fame in 1989 and has been called the greatest catcher in baseball history. After retiring from the field, Bench went on to a career in sports broadcasting, did some acting work, and appeared in commercials for Krylon paint.

Reference: *Vanity Fair*

> **Stan:** Blanche, Rose, this is my little brother Ted.
>
> **Blanche:** Charmed, I'm sure. Oh, there's my new *Vanity Fair*.

Vanity Fair is a monthly magazine about popular culture and fashion, first published in 1913.

Reference: Gary Hart

> **Dorothy:** She's Gary Hart's campaign manager. It doesn't pay much, but you don't have to get out of bed to do it.

Gary Hart is a diplomat, lawyer, and politician who represented the state of Colorado in the US Senate from 1975 to 1987. Born in Kansas in 1936, Hart graduated from Yale Law School and pursued a legal career in Denver before entering the political arena as Senator George McGovern's campaign manager for his 1972 run for president. In 1986, Hart announced his intention to seek the Democratic presidential nomination in the 1988 election. He was widely viewed as the clear front-runner until rumors began circulating that labeled him a womanizer, and reports surfaced of an extramarital affair with model, actress, and pharmaceutical sales representative Donna Rice. The alleged scandal hit the tabloids and quickly gained momentum, resulting in Hart withdrawing from the race. He went on to continue work in politics, has authored several books, and in 2014 was named the US special envoy for Northern Ireland. The 1987 scandal, however, has continued to follow him. It was the subject of the 2014 book *All the Truth Is Out: The Week Politics Went Tabloid* by Matt Bai, which became the basis for the 2018 film *The Front Runner*, starring Hugh Jackman.

References: Janet Jackson, La Toya Jackson, Tito Jackson, Stonewall Jackson, the Victory Tour

> **Rose:** I started counting the members of the Jackson family: Michael, Janet, La Toya, Tito. Then there's Stonewall Jackson, but I don't remember him on the Victory Tour.

Pop icon Janet Jackson began her career in the 1970s with acting roles on shows like *Good Times*, *Diff'rent Strokes*, and *Fame* before launching a highly successful recording career in the 1980s. Among her many hits are "Nasty," "What Have You Done for Me Lately," "Miss You Much," "Rhythm Nation," "That's the Way Love Goes," and many others. She also continued acting over the decades, with roles in such films as *Poetic Justice* and *The Nutty Professor II: The Klumps*. She continues to tour and record. Singer La Toya Jackson is known less for her music and more for such activities as posing nude for *Playboy*, being a spokesperson for the Psychic Friends Network, and other publicity stunts. More recently, she's dabbled in reality television, including a 2019 run on *The Masked Singer*. Tito Jackson is an original member of the Jackson 5. Stonewall Jackson (1824–1863) was a Confederate general during the American Civil War. The Victory Tour was a concert tour featuring all six of the famous Jackson brothers—Michael, Randy, Jermaine, Tito, Marlon, and Jackie—which took place between July and December 1984.

Reference: Sominex

> **Sophia:** We call this Sicilian Sominex.

Sominex is an over-the-counter nighttime sleep aid.

References: Roseland Ballroom, the jitterbug

> **Dorothy:** We went to Roseland, and you and I did the jitterbug.

The Roseland Ballroom was a multipurpose hall in New York's theater district built in 1922 and closed in 2014. The jitterbug is a type of swing dance popularized during World War II.

Reference: Coney Island

> **Dorothy:** The last time I went to Coney Island, I got pregnant.

Coney Island is a residential and commercial neighborhood in Brooklyn, New York, known as an entertainment destination where tourists and locals crowd its boardwalk, beach, and amusement park rides, such as the famed Cyclone roller coaster.

Reference: The Allied invasion

> **Sophia:** One swig and he slept through the Allied Invasion.

The Allied invasion was when 156,000 Allied forces invaded the beaches of Normandy during World War II. See "D-Day."

Repeat References: A&P *(Episode 2.6: Big Daddy's Little Lady)*, Oreos *(Episode 1.16: The Truth Will Out)*, Michael Jackson *(Episode 3.6: Letter to Gorbachev)*, Johnny Carson *(Episode 3.3: Bringing Up Baby)*, The Godfather *(Episode 2.4: It's a Miserable Life)*, Hamlet *(Episode 1.5: The Triangle)*

EPISODE 3.9: A VISIT FROM LITTLE SVEN
Directed by Terry Hughes. Written by David Nichols. Original airdate: November 21, 1987.
Blanche's visiting cousin, Sven, becomes smitten with Blanche and decides to call off his pending nuptials.

References: *Jaws, Jaws 2, Psycho II*

> **Blanche:** Doesn't that get confusing, having two Big Svens?
>
> **Rose:** There aren't, Blanche. There's Big Sven and Big Sven 2, like *Jaws* and *Jaws 2*.
>
> **Dorothy:** Rose, are any of your relatives named *Psycho* and *Psycho II*?

Jaws is a 1975 Steven Spielberg film starring Richard Dreyfuss, based on the Peter Benchley novel of the same name, about a man-eating shark attacking beachgoers at a resort town. *Jaws 2* is the 1978 sequel to *Jaws*, which pretty much follows the same formula, only without Spielberg and Dreyfuss. *Psycho*

II is the 1983 horror film sequel to 1960's *Psycho*, in which Norman Bates is released from a mental institution and attempts to return to normal life at the Bates Motel.

Reference: Howie Mandel

> **Dorothy:** It's like living in a house full of Howie Mandels.

Howie Mandel is a comedian, host, and actor who rose to fame in the late 1970s as a stand-up comedian and actor. He starred in the series *St. Elsewhere* in the 1980s; created, voiced, and starred in the children's cartoon *Bobby's World* in the 1990s; and is known more recently as host of NBC's *America's Got Talent*.

Reference: Mr. Whipple

> **Dorothy:** Did you get a picture of him with that Mr. Whipple cutout at the A&P?

Mr. Whipple is a fictional supermarket manager portrayed by actor Dick Wilson in a series of radio, print, and television ads for Charmin toilet paper from 1964 to 1985. He's best remembered for warning customers not to squeeze the Charmin.

Reference: The Cape of Good Hope

> **Sven:** I've never sailed around the Cape of Good Hope this time of year.

The Cape of Good Hope is a rocky headland on the Atlantic coast of South Africa. It's often mistaken for being the southernmost tip of Africa, but that's actually Cape Agulhas.

Reference: "Sweet Georgia Brown"

> **Dorothy:** To this day, he can belch out the chorus to "Sweet Georgia Brown" on one Dr. Pepper.

"Sweet Georgia Brown" is a jazz standard written by Ben Bernie, Maceo Pinkard, and Kenneth Casey, which has been recorded by such artists as Cab Calloway, Bing Crosby, Nancy Sinatra, Jerry Lee Lewis, and many others.

Repeat References: Burt Reynolds *(Episode 1.5: The Triangle)*, Magic Johnson *(Episode 2.13: The Stan Who Came to Dinner)*, Mercedes-Benz *(Episode*

3.3: Bringing Up Baby), A&P *(Episode 2.6: Big Daddy's Little Lady)*, Psycho *(Episode 1.25: The Way We Met)*, Deliverance *(Episode 2.2: Ladies of the Evening)*, the Pope *(Episode 2.18: Forgive Me, Father)*, Dr. Pepper *(Episode 1.23: Blind Ambitions)*

EPISODE 3.10: THE AUDIT
Directed by Terry Hughes. Written by Winifred Hervey Stallworth. Original airdate: November 28, 1987.
Dorothy and Stan prepare for an audit from the IRS. Rose and Blanche take a Spanish class.

Reference: *Amos 'n' Andy*

> **Rose:** Guess what I'll be doing for three hours every Tuesday and Thursday night?
>
> **Dorothy:** Cutting up your black pantyhose and putting on an *Amos 'n' Andy* puppet show?

Amos 'n' Andy is a comedy series that began as a radio show, running from 1928 to 1960, about two Black characters voiced by Freeman Gosden and Charles Correll, both white. It was reworked with Black actors as a television sitcom from 1951 to 1953. The radio show became hugely popular among listeners while also drawing protests from the likes of the NAACP and the African Methodist Episcopal Zion Church for its racist stereotyping.

Reference: Ziploc

> **Rose:** Being bilingual really gets me confused.
>
> **Sophia:** Ziploc bags get you confused.

Ziploc is a brand of plastic zipper storage bags introduced in 1968.

Reference: *Fortune*

> **Stan:** So I didn't make the cover of *Fortune*.

Fortune is multinational business magazine founded by Henry Luce in 1929.

Reference: Palookaville

> **Stan:** All of our friends were moving up, and we were stuck with a one-way ticket to Palookaville.

Palookaville is a fictional town said to be the home of the generally incompetent.

Reference: *On the Waterfront*

Dorothy: Stanley, did you just rent *On the Waterfront*?

On the Waterfront is a 1954 crime drama starring Marlon Brando about union violence and corruption among longshoremen on the New Jersey waterfront.

Reference: The Rainbow Coalition

Stan: Did I mention the fact that I'm a member of the Rainbow Coalition?

The Rainbow Coalition is an organization founded by Jesse Jackson in 1984 that sought equal rights for African Americans, women, and homosexuals.

Reference: The Elephant Man

Blanche: Still worried about the money you owe the government?

Dorothy: No, Blanche. I'm worried about whether Michael Jackson will be able to buy the remains of the Elephant Man.

Joseph Carey Merrick (1862–1890) was an English man known for severe deformities that led to him being exhibited at a freak show as the "Elephant Man." He later met prominent British surgeon Frederick Treves and lived out his days at the Royal London Hospital. His health deteriorated and he died in 1890 at the age of twenty-seven. Various plays and films have been inspired by Merrick's life. In 1987, singer Michael Jackson, apparently profoundly affected by Merrick's story, allegedly attempted and failed to buy Merrick's skeleton, which was preserved at the Royal London Hospital, for $1 million.

Reference: *Ishtar*

Sophia: Don't go see *Ishtar*. Woof.

Ishtar is a 1987 adventure-comedy film starring Warren Beatty and Dustin Hoffman as a pair of songwriters who become embroiled in a Cold War standoff in Morocco. It was a critical and commercial disaster and is considered one of the worst films ever made.

Reference: Ellis Island

> **Blanche:** Maybe they stopped off at the Ellis Island gift shop.

Ellis Island is an island in New York Harbor owned by the federal government and at one time the country's busiest immigration inspection station. From the late nineteenth century through the mid-twentieth century, more than ten million immigrants arrived at the port. Today it is part of the Statue of Liberty National Monument.

Reference: Karl Malden

> **Dorothy:** I think I'm going to cry.
>
> **Blanche:** Don't do that. Your eyes will get all beady and your nose will swell up like Karl Malden's.

Karl Malden (1912–2009) was an Oscar-winning actor known for such films as *A Streetcar Named Desire*, *On the Waterfront*, *Pollyanna*, *How the West Was Won*, *Gypsy*, and *Patton*.

Reference: Toyota

> **Stan:** I guess I finally became what I always feared most—another middle-aged bald guy who drives a Toyota.

Toyota is a Japanese automobile manufacturer founded in 1937.

Repeat References: Julio Iglesias *(Episode 1.1: Pilot)*, Corvette *(Episode 2.7: Family Affair)*, Jazzercise *(Episode 1.3: Rose the Prude)*, Uncle Sam *(Episode 2.10: Love, Rose)*, Michael Jackson *(Episode 3.6: Letter to Gorbachev)*, Harry Belafonte *(Episode 1.2: Guess Who's Coming to the Wedding?)*

EPISODE 3.11: THREE ON A COUCH

Directed by Terry Hughes. Written by Jeffrey Ferro and Fredric Weiss. Original airdate: December 5, 1987.

The girls seek professional counseling to deal with their constant bickering.

Reference: *Designing Women*

> **Sophia:** You know what I can't stand anymore? That phony accent of yours. What is this, *Designing Women*?

A CBS sitcom that ran from 1986 to 1993, *Designing Women* focused on a group of Southern women who ran an interior decorating firm in Atlanta, Georgia. The series starred Delta Burke, Dixie Carter, Annie Potts, Jean Smart, Meshach Taylor, and Alice Ghostley in a recurring role, and tackled a variety of topical issues. Episodes often climaxed with a lengthy liberal diatribe by Carter's Julia Sugarbaker. Burke's issues with weight gain and erratic behavior on set made her tabloid fodder, and a public feud with producers led to her departure in 1991, along with Smart's. Actresses Julia Duffy, Jan Hooks, and Judith Ivey filled in over the ensuing years.

Reference: Buckwheat

> **Blanche:** Dorothy, you've looked much worse than this. Remember that time you gave yourself a home perm, burnt your hair right down to the roots, and ended up looking like Buckwheat?

Buckwheat is a fictional character from the *Our Gang* / *Little Rascals* short films of the 1930s and 1940s, portrayed by Billie Thomas Jr. While some praised the character—and other minorities from the series—for being a film representation of African Americans during the era, the character eventually became associated with negative stereotypes.

References: Chevron, Chrysler LeBaron, Pappagallo

> **Blanche:** I have been waiting for Larry to ask me out ever since our eyes first met at Del's Route One Chevron and I climbed up on the hood of his LeBaron and wrote my phone number on his windshield with the heel of my Pappagallo pump.

Chevron is a multinational energy corporation founded in 1879. While it's engaged in every aspect of the oil and natural gas industries, it is with the company's many gas stations that most of us are familiar. Originally a classic luxury car in the 1930s, the Chrysler LeBaron had many incarnations throughout its six-decade existence. Pappagallo was a line of women's shoes popular in the mid- to late twentieth century.

Reference: Toto the dog

> **Carl:** Just Toto. You're Dorothy and I'm Toto, at least for the next eight dollars.

Toto is the fictional terrier companion to Dorothy Gale in L. Frank Baum's 1900 novel *The Wonderful Wizard of Oz*, as well as its various sequels and many screen and stage adaptations.

References: Wesson, Florence Henderson

> **Dorothy:** It's right under an ad that reads, "History professor seeking non-smoking Oriental woman who is into Wesson oil and bears a resemblance to Florence Henderson."

Beloved actress and singer Florence Henderson (1934–2016) is best remembered as Carol Brady on *The Brady Bunch*, as well as its many spinoffs and specials. She was also a frequent game show panelist, hosted her own cooking show and talk show, and was a spokesperson for Wesson, a brand of cooking oil, from 1974 to 1996.

References: *Aliens*, Sigourney Weaver

> **Blanche:** Rose and I rented that movie *Aliens* and it just scared us half to death.
>
> **Sophia:** It scared me, too. That Sigourney Weaver's a sweet girl, but she really shouldn't go without makeup.

Aliens is a 1986 sci-fi/horror sequel to 1979's *Alien*, which centered around a group of astronauts—including a makeup-less Sigourney Weaver—battling the titular alien, who is set loose on the ship. Her character, Ellen Ripley, was (spoiler alert) the sole survivor of that flick, and when it really bolstered Weaver's box office draw, she helmed the sequel. Unlike many a sequel, the film was critically acclaimed and a financial hit and several films followed. The franchise is still going today, with new projects in development. Weaver is an actress known for her work in this *Alien* franchise, as well as *Ghostbusters*, *Gorillas in the Mist*, and *Working Girl*.

Reference: Milk of Magnesia

> **Sophia:** I'm just drawing a line on the Milk of Magnesia bottle.

Milk of Magnesia is a medication used as a laxative and to treat heartburn and indigestion.

References: Brigitte Nielsen, Rolls-Royce, Robert Goulet, *Bambi*

> **Sophia:** Picture it: Sicily 1922. A beautiful young woman with breasts not unlike Brigitte Nielsen, except hers moved when she skipped. She comes walking down a picturesque country road when suddenly a yellow Rolls-Royce pulls up and blocks her path.
>
> **Blanche:** Oh, who was in the Rolls?
>
> **Sophia:** Robert Goulet, for all I know! It's not important to the story. Anyway, the Rolls-Royce moves on, and the girl finds her pepperoni is missing.
>
> **Rose:** What happened to it, Sophia?
>
> **Sophia:** Bambi ate it! How should I know?

Brigitte Nielsen is a Danish actress and model who appeared in the films *Red Sonja*, *Rocky IV*, and *Beverly Hills Cop II* in the 1980s. She was married to Sylvester Stallone from 1985 to 1987. Rolls-Royce is a luxury automobile maker founded in the early twentieth century. Robert Goulet (1933–2007) was a singer and actor who gained fame as Sir Lancelot in the original 1960 Broadway production of *Camelot*, which he followed with appearances on *The Danny Thomas Show* and *The Ed Sullivan Show* and a 1962 Grammy Award for Best New Artist. Goulet's nearly six-decade career spanned several albums, stage productions, and film and TV roles. Released in 1942, *Bambi* is one of Disney's earliest animated films, about the titular young deer.

Repeat References: Lucille Ball *(Episode 1.11: Stan's Return)*, Vicks Vapo-Rub *(Episode 1.6: On Golden Girls)*, the Duke and Duchess of Windsor *(Episode 2.18: Forgive Me, Father)*, Tammy Faye Bakker *(Episode 3.7: Strange Bedfellows)*, hot toddy *(Episode 1.21: The Flu)*, Madonna *(Episode 1.8: Break-In)*, Polaroid *(Episode 1.5: The Triangle)*

EPISODE 3.12: CHARLIE'S BUDDY

Directed by Terry Hughes. Written by Kathy Speer and Terry Grossman. Original airdate: December 12, 1987

Rose begins dating an old army buddy of her late husband, Charlie.

Reference: The Alamo

> **Dorothy:** It's a dress, Blanche. It's not the Alamo.

The Alamo is a Franciscan mission in San Antonio, Texas, which was besieged in 1836, during the Texan war for independence from Mexico. A group of volunteer Texan soldiers, who were occupying the site, found themselves trying to defend it against a Mexican army numbering in the thousands. They held out for thirteen days before finally being overtaken. The battle became an enduring symbol of resistance to oppression, as did the phrase "Remember the Alamo!" during the Mexican-American War in the 1840s. Today the Alamo is a popular tourist destination.

Reference: Haley's M-O

> **Dorothy:** Oh, Ma, good news!
>
> **Sophia:** They changed the flavor of Haley's M-O?

Haley's M-O is an over-the-counter laxative made from magnesium hydroxide and mineral oil.

Reference: Jimmy Carter

> **Dorothy:** Blanche, have you ever met a man you didn't think was giving you the eye?
>
> **Blanche:** Once in 1976, but it was only two days later that Mr. President Jimmy Carter admitted he *had* secretly lusted in his heart.

Democratic politician Jimmy Carter served as the thirty-ninth president of the United States from 1977 to 1981. Prior to the presidency, he'd served as the governor of Georgia and as a Georgia state senator. Since his time in office, Carter has become well known for his philanthropic work. He's a major figure with Habitat for Humanity, doing everything for the charitable organization from fund-raising to publicity to the actual building of homes.

Reference: Shillelagh

> **Sophia:** Ever since that guy hit town she spends most of her time out polishing his shillelagh.

A shillelagh is a wooden walking stick closely associated with Ireland and Irish folklore.

Reference: The Pointer Sisters

> **Sophia:** Pick up one for Rose. You can go as the Pointer Sisters.

The Pointer Sisters are a Grammy-winning R&B singing group originally consisting of sisters June, Bonnie, and Anita Pointer, who rose to fame in the 1970s. Sister Ruth joined eventually, and Bonnie left some years later. It was this incarnation with which the group was most successful, charting a string of hits in the 1980s like "I'm So Excited," "Jump (For My Love)," "Automatic," "Fire," "He's So Shy," "Slow Hand," and "Neutron Dance."

References: Pudding Pops, the Eiffel Tower

> **Dorothy:** Last weekend you ate so many Pudding Pops, you could've built the Eiffel Tower with the sticks.

Pudding Pops were a line of frozen ice pop treats introduced in the 1970s by Jell-O. They were available in chocolate, vanilla, and swirl flavors. The Eiffel Tower is a wrought-iron lattice tower in Paris, France, named after engineer Gustave Eiffel. It was constructed between 1887 and 1889 as the entrance to the 1889 World's Fair and is considered one of the most recognizable structures—and most popular tourist attractions—in the world.

References: Yarmulke, Hefty bag

> **Dorothy:** What do they expect to see me in, a yarmulke and a Hefty bag?

A yarmulke is a skullcap worn by Jewish men. Hefty is a well-known brand of trash bags and food storage bags, among other household items, founded by the Mobil Chemical Co.

Reference: CBS

> **Sophia:** I may live to see CBS come up with a morning show yet.

Broadcast TV and radio network CBS, standing for Columbia Broadcasting System, was founded in 1927. With its distinctive eye logo, in use since the 1950s, CBS has been one of the major networks in broadcasting for decades.

Reference: *The Three Musketeers*

> **Rose:** I feel like I'm breaking up *The Three Musketeers*.

The Three Musketeers is an adventure novel written in 1844 by Alexandre Dumas about a trio of chivalrous swordsmen.

Reference: Kim Basinger

> **Blanche:** I am wearing this dress. Dorothy, it deserves to be displayed on a devastatingly beautiful body.
>
> **Dorothy:** Who are you going to send it to, Kim Basinger?

Actress and model Kim Basinger was hailed as a sex symbol after rising to fame in the 1980s in films such as *Never Say Never Again*, *The Natural*, and Tim Burton's *Batman*. She won both a Golden Globe and an Oscar for her role in 1997's *L.A. Confidential.* That makes her the only actress to have both won an Oscar and posed nude in *Playboy*.

Reference: Chips Ahoy!

> **Blanche:** We're out of Chips Ahoy! I'm going to get out of this girdle and go down to the market for some cookies and bean dip.

A brand of cookies from the Nabisco company that debuted in 1963, Chips Ahoy!—a nod to the nautical term "Ships Ahoy!"—have long been a popular cookie choice in the grocery-store snack aisle. The original, and still flagship, Chips Ahoy! is a basic, crunchy chocolate chip cookie. Over the years, additional flavors and varieties have been introduced, like chewy and chunky options, cookies with peanut butter cups or sprinkles added, or—well, you get the idea.

Reference: World War II

> **Buddy:** I thought you meant they wouldn't believe there are any dinosaurs around from World War II.

World War II was a global war from 1939 to 1945, involving all the world's great powers who formed two opposing military alliances—the Allies (United States, United Kingdom, Soviet Union, and China) and the Axis powers (Germany, Italy, Japan), with the former emerging victorious.

Reference: The Met

> **Dorothy:** Ma, I need to talk to someone.
>
> **Sophia:** Sure, come in. I can hear Pavarotti live from The Met anytime.

The Metropolitan Opera is a famous American opera company based in New York City, founded in 1883.

Repeat References: Michael Jackson *(Episode 3.6: Letter to Gorbachev)*, Burdines *(Episode 2.11: 'Twas the Nightmare Before Christmas)*, Luciano Pavarotti *(Episode 1.10: The Heart Attack)*, Winston Churchill *(Episode 2.4: It's a Miserable Life)*

Episode 3.13: The Artist
Directed by Terry Hughes. Written by Christopher Lloyd. Original airdate: December 19, 1987.
Dorothy, Blanche, and Rose begin secretly posing nude for a sculptor.

Reference: Del Monte

> **Sophia:** He tells me to sniff his carnation for good luck. I take one whiff and *bingo*!
>
> **Dorothy:** He squirted your dress with ink!
>
> **Sophia:** Actually, it was Del Monte prune juice.

Founded in 1886, Del Monte Foods is one of the largest producers and distributors of processed foods in the United States, including fruit snacks, prune juice, and canned fruits and vegetables.

Reference: Volaré

> **Dorothy:** That's exactly what she said when that shoe salesman took Polaroids of her in the backseat of his Volaré.

Volaré was a car produced by Plymouth in the 1970s.

Reference: Mikhail Baryshnikov

> **Sophia:** I got the mind of a fox and the butt muscles of Baryshnikov.

Mikhail Baryshnikov is a Russian dancer, choreographer, and actor known as one of the greatest male ballet dancers in history. He moved to the West in the 1970s, where he soon danced with such groups as the American Ballet Theatre and the New York City Ballet. He eventually became artistic director of the former. He became a naturalized US citizen in 1986 and was nominated for an Academy Award for his role in *The Turning Point*.

Reference: Pablo Picasso

> **Blanche:** You know that famous Picasso painting *Nude Woman Playing the Violin*?

Laszlo: Well, of course.

Blanche: Well, originally, it was called *Blanche Playing the Violin*. Only it wasn't a violin. You think about that the next time you're standing around with your chisel in your hand.

Spanish painter and sculptor Pablo Picasso (1881–1973) cofounded the Cubist movement and is regarded as one of the most influential artists of the twentieth century.

Repeat References: Howie Mandel *(Episode 3.9: A Visit from Little Sven)*, Polaroid *(Episode 1.5: The Triangle)*, SeaWorld *(Episode 1.25: The Way We Met)*

EPISODE 3.14: BLANCHE'S LITTLE GIRL

Directed by Terry Hughes. Written by Kathy Speer and Terry Grossman. Original airdate: January 2, 1988.
Blanche is shocked to learn that her estranged daughter, Rebecca, a former model, has gained weight—and is even more shocked after meeting Rebecca's abusive boyfriend. Sophia battles her obnoxious boss at a fast-food restaurant.

Reference: *Butch Cassidy and the Sundance Kid*

Sophia: Oh boy, what a day.

Dorothy: What happened, Ma? Butch and Sundance steal your seat on the bus?

Butch Cassidy and the Sundance Kid is a 1969 Western film loosely based on fact that tells the story of real-life nineteenth-century outlaws Robert LeRoy Parker (aka Butch Cassidy) and his partner, Harry Longabaugh. Paul Newman and Robert Redford played the train robbers in the Academy Award–winning flick.

Reference: F. Murray Abraham

Blanche: I don't know what to say to her.

Rose: Johnny Carson had that same problem the other night with F. Murray Abraham.

F. Murray Abraham is an actor probably best known for his Oscar-winning role as composer Antonio Salieri in 1984's *Amadeus*. Abraham was born without the F. He added it to honor his father, Fahrid, and to give "Murray Abraham" a little more panache. Abraham has worked steadily in Hollywood for decades, including a recent Emmy-nominated stint on the Showtime series *Homeland*.

Reference: Erik the Red

> **Rose:** I haven't heard anyone insult someone like that since Lars Svenson accused Erik the Red of being a coward and called him yellow.
>
> **Dorothy:** Wouldn't that make him Erik the Orange?

Erik the Red (c. 950–c. 1003) was a Norwegian Viking who founded the first settlement in Greenland. Born Erik Thorvaldsson, he allegedly gained the "Red" nickname due to the color of his hair and beard.

Reference: The Dodgers

> **Rebecca:** Mama offered to drive us over to Vero Beach to see the Dodgers play.

The Dodgers are a Major League Baseball team established in 1883 in Brooklyn that relocated to Los Angeles before the 1958 season.

Reference: *Rebecca of Sunnybrook Farm*

> **Jeremy:** I know things move kind of slow here at Sunnybrook Farm, but we have a plane to catch.

Rebecca of Sunnybrook Farm is a classic children's novel written by Kate Douglas Wiggin in 1903, about a girl and her two aunts living in a fictional Maine village.

Reference: *Marblehead Manor*

> **Dorothy:** She's depressed because *Marblehead Manor* is only on once a week.

Marblehead Manor is a syndicated sitcom that ran from 1987 to 1988, starring Paxton Whitehead, Phil Morris, and a pre-*Seinfeld* Michael Richards, about the happenings at the posh estate of a corn oil fortune heir.

Repeat References: World War II *(Episode 3.12: Charlie's Buddy)*, Johnny Carson *(Episode 3.3: Bringing Up Baby)*, Tommy Lasorda *(Episode 2.4: It's a Miserable Life)*, Oreos *(Episode 1.16: The Truth Will Out)*, the Yalta Conference *(Episode 2.4: It's a Miserable Life)*

EPISODE 3.15: DOROTHY'S NEW FRIEND

Directed by Terry Hughes. Written by Robert Bruce and Martin Weiss. Original airdate: January 16, 1988.
Dorothy develops a friendship with local author Barbara Thorndike, who struggles to bond with Blanche and Rose.

Reference: The Big Bopper

> **Rose:** It says here that since Michael Jackson can't buy the Elephant Man, he's now put in a bid for the remains of the Big Bopper.

The Big Bopper (1930–1959) was the stage name of singer and musician Jiles Perry "J. P." Richardson Jr. Among his best-known tunes are "Chantilly Lace" and "White Lightning," the latter becoming the first number-one hit for country music legend George Jones. Richardson was killed in a 1959 plane crash along with Ritchie Valens and Buddy Holly, an event that became referred to as "The Day the Music Died" in Don McLean's song "American Pie."

References: William Faulkner, F. Scott Fitzgerald

> **Dorothy:** When I think of great literary figures of our time, it's usually Faulkner, Fitzgerald, and Schwarzenegger.

Great American author and Nobel Prize laureate William Faulkner (1897–1962) penned such classics as *The Sound and the Fury*, *As I Lay Dying*, *Absalom, Absalom!*, *The Reivers*, and many other novels, stories, essays, and poems. F. Scott Fitzgerald (1896–1940) was a celebrated novelist and essayist best known for penning *The Great Gatsby* in 1925, as well as other novels like *This Side of Paradise* and *Tender Is the Night* and short story "The Curious Case of Benjamin Button."

Reference: Bernard Malamud

> **Blanche:** Dorothy tells us you're an author.

> **Barbara:** I'm just a writer. Malamud's an author.

Bernard Malamud (1914–1986) was a Pulitzer Prize–winning novelist known for works such as *The Natural* and *The Fixer*.

Reference: Eve

> **Blanche:** I'm going as Eve from the Garden of Eden. All I'll need is a few strategically placed leaves.

A figure in the Book of Genesis in the Bible, Eve is considered to be the first woman. She lived in the Garden of Eden with Adam.

References: Dorothy Parker, Alexander Woollcott

> **Barbara:** And so Dorothy Parker turned to Alexander Woollcott and said, "If you laid every woman in this room, end to end, I wouldn't be a bit surprised."

Witty New York writer Dorothy Parker (1893–1967) was a founding member of the Algonquin Round Table. Alexander Woollcott (1887–1943) was a critic and commentator for *The New Yorker* magazine and also a member of the Algonquin Round Table.

Reference: Hide-and-go-seek

> **Rose:** It's an adult version of hide-and-go-seek.
>
> **Barbara:** And how does it differ from the children's version?
>
> **Rose:** Adults play it.

Hide-and-go-seek is a popular children's game in which one player is "it," which means they close their eyes and wait while the rest of the players hide. It is then up to the "it" player to find the others.

Reference: *Three's Company*

> **Dorothy:** I think I saw Jack and Janet give Chrissy this treatment on an episode of *Three's Company*.

Three's Company is a sitcom farce that ran on ABC from 1977 to 1984. It originally starred John Ritter, Joyce DeWitt, and Suzanne Somers as Jack, Janet, and Chrissy, platonic roommates who shared a Santa Monica apartment. Somers eventually left, replaced first by Jenilee Harrison, then by Priscilla Barnes.

References: Angie Dickinson, *Dressed to Kill*

> **Blanche:** I think she's a phony.

Dorothy: This from a woman who tells her dates that she was Angie Dickinson's body double in *Dressed to Kill*.

Actress Angie Dickinson rose to fame in the 1950s for roles in *Gun the Man Down* and *Rio Bravo*. Her six-decade career includes a string of classic film roles and a Golden Globe Award–winning performance as Sergeant Pepper Anderson on NBC's *Police Woman* series from 1974 to 1978. In 1991, she guest-starred in an episode of *The Golden Girls* spinoff series *Empty Nest* as a girlfriend of Dr. Harry Weston. *Dressed to Kill* is a 1980 slasher film starring Michael Caine and Dickinson as a psychiatrist and the sex-starved housewife who attempts to seduce him. An opening scene in a shower, depicting Dickinson's character in the nude, featured body double Victoria Lynn Johnson, a *Penthouse* model.

References: *The Grapes of Wrath*, *The Old Man and the Sea*, *For Whom the Bell Tolls*, *The Catcher in the Rye*, George Bernard Shaw

Dorothy: Everything sounds so good. The Crepes of Wrath. The Old Man and the Seafood Salad. I think I will have the For Whom the Stuffed Bell Pepper Tolls.

Barbara: And I'll have a turkey sandwich with Catcher in the Rye Bread and a side order of George Bernard Slaw.

The Grapes of Wrath is a 1939 John Steinbeck novel that won both the National Book Award and Pulitzer Prize for Fiction. Set during the Great Depression, the book follows the Joad family, a group of farmers attempting to escape the Dust Bowl for California. The book was adapted for a film in 1940 that starred Henry Fonda and Jane Darwell, was nominated for seven Academy Awards (winning two), and is widely considered a classic. *The Old Man and the Sea* is a 1952 short novel by Ernest Hemingway about a Cuban fisherman and a giant marlin. *For Whom the Bell Tolls* is a 1940 Ernest Hemingway novel about a young American fighting in the Spanish Civil War. A quintessential story of alienation and teen angst, *The Catcher in the Rye* is a 1951 novel by J. D. Salinger focusing on the life of protagonist Holden Caulfield. While published for adults, the book has long been popular among teen readers. George Bernard Shaw (1856–1950) was a Nobel Prize–winning Irish playwright, critic, and activist who wrote over sixty plays, including *Man and Superman* and *Pygmalion*.

References: Edgar Allan Poe, *The Iceman Cometh*

> **Waiter:** Oh yes, you had the Edgar Allan Poe-tatoes. And the ice water cometh.

Edgar Allan Poe (1809–1849) was a writer of mystery and the macabre, known for his poetry and short stories. Among his most famous works are the poems "The Raven" and "Annabel Lee," and the tales *The Fall of the House of Usher*, *The Purloined Letter*, and *The Tell-Tale Heart*. *The Iceman Cometh* is a play written in 1939 by Eugene O'Neill which premiered on Broadway in 1946, about a group of bar patrons in an early twentieth-century New York saloon.

Reference: Mike Tyson

> **Dorothy:** I don't know Mike Tyson well enough to borrow his jewelry.

Mike Tyson is a former professional boxer who competed from 1985 to 2005 and was heavyweight champion from 1987 to 1990. His popularity inspired a Nintendo video game named after him. He was convicted of rape in 1992 and served three years in prison. In 1997, during a match against Evander Holyfield, Tyson was disqualified after biting off part of his opponent's ear.

Repeat References: Michael Jackson *(Episode 3.6: Letter to Gorbachev)*, the Elephant Man *(Episode 3.10: The Audit)*, Elvis Presley *(Episode 1.18: The Operation)*, Arnold Schwarzenegger *(Episode 2.21: Dorothy's Prized Pupil)*, Mallomars *(Episode 1.12: The Custody Battle)*, A&P *(Episode 2.6: Big Daddy's Little Lady)*, ALF *(Episode 3.7: Strange Bedfellows)*, Dramamine *(Episode 1.6: On Golden Girls)*, Norman Mailer *(Episode 1.21: The Flu)*

EPISODE 3.16: GRAB THAT DOUGH

Directed by Terry Hughes. Written by Winifred Hervey Stallworth. Original air-date: January 23, 1988.
The girls fly to Hollywood to appear on the game show *Grab That Dough*.

References: Gene Rayburn, Chuck Woolery, Bob Eubanks

> **Rose:** He's like Gene Rayburn, Chuck Woolery, and Bob Eubanks all rolled into one.

Gene Rayburn (1917–1999) was a radio and television personality best known for hosting the game show *Match Game*. Chuck Woolery is a former game show and talk show host, known for being the original host of *Wheel of Fortune*, as well as *Love Connection* and *Scrabble*. TV personality and game show host Bob Eubanks is known for hosting such shows as *The Newlywed Game* and *Card Sharks* from the 1960s through the 1990s, as well as plenty of other shows along the way.

Reference: The Iron Curtain

> **Blanche:** I have altered my appearance for a very important movie role.
>
> **Dorothy:** It's about a woman who eats her way from behind the Iron Curtain.

The Iron Curtain was initially an imaginary boundary that divided Europe into two areas from the end of World War II until the end of the Cold War in 1991. It later referred to the actual physical barrier of walls and fences between the East and West, including the Berlin Wall.

Reference: Adolf Hitler

> **Sophia:** Mussolini asked the questions, and you'd better have the right answers. Things like, "Who do you like better, me or Hitler?" "Who's got the snappiest boots, me or Hitler?" "Who's got the cutest girlfriend, me or Hitler?"

Adolf Hitler (1889–1945) was leader of the Nazi Party and Führer of Germany from 1934 to 1945. He initiated World War II by invading Poland in 1939 and was responsible for the genocide of approximately six million Jews. He died from a self-inflicted gunshot wound in 1945.

References: Goodson-Todman Productions, *Tattletales*

> **Dorothy:** Come on, Ma, you're making this up.
>
> **Sophia:** Like hell. Goodson-Todman brought it to the United States, changed a few of the rules, and called it *Tattletales*.

Goodson-Todman Productions is a television production company founded in 1946 by Mark Goodson and Bill Todman. The company produced some of the most successful game shows in history, such as *The Price Is Right*, *What's My Line?*, *Beat the Clock*, *Password*, *Match Game*, *Concentration*, *Family Feud*, and *Card Sharks*. *Tattletales* was another of their shows. Hosted by Bert Convy, the show ran from 1974 to 1984 and focused on questions about the lives of celebrity couples.

Reference: Clark Gable, *It Happened One Night*

> **Blanche:** I can lift up my skirt like in that Clark Gable movie *It Happened One Night.*

Sometimes called "The King of Hollywood," Clark Gable (1901–1960) is one of the most celebrated actors in Hollywood history, with sixty films to his credit, many as the leading man. His most well-known roles include *Mutiny on the Bounty, San Francisco, Manhattan Melodrama*, and as Rhett Butler in *Gone with the Wind. It Happened One Night* is a 1934 romantic comedy starring Claudette Colbert and Gable as a pampered socialite and the reporter she falls in love with. It won all five major Academy Awards: Best Picture, Best Director, Best Actor, Best Actress, and Best Adapted Screenplay.

References: Big Ben, English bobby

> **Blanche:** Was that a real English bobby spanking you there in front of Big Ben?

Big Ben is the nickname for the Great Bell of the striking clock at the Palace of Westminster in London. Big Ben is typically mentioned in reference both to the clock and the clock tower, but the tower itself is actually called Elizabeth Tower. The tower was designed by Augustus Pugin and was completed in 1859, at the time the largest and most accurate such clock in the world. A bobby is a slang term for members of London's Metropolitan Police, derived from the name of the force's creator, Sir Robert Peel.

Reference: The Gatlin Brothers

> **Rose:** You and Dorothy are joining a country-and-western band?
>
> **Dorothy:** That's the Gatlin Brothers, Rose.

The Gatlin Brothers are a Grammy-winning country music trio consisting of brothers Larry, Steve, and Rudy Gatlin. They've been entertaining audiences for more than sixty years with hits like "All the Gold in California," "Broken Lady," and "Night Time Magic."

Reference: The AMC Pacer

> **Sophia:** You, Dorothy, are the biggest disappointment to hit the streets since the AMC Pacer.

The Pacer was a small car model produced by AMC during the 1970s. It was wider and more cab-forward than its counterpart, the Gremlin, which was apparently a selling point? Labeled futuristic in its early years, the Pacer was likened to a jelly bean and something George Jetson would drive. Younger folks may recognize the Pacer from the *Wayne's World* movies or, for even younger folks, *Cars 2*.

References: Tennessee Williams, *The Glass Menagerie*

> **Guy:** What famous Tennessee Williams play was recently made into a film by Paul Newman?
>
> **Rose:** Was it *The Glass Menagerie*?

Tennessee Williams (1911–1983) was a Pulitzer Prize–winning playwright known for such classics as *A Streetcar Named Desire* and *Cat on a Hot Tin Roof*. *The Glass Menagerie* is a 1944 play by Williams about an aspiring poet who works to support his mother and fragile sister, who maintains a beloved collection of glass animals.

Reference: Henry Ford

> **Guy:** What famous industrialist invented the assembly line?
>
> **Sophia:** Henry Ford!

Henry Ford (1863–1947) was an American industrialist and businessman who founded the Ford Motor Company in 1903.

References: Charles Schulz, *Peanuts*, George Washington Carver, George Shultz

> **Guy:** Who is the current Secretary of State? Willard?
>
> **Willard:** Charles Schulz!
>
> **Dorothy:** He created *Peanuts*!
>
> **Willard:** I thought that was George Washington Carver?
>
> **Rose:** Is the correct answer George Shultz?

Charles Schulz (1922–2000) was the cartoonist who created the comic strip *Peanuts*, which ran from 1950 to 2000 and continues in repeats. It features the classic characters Snoopy, Charlie Brown, Linus, Lucy, and the rest, who have been adapted into animated specials, series, films, merchandise, and general pop culture icons. A famed agricultural scientist and inventor,

George Washington Carver (1860s–1943) was a proponent of alternative crops to cotton, developed methods to prevent soil depletion, and served as the head of the agriculture department at Tuskegee University (then Tuskegee Institute), where he taught for forty-seven years. He's considered one of the most prominent Black scientists of the twentieth century. George Shultz is a Republican politician who served in such roles as US secretary of labor from 1969 to 1970, US secretary of the treasury from 1972 to 1974, and US secretary of state from 1982 to 1989.

Reference: *The Three Amigos*

> **Rose:** We made up on the plane.
>
> **Dorothy:** There was nothing else to do. It was either that or watch *Three Amigos* with a headset.

The Three Amigos is a 1986 Western comedy starring Steve Martin, Chevy Chase, and Martin Short as three silent film stars mistaken for real heroes by the residents of a small Mexican village.

Repeat References: Angie Dickinson *(Episode 3.15: Dorothy's New Friend)*, Benito Mussolini *(Episode 3.7: Strange Bedfellows)*, Ovaltine *(Episode 1.4: Transplant)*, Paul Newman *(Episode 3.2: One for the Money)*

EPISODE 3.17: MY BROTHER, MY FATHER
Directed by Terry Hughes. Written by Barry Fanaro and Mort Nathan. Original airdate: February 6, 1988.
Sophia's brother Angelo, a priest, visits just as a hurricane strikes Miami. Blanche and Rose rehearse for a local production of *The Sound of Music*.

Reference: *The Sound of Music*

> **Rose:** We're doing *Sound of Music* and Blanche is mad because she didn't get the lead.

The Sound of Music is a 1959 Broadway musical by Rodgers and Hammerstein based on the 1949 memoir of Maria von Trapp, who takes a job as a governess for a large family while deciding whether or not to become a nun. The original production starred Mary Martin and won five Tony Awards, including Best Musical. It was then made into a 1965 film starring Julie Andrews, which has itself become a classic.

Reference: NBA

> **Blanche:** A gay theater director. Did you ever hear of such a thing?
>
> **Dorothy:** It's absolutely shocking. Next thing you know, they'll have Black basketball players in the NBA.

The National Basketball Association is a men's professional basketball league founded in 1946.

Reference: Nazis

> **Rose:** The Nazis are coming! The Nazis are coming!

Nazism is an ideology associated with the far-right Nazi political party in Germany, active between 1920 and 1945 and led by Adolf Hitler, characterized by fascism and a disdain for liberal democracy.

Reference: Caesars Palace

> **Dorothy:** It's really coming down.
>
> **Rose:** What's coming down?
>
> **Dorothy:** The Liberace marquee at Caesars Palace.

Caesars Palace is a luxury hotel and casino in the Las Vegas strip, established in 1966 and modeled after the Roman Empire, or perhaps the kitschy Vegas version of such.

Reference: The Boston Philharmonic

> **Stan:** I was a little disappointed Michael didn't want to go into the novelty business with me.
>
> **Dorothy:** It was a crushing blow when he decided to join the Boston Philharmonic instead of selling rubber dog poop door-to-door.

The Boston Philharmonic Orchestra is a semiprofessional orchestra based in Boston, Massachusetts, and founded in 1979.

Reference: Jessica Hahn

> **Angelo:** Please, I am begging you as a man of the cloth.
>
> **Dorothy:** Now I know how Jessica Hahn must've felt.

Jessica Hahn became widely known in 1987 after accusing televangelist Jim Bakker of rape while employed as his church secretary in the early 1980s. She parlayed the notoriety into a modeling and acting career of sorts, posing nude for *Playboy*, guest-starring in shows like *Married . . . with Children* and *Unhappily Ever After*, and making frequent appearances on *The Howard Stern Show*.

Reference: Mastercard

> **Stan:** Women come to me!
>
> **Dorothy:** Right after they get the approval number on your Mastercard.

Mastercard is a financial services company—and maker of a popular credit card—founded in 1966.

References: "I've Got a Crush on You," "Embraceable You"

> *Stan sings both songs in an attempt to woo Dorothy.*

"I've Got a Crush on You" is a song by brothers George (1898–1937) and Ira Gershwin (1896–1983), originally used in the Broadway productions of *Treasure Girl* in 1928 and *Strike Up the Band* in 1930. It has become a standard after being recorded by the likes of Frank Sinatra and Ella Fitzgerald. "Embraceable You" is a popular jazz standard written in 1928 by the Gershwins and recorded by the likes of Billie Holiday, Nat King Cole, Bing Crosby, Ella Fitzgerald, Judy Garland, and others.

References: Berlin Wall, Cole Porter, George and Ira Gershwin

> **Sophia:** Stanley, think of me as the Berlin Wall. Try to climb over me and you'll know what barbed wire between your legs feels like.
>
> **Stan:** Gotcha.
>
> **Sophia:** Dorothy, how did this start? Cole Porter?
>
> **Dorothy:** Gershwin.
>
> **Sophia:** Thank God I came in time.

The Berlin Wall was a concrete barrier that divided Berlin, the capital of Germany, both physically and ideologically from 1961 to 1989. The Wall separated West Berlin (think: less oppressive, more affluent) from surrounding East Germany (which was under Soviet Union control). To keep easterners from fleeing west to greener pastures, the Soviet-allied German Democratic Government decided to erect a divider. At first a barbed-wire barricade, the border eventually became an actual concrete wall—well, two walls, actually—stretching ninety-six miles, thirteen feet tall, with a heavily guarded corridor between them. By 1989, the Wall was lined with hundreds of watchtowers, and guards shot down anyone who dared to try to cross. By 1989, civil unrest and political changes pressured the East German government to loosen restrictions, and that November, it was announced that people would be free to cross the borders. People flocked to the Wall for what some called "the greatest street party in the history of the world." People began to destroy the Wall, and by 1990, East and West Germany were officially reunified.

Cole Porter (1891–1964) was a composer and songwriter whose works have become standards ("Night and Day," "I Get a Kick out of You," "Begin the Beguine") and whose scores have become stage classics (*Kiss Me, Kate*; *Anything Goes*). George Gershwin (1898–1937) was a renowned composer who collaborated with his lyricist brother Ira (1896–1983) on several classic songs and musicals.

Repeat References: Dan Rather *(Episode 1.22: Job Hunting)*, Liberace *(Episode 2.15: Before and After)*, St. Francis of Assisi *(Episode 2.26: Empty Nests)*

Episodes 3.18 and 3.19: Golden Moments (Parts 1 and 2)

Directed by Terry Hughes. Teleplay by Mort Nathan and Barry Fanaro. Story by Kathy Speer and Terry Grossman. Original airdate: February 13, 1988.
Sophia announces that she's moving in with her son, Phil, prompting the girls to reminisce about their time together.

Reference: Willie Shoemaker

Sophia: You've ridden more winners than Willie Shoemaker.

Willie Shoemaker (1931–2003) was a jockey who, for twenty-nine years, held the record for total professional victories.

Reference: The Wizard of Oz

Rose: What about me?
Sophia: You? You need the Wizard of Oz.

The Wonderful Wizard of Oz is a 1900 L. Frank Baum novel about a young girl who gets transported via cyclone from her dull Kansas prairie farm to a magical land full of Munchkins, witches, and flying monkeys. It's been adapted countless times, including into the classic 1939 movie musical version starring Judy Garland.

Reference: *Little House on the Prairie*

> **Sophia:** What, this is *Little House on the Prairie*? We're at each other's throats all the time.

Little House on the Prairie is a historical drama series that ran on NBC from 1974 to 1983 about a Minnesota farm family in the 1800s. It starred Michael Landon, Melissa Gilbert, and Karen Grassle, and was based on the book series by Laura Ingalls Wilder.

Repeat Reference: Caesars Palace *(Episode 3.17: My Brother, My Father)*

EPISODE 3.20: AND MA MAKES THREE
Directed by Terry Hughes. Written by Winifred Hervey Stallworth. Original airdate: February 20, 1988.
Sophia's constant presence puts a strain on Dorothy's new relationship.

Reference: *Thirtysomething*

> **Sophia:** I'm upset because I can't relate to *Thirtysomething*.

Thirtysomething was a drama series that ran on ABC from 1987 to 1991, about a group of Philadelphia baby boomers in their thirties. Ken Olin, Mel Harris, Timothy Busfield, and Patricia Wettig starred. A potential reboot was announced in 2020 but failed to materialize.

Reference: Venus flytrap

> **Dorothy:** I have a date to play this morning.
> **Blanche:** With a man?
> **Dorothy:** No, Blanche, with a Venus flytrap.

A Venus flytrap is a carnivorous plant that traps its prey—insects—by closing its leaves around them.

Reference: Pinky Lee

> **Sophia:** Lillian is still around, but she thinks she's Pinky Lee.

Pinky Lee (1907–1993) was a burlesque comedian who hosted *The Pinky Lee Show*, a children's program, in the 1950s.

Reference: Chiclets

> **Sophia:** I have a Chiclet here somewhere if you're fighting over a piece of gum.

Chiclets is a brand of little, square, candy-coated chewing gum introduced in 1900. The name is derived from chicle, a natural gum used in its making.

References: Giorgio Armani, Ed Sullivan

> **Blanche:** You thought Giorgio Armani was a puppet on *Ed Sullivan*.

Giorgio Armani is an Italian designer of high-end and red-carpet fashions. He founded the Armani company in 1975 and over the years has expanded his luxury brand into hotels, music, and sports. Ed Sullivan (1901–1974) was a television personality and columnist best known for creating and hosting his own variety show, which ran from 1948 to 1971. It's been called one of the greatest TV shows of all time, luring the likes of The Beatles, Elvis Presley, and The Muppets. Everyone who was anyone appeared on the show over the years, from popular musicians to opera stars, from comedians and actors to ballet dancers and circus acts.

Reference: Jimmy the Greek

> **Rose:** You're dumping your own mother?
>
> **Dorothy:** Faster than CBS dumped Jimmy the Greek.

Jimmy "the Greek" Snyder (1918–1996) was a sports commentator and regular contributor to the CBS show *The NFL Today* beginning in 1976. His controversial, racist remarks about Black athletes led to his immediate firing in 1988.

Reference: Charles de Gaulle

> **Sophia:** It reminds me of the place I met Charles de Gaulle. We were lovers, you know.

Charles de Gaulle (1890–1970) was a prominent French army officer and statesman who led the French Forces against Nazi Germany in World War II and served as president of France from 1959 to 1969.

Reference: Itzhak Perlman

> **Sophia:** Move it along, would you, Itzhak? We're trying to have a conversation here.

Itzhak Perlman is a celebrated conductor, violinist, and music teacher who has performed at such prestigious events as the inauguration of President Barack Obama and at a dinner honoring Queen Elizabeth II. He's won sixteen Grammys and four Emmys.

Reference: "Day-O (The Banana Boat Song)"

> *Sophia sings the song when learning of a trip to the Bahamas.*

"Day-O (The Banana Boat Song)" is a traditional Jamaican folk song. The best-remembered version is probably Harry Belafonte's 1955 hit rendition that Catherine O'Hara and company danced around the table to in *Beetlejuice*.

Reference: Wally and the Beaver

> **Dorothy:** Who are we, Wally and the Beaver?

These are characters from *Leave It to Beaver*, a beloved sitcom (1957–1963) about the adventures of young "Beaver" Cleaver and his suburban family, parents Ward and June and brother Wally. It was created by Joe Connelly and Bob Mosher and starred Barbara Billingsley, Hugh Beaumont, Tony Dow, and Jerry Mathers as The Beaver. The show has long held its iconic status, with a made-for-TV movie in 1983, a reboot series, *The New Leave It to Beaver* (1985–1989), and a 1997 feature film.

References: Tom Selleck, Steve Guttenberg, *Three Men and a Baby*

> **Blanche:** I was stranded on a desert island with Tom Selleck, Ted Danson, and Steve Guttenberg. Three men and oooh baby.

Tom Selleck is an actor who rose to fame as the lead in the 1980s crime series *Magnum, P.I.* Other notable roles include *Quigley Down Under* and a recurring role as Monica's boyfriend, Richard, on *Friends*. He's also a spokesperson for the National Rifle Association. Actor Steve Guttenberg also rose to fame in the 1980s for a string of successful films, including *Police Academy*, *Cocoon*, and *Short Circuit*. Selleck and Guttenberg costarred with Ted Danson in the 1987 comedy *Three Men and a Baby* and its 1990 sequel, *Three Men and a Little Lady*.

Reference: Joe Frazier

> **Sophia:** I always wanted to have a nose like Joe Frazier.

"Smokin' Joe" Frazier (1944–2011) was a popular professional boxer active from 1965 to 1981. He was the heavyweight champion from 1970 to 1973, won an amateur gold medal at the 1964 Summer Olympics, and was the first boxer to beat Muhammad Ali.

Reference: Der Wienerschnitzel

> **Sophia:** I swear on your father's grave. Or what used to be your father's grave. Now it's a Der Wienerschnitzel.

Der Wienerschnitzel is a fast-food restaurant chain founded in 1961 that specializes in hot dogs. The company dropped the "Der" in 1977.

Repeat References: CBS *(Episode 3.12: Charlie's Buddy)*, Ted Danson *(Episode 2.23: Son-in-Law Dearest)*, Richard Nixon *(Episode 2.2: Ladies of the Evening)*

EPISODE 3.21: LARCENY AND OLD LACE
Directed by Terry Hughes. Teleplay by Robert Bruce and Martin Weiss. Story by Jeffrey Ferro and Fredric Weiss. Original airdate: February 27, 1988.
Dorothy is distrustful of Sophia's new boyfriend, Rocco, a supposed former mobster. Blanche and Dorothy read Rose's diary and are shocked by what she has written about them.

Reference: Spuds Mackenzie

> **Dorothy:** They caught him on a billboard spray-painting something obscene on Spuds Mackenzie.

Spuds MacKenzie was a fictional dog character used in a series of popular advertisements for Bud Light beer in the late 1980s.

References: Frank Nitti, Dutch Schultz

> **Sophia:** You really knew Frank Nitti?
> **Rocco:** Sure. Frank Nitti, Dutch Schultz, Al Capone.

Frank Nitti (1886–1943) was an Italian American Chicago gangster and one of Al Capone's top henchmen. He became boss of the Capone Gang after being released from prison in 1932 since Capone still had years left to serve. Dutch Schultz (1902–1935) was another New York mobster in the 1920s and 1930s.

Reference: Donald Trump

> **Sophia:** Who do you think you are, Donald Trump? You don't own this casino.

Before becoming a reality television show host and the forty-fifth president of the United States, Donald Trump was a well-known and wealthy businessman during *The Golden Girls* era.

Reference: Spiro Agnew

> **Rose:** You mean Rocco?
>
> **Dorothy:** No, Rose. I mean Spiro Agnew.

Spiro Agnew (1918–1996) was US vice president under Richard Nixon from 1969 until his resignation in 1973. That resignation, however, was separate from the Watergate scandal that cinched Nixon's own resignation a year later. Agnew's troubles stemmed from his tenure as governor of Maryland prior to becoming veep. A corruption investigation ensued with Agnew maintaining his innocence. He eventually pleaded no contest to a federal tax evasion charge, resigned the vice presidency, published a memoir in 1980 professing his innocence, and maintained a relatively quiet life until his death from leukemia in 1996.

Reference: Gelusil

> **Blanche:** Doesn't it bother you?
>
> **Dorothy:** Not if I take a little Gelusil.

Gelusil is an over-the-counter medicine used to treat heartburn and acid indigestion.

Reference: Mrs. Cleaver

> **Dorothy:** I want you to leave the door open.
>
> **Rocco:** Yes, Mrs. Cleaver.

Mrs. Cleaver is a reference to the mother on the sitcom *Leave It to Beaver*, which was explained in the previous episode. This line was often uttered by the character Eddie Haskell, the best friend of Wally Cleaver.

Reference: George Bush

> **Blanche:** Rose, whatever it is you're thinking, it isn't true.
>
> **Rose:** Good, then George Bush isn't married to his mother?

George H. W. Bush served as the forty-first president of the United States from 1989 to 1993. He also served as vice president during the administration of Ronald Reagan.

Reference: Depilatory

> **Sophia:** You should have never stopped using that depilatory.

A depilatory is a cosmetic used to remove unwanted hair.

Reference: 7-Eleven

> **Sophia:** What do you think this is, the 7-Eleven? I'm not open all night.

The 7-Eleven chain of convenience stores was founded in 1927.

Reference: Camel

> **Sophia:** Three close friends are haggling over a Camel.
>
> **Rose:** How many humps?
>
> **Sophia:** None. I'm talking about a cigarette.

Camel is a popular brand of cigarettes introduced in 1913 and still being sold today. It was founded by R. J. Reynolds, the innovator of the packaged cigarette.

Reference: The Colonel

> **Sophia:** The next time we go to the Colonel, I'm getting all white meat *and* a biscuit.

Colonel Harland David Sanders (1890–1980), or simply The Colonel, was a businessman who, in 1930, founded the fast-food chain Kentucky Fried Chicken, or KFC. He served as the company's brand ambassador and remains part of its visual identity to this day. In fact, some refer to the restaurant itself as The Colonel. The title of colonel refers not to military rank but to a title bestowed to certain renowned citizens by the Commonwealth of Kentucky. Today, Colonel Sanders has become a spokes-character for the KFC brand, with various actors portraying the white-suited, white-haired gentleman.

Reference: Diuretics

> **Sophia:** The man is taking diuretics for a prostate problem. His whole life is a fifty-yard dash.

Diuretics are water pills which increase the amount of water and salt expelled from the body through urine.

Reference: Packard

> **Blanche:** When George and I were courting, and it was getting to the intimate stage, we went for a date in his big old Packard. Well, halfway home we ran out of gas.

Packard was a luxury automobile founded in 1899 and defunct since 2007.

Reference: Dom Pérignon

> **Dorothy:** When I returned to the table there was an open bottle of Dom Pérignon and two filled glasses.

Dom Pérignon is a prestigious brand of champagne named after a Benedictine monk who pioneered a variety of winemaking techniques but not, surprisingly enough, actual champagne sparkling wine.

Reference: The Home Shopping Network

> **Rose:** Where'd it turn up, Dorothy?
>
> **Dorothy:** On the Home Shopping Network, Rose.

The Home Shopping Network is a television network launched in 1982 as a series of televised sales pitches for consumer goods and services.

Reference: Harley-Davidson

> **Rocco:** Get ready, you're coming with me. I've got a brand-new Harley-Davidson out in the driveway.

Harley-Davidson is a major American motorcycle manufacturer founded in Milwaukee, Wisconsin, in 1903.

References: Tampa Bay Buccaneers, Joe Namath

> **Rose:** What famous football player wore pantyhose . . .
>
> **Blanche:** Doug Kuriloff, Tampa Bay Bucks, New Year's Eve. We were at a Holiday Inn near the airport.
>
> **Dorothy:** The complete question is who wore pantyhose in a magazine advertisement?
>
> **Blanche:** Well, how the hell would I know? If I want to see a man in pantyhose I don't have to go out and buy a magazine.
>
> **Dorothy:** Joe Namath.

The Tampa Bay Buccaneers are a professional football team out of Tampa Bay, Florida, that joined the NFL in 1976. Joe Namath is a former professional football player of the 1960s and 1970s who played for such teams as the New York Jets and the Los Angeles Rams. He was elected to the Pro Football Hall of Fame in 1985. In the 1970s he did an ad for Hanes's Beautymist pantyhose, with the hook being, "If they can make my legs look good, imagine what they can do for yours."

References: Wolfgang Amadeus Mozart, *Eine kleine Nachtmusik*, *The Bugs Bunny / Road Runner Show*, Elmer Fudd

> **Blanche:** What famous Mozart composition, completed in 1787, is a serenade in G for two violins, viola, cello, and double bass, in four movements?
>
> **Rose:** *Eine kleine Nachtmusik.*
>
> **Blanche:** That's right. How did you know that?
>
> **Rose:** They always play it during the chases on *The Bugs Bunny / Road Runner Show*. There was this one where Elmer Fudd was chasing Bugs, and he stuck his gun down a hole in the ground . . .

Wolfgang Amadeus Mozart (1756–1791) was a composer of the Classical period who was already prolific in multiple instruments and composing works by the age of five. *Eine kleine Nachtmusik* is a piece of classical music dating back to 1787 and composed by Mozart. The German title means "a little serenade," or "a little night music." It's been widely recorded and used in films like *Batman*, *Alien*, and *Ace Ventura: Pet Detective*. *The Bugs Bunny / Road Runner Show* is one of several incarnations of anthology shows featuring the Warner Bros.–produced *Looney Tunes* and *Merrie Melodies* short cartoons starring the likes of Bugs Bunny, Daffy Duck, Porky Pig, the Road Runner, and others. The original cartoons were produced between 1948 and 1969. Variations of the anthology show ran both in prime time and, mostly, on Saturday mornings from the 1960s up until 2000. This specific incarnation, *The Bugs Bunny / Road Runner Show*, ran on CBS Saturday mornings from 1977 to 1985, when it moved over to ABC and changed its name again. Elmer Fudd is a fictional character in the Warner Bros. Looney Tunes / Merrie Melodies cartoon series, most often depicted as an adversary of Bugs Bunny. Typical storylines had the speech impediment–suffering Fudd hunting Bugs, whom he refers to as a "wascawwy wabbit." A bit on the dim-witted side, Fudd was an easy-enough adversary for the sharp-witted Bugs to thwart.

Repeat References: Christie Brinkley *(Episode 2.17: Bedtime Story)*, Al Capone *(Episode 3.5: Nothing to Fear but Fear Itself)*, NyQuil *(Episode 1.21: The Flu)*, Mary Poppins *(Episode 1.12: The Custody Battle)*, Willard Scott *(Episode 1.3: Rose the Prude)*, Nightline *(Episode 3.7: Strange Bedfellows)*, Holiday Inn *(Episode 2.17: Bedtime Story)*

EPISODE 3.22: ROSE'S BIG ADVENTURE

Directed by Terry Hughes. Written by Jeff Abugov. Original airdate: March 12, 1988.

Rose plans a cruise around the world with her newly retired boyfriend. The girls attempt to remodel the garage into a guest bedroom.

Reference: The St. Valentine's Day Massacre

> **Sophia:** I haven't seen a crime like this in a garage since the St. Valentine's Day Massacre.

The St. Valentine's Day Massacre was the killing of seven members of Chicago's North Side Gang, who were lined up against a wall and shot by men dressed as police officers, on Valentine's Day 1929.

Reference: *Ryan's Hope*

> **Dorothy:** If you walk out that door right now, you can forget about ever coming back! I sound like I'm on *Ryan's Hope*.

Ryan's Hope is a soap opera that ran on ABC from 1975 to 1989, about an Irish American family in Manhattan.

Reference: *Moonlighting*

> **Al:** Can't it wait until after *Moonlighting*? There's a special episode on tonight. It's only been rerun three times.

Moonlighting is a comedy-drama series that ran on ABC from 1985 to 1989, starring Bruce Willis and Cybill Shepherd as a pair of private detectives rife with sexual tension.

Reference: "I Am the Walrus"

> **Sophia, translating from Italian:** I am in charge. I am the boss. I am the master. I am the walrus.

"I Am the Walrus" is a 1967 song by The Beatles for their TV movie *Magical Mystery Tour*.

Reference: The Donner Party

> **Dorothy:** Rose, if these had been offered to the Donner Party, they still would've eaten each other.

The Donner Party was a group of pioneers who migrated along the Oregon Trail from Missouri toward California via wagon train in the mid-1800s. Trapped by a harsh, snowbound Nevada winter, some of the group turned to cannibalism to survive. Eighty-seven people started out on the journey, and forty-eight survived.

Reference: Jimmy Swaggart

> **Dorothy:** No, Blanche. She's upset because Jimmy Swaggart can't cover his motel bill.

Jimmy Swaggart is a Pentecostal televangelist whose syndicated program hit its peak in the 1980s with transmission to more than three thousand stations. Sexual scandals with prostitutes in the late 1980s and early 1990s led to his defrocking by the Assemblies of God.

Reference: *Cocoon*

> **Dorothy:** Looks like the road company of *Cocoon*.

Cocoon is a 1985 science-fiction film directed by Ron Howard and starring Don Ameche (who won an Oscar for his role), Wilford Brimley, and Jessica Tandy. The plot deals with a group of elderly people rejuvenated by aliens. The film was a critical and commercial success and led to a sequel, *Cocoon: The Return*, in 1988.

Reference: The Osmond Brothers

> **Rose:** Who are all these old men?
>
> **Dorothy:** The Osmond Brothers, Rose. The years without Donny have not been kind to them.

The Osmond Brothers were a family music group popular in the 1970s, consisting—at various times—of brothers Alan, Wayne, Merrill, Donny, and Jimmy. Donny teamed with their sister, Marie, for a successful run as a singing duo and variety show hosts, while also enjoying a successful solo career. More recently, Donny appeared on a season of *The Masked Singer*.

Reference: Goofy

> **Rose:** We could just walk around and get our picture taken with Goofy.

An anthropomorphic animated dog character, Goofy has been one of Disney's most recognizable and beloved characters for decades. Characterized as dim-witted and clumsy, Goofy first appeared in the 1932 cartoon *Mickey's Revue* as "Dippy Dawg" and has been around ever since, including in his own early-1990s animated series, *Goof Troop*.

Repeat References: The Vatican *(Episode 2.9: Joust Between Friends)*, Disney World *(Episode 1.4: Transplant)*, Space Mountain *(Episode 1.16: The Truth Will Out)*

EPISODE 3.23: MIXED BLESSINGS

Directed by Terry Hughes. Written by Christopher Lloyd. Original airdate: March 18, 1988.

Dorothy's son, Michael, arrives with his fiancée, Lorraine, who happens to be Black and twice his age.

Reference: UPS

> **Dorothy:** Is the UPS man wearing his tight overalls again?

The United Parcel Service (UPS) is a package delivery company founded in 1907.

Reference: Epcot

> **Sophia:** There's my ride! I'm off to Epcot.

Epcot is a theme park at Walt Disney World Resort in Florida. It opened in 1982 as a celebration of human achievement, technological innovation, and interactional culture. Known as a "permanent world's fair," Epcot's name was conceived as an acronym for Experimental Prototype Community of Tomorrow, a sort of futuristic utopian city planned by Walt Disney. Spaceship Earth, a giant golf-ball-shaped sphere, serves as Epcot's symbolic structure.

Reference: Emilio Estevez

> **Rose:** Emilio Estevez is kind of Spanish, Dorothy.

Emilio Estevez is an actor who rose to fame in the 1980s as part of the "Brat Pack" group of young actors who appeared in such films as *The Breakfast Club*, *St. Elmo's Fire*, and *The Outsiders*. He also starred in *Stakeout*, *The Mighty Ducks*, and *Young Guns*. Estevez is the son of actor Martin Sheen and brother of Charlie Sheen, and was married for a while in the 1990s to singer/dancer Paula Abdul.

Reference: Sonny Bono

> **Dorothy:** I'm nervous because if Sonny Bono gets elected mayor of Palm Springs, he's going to make all the postmen wear leather bell-bottoms and a fur vest.

Singer, songwriter, actor, and politician Sonny Bono (1935–1998) rose to fame in the 1960s alongside his then-wife, Cher. Known as Sonny & Cher, the duo released such hit records as "I Got You Babe" and "The Beat Goes On," and starred in their own variety series, *The Sonny and Cher Comedy Hour*, from 1971 to 1974. Bono also wrote and produced several hit records, both for him and Cher and for other stars of the day. Bono and Cher divorced in 1975 but continued to perform together in the 1980s. In addition to a string of television guest appearances throughout the 1970s and 1980s, Bono moved into politics with a successful bid as mayor of Palm Springs, California. He served in the role from 1988 to 1992.

Reference: PAM

> **Rose:** Blanche says we might have better luck if we sprayed our fannies with PAM.

PAM is a brand of cooking spray made primarily from canola oil. It was introduced in 1961 by Leon Rubin and Arthur Meyerhoff, whose company, Gibraltar Industries, marketed the product. PAM is actually an acronym for Product of Arthur Meyerhoff. It's now owned by ConAgra Foods.

Reference: *Soul Train*

> **Rose:** If you don't believe me, just turn on your television set and watch a white person dance down the line on *Soul Train*.

Soul Train is a dance-music television program created by Don Cornelius that aired from 1971 to 2006, primarily featuring performances by R&B, soul, and hip-hop artists, among other genres.

Reference: Diana Ross

> **Greta:** Ever since Diana Ross started marrying white men, everyone's got to have one.

Diana Ross is an iconic singer and actress who rose to fame as the lead singer of The Supremes and enjoyed a successful solo career, with hits like "Where Did Our Love Go," "Baby Love," "Come See About Me," "Ain't No Mountain High Enough," "I'm Coming Out," and "Endless Love." Her acting successes include *Lady Sings the Blues* and *The Wiz*.

Reference: *A Raisin in the Sun*

> **Sophia:** What is this, a revival of *Raisin in the Sun*?

A Raisin in the Sun is a play written by Lorraine Hansberry about a Black family's attempts to improve their circumstances following the death of the family's father. It debuted on Broadway in 1959 with a cast that included Sidney Poitier and Ruby Dee.

Reference: Good Humor Man

> **Sophia:** Your daughter looks like she's been around the block more times than the Good Humor man.

Good Humor was a brand of ice cream introduced in 1920 as a chocolate-coated bar of vanilla ice cream on a stick, sold from ice-cream trucks. The brand was a pop culture fixture circa the 1950s, with nearly two thousand trucks delivering what had by then expanded into more than eighty treat options. Good Humor brand ice-cream treats are still available today in supermarkets.

Reference: "Abraham, Martin and John"

> **Rose:** Now, what do you say we all join hands and sing a chorus of "Abraham, Martin and John"?

"Abraham, Martin and John" is a 1968 song written by Dick Holler and first recorded by Dion as a tribute to the titular icons of social change: Abraham Lincoln, Martin Luther King Jr., and John F. Kennedy. A fourth verse brings in Bobby Kennedy as well. All four men were assassinated. The song has had many notable covers over the years, including by the likes of Marvin Gaye, Ray Charles, and Smokey Robinson.

Reference: *Judgment at Nuremberg*

> **Dorothy:** I couldn't sleep, so I thought I'd watch a little TV to unwind and take my mind off my troubles.
>
> **Rose:** What are you watching?
>
> **Dorothy:** *Judgment at Nuremberg.*

Judgment at Nuremberg is a 1961 courtroom drama starring Spencer Tracy, Burt Lancaster, Richard Widmark, and a host of other big stars, about a military tribunal for Nazi war criminals. The critically acclaimed film was nominated for eleven Academy Awards and won three.

Reference: Lillian Gish

> **Blanche:** Hell, he could marry Lillian Gish. I wouldn't care.

Lillian Gish (1893–1993) was a pioneering actress whose seven-decade career spanned the early days of silent films well into the 1980s. At the time of this joke, she would've been in her nineties—a bigger age difference than the one between Michael and Lorraine.

Reference: Ella Fitzgerald

> **Dorothy:** Do you like cheesecake?

Greta: Can Ella shatter glass?

Sometimes called The First Lady of Song, jazz singer Ella Fitzgerald (1917–1996) was one of music's greats, with hits like "Dream a Little Dream of Me," "Cheek to Cheek," and "It Don't Mean a Thing (If It Ain't Got That Swing)." In the 1970s, she appeared in a series of television commercials for Memorex cassette tapes, in which she hit a note so high while singing that she shattered a wineglass.

Repeat References: *The Cosby Show (Episode 1.23: Blind Ambitions)*, A&P *(Episode 2.6: Big Daddy's Little Lady)*, Martha and the Vandellas *(Episode 1.14: That Was No Lady)*

EPISODE 3.24: MISTER TERRIFIC
Directed by Terry Hughes. Written by Kathy Speer and Terry Grossman. Original airdate: April 30, 1988.
Rose begins dating a television superhero named Mister Terrific, who gets Dorothy a job on set.

Reference: Mark Twain

> **Sophia:** Just an observation. If my name were Mark Twain, you'd be writing this stuff down.

Mark Twain (1835–1910) was a writer known for such classics as *The Adventures of Tom Sawyer*, *The Adventures of Huckleberry Finn*, and *The Prince and the Pauper*.

Reference: Jack Kemp

> **Rose:** He was signing autographs in an empty storefront that used to be Jack Kemp's campaign headquarters.

Jack Kemp is a Republican politician who worked in the administration of President George H. W. Bush after failing to clinch the nomination himself in 1988. He also served nine terms in the US House of Representatives throughout the 1970s and 1980s and was the vice presidential nominee in the 1996 election campaign of Bob Dole.

Reference: Bozo the Clown

> **Rose:** He's not a clown, he's a superhero. You're thinking of Bozo.

Sophia: I'm talking to Bozo.

Occasionally billed as the World's Most Famous Clown, Bozo entertained generations of kids after being introduced in 1946 (and to television in 1949). The character appeared in franchised TV programs and was portrayed by various local performers. The original Bozo, however, was created by Alan W. Livingston and portrayed by Pinto Colvig. It wasn't until 1956, when the creative rights were purchased by Larry Harmon, that the character became a franchised property. *Today* show weatherman Willard Scott even portrayed the red-haired clown in the early 1960s. The most popular production of Bozo, however, was WGN-TV's *The Bozo Show* out of Chicago. The show ran from 1960 to 2001. Bob Bell played the role from 1960 to 1984, followed by Joey D'Auria.

Reference: Hilton

> **Sophia:** I haven't seen so much brass since the brass-knuckle and RV show at the Palermo Hilton.

Hilton is a global brand of hotels and resorts founded in 1919 by Conrad Hilton.

Reference: Dave Garroway

> **Sophia:** Dave Garroway told me if I treated him right I'd be his sidekick on the *Today* show. I said no, and he ended up with a monkey. Draw your own conclusions.

Dave Garroway (1913–1982) was the original founding host and anchor of the *Today* show on NBC from 1952 to 1961, who often appeared alongside the show's early mascot, chimpanzee J. Fred Muggs.

References: The Smithsonian, *Spirit of St. Louis*

> **Blanche:** What do you think I ought to do with my bed?
> **Dorothy:** Put it in the Smithsonian, Blanche. It has more miles on it than the *Spirit of St. Louis*.

The Smithsonian is a group of museums in Washington, DC, administered by the federal government, first opened in 1846 and named in honor of founding donor James Smithson. The museums hold more than 150 million items. The *Spirit of St. Louis* was a custom-built, single-engine monoplane flown by Charles Lindbergh on the first transatlantic flight from New York to Paris, France.

References: Captain Kangaroo, Mr. Green Jeans

> **Mister Terrific:** The critics called me the next Captain Kangaroo. Mr. Green Jeans sent me a fan letter.

Captain Kangaroo was a fictional character created and portrayed by Bob Keeshan (1927–2004) for the CBS children's show *Captain Kangaroo*, which aired weekdays from 1955 to 1984. Captain Kangaroo, named for the big pockets in his coat, would tell stories, conduct stunts, show cartoons, and welcome various special guests—the usual kids' show fare. After being canceled in 1984, a brief revival aired for one season in the late 1990s (absent Keeshan). Mr. Green Jeans was a fictional character on *Captain Kangaroo*, portrayed by actor Hugh Brannum (1910–1987) and known for his signature green overalls.

Reference: Squeaky Fromme

> **Dorothy:** Right now, Squeaky Fromme has a better grasp on reality.

Lynette "Squeaky" Fromme, who linked up with Charles Manson at age nineteen, became a member of the Manson Family cult and attempted to assassinate President Gerald Ford in 1975, which got her sentenced to life in prison. She was paroled in 2009.

References: Lex Luthor, The Joker

> **Dorothy:** Mister Terrific, I think that Lex Luthor and The Joker are harassing an old lady in the stairwell.

Lex Luthor is a fictional supervillain from the DC Comics line, depicted as the archenemy of Superman. The character first appeared 1940. A comic book supervillain and arch nemesis of Batman, The Joker also first appeared in 1940 and is often depicted as a psychopathic criminal mastermind who wears clown makeup. He's been portrayed on-screen by the likes of Jack Nicholson, Cesar Romero, Heath Ledger, Jared Leto, and Joaquin Phoenix.

Reference: Sigmund Freud

> **Dorothy:** In St. Olaf, they think that Freud is a way to cook chicken.

Sigmund Freud (1856–1939) was a noted Austrian neurologist and founder of psychoanalysis. He introduced, among other concepts, the Oedipus complex, a child's unconscious sexual desire for the opposite sex parent.

Repeat References: *Enquirer (Episode 1.25: The Way We Met)*, Mr. Whipple *(Episode 3.9: A Visit from Little Sven)*, Neiman Marcus *(Episode 1.23: Blind Ambitions)*, New York Yankees *(Episode 3.3: Bringing Up Baby)*, Today *(Episode 1.3: Rose the Prude)*, Mikhail Baryshnikov *(Episode 3.13: The Artist)*, Morley Safer *(Episode 2.14: The Actor)*, Angie Dickinson *(Episode 3.15: Dorothy's New Friend)*, Thirtysomething *(Episode 3.20: And Ma Makes Three)*, Superman *(Episode 2.4: It's a Miserable Life)*

EPISODE 3.25: MOTHER'S DAY
Directed by Terry Hughes. Teleplay by Barry Fanaro and Mort Nathan. Story by Kathy Speer and Terry Grossman. Original airdate: May 7, 1988.
While waiting for their children to call, the girls reminisce about past Mother's Day celebrations.

Reference: Queen Elizabeth II

> **Rose, on phone:** Person to person from the Duke of Windsor to Queen Elizabeth?

Queen Elizabeth II has been queen of the United Kingdom and its Commonwealth realms since 1952.

References: John D. Rockefeller, Gary Cooper

> **Stan:** To her, I have the business sense of a Rockefeller, the looks of a Gary Cooper, and the charm of a Cary Grant.
>
> **Dorothy:** I'm not surprised. The woman drinks grain alcohol out of a measuring cup.

John D. Rockefeller (1839–1937) was a business magnate and philanthropist who founded the Standard Oil Company and is considered to have been the richest person in modern history. The name Rockefeller has become synonymous with wealth. One of the most celebrated actors during the Golden Age of Hollywood, Gary Cooper's (1901–1961) career spanned nearly four decades, from the 1920s until his death in 1961. A two-time Best Actor Oscar winner, Cooper's notable works include *Mr. Deeds Goes to Town*, *Sergeant York*, *For Whom the Bell Tolls*, and *High Noon*.

Reference: Woody Woodpecker

> **Blanche:** Black motorcycle boots, skin-tight Levi's, a match in his mouth, and white T-shirt with the sleeves rolled up to reveal his brand-new Woody the Woodpecker tattoo.

Woody Woodpecker is an anthropomorphic cartoon woodpecker created in 1940 by Ben "Bugs" Hardaway, known for appearing in a variety of cartoon shorts from the 1940s to the 1970s.

Reference: Studebaker

> **Blanche:** The next thing I knew, I was sitting next to him in that souped-up old Studebaker, racing out toward Bayou country.

Studebaker was an automobile manufacturer that launched in 1852 and was defunct by 1967.

Reference: *Reader's Digest*

> **Sophia:** Yeah, right, so sell it to the *Reader's Digest*.

Reader's Digest is a general interest magazine founded in 1922 by DeWitt Wallace and Lila Bell Wallace, published ten times per year. For years it was the best-selling consumer magazine in the United States.

Repeat References: The Duke of Windsor *(Episode 2.18: Forgive Me, Father)*, Adolf Hitler *(Episode 3.16: Grab That Dough)*, Cary Grant *(Episode 1.6: On Golden Girls)*, Rexall *(Episode 1.9: Blanche and the Younger Man)*, Levi's *(Episode 3.6: Letter to Gorbachev)*, the Dodgers *(Episode 3.14: Blanche's Little Girl)*

Season Four: 1988–1989

By this point in the series, we're scooting past what would prove to be the halfway point. You'll notice the Repeat Reference sections getting longer as more references are recycled, but the balance continues to shift between jokes that were current (Molly Ringwald, Robin Givens, Steve Garvey) and classic (Zorro, the Ritz Brothers).

A notable shift this season is the introduction of Dr. Harry Weston (Richard Mulligan) and Dreyfuss, the central character and his canine companion of the spinoff series *Empty Nest*, mercifully retooled from the Rita Moreno–led misfire from the end of the second season. We eventually see all of the *Empty Nest* characters cross over by the end of *The Golden Girls*, and Dreyfuss, who proved to be a breakout television pet of the era, is one of the most frequent references throughout the entire show.

Episode 4.1: Yes, We Have No Havanas
Directed by Terry Hughes. Written by Mort Nathan and Barry Fanaro. Original airdate: October 8, 1988.
Blanche is surprised to find herself in a love triangle with Sophia. Dorothy teaches a history class for GED candidates, including Rose.

Reference: Molly Ringwald

> **Sophia:** Why do you always come into a room and say, "Girls, girls"? Do you see Molly Ringwald sitting here?

Molly Ringwald is an actress who rose to fame in the 1980s as a member of the "Brat Pack" and teen star of movies like *Sixteen Candles*, *The Breakfast Club*, and *Pretty in Pink*. In more recent years, she's appeared on such TV series as *The Secret Life of the American Teenager* and *Riverdale*.

Reference: Rex the Wonder Horse

> **Fidel:** Do you know that at one time, I was the most famous Fidel in the entire country? Until you-know-who showed up.
>
> **Rose:** Who?
>
> **Dorothy:** Rex the Wonder Horse, Rose.

Rex the Wonder Horse was a Morgan stallion who appeared in a series of films in the 1920s and 1930s, including *No Man's Law*, *Plunging Hoofs*, and *Hoofbeats of Vengeance*.

Reference: Sake

> **Dorothy:** I thought you were pulling my leg.
>
> **Jim:** I don't think I could drink that much sake.

Sake is a Japanese rice wine.

Reference: Old Spice

> **Rose:** That afternoon I passed it along to fifty young men and one very confused female PE teacher who smelled of Old Spice.

Old Spice is a brand of grooming products for men launched by William Lightfoot Schultz in 1937 as a woman's scent. A men's version followed the next year.

Reference: Pledge of Allegiance

> *Rose leads the Pledge in her GED class.*

The Pledge of Allegiance is an expression of allegiance to the American flag, written in 1892 by Francis Bellamy and officially adopted by Congress in 1942. The phrase "under God" was added in 1954.

Reference: Red Skelton

> **Rose:** Maybe he paints, like Red Skelton.

Red Skelton (1913–1997) was a comedian best known for hosting *The Red Skelton Show*, a comedy variety show that ran from 1951 to 1971. He also painted pictures of clowns as a hobby.

Reference: MedicAlert bracelet

Sophia: We happen to be an item. I'm wearing his MedicAlert bracelet.

MedicAlert bracelets are ID bracelets produced by the MedicAlert Foundation, founded in 1956, containing the wearer's important information for medical authorities in case of an emergency.

Reference: Bruce Willis

Blanche: Some things in life defy explanation.

Rose: Yeah, like Bruce Willis's hair.

Bruce Willis is an actor who rose to fame in the 1980s in the television series *Moonlighting* before launching a highly successful film career that includes such films as *Die Hard*, *Pulp Fiction*, and *The Sixth Sense*.

Reference: *How the West Was Won*

Dorothy: If you want to talk behinds, they could show *How the West Was Won* on yours.

How the West Was Won is a star-studded 1962 epic Western film made by Metro-Goldwyn-Mayer and starring Carroll Baker, Lee J. Cobb, Henry Fonda, Karl Malden, Gregory Peck, Debbie Reynolds, James Stewart, and John Wayne.

References: Third Reich

Dorothy: Rose, the question was, "Who was the leader of the Third Reich?"

The Third Reich is a Nazi term used by the likes of Adolf Hitler, alluding to the conceit that Nazi Germany was the successor to the Holy Roman Empire and the German Empire.

Reference: Eva Braun

Rose: I'm as sure of that as I am that's Eva Braun standing next to him.

Eva Braun (1912–1945) was the longtime companion—and for less than forty-eight hours, the wife—of Hitler, who was more than two decades her senior. During the end of World War II, with Nazi Germany collapsing around them, the pair wed in a brief civil ceremony forty hours before committing suicide together in a bunker, he by a gunshot wound and she by taking cyanide.

Reference: Ruth Buzzi

> **Sophia:** Fidel is taking me to the Burt Reynolds Dinner Theatre to see Ruth Buzzi in *Evita*.

Actress and comedian Ruth Buzzi is best known for her Golden Globe–winning stint on the variety show *Rowan & Martin's Laugh-In* from 1968 to 1973. She didn't stop there. Buzzi has appeared in hundreds of series over the decades, as well as talk shows, game shows, and voiceover projects. She also had a successful traveling nightclub act and appeared in multiple films. She did not, apparently, appear in *Evita* at the Burt Reynolds Dinner Theatre, but she did play Screech's mom on *Saved by the Bell*.

Reference: Ann Miller

> **Sophia:** The man's face has more powder on it than Ann Miller's.

Ann Miller (1923–2004) was an actress and singer of the Classic Hollywood era of the 1940s and 1950s, known for roles in *You Can't Take It with You*, *Easter Parade*, *On the Town*, and *Kiss Me Kate*. During the era, she also appeared in a series of ads for Max Factor face powder.

Repeat References: Fidel Castro *(Episode 2.11: 'Twas the Nightmare Before Christmas)*, TV Guide *(Episode 2.4: It's a Miserable Life)*, Benihana *(Episode 2.19: Long Day's Journey into Marinara)*, World War II *(Episode 3.12: Charlie's Buddy)*, Adolf Hitler *(Episode 3.16: Grab That Dough)*, Kleenex *(Episode 1.4: Transplant)*, Jell-O *(Episode 1.20: Adult Education)*, Bromo-Seltzer *(Episode 2.12: The Sisters)*, Burt Reynolds Dinner Theatre *(Episode 1.5: The Triangle)*, *Evita (Episode 2.2: Ladies of the Evening)*

EPISODE 4.2: THE DAYS AND NIGHTS OF SOPHIA PETRILLO
Directed by Terry Hughes. Written by Kathy Speer and Terry Grossman. Original airdate: October 22, 1988.
While Sophia spends an active day on the town, the rest of the girls while away the hours accomplishing nothing.

Reference: Frederick's of Hollywood

> **Blanche:** I always throw open the window, uncork a bottle of Cold Duck, and slip into my Frederick's of Hollywood ostrich feather nightie.

Frederick's of Hollywood is a lingerie retail chain founded in 1947 by Frederick Mellinger, who invented the push-up bra. It was the retail leader in lingerie until Victoria's Secret stole its thunder in the 1980s. The company filed for bankruptcy in 2015 and the brand was sold and relaunched as an online-only store soon after.

Reference: Cesar Chavez

> **Claire:** Sophia?
> **Sophia:** Nah, Cesar Chavez. I got hungry.

Labor leader and Latino American civil rights activist Cesar Chavez (1927–1993) cofounded the National Farm Workers Association, which later became the United Farm Workers labor union and was prone to hunger strikes as a form of protest. During the era of *The Golden Girls*, Chavez's work increasingly focused on opposition to pesticide use on crops. He died in 1993 at age sixty-six and posthumously received the Presidential Medal of Freedom the following year.

Reference: Boy Scouts

> **Sophia:** You know who helps old ladies like us? Boy Scouts in cartoons.

Founded in 1910, the Boy Scouts of America is one of the largest youth organizations in the United States, with more than two million Scouts and a million adult volunteers.

Reference: Radio Free Europe

> **Blanche:** You could pick up Radio Free Europe with those ears.

Radio Free Europe is a US government–funded organization that broadcasts news and information to Eastern Europe, Central Asia, and the Middle East to ensure the free flow of information to countries where it is either banned by government or underdeveloped. It was created in 1949.

Reference: Mike Douglas

> **Sophia:** Haven't we learned anything from the tragic examples of Mike Douglas and Ferdinand Marcos?

Singer, actor, and entertainer Mike Douglas (1920–2006) is perhaps best remembered for hosting the long-running *Mike Douglas Show*, a daytime TV talk show that began in Cleveland in 1961, went into national syndication in 1965, and lasted until 1981. Before that, though, he had worked as a big band singer in the 1940s. When that style of music faded in the 1950s, largely replaced by rock and roll, his career suffered greatly before he bounced back as a television host. Ferdinand Marcos (1917–1989) was a dictatorial politician who served as the president of the Philippines from 1965 until he was removed from power in 1986 and fled to Hawaii.

Reference: "When the Saints Go Marching In"

> *Sophia's boardwalk band performs the song.*

"When the Saints Go Marching In" is a hymn often played by jazz bands and made famous in 1938 by Louis Armstrong and his orchestra.

Reference: Teamsters

> **Sophia:** I'm a Sunshine Lady, not a Teamster.

The International Brotherhood of Teamsters is a labor union formed in 1903.

Reference: *General Hospital*

> **Sophia:** What's the matter, you don't watch *General Hospital*? This place is a passion pit.

One of the longest-running series in television history, *General Hospital* is a daytime soap opera that debuted on ABC in 1963 and is still on the air. It's won the Daytime Emmy Award for Outstanding Drama Series thirteen times.

Reference: Borscht

> **Rose:** The town fathers mistook him for Max Brinker, the inventor of herring crispies, which by the way go great with borscht—but what doesn't?

Borscht is a sour, red soup made from beets, potatoes, carrots, and broth, among other ingredients.

References: Adlai Stevenson, Dwight D. Eisenhower

> **Dorothy:** She felt it was her personal responsibility to elect Adlai Stevenson president. She didn't care for Eisenhower.

Adlai Stevenson (1900–1965) was a lawyer and Democratic politician who served in various federal government positions in the 1930s and 1940s and twice lost the presidential election by a landslide to Republican Dwight D. Eisenhower, in 1952 and 1956. Eisenhower (1890–1969) was an army general who served as president of the United States from 1953 to 1961. He became a five-star general during World War II and planned and supervised the invasion of Normandy in 1944–1945.

Repeat References: Cold Duck *(Episode 1.25: The Way We Met)*, Valerie Harper *(Episode 3.6: Letter to Gorbachev)*, Neiman Marcus *(Episode 1.23: Blind Ambitions)*, Hugh Downs *(Episode 2.18: Forgive Me, Father)*, Today *(Episode 1.3: Rose the Prude)*, Andy Granatelli *(Episode 2.22: Diamond in the Rough)*, Jeopardy! *(Episode 3.5: Nothing to Fear but Fear Itself)*

EPISODE 4.3: THE ONE THAT GOT AWAY

Directed by Terry Hughes. Written by Christopher Lloyd. Original airdate: October 29, 1988.

Blanche vows to woo her old friend, Ham, the only man who ever turned her down. Rose and Dorothy encounter a UFO.

Reference: Oprah Winfrey

> **Rose:** Planes aren't that thin or that bright.
>
> **Dorothy:** Neither is Oprah Winfrey, but that doesn't make her a flying saucer.

Oprah Winfrey is a famed talk show host, producer, actress, and author known for hosting *The Oprah Winfrey Show* from 1986 to 2011.

Repeat References: Boy Scouts *(Episode 4.2: The Days and Nights of Sophia Petrillo)*, Chips Ahoy! *(Episode 3.12: Charlie's Buddy)*, Superman *(Episode 2.4: It's a Miserable Life)*, Doc Severinsen *(Episode 2.19: Long Day's Journey into*

Marinara), Cocoon (Episode 3.22: Rose's Big Adventure), ALF (Episode 3.7: Strange Bedfellows), Gone with the Wind (Episode 1.24: Big Daddy)

Episode 4.4: Yokel Hero

Directed by Terry Hughes. Written by Martin Weiss and Robert Bruce. Original airdate: November 5, 1988.
The girls visit St. Olaf to see Rose receive the prestigious St. Olaf Woman of the Year award.

Reference: Dan Quayle

> **Rose:** I never dreamed that someone as unqualified as I am would ever be nominated for anything so important.
>
> **Dorothy:** I guess Dan Quayle really opened the floodgates.

Dan Quayle was vice president of the United States from 1989 to 1993, under George H. W. Bush. Before that, he'd served as an Indiana representative and senator.

Reference: Regis Philbin

> **Rose:** I just found out I'm the most boring person alive.
>
> **Sophia:** Did something happen to Regis Philbin?

Regis Philbin (1931–2020) was a beloved television host best known for cohosting with Kathie Lee Gifford *Live! with Regis and Kathie Lee* beginning in 1988, which became *Live! with Regis and Kelly* in 2001 when Gifford departed and was replaced by Kelly Ripa. Additional hosting credits included the US version of *Who Wants to Be a Millionaire* and *Million Dollar Password*.

Reference: The rhythm method

> **Sophia:** Rose, you're here because the rhythm method was very popular in the twenties.

The rhythm method was used by women to monitor their body and analyze past menstrual cycles in order to determine their most fertile days.

References: Mount Rushmore, Alf Landon, Wendell Wilkie

> **Rose:** It's kind of like Mount Rushmore, except they sculpted four losers of presidential elections in the mountainside. Let's see, there was Alf Landon, Wendell Wilkie, and Adlai Stevenson and Adlai Stevenson.

Blanche: Why are there two Adlai Stevensons?

Dorothy: Oh, Blanche, isn't it obvious? He lost twice. Oh God, it's making sense.

The Mount Rushmore National Memorial is a colossal structure carved into the granite face of Mount Rushmore in Keystone, South Dakota. It was designed by sculptor Gutzon Borglum and was executed between 1927 and 1941. It depicts former US presidents George Washington, Thomas Jefferson, Theodore Roosevelt, and Abraham Lincoln. Alf Landon (1887–1987) was a Republican politician who served as the governor of Kansas from 1933 to 1937 and was the party's nominee for president in the 1936 election. He lost by a landslide to Franklin D. Roosevelt. Wendell Wilkie (1892–1944) was a lawyer and executive who was the 1940 Republican nominee for president of the United States. He also lost to incumbent Franklin D. Roosevelt.

References: Dr. Harry Weston, Dreyfuss the Dog

Harry, entering with Dreyfuss: Hello!

Blanche: Oh, Dr. Harry Weston. And I'm not dressed. Thank God!

Dr. Weston was the protagonist of spinoff series *Empty Nest*. Portrayed by Richard Mulligan, Harry was a bumbling but caring pediatrician who, at the start of the series, was mourning the loss of his late wife while coping with the fact that his three daughters had all moved out—a setup that didn't lend itself well to a weekly sitcom. Soon, two of those daughters moved back home, forcing Harry to learn to be a parent to adults. Mulligan's performance as Harry won him an Emmy Award for Best Actor in 1989. Dreyfuss was Harry's scene-stealing dog, played by a St. Bernard / golden retriever mix named Bear.

Repeat Reference: *TV Guide (Episode 2.4: It's a Miserable Life)*, Adlai Stevenson *(Episode 4.2: The Days and Nights of Sophia Petrillo)*

Episode 4.5: Bang the Drum, Stanley
Directed by Terry Hughes. Written by Robert Bruce and Martin Weiss. Original airdate: November 12, 1988.
Sophia and Stan team up to sue the baseball park after Sophia is injured at a game. Blanche and Rose prepare for roles in a local production of *Cats*.

Reference: *Cats*

> **Blanche:** We're doing the award-winning musical *Cats*.

Cats is an Andrew Lloyd Webber musical based on a 1939 poetry collection called *Old Possum's Book of Practical Cats* by T. S. Eliot. The musical debuted in 1981 and became a worldwide success, with productions taking place ever since. It ran on Broadway for eighteen years, grossing over $380 million in ticket sales. It was adapted to film in 2019 and, despite a star-studded cast including Jennifer Hudson, Taylor Swift, Sir Ian McKellen, and Dame Judi Dench, it was a massive critical and commercial disaster.

Reference: "Take Me Out to the Ball Game"

> **Dorothy:** Take me out to the ball game, Stanley.

"Take Me Out to the Ball Game" is the official anthem of North American baseball, written in 1908 by Jack Norworth and Albert Von Tilzer.

References: Club Med, Dixie cups

> **Sophia:** Please, for half the price I could go to Club Med, get a nicer room, better food, and not be forced to pee in a Dixie cup.

Club Med is a line of all-inclusive vacation resorts. The company was founded in France in 1950 and has expanded to more than seventy resort villages in locations all over the world. Dixie is a brand of disposable paper cups developed in 1907 by Boston lawyer Lawrence Luellen, who was concerned about the spread of germs by people sharing glasses at public drinking-water stations.

Reference: The Ritz Brothers

> **Sophia:** I saw The Ritz Brothers. Believe me, they're much funnier dead.

The Ritz Brothers were a comedy trio who performed in nightclubs and films from the 1920s through the 1960s, consisting of brothers Al, Jimmy, and Harry Ritz.

Reference: *Mr. Belvedere*

> **Dorothy:** Mr. Belvedere is a humble servant, Stanley. You are a horse's ass.

Mr. Belvedere is a sitcom that aired on ABC from 1985 to 1990, about the posh English butler of a suburban American family. The series starred Christopher Hewett, Bob Uecker, and Ilene Graff.

Reference: *My Fair Lady*

> **Rose:** What act?
>
> **Dorothy:** The second act of *My Fair Lady*, Rose.

My Fair Lady is a musical by Alan Jay Lerner and Frederick Loewe, based on George Bernard Shaw's play *Pygmalion*, about Eliza Doolittle, a flower girl who takes speech lessons to learn to pass as a lady. It premiered on Broadway in 1956 and was made into a popular 1964 film starring Audrey Hepburn and Rex Harrison.

Reference: Lassie

> **Sophia:** Who am I, Lassie? Next you'll lure me into a burning barn.

Lassie is a fictional dog created by author Eric Knight for a 1938 short story and 1940 novel, *Lassie Come Home*, later turned into a film, and then a popular, long-running TV series called *Lassie*. Lassie was a loyal female collie known for getting her pal, Timmy, out of jams.

Reference: *U.S. News & World Report*

> **Sophia:** My circulation is worse than *U.S. News & World Report*.

U.S. News & World Report is a media company founded as two separate news-magazines in 1933, which merged in 1948.

Repeat References: The Dodgers *(Episode 3.14: Blanche's Little Girl)*, the Eiffel Tower *(Episode 3.12: Charlie's Buddy)*, *The Exorcist (Episode 2.4: It's a Miserable Life)*, Dreyfuss the dog *(Episode 4.4: Yokel Hero)*

EPISODE 4.6: SOPHIA'S WEDDING—PART 1

Directed by Terry Hughes. Written by Barry Fanaro and Mort Nathan. Original airdate: November 26, 1988.

Dorothy and Sophia visit Brooklyn for the funeral of Sophia's old friend, Esther, and confronts Esther's husband, Max, whom Sophia blames for a past injustice. Blanche and Rose start an Elvis Presley fan club.

Reference: "Burning Love"

> **Dorothy, reading a letter:** Dear Rose Nylund, your application to start an unauthorized chapter of the Elvis Presley Hunka Hunka Burning Love Fan Club in your neighborhood and/or trailer park has been accepted.

"Burning Love" is a 1972 hit by Elvis Presley. The song was Presley's last Top 10 hit, and while several others have covered it, the song pretty much belongs to the King of Rock and Roll.

References: *Harum Scarum*, Motel 6

> **Rose:** Why should you be president?
>
> **Blanche:** I saw Elvis in *Harum Scarum* over fifty times.
>
> **Rose:** So did I.
>
> **Blanche:** I have every album he ever recorded.
>
> **Rose:** So have I. And every single.
>
> **Blanche:** I slept with him in a Motel 6 outside Chattanooga.
>
> **Rose:** Congratulations, Madame President.

Harum Scarum is a 1965 musical comedy film starring Elvis Presley as a movie star who winds up in a jam while promoting his latest picture in the Middle East. Motel 6 is a budget motel chain founded in 1962.

Reference: Knish

> **Dorothy:** Years ago, Max and my father were business partners. They ran a pizza/knish stand at Coney Island.

A knish is a Jewish snack food consisting of a filling covered in dough and baked or deep-fried. Common fillings include mashed potatoes, cheese, black beans, or spinach.

Reference: PLO

> **Blanche:** Maybe you ought to join an organization that is less fanatical in its devotion.
>
> **Dorothy:** Like what, Blanche, the PLO?

The Palestine Liberation Organization is a group founded in 1964 to liberate Palestine through armed struggle.

Reference: The Louisiana Purchase

> **Sophia:** The last time I was a virgin the Louisiana Purchase was still in escrow.

The Louisiana Purchase was the 1803 acquisition of the territory of Louisiana by the United States from France. The $15 million purchase was not for the modern-day state of Louisiana itself. In fact, it practically doubled the size of the United States at the time and consisted of area covering fifteen modern-day states.

Reference: Dick Clark

> **Sophia:** I can't get married unless I have you-know-who's blessing.
> **Rose:** Who?
> **Sophia:** Dick Clark!

Dick Clark (1929–2012) was a radio and TV broadcasting legend, known for hosting *American Bandstand* from 1956 to 1989, which became known for giving music artists some of their first national platforms. He also hosted the *Pyramid* game show in the 1970s and 1980s and *Dick Clark's New Year's Rockin' Eve* countdown every December 31 for decades. He also created and produced the American Music Awards, which launched in 1973. Clark was known for looking younger than his actual age.

Reference: Merlin Olsen, Forget-Me-Not

> **Rose:** Is that you, Sophia?
> **Sophia:** No, it's Merlin Olsen. I'm watering my forget-me-not bouquet.

Merlin Olsen (1940–2010) was a professional football player, announcer, and actor who played for the Los Angeles Rams until moving into a broadcasting and acting career, which included roles in *Little House on the Prairie* and *Father Murphy*. In the 1980s, he appeared in commercials for FTD florists; hence, this joke about forget-me-nots, which is a flower.

References: Susan Hayward, *I Want to Live!*

> **Caterer:** This is more moving than Susan Hayward's climactic speech in *I Want to Live!*

Actress Susan Hayward (1917–1975) was nominated for five Best Actress Oscars in the 1940s and 1950s for her work in *Smash-Up, The Story of a Woman, My Foolish Heart, With a Song in My Heart, I'll Cry Tomorrow*, and *I Want to Live!*, a 1958 biographical film in which she starred as Barbara Graham, a prostitute and criminal convicted of murder and facing capital punishment. A commercial and critical success, the film earned six Academy Award nominations, with Hayward winning the Best Actress trophy.

Reference: "Hawaiian Wedding Song"

> *Sung by the Elvis impersonators at Sophia and Max's wedding.*

Originally a 1926 tune by Charles E. King, "Hawaiian Wedding Song" was rewritten in its better-known form by Al Hoffman and Dick Manning and has been recorded by the likes of Elvis Presley, Bing Crosby, and Donny Osmond, among others.

Repeat References: Elvis Presley *(Episode 1.18: The Operation)*, *The Three Amigos (Episode 3.16: Grab That Dough)*, Charles Boyer *(Episode 1.3: Rose the Prude)*, Jordan Marsh *(Episode 2.11: 'Twas the Nightmare Before Christmas)*, MCI *(Episode 1.1: Pilot)*, Rambo *(Episode 1.6: On Golden Girls)*, Anita Bryant *(Episode 2.6: Big Daddy's Little Lady)*, The Ed Sullivan Show *(Episode 3.20: And Ma Makes Three)*, Mel Gibson *(Episode 3.5: Nothing to Fear but Fear Itself)*, Johnny Carson *(Episode 3.3: Bringing Up Baby)*, Donald Trump *(Episode 3.21: Larceny and Old Lace)*

EPISODE 4.7: SOPHIA'S WEDDING—PART 2

Directed by Terry Hughes. Written by Barry Fanaro and Mort Nathan. Original airdate: November 26, 1988.

Sophia and Max return from their honeymoon and announce plans to open a pizza and knish stand at the beach. A stressed-out Dorothy begins smoking.

Reference: Mrs. O'Leary

> **Rose:** I'll bet that's why Chicago burned down. Mrs. O'Leary was probably a tramp, too.

Catherine O'Leary (1827–1895) was a Chicago woman who gained fame when it was alleged that an accident involving her cow started the Great Chicago Fire of 1871. The fire began in O'Leary's family barn and, with high winds and dry conditions, ended up destroying roughly 3.3 square miles of the city and killing hundreds of people. A reporter published a claim that the fire was started when the cow kicked over a lantern while being milked. The story gained traction and is even still circulated today when the subject comes up. Two decades later, however, the reporter admitted to making up the story.

Reference: "It Had to Be You"

Max sings this to Sophia on the boardwalk.

"It Had to Be You" is a song written by Isham Jones and Gus Kahn in 1924 and recorded by the likes of Frank Sinatra, Bing Crosby, Ray Charles, and Barbra Streisand.

Reference: Julius Caesar

Rose: He had a Caesar complex. Salad, not Julius.

Roman statesman Julius Caesar (100–44 BC) played a large role in the rise of the Roman Empire back in the BC days before things went south for him. After declaring himself dictator for life, he was assassinated by a group of political rivals on the Ides of March—or March 15, as we'd say. He was stabbed twenty-three times.

Reference: Rembrandt Harmenszoon van Rijn

Max: A Rembrandt with tomato sauce!

Rembrandt Harmenszoon van Rijn (1606–1669) was a Dutch painter who is considered among the greatest visual artists in history.

Reference: *Farmers' Almanac*

Rose: A cow sitting on a gas tank reading the *Farmers' Almanac*.

The *Farmers' Almanac* is an annual periodical that's been in publication since 1818 and provides long-range weather predictions and articles on such topics as home remedies, folklore, and the best days of the year to do various activities.

Reference: *The Oprah Winfrey Show*

> **Max:** What is this, *The Oprah Winfrey Show?*

The Oprah Winfrey Show was an influential daytime talk show hosted by Oprah Winfrey that aired for twenty-five seasons from 1986 to 2011.

References: Ronald Colman, Greer Garson

> **Max:** If this was Ronald Colman and Greer Garson, there wouldn't be a dry eye in the house.

Popular from the 1920s through the 1940s, English actor Ronald Colman (1891–1958) got his start in theater and silent movies before launching a successful Hollywood career with films such as *Bulldog Drummond*, *Condemned*, *A Tale of Two Cities*, *Lost Horizon*, and *Kismet*. He won an Academy Award in 1947 for his role in *A Double Life* and was an inaugural recipient of a star on the Hollywood Walk of Fame. A major star at the Metro-Goldwyn-Mayer studios in the 1940s, England-born Greer Garson (1904–1996) received five consecutive Best Actress Oscar nominations from 1941 to 1945 (and seven total nods throughout her career). She's known for such films as *Blossoms in the Dust*, *Mrs. Miniver*, *Madame Curie*, *Mrs. Parkington*, and *The Valley of Decision*.

Reference: Saint Peter

> **Sophia:** I don't need a divorce on my record with Saint Peter in spitting distance.

One of the Twelve Apostles of Jesus Christ in the Bible. Also in the Bible, it's stated that he'll be given the keys to the kingdom of Heaven, which has led to the idea of Saint Peter being the gatekeeper at its entrance.

Repeat References: Disney World *(Episode 1.4: Transplant)*, Life Savers *(2.15: Before and After)*, 7-Eleven *(Episode 3.21: Larceny and Old Lace)*, Coney Island *(Episode 3.8: Brotherly Love)*, Lassie *(Episode 4.5: Bang the Drum, Stanley)*, Pablo Picasso *(Episode 3.13: The Artist)*, Mr. Potato Head *(Episode 2.16: And Then There Was One)*

EPISODE 4.8: BROTHER, CAN YOU SPARE THAT JACKET?
Directed by Terry Hughes. Written by Kathy Speer and Terry Grossman. Original airdate: December 3, 1988.

When a jacket containing their winning lottery ticket inadvertently gets donated to a homeless shelter, the girls spend the night there in an attempt to retrieve it.

Reference: *A Different World*

> **Sophia:** A terrible mistake is when you forget that *A Different World* follows *Cosby*.

A spinoff of *The Cosby Show*, *A Different World* ran on NBC from 1987 to 1993 and focused on the students at fictional Hillman College, a historically Black college in Virginia. The show was conceived as a vehicle for *Cosby*'s Lisa Bonet, who had become a breakout star for her role as Denise Huxtable. Bonet left after the first season, and the show became more of an ensemble piece while focusing largely on the characters of Whitley Gilbert (Jasmine Guy) and Dwayne Wayne (Kadeem Hardison).

References: Pepsi, Michael J. Fox

> **Sophia:** It's the guy from the Pepsi commercials!
>
> **Rose:** Pepsi commercials? Oh my God, that's Michael J. Fox!

Pepsi is a popular carbonated soft drink created in 1893 by Caleb Bradham. It was first called Brad's Drink, then Pepsi-Cola, and finally, as of 1961, just Pepsi. Michael Jackson appeared in an ad campaign for the brand in the 1980s. Emmy Award–winning actor Michael J. Fox did not appear in Pepsi commercials, but he became a household name in the 1980s with a career-defining role as Alex P. Keaton on the successful sitcom *Family Ties*, which ran from 1982 to 1989. Fox became a popular teen heartthrob during the show's run and launched a successful film career, most notably as Marty McFly in the *Back to the Future* trilogy. He was diagnosed with Parkinson's disease in 1991 at age twenty-nine, went public with the diagnosis in 1998, and has been a vocal advocate for the disease, founding the Michael J. Fox Foundation for Parkinson's Research in 2000.

Reference: The Concorde

> **Rose:** I guess now I'll never get to fly on the Concorde.

The Concorde was a British-French supersonic passenger airplane that had a maximum speed over twice the speed of sound. First flown in 1969, it entered service in the mid-1970s and was flown until 2003.

Reference: The Rainbow Room

> **Rose:** This isn't for dinner at the Rainbow Room. This is for ten big ones.

The Rainbow Room is an iconic dining and entertainment venue on the sixty-fifth floor of the Rockefeller Center in New York City.

References: *Mission: Impossible*, Peter Graves

> **Dorothy:** What is this, *Mission: Impossible?* Do I look like Peter Graves?

On CBS from 1966 to 1973 and starring Peter Graves (1926–2010), *Mission: Impossible* is a TV series about secret government agents. The series was revived on ABC for two seasons in 1988 and inspired a series of movies starring Tom Cruise, beginning in 1996. In addition to starring in this series, Graves's five-decade career also included roles in the *Airplane!* films, *Stalag 17*, *Savannah Smiles*, *Addams Family Values*, and as "mama's boy" news anchor Jerry Kennedy on *The Golden Girls*.

Reference: Ethan Allen

> **Sophia:** Before we leave, I want to get the model number off this cot. I'm hoping Ethan Allen makes one in knotty pine.

Ethan Allen is a furniture chain founded in 1932 by brothers-in-law Nathan Ancell and Theodore Baumritter. The company was named after the Vermont Revolutionary leader Ethan Allen in reference to the firm's style of Early American furniture.

Reference: "Brother, Can You Spare a Dime?"

> *This song plays while the girls search for their missing lottery ticket at the homeless shelter.*

"Brother, Can You Spare a Dime?" is a Great Depression–era tune written by Yip Harburg and composer Jay Gorney for the 1932 musical revue *Americana*. The song has been covered by more than fifty artists, including Bing Crosby, Rudy Vallee, Judy Collins, and Tom Waits.

Repeat References: *The Cosby Show (Episode 1.23: Blind Ambitions)*, Michael Jackson *(Episode 3.6: Letter to Gorbachev)*, Chiclets *(Episode 3.20: And Ma Makes Three)*, Hilton *(Episode 3.24: Mister Terrific)*

EPISODE 4.9: SCARED STRAIGHT
Directed by Terry Hughes. Written by Christopher Lloyd. Original airdate: December 10, 1988.
Blanche's visiting brother, Clayton, announces that he's gay.

Reference: Rich Little

> **Dorothy:** Spoke to you? How?
>
> **Sophia:** Do I look like Rich Little?

Rich Little is an actor and impressionist who has been dubbed "The Man of a Thousand Voices."

References: Barbara Eden, the College All-American Football Team

> **Sophia:** You want him to show up with Barbara Eden and the College All-American Football Team? It's a dream, not a Bob Hope special.

Star of film, stage, and screen, Barbara Eden is best remembered for playing a two-thousand-year-old genie in the sitcom *I Dream of Jeannie* from 1965 to 1970. The College Football All-American Team, its actual name, is an annual honor given to the best American college football players at their respective positions.

Reference: Roy Rogers

> **Sophia:** Fabulous. Roy and Dale are back.

Roy Rogers (1911–1998) was a singer, actor, and TV host known as "King of the Cowboys," who appeared in more than a hundred films and hosted the radio and television programs *The Roy Rogers Show* in the 1940s and 1950s. He was married to, and often appeared alongside, his wife, Dale Evans.

Reference: Gomer Pyle

> **Sophia:** Nice getting to know you, Gomer.

Gomer Pyle was a fictional character played by actor Jim Nabors on *The Andy Griffith Show*. A naive, gentle auto mechanic, Gomer first appeared on the show during its third season in 1962 and was later spun off into his own series, *Gomer Pyle, U.S.M.C.*, which ran from 1964 to 1969 and followed Gomer after he enlisted in the US Marine Corps.

Reference: Montgomery Clift

> **Clayton:** I still haven't told Blanche I was the one who stole the Montgomery Clift poster off her wall when she left for college.

A four-time Academy Award nominee, Montgomery Clift (1920–1966) was one of the leading movie stars of the 1940s, 1950s, and 1960s. Among his most notable works are *The Heiress, A Place in the Sun, I Confess, From Here to Eternity,* and *Judgment at Nuremberg.* He's considered one of the original method actors of Hollywood. A terrible car accident in 1956 had lasting impacts on Clift, leading to alcohol and painkiller abuse, erratic behavior, and additional health problems. His career never quite reached the same heights as it had in the years prior.

Reference: "Send in the Clowns"

> **Sophia:** He's the only man I ever knew who knows all the words to "Send in the Clowns."

"Send in the Clowns" is a song by Stephen Sondheim written for the 1973 musical *A Little Night Music.*

Reference: Ted Turner

> **Blanche:** Why? Because he was seduced by a bubblehead whose hair looks like it was colorized by Ted Turner?

Ted Turner is a media proprietor who founded such networks as CNN and TBS and who was an aggressive proponent of the colorization of black-and-white films in the 1980s, including a well-publicized attempt to colorize *Citizen Kane.*

Repeat References: Bengay *(Episode 1.6: On Golden Girls)*, Bob Hope *(Episode 1.9: Blanche and the Younger Man)*, Magic Johnson *(Episode 2.13: The Stan Who Came to Dinner)*, Dale Evans *(Episode 1.25: The Way We Met)*

EPISODE 4.10: STAN TAKES A WIFE

Directed by Terry Hughes. Written by Winifred Hervey-Stallworth. Original airdate: January 7, 1989.

Dorothy's feelings for Stan resurface just as he announces his engagement to another woman.

Reference: Lisa Bonet

Sophia: Lisa Bonet spent more on the ring in her nose.

Actress Lisa Bonet rose to fame as Denise Huxtable on the NBC sitcom *The Cosby Show*. She starred on the series from 1984 to 1987, when she then helmed the spinoff series *A Different World*, which saw Denise head off to college. That same year, Bonet eloped with musician Lenny Kravitz and gave birth to daughter Zoe in 1988. She left *A Different World* after its first season, returned to *The Cosby Show* in 1989, and was fired in 1991 for apparent creative differences with series star Bill Cosby. Bonet and Kravitz divorced in 1993, and she legally changed her name to Lilakoi Moon in 1995 (although she still goes by Lisa Bonet professionally). Bonet is now married to *Game of Thrones* and *Aquaman* star Jason Momoa. She still works in front of the camera, including recent appearances on *Girls* and *Ray Donovan*.

Reference: *Love Connection*

Rose: I hate when the people put each other down on *Love Connection*.

Love Connection was a dating game show in which single people attempted to connect with a compatible partner. The original run, hosted by Chuck Woolery, launched in 1983 and ended in 1994, with short-lived reboots happening in 1998 and 2017.

Reference: Nat King Cole

Dorothy: She sings opera to her sauce, except of course during the holiday season when she sings Nat King Cole.

Actor, jazz singer, and pianist Nat King Cole (1919–1965) recorded more than one hundred hit songs throughout his career and was among the first African Americans to host a TV series, *The Nat King Cole Show*, which debuted in 1956. Among his hits are "Straighten Up and Fly Right," "The Christmas Song," "Unforgettable," and "Looking Back." He died from lung cancer in 1965. In 1991, his daughter, singer Natalie Cole, recorded an album of covers of her father's songs, including a reworked version of "Unforgettable" using both her and her father's vocals.

Repeat References: Sonny Bono *(Episode 3.23: Mixed Blessings)*, *Sports Illustrated (Episode 2.16: And Then There Was One)*, *Designing Women (Episode 3.11: Three on a Couch)*, *Cheers (Episode 3.4: The Housekeeper)*

EPISODE 4.11: THE AUCTION

Directed by Terry Hughes. Written by Eric Cohen. Original airdate: January 14, 1989.

The girls attempt to purchase a painting at auction by an obnoxious artist who they have learned is dying.

Reference: Zorro

> **Blanche:** Last night, the damn ceiling caved in on my bedroom. Knocked the Zorro mask right out of poor Ed Rosen's hand.

Zorro is a fictional character created in 1919 by Johnston McCulley, typically portrayed as a vigilante in an all-black costume that includes a cape, hat, and mask. The character has appeared in multiple books, films, television series, radio dramas, stage productions, and comics.

Reference: *Murder, She Wrote*

> **Dorothy:** She has trouble following *Murder, She Wrote.*

Murder, She Wrote is a long-running CBS television series in which Angela Lansbury played Jessica Fletcher, a busybody mystery novelist with a penchant for becoming involved in, and solving, murders. The show ran from 1984 to 1996 and was followed by a series of made-for-TV movies. The show was watched by more than thirty million people at its peak, and Lansbury won four Golden Globes for the role.

Reference: Father Flanagan

> **Sophia:** You think I'm hiding Father Flanagan under here?

Father Edward J. Flanagan (1886–1948) was an Ireland-born priest who came to the United States in the early twentieth century and eventually founded Father Flanagan's Boys' Home after working with the homeless population in Omaha, Nebraska. The home eventually became Boys Town, which is still operating today.

Reference: Prime Minister Botha

> **Sophia:** I couldn't sleep so I'm having some tea, if that's okay with you, Prime Minister Botha.

Nicknamed *Die Groot Krokodil* ("The Great Crocodile"), P. W. Botha (1916–2006) was the fierce-willed prime minister of South Africa from 1978 to 1984 and its president from 1984 to 1989.

References: Sno-Caps, Devil Dogs, Ho Hos, the Twinkie defense

> **Rose:** I couldn't sleep either, but I think it was something I ate before bed.
>
> **Sophia:** What did you eat?
>
> **Rose:** Nothing out of the ordinary. A handful of Sno-Caps, a couple of Devil Dogs, some Oreos, and a Ho-Ho chopped up in a bowl of fruit cocktail with heavy syrup.
>
> **Dorothy:** Couldn't sleep? I'm surprised you didn't try to kill the mayor of San Francisco.

Sno-Caps are a brand of candy consisting of small pieces of chocolate candy covered in white sprinkles, first introduced in the 1920s. Devil Dogs are a snack food from the Drake's Cakes line of baked goods, which was founded in 1896. Devil Dogs are two pieces of devil's food cake sandwiched around vanilla-flavored cream. Ho Hos are cylindrical chocolate snack cakes with a cream filling. Dorothy's joke about the mayor of San Francisco is a reference to the "Twinkie defense," which was coined by journalists reporting the 1979 trial of Dan White, who was accused of killing San Francisco mayor George Moscone and city supervisor Harvey Milk. White's defense team claimed he was suffering from diminished capacity brought about by depression, a symptom of which was a change in his diet from healthy foods to sugary junk food. He was convicted of voluntary manslaughter, served five years of a seven-year sentence, and committed suicide in 1985.

Repeat References: Attica *(Episode 2.2: Ladies of the Evening)*, Liberace *(Episode 2.15: Before and After)*, Oreos *(Episode 1.16: The Truth Will Out)*, George H. W. Bush *(Episode 3.21: Larceny and Old Lace)*, Thirtysomething *(Episode 3.20: And Ma Makes Three)*

EPISODE 4.12: BLIND DATE
Directed by Terry Hughes. Written by Christopher Lloyd. Original airdate: January 28, 1989.
Blanche begins dating a blind man. Rose and Dorothy coach a youth football team.

References: Détente, *Masterpiece Theatre*

> **Sophia:** The man spins a big, wooden wheel for eight years, suddenly he's discussing détente with Henry Kissinger. What else happened lately? Mike Tyson hosting *Masterpiece Theatre*?

Détente was the Cold War policy of relaxing tensions between the Soviet Union and the West during the late 1960s and early 1970s. *Masterpiece Theatre* is an anthology series that premiered on PBS in 1971, presenting various acclaimed British productions, including book adaptations, biographies, mysteries, and series such as *Downton Abbey*. For its first twenty years, it was hosted by Alistair Cooke. It's now known simply as *Masterpiece*.

Reference: Lynn Redgrave

> **Sophia:** I had one of those Weight Watchers broccoli au gratins for lunch. Boy, that stuff's murder. I'm surprised Lynn Redgrave has a friend in the world.

Lynn Redgrave (1943–2010) was a Golden Globe Award–winning actress known for such films as *Tom Jones* and *Georgy Girl*. In the 1980s she appeared in a series of commercials for Weight Watchers frozen entrees.

Reference: Emmett Kelly

> **Rose:** I need help.
>
> **Sophia:** Mostly with your lipstick. Emmett Kelly applied makeup with more finesse.

Emmett Kelly (1898–1979) was a circus performer who created the Weary Willie clown character, based on the look of Depression-era hobos.

Reference: Raymond Burr

> **Dorothy:** Little bodies don't like it when big bodies fall on them.
>
> **Sophia:** Which is why Raymond Burr never married.

Actor Raymond Burr's (1917–1993) illustrious career included stage, radio, television, and film, including appearances in Alfred Hitchcock's *Rear Window* and the TV series *Ironside*. He is perhaps best remembered as playing the title role in *Perry Mason*, which ran on CBS from 1957 to 1966. He reprised the role in a successful string of TV movies from 1985 until his death in 1993. Burr was also well known for various philanthropic projects and business ventures like cultivating orchids and launching Raymond Burr Vineyards.

Reference: D-Day

> **Dorothy:** For God's sake, Rose, Eisenhower used less chalk planning D-Day!

D-Day refers to June 6, 1944, when 156,000 Allied forces invaded the beaches of Normandy during World War II. The Battle of Normandy lasted until August and resulted in the liberation of Western Europe from Nazi Germany control. D-Day is considered the beginning of the end of World War II. The term D-Day refers to a US Army designation that was used to indicate the start date for a field operation.

Reference: Frank Capra

> **Sophia:** I'm going for a moment here. You never saw a Frank Capra film?

One of the most esteemed film directors and producers of the 1930s and 1940s, Frank Capra (1897–1991) was at the helm of several classic movies, including *It Happened One Night, Mr. Smith Goes to Washington*, and *It's a Wonderful Life*.

Reference: Billy Barty

> **Sophia:** Being small isn't all bad. Take it from someone who knows.
>
> **Billy:** You mean you?
>
> **Sophia:** You see Billy Barty sitting here?

Actor Billy Barty (1924–2000) stood at three feet, nine inches, due to cartilage–hair hypoplasia dwarfism, and was usually cast in comedic roles to make use of his height. For instance, you may remember him as Rose's much-shorter-than-normal father during a dream scene in season one's "A Little Romance." Barty's filmography spans decades, from the 1930s all the way to the turn of the twenty-first century.

Reference: Danny DeVito

> **Sophia:** You think Danny DeVito got to be famous with his good looks?

Actor, director, and producer Danny DeVito rose to fame in the 1970s portraying taxi dispatcher Louie De Palma in the TV series *Taxi* and has had a successful film and television career ever since. Among his notable works are roles in *One Flew Over the Cuckoo's Nest, Terms of Endearment, Throw Momma from the Train, Twins, Batman Returns, Matilda, Man on the Moon,* and more. Standing at four feet, ten inches, DeVito is known for his short stature. He was married for decades to *Cheers* actress Rhea Perlman. The pair separated in 2017. In 2006, he joined the cast of *It's Always Sunny in Philadelphia*, the longest-running live-action comedy series in television history.

Repeat References: Pat Sajak *(Episode 1.18: The Operation)*, *Wheel of Fortune (Episode 2.19: Long Day's Journey into Marinara)*, Henry Kissinger *(Episode 2.7: Family Affair)*, Mike Tyson *(Episode 3.15: Dorothy's New Friend)*, Weight Watchers *(Episode 2.26: Empty Nests)*, George H. W. Bush *(Episode 3.21: Larceny and Old Lace)*, Dwight D. Eisenhower *(Episode 4.2: The Days and Nights of Sophia Petrillo)*, Benito Mussolini *(Episode 3.7: Strange Bedfellows)*, World War II *(Episode 3.12: Charlie's Buddy)*

EPISODE 4.13: THE IMPOTENCE OF BEING ERNEST
Directed by Steve Zuckerman. Teleplay by Rick Copp and David A. Goodman. Story by Kevin Abbott. Original airdate: February 4, 1989.
Rose wonders why her new boyfriend refuses to be intimate. Sophia must settle an old Sicilian vendetta.

Reference: Pizza Hut

Sophia: They must've painted the men's room walls at the Pizza Hut.

Pizza Hut is a restaurant chain founded in 1958 by Dan and Frank Carney, known for an Italian American menu of pizza, pasta, side dishes, and desserts.

Reference: *South Pacific*

Dorothy: A dead rabbit means "My husband knows, get out of town."
Rose: Knows what?
Dorothy: The score to *South Pacific*, Rose.

South Pacific is a 1949 Broadway musical by Rodgers and Hammerstein based on the James A. Michener book *Tales of the South Pacific*, about a nurse who falls in love with an expatriate plantation owner.

Reference: Robin Givens

> **Blanche:** I cannot believe a man like that would be interested in Rose.
>
> **Dorothy:** Well, I guess he's not perfect after all.
>
> **Blanche:** That's right, Dorothy! Thank you. I feel so much better.
>
> **Dorothy:** We're living with Robin Givens.

Actress Robin Givens rose to fame in the 1980s as a cast member of the ABC sitcom *Head of the Class*, which debuted in 1986 and ran for five seasons. In 1987, she began a high-profile relationship with boxer Mike Tyson. The pair wed in February 1988, but by that fall accusations of physical abuse surfaced. Givens filed for divorce in October 1988, citing spousal abuse.

Reference: *The People's Court*

> **Sophia:** It's a vendetta, not *The People's Court*.

The People's Court is a reality court TV show launched in 1981. It was presided over by Judge Joseph Wapner until 1993. Judges Ed Koch, Jerry Sheindlin, and Marilyn Milian have also presided, with Milian holding the bench since 2001.

Reference: The Human Torch

> **Blanche:** Sometimes you have to stoke a man's fire a little bit.
>
> **Sophia:** Words of wisdom from the Human Torch.

The Human Torch is a fictional superhero in Marvel Comics titles, such as *The Fantastic Four*. The character first appeared in 1961 and is known for the ability to engulf his entire body in flames.

Reference: *Citizen Kane*

> **Rose:** Through most of *Citizen Kane*, we all thought everybody was looking for a rowboat.

A 1941 drama film produced, cowritten, directed, and starring Orson Welles, *Citizen Kane* is the story of tycoon Charles Foster Kane, who, on his death-bed, utters the word "Rosebud" (not rowboat). The film is considered by many to be the greatest of all time and was nominated for Academy Awards in nine categories.

Reference: Peter Allen

> **Dorothy:** A tan bamboo purse was found at the scene. Do you know what that means?
>
> **Blanche:** The man was murdered on his way to a Peter Allen concert?

Peter Allen (1944–1992) was an Australian singer/songwriter/entertainer known for lavish costumes and a flamboyant stage persona. He cowrote the Oscar-winning theme to the movie *Arthur*, had a hit with "I Go to Rio" and other tunes, and had his songs covered by the likes of Olivia Newton-John. He married Liza Minnelli in 1967. They divorced seven years later, and he then began a longtime relationship with model Gregory Connell. Allen died of AIDS-related throat cancer in 1992. A musical about his life, called *The Boy from Oz*, won Hugh Jackman a 2004 Tony award for Best Actor in a Musical.

Reference: Etch A Sketch

> **Sophia:** I'll get the Etch A Sketch. At my age, I need a visual aid.

An Etch A Sketch is a mechanical drawing toy introduced in 1960 and consisting of a flat gray screen in a red plastic frame with two round knobs in the lower front corners. Twisting the knobs operates them like a stylus to displace aluminum powder onto the back of the screen, which makes a solid line and allows the user to sketch beautiful artwork—or, more likely, ugly squiggly lines.

Repeat References: Ed McMahon *(Episode 2.2: Ladies of the Evening)*, Barbara Walters *(Episode 1.20: Adult Education)*, Gandhi *(Episode 1.13: A Little Romance)*

EPISODE 4.14: LOVE ME TENDER
Directed by Terry Hughes. Written by Richard Vaczy and Tracy Gamble. Original airdate: February 6, 1989.
Sophia objects to Dorothy's strictly physical relationship with her new beau. Blanche and Rose volunteer to mentor two teenage girls.

Reference: Janet Gaynor

> **Sophia:** I didn't send in your picture, I sent the picture that came with my wallet.

Dorothy: Ma, I am furious with you.

Sophia: Think how mad your date's going to be when he finds out he's not going out with Janet Gaynor.

Actress Janet Gaynor (1906–1984) began working in the silent film era and successfully transitioned into sound films in the 1920s, becoming the first actress to win the Academy Award for Best Actress. Her notable films include *7th Heaven, Sunrise: A Song of Two Humans*, and *Street Angel*. She died in 1984 from injuries sustained during a car accident.

Reference: Dear John letter

Eddie: After twenty-five years of marriage, my wife, Roberta, sent me a Dear John letter.

Rose: That's terrible. Married twenty-five years and she doesn't know your name is Eddie?

A Dear John letter is written from a wife or girlfriend to her significant other informing him that she's leaving him for someone else. While the origin of the phrase is unknown, it's believed to have surfaced during World War II, when women on the home front wrote letters dumping their soldier spouses and boyfriends. The phrase was also used in the title of a 1980s British sitcom which ran for two seasons and was adapted for US television in 1989. The US version, which starred *Taxi*'s Judd Hirsch, ran for four seasons.

References: *Oliver & Company, Who Framed Roger Rabbit, Tequila Sunrise*

Jackie: Would it be asking too much to see a movie?

Rose: Oh, no. We can go see *Oliver & Company* or *Roger Rabbit*.

Jackie: Or *Tequila Sunrise*! I hear Mel Gibson takes his shirt off a lot.

Oliver & Company is a 1988 animated Disney musical based on the Charles Dickens novel *Oliver Twist*, about a homeless kitten who befriends a group of dogs on the streets of New York. *Who Framed Roger Rabbit* is an Academy Award–winning 1988 comedy-mystery film that blended live action and animation, set in a 1940s version of Hollywood where cartoon characters and people coexisted. The plot centers around a detective's attempt to exonerate a cartoon rabbit accused of murdering a wealthy businessman. Bob Hoskins, Christopher Lloyd, and Joanna Cassidy starred. *Tequila Sunrise* is a 1988 crime thriller starring Mel Gibson, Michelle Pfeiffer, and Kurt Russell.

Reference: *Dumbo*

> **Blanche:** I do think I should caution you, they were meant for petite ears.
>
> **Dorothy:** They'll just have to do until Disney unveils their *Dumbo* line.

Dumbo is a 1941 animated film from Disney depicting a young circus elephant with giant floppy ears, a source of ridicule until he realizes those ears afford him the ability to fly.

Reference: "There's something rotten in the state of Denmark."

> **Blanche:** You know, there's something rotten in the state of Denmark.
>
> **Rose:** It's their cheese. They refuse to use preservatives.

This is a line from William Shakespeare's *Hamlet*, which has come to generally describe a situation in which something is wrong.

Reference: Nelson Mandela

> **Dorothy:** You're a regular Nelson Mandela, Rose.

Nelson Mandela (1918–2013) was a South African anti-apartheid revolutionary and political leader who served as South Africa's president from 1994 to 1999.

Reference: Bing Crosby

> **Sophia:** Boy, I wish I'd married Bing Crosby when I had the chance.
>
> **Blanche:** Why, because he was such a strict disciplinarian?
>
> **Sophia:** No, because now I'd be a wealthy widow with my own place in Pebble Beach, so I wouldn't have to listen to that crap.

Actor, comedian, and singer Bing Crosby (1903–1977) made over seventy films and recorded well over a thousand songs during his five-decade career. Among his most notable works are *Going My Way*, for which he won an Oscar, *The Country Girl*, and a series of musical comedy films alongside Bob Hope. His recording of "White Christmas" and the film of the same name in which he starred, alongside Danny Kaye, Rosemary Clooney, and Vera-Ellen, are holiday staples.

References: *Miami Herald*

> **Sophia:** I'd feel terrible if you came home one morning and found me on the doorstep instead of the *Miami Herald*.

The *Miami Herald* is Miami's daily newspaper, established in 1903.

References: Pearl Harbor, Colonel Gaddafi

> **Sophia:** Don't underestimate me. I could make you feel guilty about bombing Pearl Harbor if I wanted. The point is, I don't want you to feel guilty. There's nothing wrong with a physical relationship.
>
> **Dorothy:** Then what about what you said last night?
>
> **Sophia:** If you'd let me finish my thought, Colonel Gaddafi, you might've understood.

Pearl Harbor is a harbor in Hawaii that was the site of a surprise military attack by the Japanese upon the United States, which led to the latter's formal entry into World War II. The attack led to the death of 2,403 Americans. Muammar Gaddafi (1942–2011) was a Libyan revolutionary and politician who served as Brotherly Leader and Guide of the Revolution of Libya from 1977 until his assassination in 2011.

Repeat References: Jim and Tammy Faye Bakker *(Episode 3.7: Strange Bedfellows)*, Old Spice *(Episode 4.1: Yes, We Have No Havanas)*, Bambi *(Episode 3.11: Three on a Couch)*

EPISODE 4.15: VALENTINE'S DAY
Directed by Terry Hughes. Written by Kathy Speer, Terry Grossman, Barry Fanaro, and Mort Nathan. Original airdate: February 11, 1989.
The girls reminisce about past Valentine's Day celebrations.

Reference: C. Everett Koop

> **Sophia:** Big deal. We took a bite out of the same piece of chocolate. Call C. Everett Koop.

C. Everett Koop (1916–2013) was a prominent pediatric surgeon who served as the surgeon general of the United States under President Ronald Reagan.

Reference: Cold-water flat

> **Sal:** I'll have us out of here in no time.

Papa Angelo: The same words he used when he moved you into that crummy cold-water flat twelve years ago.

A cold-water flat was an apartment with no running hot water that was common in such cities as Detroit, Chicago, and New York until the mid-twentieth century. Today's building codes make them illegal.

Reference: Studs Terkel

Sophia: In those days, Chicago stood for two things.

Rose: What were they?

Sophia: How the hell should I know? What am I, Studs Terkel?

Studs Terkel (1912–2008) was an author, actor, and radio host who received the Pulitzer Prize in 1985 for *The Good War*, an oral history of World War II.

References: Pinkerton guard, Nestlé Crunch, Dentu-Grip

Blanche: It might be a good idea to take along some protection.

Rose: What kind of protection?

Dorothy: Two armed Pinkerton guards! No, Blanche is talking about . . . (*points*)

Rose: A Nestlé's Crunch?

Dorothy: One over.

Rose: An enema bag?

Dorothy: To the right.

Rose: Dentu-Grip?

Dorothy: Condoms, Rose! Condoms! Condoms! Condoms!

A Pinkerton guard is a private security guard with the Pinkerton National Detective Agency, founded by Scotsman Allan Pinkerton in 1850. Nestlé Crunch is a popular candy bar introduced in 1928, consisting of milk chocolate and crisped rice. Dentu-Grip is a denture adhesive that first appeared in the 1940s.

Reference: Coors Light

Sophia: Of course I was. These dimwits' idea of romance is a Coors Light and a *Love Boat* rerun.

Coors Light is a light beer introduced by the Coors Brewing Company in 1978.

Reference: Marzipan

> **Sophia:** You got a marzipan bar in your ear?

Marzipan is a candy-like mixture used in baking, typically consisting of finely ground almonds, sugar, corn syrup, and egg whites.

Reference: "Begin the Beguine"

> **Sophia:** Once we hit Wolfie's deli, I would appreciate it if you would serenade me with "Begin the Beguine."

"Begin the Beguine" is a 1930s tune written by Cole Porter and covered by everyone from Artie Shaw and His Orchestra to Frank Sinatra. The beguine is a dance akin to the rhumba.

Repeat References: St. Valentine's Day Massacre *(Episode 3.22: Rose's Big Adventure)*, David Horowitz *(Episode 2.10: Love, Rose)*, Julio Iglesias *(Episode 1.1: Pilot)*, *The Love Boat (Episode 2.19: Long Day's Journey into Marinara)*, Wolfie's *(Episode 2.1: End of the Curse)*

EPISODE 4.16: TWO RODE TOGETHER
Directed by Terry Hughes. Written by Robert Bruce and Martin Weiss. Original airdate: February 18, 1989.
Dorothy takes Sophia to Disney World for quality bonding time. Rose and Blanche collaborate on a children's book.

Reference: Marilyn Quayle

> **Rose:** It made Toonder's wife miserable that her husband was best known for being mediocre.
>
> **Blanche:** I understand Marilyn Quayle feels the same way.

Marilyn Quayle is the wife of former vice president Dan Quayle.

Reference: The Bates Motel

> **Sophia:** She told me we were going to a resort. We pull up to this place that looks like the Bates Motel, two goons in white coats drag

me inside, and for the next year and a half I'm forced to make lanyards against my will.

The Bates Motel is the fictional roadside stop overseen by proprietor Norman Bates in Alfred Hitchcock's 1960 thriller *Psycho* (itself based on a 1959 novel by Robert Bloch). The film, starring Anthony Perkins and Janet Leigh, is considered a classic and among Hitchcock's best works. The movie has garnered several sequels, a 1998 remake, and a prequel series, titled *Bates Motel*, which ran for five seasons.

Reference: Bill Moyers

> **Sophia:** A journal? Who the hell are you, Bill Moyers?

Bill Moyers is a journalist and political commentator who served as White House press secretary from 1965 to 1967, under the Johnson administration, and has worked on or hosted many television news programs.

Reference: "Hey Sam, what's that you're playing?"

> *Sophia says this to the piano player at the hotel bar.*

This whole bit is a spin on an exchange between nightclub owner Rick Blaine (Humphrey Bogart) and pianist Sam (Dooley Wilson) from the 1942 classic film *Casablanca*.

Reference: *On Golden Pond*

> **Sophia:** Dorothy, this isn't *On Golden Pond*. And you're not Jane Fonda.

On Golden Pond is a 1981 drama film based on the play of the same name, starring Katharine Hepburn and Henry Fonda as an elderly couple who summer at an idyllic New England vacation home.

References: "A thousand points of light," Barbara Bush

> **Sophia:** I tell you, I saw a thousand points of light. It was a kinder, gentler America. I turned to my wife, Barbara, and I said—
> **Dorothy:** Ma, what the hell are you talking about?

"A thousand points of light" is a phrase popularized by President George H. W. Bush in his speech accepting the 1988 Republican presidential nomination, describing America's volunteer organizations and clubs as "a thousand points of light in a broad and peaceful sky." The First Lady of the United

States from 1989 to 1993, Barbara Bush (1925–2018) married George H. W. Bush in 1945. During *The Golden Girls* era, Bush was serving as Second Lady of the United States during the two-term presidency of Ronald Reagan before George announced his own candidacy in 1988.

Reference: Kodak

> **Sophia:** It's the same with all magical moments. You can't capture them forever, no matter what Kodak tells you.

Kodak is a company founded in 1888 and best known during *The Golden Girls* era for its dominant position in the industry of photographic film. It has since moved into other business segments like print systems, 3-D printing, and software.

Repeat References: Johnny Cash *(Episode 3.4: The Housekeeper)*, Disney World *(Episode 1.4: Transplant)*, Space Mountain *(Episode 1.16: The Truth Will Out)*, The Ed Sullivan Show *(Episode 3.20: And Ma Makes Three)*, Howard Johnson *(Episode 2.6: Big Daddy's Little Lady)*, "It's a Small World (After All)" *(Episode 2.19: Long Day's Journey Into Marinara)*, Jane Fonda *(Episode 2.18: Forgive Me, Father)*, George H. W. Bush *(Episode 3.21: Larceny and Old Lace)*, Mr. Belvedere *(Episode 4.5: Bang the Drum, Stanley)*

EPISODE 4.17: YOU GOTTA HAVE HOPE

Directed by Terry Hughes. Written by Barry Fanaro and Mort Nathan. Original airdate: February 25, 1989.

Rose attempts to secure Bob Hope to emcee a local talent show after announcing that she believes him to be her estranged father. Sophia attempts to get her new boyfriend into the show.

References: "Puff the Magic Dragon," Barbara Mandrell

> **Bodybuilder, after singing "Puff":** If I increase my steroids by one hundred milligrams, I can sing just like Barbara Mandrell.

"Puff the Magic Dragon" is a song released in 1963 by folk trio Peter, Paul and Mary, based on a poem by Leonard Lipton. It was adapted into a 1978 TV special. Barbara Mandrell is a country music icon known for a series of hits in the 1970s and 1980s, including "Sleeping Single in a Double Bed" and "I Was Country When Country Wasn't Cool." With sisters Irlene and Louise, she hosted her own prime-time variety series in the early 1980s, *Barbara*

Mandrell and the Mandrell Sisters, and was the first person to win the County Music Association's Entertainer of the Year award twice—not to mention a slew of other accolades, including two Grammys.

References: Ricky Ricardo, Ryan O'Neal

> **Sophia:** "You can't be in the show, you can't be in the show." Who are you, Ricky Ricardo? For your information, I'm not here to audition.
>
> **Rose:** Why are you here?
>
> **Sophia:** I realized I had no talent, so I decided to become an agent. Why Ryan O'Neal hasn't come to the same conclusion, I'll never understand.

Ricky Ricardo was a fictional character on the classic sitcom *I Love Lucy,* played by Desi Arnaz. Ricky, a bandleader, was always trying to stop Lucy from performing in his shows. Ryan O'Neal is an actor and former boxer who starred in *Peyton Place, Love Story, What's Up, Doc?, Paper Moon,* and other films. More recently, he had a recurring role on the Fox series *Bones.*

References: "Neutron Dance," the Del Rubio Triplets

> *The song is performed by the Donatello Triplets at the talent show audition.*

"Neutron Dance" was a Top 10 hit by the Pointer Sisters, written by Allee Willis and Danny Sembello. It was released by the group in 1983 and became a hit once featured on the soundtrack to *Beverly Hills Cop.* On *The Golden Girls,* the song was covered by the Del Rubio Triplets, playing the Donatello Triplets. In real life, the triplets were singing sisters Eadie, Elena, and Milly Del Rubio, who rose to fame in the 1980s with their campy look and television appearances on shows like *Pee-wee's Playhouse* and various Bob Hope specials.

References: *The Accidental Tourist,* Critic's Corner

> **Blanche:** He wandered over to the Critic's Corner and lost his cookies on Gene Shalit. Gene thought it was because Willard disagreed with his review of *The Accidental Tourist.*

The Accidental Tourist is a 1988 drama film starring William Hurt, Kathleen Turner, Bill Pullman, and Geena Davis, in a role that won the latter an Oscar. In fact, the film scored four Oscar nods in all, including Best Picture. The Critic's Corner was Gene Shalit's review segment on the *Today* show.

References: *Phantom of the Opera*, W. Somerset Maugham

> **Sophia:** The two of you have a look on your face like you paid for *Phantom of the Opera* tickets. Excuse me for not being Somerset Maugham.

Phantom of the Opera was originally a 1910 novel by French writer Gaston Leroux, but it's perhaps best known for its successful 1986 stage adaptation by Andrew Lloyd Webber, Charles Hart, and Richard Stilgoe. Its plot revolves around a young singer's obsession with a mysterious, disfigured man living beneath the Paris Opera House. W. Somerset Maugham (1874–1965) was an author and playwright known for such works as *Of Human Bondage*, *The Painted Veil*, and *The Razor's Edge*.

Reference: *Miracle on 34th Street*

> **Dorothy:** Rose, this is not *Miracle on 34th Street*!

Miracle on 34th Street is an Oscar-winning 1947 Christmas movie based on a story by Valentine Davies, about a Macy's Department Store Santa Claus who may or may not be the real thing. The film starred Maureen O'Hara, John Payne, Edmund Gwenn, and Natalie Wood. A remake was released in 1994.

Reference: Sam Snead

> **Dorothy:** He's not going to do a favor for three people who look like Sam Snead with a hormone problem.

Sam Snead (1912–2002) was a professional golfer who was regarded as one of the best players of all time.

Reference: "These Boots Are Made for Walkin'"

> *This song is sung by the Donatello Triplets.*

"These Boots Are Made for Walkin'" is a 1966 hit song written by Lee Hazlewood and recorded by Nancy Sinatra.

Reference: Franklin Delano Roosevelt

> **Bob Hope:** Reagan left office with the highest popularity rating since FDR.

Franklin D. Roosevelt (1882–1945), often referred to as FDR, was the president of the United States from 1933 until his death in 1945, winning a record four presidential elections and known for implementing his New Deal domestic agenda following the Great Depression.

Reference: Sam Donaldson

> **Bob Hope:** Earthquakes don't bother the president. If Sam Donaldson couldn't shake him up, nothing will.

Sam Donaldson is a former reporter and news anchor who worked for ABC News from 1967 until his retirement in 2013. He was the network's White House correspondent for several years and coanchored the Sunday program *This Week.* In addition to his storied career as a journalist, Donaldson was also known for his prominent eyebrows.

Repeat References: Willard Scott and *Today (Episode 1.3: Rose the Prude)*, Gene Shalit *(Episode 3.4: The Housekeeper)*, Bob Hope *(Episode 1.9: Blanche and the Younger Man)*, NBC *(Episode 1.20: Adult Education)*, Joan Collins *(Episode 2.1: End of the Curse)*, vaudeville *(Episode 2.26: Empty Nests)*, Ronald Reagan *(Episode 3.6: Letter to Gorbachev)*, Tammy Faye Bakker *(Episode 3.7: Strange Bedfellows)*, Maybelline *(Episode 1.9: Blanche and the Younger Man)*, Nancy Reagan *(Episode 1.4: Transplant)*

EPISODE 4.18: FIDDLER ON THE ROPES

Directed by Terry Hughes. Written by Kathy Speer and Terry Grossman. Original airdate: March 4, 1989.
Sophia uses the other girls' investment money to purchase a prizefighter.

Reference: Social Security

> **Blanche:** I wonder if you can collect Social Security at forty-nine, fifty.
>
> **Dorothy:** Forty-nine fifty. What is that, Blanche, the address of the Social Security building?

Social Security refers to the federal Old-Age, Survivors, and Disability Insurance program, originally signed into law by Franklin D. Roosevelt in 1935.

Reference: Harriet Nelson

> **Sophia:** Okay, so I don't turn a phrase like Harriet Nelson.

Harriet Nelson (1909–1994) was an actress and singer best known for her role on the sitcom *The Adventures of Ozzie and Harriet*, which aired on ABC from 1952 to 1966 and starred the real-life Nelson family—husband Ozzie, wife Harriet, and their sons.

References: Golda Meir, Oscar Mayer

> **Dorothy:** Ma, you never met Golda Meir.
>
> **Sophia:** Please, I almost married her husband, the man who perfected the hot dog.
>
> **Both:** Oscar Mayer.

Golda Meir (1898–1978) was prime minister of Israel from 1969 to 1974. Oscar Mayer is a meat and cold-cut company known for hot dogs and other processed-meat items, founded in 1883 by its namesake, Oscar F. Mayer (1859–1955).

Reference: Everlast

> **Dorothy:** Blanche, Everlast is a brand name, not a nickname.

Everlast is a popular brand of boxing, martial arts, and fitness clothing, shoes, and accessories founded in 1910.

Reference: "Hath not a Jew eyes?"

> **Pepe:** I am a Cuban, but hath not a Cuban eyes?

This monologue is a spin on a famous William Shakespeare–penned speech from *The Merchant of Venice*.

Reference: Chevy Chase

> **Sophia:** Why does every fighter become an actor? Just once I'd like it the other way around, if for no other reason than to see Chevy Chase get his butt kicked.

Actor, writer, and comedian Chevy Chase rose to fame in the 1970s as a cast member and writer on *The National Lampoon Radio Hour*, which he followed up with a gig as an original cast member on *Saturday Night Live*, which launched in 1975. Chase went on to a successful career in films throughout the 1980s, including his iconic role as Clark Griswold in a series of National Lampoon "Vacation" films. The 1990s weren't too kind to him, with a string of box office duds and an ill-fated late-night talk show, but he rebounded with a role in the 2009 NBC series *Community*. Long known to be volatile presence on sets, he left the show in its fourth season after a public feud with its creator.

Reference: *Golden Boy*

> **Dorothy:** Are we back to real life or are the two of you performing a scene from *Golden Boy*?

Golden Boy is a 1964 musical with a book by Clifford Odets and William Gibson, lyrics by Lee Adams, and music by Charles Strouse, adapted from Odets's 1937 stage play. It's about a young man from Harlem who turns to prizefighting to escape his ghetto roots.

Repeat References: Robin Givens *(Episode 4.13: The Impotence of Being Ernest)*, Don King *(Episode 1.20: Adult Education)*, Sylvester Stallone *(Episode 1.6: On Golden Girls)*, Jimmy Swaggart *(Episode 3.22: Rose's Big Adventure)*, Macbeth *(Episode 1.12: The Custody Battle)*

Episode 4.19: 'Til Death Do We Volley
Directed by Terry Hughes. Written by Richard Vaczy and Tracy Gamble. Original airdate: March 18, 1989.
Dorothy's reunion with her competitive friend, Trudy, is marred when Trudy collapses during a tennis match.

Reference: The Nobel Prize

> **Dorothy:** Didn't you go to school with that brilliant doctor who won the Nobel Prize?
>
> **Blanche:** Oh yes, but she let her looks go to hell.

The Nobel Prize is a prestigious annual award bestowed by Swedish and Norwegian institutions, honoring outstanding contributions for humanity in areas such as chemistry, literature, physics, medicine, and peace. It was first awarded in 1901.

Reference: Scotch Tape

> **Rose:** In our breakfast room we had one whole wall covered in "Kick Me" signs we had collected. There was a story attached to each one of them, and in some cases the original Scotch Tape.

Scotch Tape is a brand of pressure-sensitive tape manufactured by 3M, first introduced in 1930.

Reference: *Nova*

> **Sophia:** What is this, *Nova?* I don't have all the answers.

Nova is a popular science television show broadcast on PBS since 1974.

Reference: The Daughters of the Confederacy

> **Blanche:** My mama took one look at Kathie Lee and forbade me ever to see her again.
>
> **Rose:** Why?
>
> **Blanche:** Her mother was not in the Daughters of the Confederacy.

The United Daughters of the Confederacy may have been good for a Blanche joke in the 1980s, but the actual association of Southern women, established in Nashville in 1894, has been labeled a white supremacist group by some for its efforts aimed at commemorating and erecting statues for Confederate soldiers.

Reference: Cadillac Eldorado

> **Blanche:** Years later, to get back at me, Kathie Lee slept with my daddy. That was something I had to accept. Mama accepted it, too, along with a brand-new Cadillac Eldorado for her birthday.

The Cadillac Eldorado was a luxury automobile manufactured by Cadillac from 1952 to 2002.

References: The House of Savoy, Giuseppe Garibaldi, the Crimean War

> **Sophia:** It was mid-century and a disillusioned Italy looked to the House of Savoy for leadership. Giuseppe Garibaldi, our courageous leader, and not a bad dresser, thought, let's regain some national pride and jump into this Crimean War thing.

The House of Savoy was a royal dynasty dating back to 1003 in the historical Savoy region in Europe. Giuseppe Garibaldi (1807–1882) was an Italian general who led a movement that helped unify Italy. The Crimean War was a military conflict fought over religious rights between Russia and an alliance of the Ottoman Empire, the United Kingdom, Sardinia, and France. The war began in 1853 and lasted until 1856, when Russia lost.

Repeat Reference: Jane Fonda *(Episode 2.18: Forgive Me, Father)*

Episode 4.20: High Anxiety

Directed by Terry Hughes. Written by Martin Weiss and Robert Bruce. Original airdate: March 25, 1989.

Rose battles an addiction to painkillers. Dorothy and Sophia are hired to appear in a pizza commercial.

Reference: Soda jerk

> **Dorothy:** Didn't I tell you I used to work in a malt shop in high school?
>
> **Blanche:** Soda jerk?
>
> **Rose:** No thanks, I'll have a malted.

A soda jerk was the person who operated the soda fountain in a drugstore.

Reference: Krugerrand

> **Sophia:** Once upon a time, I had a butt you could bounce a quarter on. Now you could lose a Krugerrand in the creases.

A Krugerrand is a South African gold coin first minted in 1967.

Reference: Roseanne Barr

> **Sy:** If I wanted this kind of abuse, I'd be directing the Roseanne Barr show.

Brash stand-up comedian Roseanne Barr catapulted to fame in 1988 as the star of her own self-titled sitcom, *Roseanne*, which ran for nine seasons. Costarring John Goodman and Laurie Metcalf, the show followed the fictional Conners, a working-class family in a struggling factory town outside Chicago. In more recent years, Barr, the previously liberal actress, did an about face and became a rather radically vocal conservative known for ill-timed and occasionally incoherent statements. In 2018, though, things looked up when *Roseanne* was rebooted for ABC and debuted to tremendous ratings. Barr's penchant to speak before thinking, however, embroiled her in a controversy later that year when she tweeted a racist remark about Valerie

Jarrett, an advisor during the Obama administration. ABC fired Barr from the series bearing her name, killed off her character, and rebooted the reboot as *The Conners.*

References: Betty Ford, Liza Minnelli, *Arthur 2: On the Rocks*

> **Dorothy:** What is there to be ashamed of? You have a medical problem. Was Betty Ford embarrassed? Was Liza Minnelli embarrassed?
>
> **Sophia:** She should've been. Did you see *Arthur 2?*

The wife of Gerald Ford, Betty Ford (1918–2011) served as First Lady of the United States from 1974 to 1977. She was quite active in political issues, a Republican with moderate to liberal stances on issues such as women's rights, equal pay, abortion, and gun control. Following her White House years, Ford—who had admitted to her own battles with drug and alcohol abuse—founded the Betty Ford Center for substance abuse and addiction and was awarded the Congressional Gold Medal and the Presidential Medal of Freedom.

Liza Minnelli is an Emmy-, Grammy-, Oscar-, and Tony-winning actress and singer best known for her roles in *Cabaret, Flora, the Red Menace, Liza with a Z, Arthur, Arrested Development,* and for being the daughter of Judy Garland. *Arthur 2: On the Rocks* is a good example of a sequel not living up to its predecessor. This 1988 comedy reunited Dudley Moore and Minnelli as drunken millionaire Arthur Bach and his wife, Linda. The 1981 original film, a box office hit whose theme song won an Oscar, saw the wealthy Arthur jilt his fiancée to be with the lower-class Linda. The sequel deals with the couple's attempts to adopt a child and fend off the out-for-revenge jilted ex and her family. The film was a critical and box office dud for Dudley.

Reference: Monopoly

> **Blanche:** You said we were going to play Monopoly.
>
> **Rose:** I said it was like Monopoly, only instead of Atlantic City they use St. Olaf geography.

Monopoly is a classic real estate–themed board game introduced in 1935, in which players move around a board buying, trading, and developing properties in an attempt to bankrupt the other players.

Reference: Fred Flintstone

> **Dorothy:** This is Fred Flintstone. His nose is dissolved, but it's definitely Fred Flintstone.

Fred Flintstone was the animated protagonist of *The Flintstones*, an animated prime-time sitcom set in the Stone Age, focusing on Fred and his wife, Wilma. Fred worked in a quarry, Wilma kept house, and the pair frequently socialized with their next-door neighbors Barney and Betty Rubble while facing then-modern situations in their prehistoric setting. The show ran for six seasons from 1960 to 1966 and spawned decades' worth of spinoffs, animated films, merchandise, theme park attractions, and a live-action 1993 film starring John Goodman as Fred. In addition to the show, the characters are cemented in pop culture history thanks to the enduringly popular Flintstones brand of chewable vitamins for kids.

Reference: Broadway

> **Rose:** Gordon could cluck the scores of all the big Broadway musicals. I've heard a lot of poultry do show tunes, but nobody could hold a candle to him. Of course, no chicken likes to be that near an open flame.

Broadway refers to the live stage performances of musicals and plays presented in New York City's theater district along Broadway (the street) in Midtown Manhattan. Like London's West End, Broadway is considered the highest level of success in US live theater.

Reference: Gilbert and Sullivan

> **Rose:** Oh how he loved music. Especially Gilbert and Sullivan.

Playwright W. S. Gilbert (1836–1911) and composer Arthur Sullivan (1842–1900) teamed up for a series of comic operas near the turn of the twentieth century, including the well-known *H.M.S. Pinafore*, *The Pirates of Penzance*, and *The Mikado*.

Repeat Reference: NBA *(Episode 3.17: My Brother, My Father)*

Episode 4.21: Little Sister
Directed by Terry Hughes. Written by Christopher Lloyd. Original airdate: April 1, 1989.

Rose feels left out of the friendship between her visiting sister Holly and Dorothy and Blanche. In a crossover with *Empty Nest*, Sophia agrees to take care of Harry Weston's dog, Dreyfuss.

Reference: "I Have a Dream" speech

> **Sophia:** That's emphasis. You never heard the "I Have a Dream" speech?

The "I Have a Dream" speech is an iconic public speech delivered by civil rights activist Martin Luther King Jr. during the 1963 March on Washington for Jobs and Freedom, in which he called for civil rights and an end to racism.

Reference: Aetna

> **Sophia:** Hospital? Like your father was a member of the Aetna family.

Aetna is a health insurance provider.

Reference: Steve Garvey

> **Sophia:** I just hope I'm not carrying Steve Garvey's baby.

Steve Garvey is a former professional baseball player who played with the Los Angeles Dodgers and the San Diego Padres throughout the 1970s and 1980s. Garvey was known for a wholesome image throughout his time on the field, which ended when he retired in 1987. That image took a hit in 1989, when two women came forward claiming to be carrying his child while he'd recently gotten married to a third, and the accusations became comedic fodder, with radio stations putting out bumper stickers reading "Honk if you're carrying Steve Garvey's baby."

Reference: Rabbinical students

> **Sophia:** Now I can save what I know about you and the twin rabbinical students for another time.

A rabbinical school is one that prepares students to become rabbis.

Reference: Rodan

> **Dorothy:** Lately you've been eating like a bird.
> **Sophia:** Yeah, Rodan.

Rodan is a fictional flying, prehistoric monster introduced in the 1956 film *Rodan* who went on to appear in multiple *Godzilla* films.

Reference: Twinkie

> **Blanche:** Her hair's not the color of a Twinkie.

A Twinkie is a snack cake introduced in 1930, consisting of a golden sponge cake with a creamy filling.

Reference: Socrates

> **Sophia:** Socrates sat under an olive tree in a sheet for years thinking about this kind of stuff. I'm a poor immigrant with a third-grade education. Give me two minutes!

Socrates (470–399 BC) was an ancient Greek philosopher known as one of the founders of Western philosophy.

Reference: Gap

> **Blanche:** Where did those pants come from?
>
> **Dorothy:** According to the label, the Gap.

Gap is a clothing store chain founded by Donald and Doris H. Fisher. The first Gap opened in San Francisco in 1969. The store expanded throughout the 1970s and became a popular mall hot spot throughout the 1980s and 1990s.

Repeat References: Dr. Harry Weston and Dreyfuss *(Episode 4.4: Yokel Hero)*, Oscars *(Episode 2.2: Ladies of the Evening)*

EPISODE 4.22: SOPHIA'S CHOICE
Directed by Terry Hughes. Written by Richard Vaczy and Tracy Gamble. Original airdate: April 15, 1989.
Sophia attempts to help her friend, Lillian, who has been moved into an ill-equipped nursing home. Blanche hopes to use a bonus at work to fund breast augmentation surgery.

Reference: Sing Sing

> **Sophia:** Oh, you remember Shady Pines? That retirement home you stuck me in that resembles Sing Sing.

Sing Sing Correctional Facility is a maximum-security prison in Ossining, New York, opened in 1826.

Reference: Kaopectate

> **Sophia:** It's every old person's nightmare. That and a childproof cap on the Kaopectate bottle.

Kaopectate is an over-the-counter medication used to treat diarrhea.

Reference: *War and Remembrance*

> **Sophia:** You have to get into it more before you realize how bad it really is—just like *War and Remembrance*.

War and Remembrance is a 1988–1989 World War II miniseries based on the 1978 Herman Wouk novel of the same name.

Reference: *Chinatown*

> **Sophia:** If you want to get a clearer picture, I suggest you rent the cassette of *Chinatown*.

Chinatown is a 1979 neo-noir mystery/drama film directed by Roman Polanski and starring Jack Nicholson and Faye Dunaway. Set in 1937, it deals with the manipulation of a municipal resource—water—for financial gain.

References: "Remember the *Maine*!," HBO

> **Sophia:** Remember the *Maine*? She didn't. She was a frogman and swam right into the bulkhead. They put a metal plate in her head. Now she gets HBO through her eyeballs.

The USS *Maine* was a US Navy ship that sank in the Havana Harbor in 1898, which contributed to the outbreak of the Spanish-American War. The sentiment "Remember the Maine! To hell with Spain!" became a rallying cry for action, propelled by inaccurate reporting by the media that suggested the ship sank as a result of an external attack. It was eventually discovered that the source of the explosion was an accident aboard the ship, not from Spanish attack. Home Box Office is a premium cable network and entertainment company founded in 1973. Originally known for showing movies, HBO has continuously expanded over the years to produce award-winning original films, documentaries, and series, and has spun off into various subnetworks like HBO Family and streaming services, like HBO Max.

Reference: Eubie Blake

> **Sophia:** I ask for Lillian, you bring me Ubie Blake's parents.

James Hubert "Eubie" Blake (1887–1983) was a prominent composer, lyricist, and musician responsible for such hits as "Love Will Find a Way," "Memories of You," and "I'm Just Wild About Harry." Along with his longtime collaborator Noble Sissle, he wrote *Shuffle Along*, one of the first Broadway musicals written and directed by African Americans.

Reference: The Ziegfeld Follies

> **Blanche:** Lillian, Sophia tells me that you were in the Ziegfeld Follies.

The Ziegfeld Follies was a series of theatrical revue productions on Broadway from 1907 to 1931.

Reference: Jethro Bodine

> **Dorothy:** In English, Jethro!

Jethro Bodine is the fictional dim-witted, good-hearted nephew of Jed Clampett on the 1960s sitcom *The Beverly Hillbillies*. Portrayed by actor Max Baer Jr., Jethro and the rest of the Clampett brood have become synonymous with the Hollywood portrayal of a hillbilly.

Reference: "We Are the World"

> **Mr. Cummings:** Problems, problems, problems. The world is bringing me problems. And you are?
> **Sophia:** We are the world.

"We are the World" is a 1985 charity single for African famine relief, recorded by the supergroup USA for Africa. It was written by Michael Jackson and Lionel Richie and featured many of the biggest musical stars of the 1980s, including Billy Joel, Diana Ross, Ray Charles, Bruce Springsteen, Cyndi Lauper, Tina Turner, and many others.

Repeat References: Pablo Picasso *(Episode 3.13: The Artist)*, Mike Tyson *(Episode 3.15: Dorothy's New Friend)*

Episode 4.23: Rites of Spring

Directed by Terry Hughes. Written by Eric Cohen. Original airdate: April 29, 1989.
While discussing dieting plans in preparation for an upcoming pool party, the girls recall previous times they've attempted to lose weight.

Reference: Nabisco

> **Dorothy:** It's nine o'clock in the morning. You're eating pasta?
>
> **Sophia:** No, I'm eating a bowl of Nabisco Ziti-Os.

Nabisco is a manufacturer of snacks and cookies founded in 1898 and responsible for such mainstays as Chips Ahoy!, Oreos, Ritz Crackers, Fig Newtons, and others.

Reference: René Descartes

> **Dorothy:** Ma, you lost one pound.
>
> **Sophia:** Thank you, René Descartes. I'm looking for advice, not arithmetic.

René Descartes (1596–1650) was a seventeenth-century French philosopher, mathematician, and scientist, widely regarded as one of the founders of modern philosophy.

Reference: Chrysler New Yorker

> **Dorothy:** Blanche, sticking your feet out of the sunroof of a Chrysler New Yorker doesn't count.

The Chrysler New Yorker was an automobile produced by Chrysler from 1940 to 1996 and was, for several years, the company's flagship model.

Reference: PF Flyers

> **Rose:** I'm going to stick with my sweat suit and my PF Flyers.

PF Flyers are a brand of shoes introduced in 1937 by B. F. Goodrich. The "PF" stands for its patented Posture Foundation arch-support insole.

Reference: Audrey Hepburn

> **Eduardo:** For you, I see a saucier cut. An Audrey Hepburn look.

Audrey Hepburn (1929–1993) was an actress and humanitarian who rose to fame in the 1950s. She is known for her roles in *Roman Holiday, Sabrina, Funny Face, The Nun's Story, Charade, My Fair Lady,* and her iconic performance as Holly Golightly in *Breakfast at Tiffany's*. She also was a supporter of UNICEF and received the Presidential Medal of Freedom shortly before her death for her work as a UNICEF Global Ambassador.

Reference: Starship *Enterprise*

> **Blanche:** How do I look?
>
> **Dorothy:** Like something that came out of the air duct of the Starship *Enterprise*.

The Starship *Enterprise* is the spaceship from the *Star Trek* science-fiction film and television franchise.

Reference: Ram Dass

> **Sophia:** Oh really, Ram Dass? If it's all so easy, let's hear you answer this question.

Ram Dass (1931–2019) was a spiritual teacher, psychologist, and author of the 1971 book *Be Here Now*, which helped to popularize yoga and Eastern spirituality.

Repeat References: The Amazing Kreskin *(Episode 1.14: That Was No Lady)*, Rolls-Royce *(Episode 3.11: Three on a Couch)*

EPISODE 4.24: FOREIGN EXCHANGE
Directed by Terry Hughes. Written by Harriet B. Helberg and Sandy Helberg. Original airdate: May 6, 1989.
Sophia and Dorothy reel from the news that Dorothy may have been switched with another baby at the hospital where she was born. Rose and Blanche take a course in dirty dancing.

References: *Dirty Dancing, Lawrence of Arabia*

> **Blanche:** Dorothy, have you ever heard of something called dirty dancing?
>
> **Dorothy:** Well, of course, Blanche. They did it in that movie.
>
> **Rose:** What movie?

Dorothy: *Lawrence of Arabia*, Rose.

Dirty Dancing is a 1987 blockbuster starring Jennifer Grey as a young woman who falls in love with her dance instructor (Patrick Swayze) at a holiday resort. The film grossed more than $200 million during its theatrical run, was the first to sell more than a million copies on the home-video market, and its soundtrack—featuring the hit "(I've Had) The Time of My Life"—went multi-platinum and won both an Academy Award and a Grammy. Enduringly popular, the film has inspired a stage version, a prequel film, and a made-for-TV remake.

Lawrence of Arabia is a 1962 epic historical drama based on the life of T. E. Lawrence, a British army intelligence officer who fought alongside Arab guerrilla forces in World War I. The film stars Alec Guinness and Anthony Quinn and is widely considered a classic, winning seven Oscars, including Best Picture.

References: Tic Tac, Kmart

Sophia: Tic Tac?

Dorothy: Does it say Kmart on the back of my nightgown?

Sophia: As a matter of fact, it does, you cheapskate.

Tic Tac is a brand of small mints introduced in 1968. Kmart is a big-box department store chain founded in 1899. The store was at its peak in the 1980s and early 1990s, with thousands of stores operating globally at the time, but has seen a continuous decline over the past two decades.

Reference: Orkin

Blanche: I've never been so humiliated in my whole life.

Rose: That's not true. What about the time you got caught with the Orkin man?

Orkin is a pest-control services company founded in 1901.

Reference: Phil Rizzuto

Dorothy: I just keeping thinking about Ma and whose mother she really is.

Rose: You're worried she might be Gina's?

Dorothy: No, I'm worried she might be Phil Rizzuto's. I notice the phrase "Holy cow!" creeping into her conversation a lot.

Phil Rizzuto (1917–2007) was a shortstop with the New York Yankees baseball team from 1941 to 1956, who moved into a four-decade career as an announcer for the team following his retirement from the field. He was known for his trademark expression, "Holy cow!"

Reference: Wildcat drilling

Dorothy: Ma, what took you so long? All they did was draw a little blood.

Sophia: At my age, that's like wildcat drilling for oil.

Wildcat drilling is a form of high-risk, exploratory drilling for oil or natural gas.

EPISODE 4.25 AND 4.26: WE'RE OUTTA HERE—PARTS 1 AND 2
Directed by Terry Hughes. Written by Barry Fanaro, Mort Nathan, Kathy Speer, and Terry Grossman. Original airdate: May 13, 1989.
Blanche considers accepting an offer on the house after a "For Sale" sign mistakenly gets placed in the yard, leading the girls to reminisce about their time together.

References: Lee J. Cobb, *Death of a Salesman*, Marlon Brando, *A Streetcar Named Desire*, Dick Butkus, *Pal Joey*

Blanche: I missed Mr. Lee J. Cobb in *Death of a Salesman*. I missed Mr. Marlon Brando in *A Streetcar Named Desire*. Well, I was damned if I was going to miss Mr. Dick Butkus in *Pal Joey*.

Lee J. Cobb (1911–1976) was an esteemed actor known for roles in *The Brothers Karamazov*, *On the Waterfront*, *12 Angry Men*, *The Exorcist*, and for playing Willy Loman in the original Broadway production of Arthur Miller's *Death of a Salesman*, a 1949 stage play that won both the Pulitzer Prize for Drama and a Tony for Best Play. An Academy Award–winning actor and director with a career spanning six decades, Marlon Brando (1924–2004) is one of the screen's most influential performers. Notable roles include *On the Waterfront*, *Julius Caesar*, *Last Tango in Paris*, *Superman*, *The Godfather*, and *A Streetcar Named Desire*, a Tennessee Williams play that debuted on Broadway in 1947, about privileged Southern belle Blanche DuBois, who moves in with her sister in a shabby New Orleans apartment.

Professional football player, sports commentator, and actor Dick Butkus was a linebacker for the Chicago Bears from 1965 to 1973. An injury forced him into retirement at the age of thirty-one, at which point commentating and acting became his focus. He's appeared in such films as *The Longest Yard*, *Necessary Roughness*, and *Gremlins 2: The New Batch*, and TV shows, like *My Two Dads*. *Pal Joey* is a 1940 Rodgers and Hart musical about the affair between an ambitious nightclub performer and a wealthy, married woman. It was adapted into a 1957 film starring Frank Sinatra and Rita Hayworth.

Reference: Domino's Pizza

Stan: I can deliver a pizza faster to your house than Domino's.

Domino's Pizza is an international pizza chain founded in Michigan in 1960 by brothers Tom and James Monaghan. After purchasing a small chain called DomiNick's, James soon split to focus on his job as a postman. Tom later renamed the company Domino's in 1965 and began expansion, with thousands of locations all over the world. In 1984, the chain launched a program guaranteeing delivery in a half-hour or less. A 1989 accident, in which a woman was struck by a delivery driver, led to a substantial court settlement and the program's end in 1993.

References: Joe Piscopo, *Rain Man*

Rose: Are you upset because Blanche is going to sell the house and we can't live together?

Dorothy: No, I'm upset because Joe Piscopo didn't get the lead role in *Rain Man*.

Joe Piscopo is a comedian and actor best known for his work on *Saturday Night Live* in the early 1980s. Later in the decade he became a bodybuilding enthusiast. *Rain Man* is a 1988 film starring Dustin Hoffman and Tom Cruise as an autistic savant and his selfish brother who learn of one another's existence after the death of their father. The film was a box office success and won four Oscars, including Best Picture.

Reference: *Stalag 17*

Dorothy: Ma, it's two a.m. Where have you been?

Sophia: I stuffed pillows under the sheets so I could fool you during bed check. What is this, *Stalag 17?*

Stalag 17 is a 1953 war film about a group of American airmen held in a German prisoner of war camp during World War II. It was adapted from a Broadway play of the same name and starred William Holden in an Oscar-winning role.

Reference: Charlie Callas

> **Sophia:** Take the advice of a wise old Sicilian.
> **Rose:** You, Sophia?
> **Sophia:** No, Charlie Callas.

Rubber-faced comedian and actor Charlie Callas (1927–2011) was known for working alongside fellow legends Jerry Lewis, Dean Martin, and Mel Brooks in such films as *High Anxiety* and *History of the World, Part I*, series such as *Switch*, and his string of talk show appearances throughout the 1970s. He also voiced Elliott the dragon in Disney's *Pete's Dragon* in 1977.

Reference: Søren Kierkegaard

> **Blanche:** Sophia, you're not making any sense.
> **Sophia:** Excuse me, Mrs. Kierkegaard. It's four a.m.

Søren Kierkegaard (1813–1855) was a nineteenth-century Danish existentialist philosopher, poet, and social critic.

Repeat References: Howard Johnson *(Episode 2.6: Big Daddy's Little Lady)*, Scarlett O'Hara *(Episode 1.5: The Triangle)*, Suzanne Somers *(Episode 2.3: Take Him, He's Mine)*, The Vatican *(Episode 2.9: Joust Between Friends)*, the Landers sisters *(Episode 2.19: Long Day's Journey into Marinara)*

Season Five: 1989–1990

Perceptive viewers will notice a shift in the tone of the show with season five, and that's because a new batch of writers is introduced. From here on out, the writing focuses slightly less on topical references—although there are still plenty in each episode—and relies more on issue-heavy storylines.

Dorothy battles chronic fatigue syndrome, Rose worries that she may have gotten a transfusion with HIV-infected blood, Sophia begins losing her memory, Blanche gets a pacemaker, and Stan winds up homeless on Christmas morning. There's also suicide, artificial insemination, the death of a parent, teenage pregnancy, and the Czechoslovakian revolution.

Grab the tissues. It's a heavy season.

Episode 5.1: Sick and Tired—Part 1
Directed by Terry Hughes. Written by Susan Harris. Original airdate: September 23, 1989.
Dorothy attempts to receive a diagnosis for her worsening fatigue and pain symptoms. Blanche announces her intent to become a great Southern novelist.

Reference: Wite-Out

> **Dorothy:** They were too busy sniffing the Wite-Out they stole from typing class.

Wite-Out is a brand of correction fluid launched in 1966, originally created for use with photocopies.

Reference: *Win, Lose or Draw*

> **Dr. Stevens:** If this was *Win, Lose or Draw*, I'd draw a crown.

Win, Lose or Draw was a game show that ran in syndication and on NBC from 1987 to 1990, featuring two teams of three, two of whom were charged with guessing what the third player was drawing. Teams were split into men and women, with one contestant being paired with two celebrities. The show was produced by Burt Reynolds's production company, with the first episode of the syndicated version featuring Reynolds and Dom DeLuise against Betty White and Annie Potts. Bert Convy hosted the syndicated version, while Vicki Lawrence hosted the NBC daytime version. The set was modeled after Reynolds's real-life living room.

Reference: Ernest Hemingway

Blanche: Now I know why Hemingway killed himself.

Ernest Hemingway (1899–1961) was a celebrated author who released a string of prominent works from the 1920s to the 1950s and won the Nobel Prize in Literature in 1954. Among his most famous works are *The Sun Also Rises*, *A Farewell to Arms*, *For Whom the Bell Tolls*, and *The Old Man and the Sea*. He committed suicide in 1961.

Reference: The Algonquin

Blanche: New York is a writer's city. I could hang out at the Algonquin, talk to my colleagues.

A fancy New York City hotel opened in 1902, the Algonquin in Times Square became a magnet for the literati and developed a reputation for hosting many literary and theater notables, including the members of the Algonquin Round Table. The group consisted of writers, critics, actors, and the like who gathered regularly for lunch at the hotel in the 1920s to engage in wit and wordplay. The hotel is also known for having a resident feline, a tradition that began in the 1920s. The hotel was designated a New York City Historic Landmark in 1987 and a national literary landmark in 1996.

References: Bloomingdale's, Empire State Building, King Kong

Rose: I went to Bloomingdale's, the store. I swear St. Olaf could fit into it. I went to the top of the Empire State Building. You know what I don't understand? How come the fall didn't kill King Kong instantly?

Bloomingdale's is a luxury department store chain founded in 1861 by brothers Joseph and Lyman Bloomingdale. Now owned by parent company

Macy's, Inc., there are just over fifty Bloomingdale's locations, including its flagship store in New York. A 102-story skyscraper in Midtown Manhattan, the Empire State Building was designed by Shreve, Lamb & Harmon and constructed in the early 1930s. The building was at one time the tallest in New York City and is a popular draw for tourists, with millions of annual visitors making their way to the top to enjoy the view. King Kong is a giant gorilla, first appearing in 1933's *King Kong*. The film was such a success that multiple sequels and remakes have persisted for years.

Reference: Dr. Seuss

Rose: After all, Dr. Seuss was a doctor, too.

Dr. Seuss was the pen name of Theodor Seuss Geisel (1904–1991), who authored classic children's books like *The Cat in the Hat*, *Horton Hears a Who!*, *Green Eggs and Ham*, and *How the Grinch Stole Christmas*. In 2021, Dr. Seuss Enterprises, the company that controls the author's books and characters, announced they would cease publishing of six of his titles that portray Asian and Black people "in ways that are hurtful and wrong."

Reference: The Black Plague

Sophia: You think they had a name for the Black Plague when one guy had it?

The Black Plague, or the Black Death, was one of the deadliest pandemics in recorded human history, resulting in the deaths of anywhere from 75 to 200 million people in Europe, Asia, and Africa in the fourteenth century. Caused by a bacteria that resulted in the bubonic plague, the Black Death peaked in Europe in the mid-1300s.

EPISODE 5.2: SICK AND TIRED—PART 2
Directed by Terry Hughes. Written by Susan Harris. Original airdate: September 30, 1989.
Dorothy finally learns what is causing her unrelenting fatigue. Blanche's attempts to write her novel are unsuccessful.

Reference: Nurse Laverne Todd

Laverne, regarding a urine sample: He doesn't mind doing it in his own bed but there's something about doing it in a public place.

Harry: Kind of like sex.

Laverne: Maybe where you come from.

Laverne Todd was the sarcastic Southern nurse to Dr. Harry Weston on *Empty Nest*, portrayed by actress Park Overall. The character proved a break-out role for Overall, who received a Golden Globe nomination and was, for a time, rumored to be ripe for a spinoff of her own.

Reference: Vincent van Gogh

> **Blanche:** They can publish it after I'm dead, like Vincent van Gogh. . . . He cut off his hair; maybe I'll cut off mine.
>
> **Dorothy:** He cut off his ear.
>
> **Blanche:** I have too many earrings.

Vincent van Gogh (1853–1890) was a Dutch painter considered one of the most influential figures in Western art. He's known for works like *Starry Night* and for cutting off his own ear.

Reference: "To sleep perchance to dream."

> **Blanche:** To sleep perchance to dream. My God, what a wonderful line! I'm getting so good I can't stand it!

This is a line from William Shakespeare's *Hamlet*, spoken by the title character to himself as he wonders whether it's better to give up and die rather than face his troubles.

References: *Silas Marner*, Paul Bunyan

> **Blanche:** You're from Minnesota. What have you read, for God's sake, *Silas Marner*? *Paul Bunyan*?

Silas Marner is an 1861 novel by Mary Ann Evans, using her pen name George Eliot, about a linen weaver. Paul Bunyan is a giant, super-strong lumberjack in American and Canadian folklore, often accompanied by his companion, Babe the Blue Ox. Originating through oral tales told by North American loggers, and popularized in a promotional pamphlet released by a lumber company in 1916, Paul Bunyan has gone on to be the subject of songs, stage productions, movies, and more.

Reference: Glenn Close

> **Blanche:** I will not have my words coming out of Glenn Close's mouth. I'd rather die.

Glenn Close is regarded as one of the greatest actresses to ever grace the screen. She has received three Emmys, three Tonys, and three Golden Globes. Despite eight Academy Award nominations, however, she has never been a recipient; in fact, she holds the record for most nominations with no wins. Among her most notable films are *The Big Chill*, *The Natural*, *Fatal Attraction*, and *Dangerous Liaisons*.

Reference: *Flower Drum Song*

> **Sophia:** The man is a genius. By the way, I loved *Flower Drum Song*!

A Rodgers and Hammerstein musical based on the 1957 C. Y. Lee novel of the same name, *Flower Drum Song* debuted on Broadway in 1958 and was adapted into a 1961 film. It focuses on Wang Ta, a young man torn between his Chinese roots and American culture. The original production was nominated for six Tonys, winning one.

Reference: MSG

> **Sophia:** When I order at Fung Chow's and say no MSG, do they really put it in anyway?

MSG stands for monosodium glutamate, a common flavor enhancer often added to things like Chinese food or canned foods.

Repeat References: Dr. Harry Weston *(Episode 4.4: Yokel Hero)*, Sears *(Episode 1.13: A Little Romance)*, Harvard *(Episode 2.1: End of the Curse)*

EPISODE 5.3: ACCURATE CONCEPTION
Directed by Terry Hughes. Written by Gail Parent. Original airdate: October 14, 1989.
Blanche's daughter, Becky, announces her plans to be artificially inseminated. Sophia refuses to get her annual checkup.

Reference: Pavlov's dog

> **Sophia:** I had to lie to you and tell you we were going on the pony rides, and you fell for it time after time. Just like Pavlov's dog, only dumber.

Ivan Pavlov (1849–1936) was a Russian physiologist whose experiments with canines led to the development of classical conditioning, which is learning through associations between an environmental and a naturally occurring stimulus. While dogs naturally salivate at the sight of food, Pavlov found that they can associate a stimulus—in his case, the sound of a metronome—with food—even if there wasn't food present—through conditioned behavior. He played the metronome with the food with enough frequency that the dogs salivated at the mere sound of it.

Reference: Egg cream

> **Dorothy:** I'll take you to Wolfie's for an egg cream.

An egg cream is a cold beverage made of milk, carbonated water, and flavored syrups, like chocolate. Despite its name, the drink features neither eggs nor cream.

Repeat References: Wolfie's *(Episode 2.1: End of the Curse)*, Star Search *(Episode 2.17: Bedtime Story)*, San Gennaro Festival *(Episode 1.7: The Competition)*, Tony Bennett *(Episode 1.7: The Competition)*, the Dodgers *(Episode 3.14: Blanche's Little Girl)*

EPISODE 5.4: ROSE FIGHTS BACK
Directed by Terry Hughes. Written by Marc Sotkin. Original airdate: October 21, 1989.
Rose turns to a consumer reporter for help with an age discrimination complaint. Sophia begins shopping at a discount warehouse store.

Reference: Corinthian leather

> **Blanche:** I'd love to get him on a couch made out of Corinthian leather.

Corinthian leather is not a type of leather, but was actually a term coined by a marketing firm to promote the upholstery used in Chrysler luxury automobiles beginning in 1974. The term really gained traction thanks to a series of ads for the Chrysler Cordoba in the mid-1970s, featuring actor Ricardo Montalbán.

Reference: Rabbit test

> **Sophia:** I think I'm pregnant.
>
> **Dorothy:** What happened, the rabbit died laughing?

The rabbit test was a pregnancy test developed in 1931 by Maurice Harold Friedman and Maxwell Edward Lapham, in which a woman's urine was injected into rabbits in an effort to test for the hormone human chorionic gonadotropin. If the woman was pregnant, and therefore the hormone present, the rabbit's ovaries would enlarge. A few days after injection, the rabbits were dissected for examination.

Reference: Imelda Marcos

> **Dorothy:** This is how Imelda Marcos got started with that shoe thing.

Imelda Marcos was the wife of Ferdinand Marcos and First Lady of the Philippines from 1965 to 1986, known for living a lavish lifestyle amid her country's civil unrest and economic troubles, spending much of the country's money on trips, jewelry, and a massive shoe collection.

References: Union Stock Yards, Crisco

> **Rose:** One year we went to Chicago to tour the Stock Yards, but it was our twentieth anniversary. We had a romantic trip coming. . . . We even got to see where Crisco is made.

The Union Stock Yards refers to the meatpacking district of Chicago, which handled the slaughtering, processing, packaging, and distribution of meat. It opened in 1865 and closed in 1971. The Union Stock Yard Gate was designated a Chicago landmark in 1972 and a National Historic Landmark in 1981. Crisco was originally a brand of shortening—a fat that is solid at room temperature and used in making food products—launched in 1911. While the shortening is still around today, the brand has expanded to include various cooking sprays and oils as well.

Reference: Gremlin

> **Rose:** I am the battered consumer. I drive a Gremlin, for God's sake!

A subcompact hatchback car, the oddly named Gremlin was produced by American Motors Corporation from 1970 to 1978. A popular car throughout the decade, former presidents Bush (dad owned, son drove) and Clinton had Gremlins back in the day, and the car inspired a Hot Wheels version. The model has since become a hot item among collectors.

Repeat References: Canasta *(Episode 2.15: Before and After)*, Zorro *(Episode 4.11: The Auction)*, Ricky Ricardo *(Episode 4.17: You Gotta Have Hope)*, Milton Berle *(Episode 2.19: Long Day's Journey into Marinara)*

EPISODE 5.5: LOVE UNDER THE BIG TOP

Directed by Terry Hughes. Written by Richard Vaczy and Tracy Gamble. Original airdate: October 28, 1989.

Dorothy's successful lawyer boyfriend announces that he's leaving his practice to become a clown. Rose puts together a protest to save dolphins.

Reference: " 'O Sole Mio"

> **Sophia:** Some guy from Palermo forgot his accordion, so he sat around singing " 'O Sole Mio" while squeezing a monkey.

" 'O Sole Mio" is an 1898 Neapolitan song by Giovanni Capurro and Eduardo di Capua.

Reference: Lincoln

> **Dorothy:** You are driving the Lincoln tonight, aren't you?

Lincoln is a brand of luxury automobiles under the Ford umbrella, founded in 1917.

Reference: *Flipper*

> **Dorothy:** Caught a rerun of *Flipper* on cable, did you?

Flipper is an NBC series about a family and their pet bottlenose dolphin that aired from 1964 to 1967.

Repeat Reference: Gandhi *(Episode 1.13: A Little Romance)*

EPISODE 5.6: DANCING IN THE DARK

Directed by Terry Hughes. Written by Phillip Jayson Lasker. Original airdate: November 4, 1989.

Rose becomes enamored with her ballroom dancing partner, Miles, but isn't sure she fits in with his intellectual friends.

Reference: "Jeepers Creepers"

Sophia: How would you like to hold Mr. Morelli up for two choruses of "Jeepers Creepers"?

"Jeepers Creepers" is a popular standard written by Harry Warren and Johnny Mercer for the 1938 movie *Going Places* and popularized by Louis Armstrong.

References: Robert and Elizabeth Barrett Browning

Gayle: Lillian picked Winston Churchill and Browning without his wife.

Robert Browning (1812–1889) was an English poet and playwright, and husband of fellow renowned poet Elizabeth Barrett Browning (1806–1861), who is considered among the most renowned Victorian era poets.

Reference: *Moby-Dick*

Elise: Now Harv, *Moby-Dick* is about self-fulfilling prophecy.

Moby-Dick is an 1851 novel by Herman Melville about the obsessive quest of a sea captain seeking revenge on the whale who bit off his leg.

Reference: Dmitri Shostakovich

Miles: The university is playing Shostakovich.

Rose: I'd love to go. And I bet we beat them!

Dmitri Shostakovich (1906–1975) was a renowned Russian composer and pianist.

Reference: Fred Astaire

Dorothy: Ma, where are my dancing shoes?

Sophia: In the Smithsonian, right next to Fred Astaire's.

Fred Astaire (1899–1987) was a famous singer, actor, choreographer, and—perhaps most of all—dancer. His run of musicals with costar Ginger Rogers, among his multitude of other performances, has garnered him the reputation of being the most influential dancer in film.

Repeat References: The Great Depression *(Episode 2.6: Big Daddy's Little Lady)*, Ernest Hemingway *(Episode 5.1: Sick and Tired—Part 1)*, Winston Churchill *(Episode 2.4: It's a Miserable Life)*, the Smithsonian *(Episode 3.24: Mister Terrific)*, Glenn Miller *(Episode 1.3: Rose the Prude)*

EPISODE 5.7: NOT ANOTHER MONDAY

Directed by Terry Hughes. Written by Gail Parent. Original airdate: November 11, 1989.

Sophia's friend, Martha, announces her plans to commit suicide. The girls babysit for a neighbor.

References: Manhattan, Harvey Wallbanger

> **Sophia:** I'll have a Manhattan—and I'm watching, so don't slip me any of the cheap stuff.
>
> **Martha:** I'll have another Harvey Wallbanger.

A Manhattan is a classic cocktail consisting of whiskey, sweet vermouth, and bitters, garnished with a maraschino cherry. A Harvey Wallbanger is a cocktail made from vodka, orange juice, and Galliano, an herbal liqueur. There is some debate about its origins, one being that a bartender in a Los Angeles bar invented it in the 1950s and named it after a frequent customer. Another, apparently more plausible theory is that it was created by the marketing team at McKesson Imports Company in the 1970s, which at the time distributed Galliano, and Harvey Wallbanger was a character created for the campaign.

Reference: "Mr. Sandman"

> *The girls sing the song while trying to get the baby to go to sleep.*

"Mr. Sandman" is a song written in 1954 by Pat Ballard and first recorded by Vaughn Monroe & His Orchestra. It's been recorded since by the likes of The Chordettes, The Four Aces, Chet Atkins, and Emmylou Harris.

Repeat References: Miami Dolphins *(Episode 1.3: Rose the Prude)*, canasta *(Episode 2.15: Before and After)*, Dr. Harry Weston *(Episode 4.4: Yokel Hero)*

EPISODE 5.8: THAT OLD FEELING

Directed by Terry Hughes. Written by Tom Whedon. Original airdate: November 18, 1989.

Blanche is visited by her brother-in-law, Jamie, and is shocked by how much he resembles her deceased husband, George. Sophia secretly begins driving.

Reference: Mr. Magoo

> **Dorothy:** You drive like Mr. Magoo.

A cartoon character introduced in 1949 and voiced by Jim Backus, Mr. Magoo was an old, short, rich man whose nearsightedness got him into many a jam.

Repeat References: Buick *(Episode 3.3: Bringing Up Baby)*, the Statue of Liberty *(Episode 2.12: The Sisters)*, Bobby Vinton *(Episode 3.6: Letter to Gorbachev)*, *The Grapes of Wrath (Episode 3.15: Dorothy's New Friend)*

EPISODE 5.9: COMEDY OF ERRORS

Directed by Terry Hughes. Written by Don Reo. Original airdate: November 25, 1989.

After discovering an old list of life goals, Dorothy attempts to try her hand at stand-up comedy. Blanche faces an audit from the IRS.

Reference: Burt Lancaster

> **Dorothy:** A list I made of things I wanted to do with my life.
>
> **Blanche:** I had a list like that, and I've done most of them. Except for Burt Lancaster.

Burt Lancaster (1913–1994) was an Oscar-winning actor with a four-decade career, including the films *The Killers*, *From Here to Eternity*, *The Rainmaker*, *Elmer Gantry*, and *Birdman of Alcatraz*.

Reference: Greenpeace

> **Dorothy:** Charitable deductions? Blanche, that's great. What was it, the United Fund? Greenpeace? Do you remember?
>
> **Blanche:** In 1985, I bought the "We Are the World" album.

Greenpeace is a nongovernmental environmental organization founded in 1971 that campaigns on issues such as climate change, deforestation, commercial whaling, and anti-nuclear issues, among others.

References: Martha Raye, Madge

> **Sophia:** Dorothy, have you seen my teeth?

Dorothy: They're in your mouth, Ma.

Sophia: I know that. Don't they look good today? I ran them through the dishwasher.

Dorothy: Ma, listen to me. You got Martha Raye and Madge mixed up again.

Martha Raye (1916–1994) was a comic actress who appeared on Broadway and in various roles before, later in her career, appearing in a series of television commercials for Polident denture cleaner in the 1970s and 1980s. Madge was a fictional manicurist played by actress Jan Miner (1917–2004) in a series of Palmolive dishwashing liquid commercials beginning in the 1960s.

Reference: Siegfried & Roy

Jimmy: I want to bring out a lady who actually claims to know which one is Siegfried and which one is Roy!

Siegfried Fischbacher and Roy Horn (1944–2020) were a pair of magicians and entertainers known for their appearances with white lions and white tigers at the Mirage Resort and Casino in Las Vegas.

Repeat References: "We Are the World" *(Episode 4.22: Sophia's Choice)*, Merv Griffin *(Episode 2.13: The Stan Who Came to Dinner)*, Lisa Bonet *(Episode 4.10: Stan Takes a Wife)*

EPISODE 5.10: ALL THAT JAZZ

Directed by Terry Hughes. Written by Robert Bruce and Martin Weiss. Original airdate: December 2, 1989.

Dorothy's son, Michael, arrives with the news that he and his wife have separated. A stressed-out Rose asks her boss to cut back on her workload.

Reference: Jimmy Smits

Sophia: Look! It's Jimmy Smits!

Jimmy Smits is an actor best known for his roles on *L.A. Law* and *NYPD Blue*.

Reference: Rose Kennedy

Sophia: Hell, I was the Rose Kennedy of Brooklyn.

Rose Kennedy (1890–1995) was the matriarch of the Kennedy family and mother to President John F. Kennedy and senators Robert and Ted Kennedy.

Reference: Obsession

> **Dorothy:** I am very upset.
>
> **Rose:** Is it because you threw Michael out?
>
> **Dorothy:** No, it's because I can't make any sense out of those commercials for Obsession.

Obsession is a fragrance made by Calvin Klein. In the late 1980s and early 1990s, the brand was as known for its scent as it was for its unusual television commercials, some of which were directed by famed director David Lynch.

Reference: The life of Riley

> **Stan:** He's fine. He's living the life of Riley.

The origins of this phrase, which refers to someone living a life of ease and comfort, have varied and date back to the 1800s, possibly referring to a real-life Irishman named Willy Reilly and the folk ballad written about him. The phrase began to show up in the United States in print in the early 1900s, with the spelling changed to Riley, and it gained momentum during World War I. The phrase had permeated the culture enough by the 1940s that a radio comedy series called *The Life of Riley* debuted in 1944. It was adapted into a 1949 feature film, and a TV series and comic book in the 1950s.

Reference: Walter Cronkite

> **Enrique:** More around the eyes. Make me Cronkite.

Often cited as "the most trusted man in America," Walter Cronkite (1916–2009) was a broadcast journalist who anchored the *CBS Evening News* from 1962 until his retirement in 1981. He continued to make appearances afterwards as a correspondent, and would occasionally pop up as himself on shows like *Murphy Brown*.

Repeat Reference: Ted Koppel *(Episode 2.10: Love, Rose)*

EPISODE 5.11: EBB TIDE
Directed by Terry Hughes. Written by Marc Sotkin. Original airdate: December 9, 1989.

Blanche returns to her family home for the funeral of her father, Big Daddy. Sophia rents out rooms in the house to raise funds for a new television.

Reference: Leona Helmsley

> **Dorothy:** It's for you, Leona.

Nicknamed "The Queen of Mean," flamboyant businesswoman Leona Helmsley (1920–2007) was a prominent real estate mogul and hotelier with a reputation for tyrannical behavior. When hired contractors accused her of nonpayment, the subsequent investigation led to a conviction of federal income tax evasion in 1989. She served nineteen months in prison and two months under house arrest and spent her later years in relative isolation.

Reference: Bourbon and Branch

> **Blanche:** Generations of Hollingsworths would gather around Big Daddy with his Bourbon and Branch.

Bourbon and Branch is a cocktail combining bourbon whiskey and plain water.

Reference: "Fat, Fat, the Water Rat"

> *Dorothy recites this rhyme while looking at photos of a young Blanche.*

While the origin of this rhyme is unclear, it was a typical schoolyard taunt dating back at least as far as the 1930s.

Reference: "Hinky dinky parlez-vous"

> *Sophia leads this in a sing-along with party guests.*

This is a line from the English song "Mademoiselle from Armentières," made popular during World War I.

Repeat References: Graceland *(Episode 1.18: The Operation)*, the friendly skies *(Episode 1.18: The Operation)*

EPISODE 5.12: HAVE YOURSELF A VERY LITTLE CHRISTMAS
Directed by Terry Hughes. Written by Tom Whedon. Original airdate: December 16, 1989.
The girls volunteer at a soup kitchen on Christmas Day, only to discover that Stan is among those in line for food.

Reference: "Jingle Bells"

Blanche: Rose, for the past half-hour you've been humming "Jingle Bells" and yelling "Hey!" Now why must you do that?

Rose: Because it's too hard to hum the "Hey!"

"Jingle Bells" is a popular Christmas carol written by James Lord Pierpont in 1857.

Reference: Batman

Dorothy: Robby wants a Batman hat. I went to six different stores. They were all sold out.

Batman is the fictional "Caped Crusader" superhero of DC comic books, movies, TV shows, cartoons, and more. Batman originally appeared in *Detective Comics* #27 in 1939. Unlike a lot of his contemporaries, Batman didn't possess any actual superpowers. The character is the alter ego of Gotham City businessman Bruce Wayne, who uses his intellect, physical prowess, and immense wealth to finance his crime fighting. The character was a hit from the get-go and has been a pop culture phenomenon ever since, with comic books expanding into a campy 1960s television series, multiple animated shows, blockbuster films, toys, video games, and more. The character has been portrayed on-screen by the likes of George Clooney, Val Kilmer, Ben Affleck, and Adam West, but the era of his reference in *The Golden Girls* was during the popularity of Tim Burton's 1989 *Batman* film, which starred Michael Keaton in the title role.

Reference: The Seven Dwarfs

Dorothy: Do you remember that Christmas they gave me soap in the shape of the Seven Dwarfs?

The Seven Dwarfs are a fictional group of dwarfs from the Snow White fairy tale. They were given names in the Disney version of the tale: Doc, Happy, Sneezy, Sleepy, Bashful, Dopey, and Grumpy.

Reference: The Oak Ridge Boys

Rose: If we draw names out of a hat, whose names are they going to be anyway?

Dorothy: The Oak Ridge Boys, Rose.

The Oak Ridge Boys are a musical quartet founded in the 1940s that gained momentum in the 1950s as a gospel act. They switched to country music in the 1970s and rose to fame with hits like "Elvira," "Bobbie Sue," and "Gonna Take a Lot of River."

References: Macy's, Radio City Music Hall, Mitsubishi Center

> **Dorothy:** When I think of Christmas, I think of Christmas in New York. The decorations in Macy's window, the show at Radio City, skaters on the ice at Mitsubishi Center.

Macy's is a department store chain founded in New York City in 1858 by Rowland Hussey Macy. Radio City Music Hall is an entertainment venue in Midtown Manhattan, nicknamed the Showplace of the Nation. The reference to Mitsubishi Center is a nod to the fact that, in 1989, the Mitsubishi Estate Company of Tokyo purchased control of the Rockefeller Group, the owner of Rockefeller Center and other New York City properties. It was never renamed but made for a timely joke.

References: L.L.Bean, Victoria's Secret

> **Sophia:** This stinks. After the swell gift I sent him.
> **Blanche:** What was it?
> **Sophia:** A catalog item.
> **Blanche:** L.L.Bean?
> **Sophia:** Victoria's Secret.

L.L.Bean is a retail company founded in 1912 by Leon Leonwood Bean that sells primarily clothing and outdoor recreation equipment. Victoria's Secret is a lingerie, clothing, and beauty retailer founded by Roy and Gaye Raymond in 1977.

Reference: *Scarface*

> **Dorothy:** Ma, are you coming?
> **Sophia:** But I rented *Scarface*.

Scarface is a 1983 crime drama starring Al Pacino as a Cuban refugee who becomes a powerful drug lord. It's a remake of the 1932 original.

References: *Jim Thorpe—All-American, King of Kings*

> **Dorothy:** You turned on the television and they were playing *Jim Thorpe—All-American*, and you told the kids it was *King of Kings*.

Jim Thorpe—All-American is a 1951 biographical film about Native American athlete Jim Thorpe, a 1912 Olympic gold medalist for the pentathlon and decathlon. Burt Lancaster played the title role. *King of Kings* is a 1961 epic film telling the life story of Jesus of Nazareth. The film starred Jeffrey Hunter as Jesus, Siobhan McKenna as Mary, and Robert Ryan as John the Baptist.

Reference: "Say it with flowers"

> **Stan:** When I apologized, I said it with flowers.

This was a popular slogan dating back to the early 1900s, encouraging the sending of flowers as gifts.

Repeat References: *Sports Illustrated (Episode 2.16: And Then There Was One)*, George H. W. Bush *(Episode 3.21: Larceny and Old Lace)*, USO *(Episode 1.11: Stan's Return)*, Bob Hope *(Episode 1.9: Blanche and the Younger Man)*

EPISODE 5.13: MARY HAS A LITTLE LAMB
Directed by Terry Hughes. Written by Harold Apter. Original airdate: January 6, 1989.
The girls take in their pregnant sixteen-year-old neighbor when her father throws her out. Blanche worries when her prison pen pal is paroled.

Reference: *This Old House*

> **Dorothy:** Just because the plumbing is in doesn't mean the house is ready to occupy.
>
> **Mary:** I think I know what you're getting at.
>
> **Dorothy:** Good, because I really didn't make that up myself. I heard it on *This Old House*.

This Old House is a long-running home improvement television series (and now media brand that includes a magazine and website), which debuted in 1979 and was hosted throughout *The Golden Girls* era by Bob Vila.

Reference: Nash

> **Sophia:** Let me tell you what a slut is. A slut is someone who gets knocked up in the backseat of a Studebaker at a drive-in movie. It was a Studebaker wasn't it, Dorothy?
>
> **Dorothy:** It was a Nash, Ma.

Nash was a former automobile manufacturer that existed from 1916 to 1954.

Reference: The Sandinistas

> **Dorothy, finding Sophia bound and gagged:** Who did this to you?
>
> **Sophia:** The Sandinistas!

The Sandinistas were a socialist Nicaraguan political organization founded by Carlos Fonseca in 1961 that ruled the country from 1979 to 1990.

Reference: Lamaze

> **Rose:** Don't forget, Tuesday we have mime class.
>
> **Dorothy:** Mime class?
>
> **Rose:** The Lamaze class was all filled up.

Lamaze is a technique to help build a woman's confidence in her ability to manage the pain of childbirth. It was developed by French obstetrician Dr. Fernand Lamaze in the 1950s and was a very popular source of pregnancy jokes in 1980s and 1990s sitcoms.

Repeat References: *Hindenburg* disaster *(Episode 2.22: Diamond in the Rough)*, Dan Quayle *(Episode 4.4: Yokel Hero)*, Fred Astaire *(Episode 5.6: Dancing in the Dark)*, Studebaker *(Episode 3.25: Mother's Day)*

EPISODE 5.14: GREAT EXPECTATIONS
Directed by Terry Hughes. Written by Robert Bruce and Martin Weiss. Original airdate: January 13, 1990.
Blanche is reluctant to commit to her boyfriend following his heart attack. Rose joins a positive-thinking support group.

Reference: B'nai B'rith

> **Blanche:** My date is a real-live cowboy.
>
> **Dorothy:** Morty Fishbein is a real-live cowboy?

Blanche: He's from Amarillo, Texas. He was the grand marshal of the B'nai B'rith rodeo three years straight.

B'nai B'rith is a Jewish service organization founded in 1843. From community service to educational programs to scholarships and international affairs, the organization is committed to the security and continuity of Jewish people. They do not, despite Blanche's claim, host an annual rodeo.

Reference: Melanie Griffith

Dorothy: I'm Dorothy Zbornak.
Sophia: I'm Melanie Griffith.

Actress Melanie Griffith rose to fame in the 1980s in films such as *Body Double*, *Something Wild*, and *Working Girl*, which earned her an Academy Award nomination and Golden Globe win for Best Actress.

Reference: Rams

Dorothy: I have some incredible news!
Sophia: You've been traded to the Rams?

The Rams are a professional football team based in Los Angeles.

Reference: Tommy Newsom

Rose: I feel the same way when I hear the words, "And filling in for Doc, Tommy Newsom!"

Tommy Newsom (1929–2007) was a saxophonist in the NBC Orchestra on *The Tonight Show Starring Johnny Carson*. He eventually was promoted to assistant director and would frequently fill in whenever regular leader Doc Severinsen was away.

Reference: Boilermaker

Sophia: They laugh. They sing. They slam down a few boilermakers.

A boilermaker is a drink consisting of a glass of beer and a shot of whiskey, either by mixing them together or by chasing the whiskey with the beer.

Repeat References: "Sunrise, Sunset" *(Episode 2.17: Bedtime Story)*, Doc Severinsen *(Episode 2.19: Long Day's Journey into Marinara)*, Pablo Picasso *(Episode 3.13: The Artist)*

Episode 5.15: Triple Play
Directed by Terry Hughes. Written by Gail Parent. Original airdate: January 27, 1990.

Blanche attempts to woo men by pretending to sell a car. Rose meets Miles's daughter. Sophia begins hoarding money she is mistakenly receiving from Social Security.

Reference: *Hee Haw*

> **Miles:** Rose, I have never met anyone like you.
>
> **Sophia:** Check the cornfield on *Hee Haw*.

Hee Haw is a country music–themed television musical and comedy variety show set in the fictional Kornfield Kounty. The show, hosted by Roy Clark and Buck Owens, aired on CBS from 1969 to 1971, in syndication from 1971 to 1993, and on the TNN network from 1996 to 1997. It blended corn-pone humor, slapstick comedy, and performances by the hottest country stars of the day, who also appeared in the comedy sketches.

Reference: Haberdashery

> **Rose:** That was my uncle, the owner of St. Olaf's most famous haberdashery.

A haberdashery is an old-fashioned term for a men's clothing shop.

Reference: Warren Beatty

> **Dorothy:** Did you sleep well?
>
> **Sophia:** No, I had that recurring nightmare. You know, the one where I'm in bed with Warren Beatty, and he says, "Sorry, this is too sick even for me."

Actor, writer, director, and producer with a career spanning six decades, Warren Beatty has been nominated for fifteen Academy Awards, including four Best Actor nods. Notable roles include *Bonnie and Clyde*, *Shampoo*, *Heaven Can Wait*, *Reds* (for which he won the Best Director Oscar), and more. In addition to his work, Beatty's personal life, womanizing ways, and connections to the likes of Joan Collins, Carly Simon, and others were common tabloid fare for years. He's been married to actress Annette Bening since 1992.

Reference: Red Hots

> **Rose:** I could never serve store-bought candied herring. Besides, I have my own special recipe. I use Red Hots for the eyes.

Red Hots are small cinnamon candies introduced by the Ferrara Pan Candy Company in the 1930s.

Reference: Frick and Frack

> **Dorothy:** You go over there with Frick and Frack and try to ditch them.

Frick and Frack were a pair of Swiss skaters who came to the United States in the late 1930s as part of the original Ice Follies show of comedy ice skaters. Their names, surprisingly enough, were not Frick and Frack but rather Werner Groebli (1915–2008) and Hansruedi Mauch (1919–1979). The term "Frick and Frack" has become slang for any two people close enough to pretty much be indistinguishable.

Reference: The Apostles

> **Dorothy:** Everybody named after an Apostle, come with me.

The Apostles were a dozen disciples of Jesus Christ from the New Testament of the Bible, and the folks depicted having a meal with him in the painting *The Last Supper*. The group consisted of Simon, Andrew, James, John, Philip, Bartholomew, Thomas, Matthew, Thaddaeus, another James, another Simon, and Judas.

References: *Totally Hidden Video*, Kaye Ballard

> **Sophia:** Have you guys ever heard of *Totally Hidden Video*? Well, underneath this gray wig is comedian Kaye Ballard.

Totally Hidden Video is a hidden-camera comedy series that aired on Fox from 1989 to 1992. Actress, singer, and comedian Kaye Ballard (1925–2019) began her career in the 1940s, becoming known for her skills in stand-up and broad physical comedy. She appeared in various film, stage, and television roles from the 1950s well into the early twenty-first century, and for many years was a fixture on late-night talk shows and game shows.

Repeat References: Mercedes-Benz *(Episode 3.3: Bringing Up Baby)*, *The Glass Menagerie* and Tennessee Williams *(Episode 3.16: Grab That Dough)*,

Phil Rizzuto *(Episode 4.24: Foreign Exchange)*, Spanish fly *(Episode 2.1: End of the Curse)*, the Statue of Liberty *(Episode 2.12: The Sisters)*

Episode 5.16: Clinton Avenue Memoirs

Directed by Terry Hughes. Written by Richard Vaczy and Tracy Gamble. Original airdate: February 3, 1990.

Dorothy and Sophia visit their old apartment in Brooklyn in hopes of stirring Sophia's memory. Rose hires Blanche to help with a work project.

Reference: Conway Twitty

> **Blanche:** He was the first person ever to use mousse.
>
> **Rose:** I'd check my facts if I were you, Blanche. Mr. Ingrid of St. Olaf has been using moose ever since I can remember. Of course, it's his own professional secret which part of the moose he uses. But it'll keep your hair in place in winds up to 130 miles an hour.
>
> **Blanche:** I just don't believe you, Rose.
>
> **Rose:** Ask Conway Twitty.

Conway Twitty (1933–1993) was a country music singer known for hits like "Hello Darlin'" and for duets with Loretta Lynn like "After the Fire Is Gone" and "Louisiana Woman, Mississippi Man." He also had hair that never moved.

Reference: Alan Alda

> **Dorothy:** I never thought Ma would lose her memory. Of course, I never thought Alan Alda would get on my nerves.

Alan Alda is a six-time Emmy and Golden Globe Award–winning actor, writer, director, comedian, and philanthropist who shot to fame portraying Hawkeye Pierce on *M*A*S*H*, a role for which he's most remembered, but he's done tons of things before and since, including more recent roles on *The West Wing* and *30 Rock*. In the 1970s, Alda was a vocal advocate of women's rights and spoke out against toxic masculinity. While his progressive views might be less shocking (and yet no less needed) today, you can imagine how some responded at the time, derogatorily labeling him the "sensitive man" type who cooks and cleans and eats quiche.

Reference: Jean Harlow

> **Dorothy:** Pop was a big fan of Jean Harlow's back then. You hated it when he made sand breasts in front of the children.

Actress and sex symbol nicknamed the "Blonde Bombshell," Jean Harlow (1911–1937) was one of the biggest stars in 1930s Hollywood, known for such films as *Hell's Angels*, *Red-Headed Woman*, *Red Dust*, *Dinner at Eight*, and *Suzy*.

Reference: John F. Kennedy

> **Sophia:** I could've slept with JFK and don't even know it.

John F. Kennedy (1917–1963) was the thirty-fifth president of the United States from 1961 until his assassination. Kennedy—or JFK, as he's often called—had served as a Democratic member of the US House of Representatives and Senate prior to his presidency.

References: Fig Newtons, Norm Crosby

> **Sal:** I'm not really here. I'm just a Fig Newton of your imagination.
>
> **Sophia:** Oh Sal, it's been so long I'd forgotten how much you used to like Norm Crosby.

Invented in 1891, Newtons are little square cookies filled with fruit paste, named after the town of Newton, Massachusetts, not Isaac Newton. While several Newton flavors exist, like apple cinnamon and strawberry, it's the fig version that's most often associated with the Nabisco-made product. A popular comedian of the 1970s, Norm Crosby is known as the "Master of Malaprop," which is a mistaken use of an incorrect word in place of a word that sounds the same, which results in a nonsensical statement.

Reference: Charlemagne

> **Sal:** Gladys says hello.
>
> **Sophia:** You fooling around with Gladys?
>
> **Sal:** Of course not. Gladys is going out with Charlemagne.

Charlemagne (748–814) was a European emperor in the Early Middle Ages who held such roles as King of the Franks, King of the Lombards, and Emperor of the Romans.

Repeat References: Pablo Picasso *(Episode 3.13: The Artist)*, the Dodgers *(Episode 3.14: Blanche's Little Girl)*

EPISODE 5.17: LIKE THE BEEP BEEP BEEP OF THE TOM-TOM
Directed by Terry Hughes. Written by Phillip Jayson Lasker. Original airdate: February 10, 1990.
Blanche fears intimacy after having a pacemaker implanted.

Reference: Infiniti

> **Dorothy:** Ma, I never knew you were so philosophical.
>
> **Sophia:** I'm not. It's those damn Infiniti commercials. They're driving me crazy.

Infiniti is an automobile in the Nissan family released in 1989 with a series of oblique and pretentious television commercials that attempted to appeal to a premium audience.

References: Tip O'Neill, Jesse Helms

> **Sophia:** Dorothy, have you been fooling around with my Tip O'Neill calendar?
>
> **Dorothy:** No, Ma, I haven't.
>
> **Sophia:** Come on. I'm missing March. It's the month where he's playing volleyball with Jesse Helms.

Tip O'Neill (1912–1994) was a Democratic politician who served as the Speaker of the US House of Representatives from 1977 to 1987. Jesse Helms (1921–2008) was a Republican US senator from North Carolina in office from 1973 to 2003, known for strong Christian views as well as his opposition to civil rights and homosexuality.

Reference: "Over There"

> *Rose sings this song to comfort Blanche.*

"Over There" is a patriotic 1917 George M. Cohan song popular with the US military during both world wars.

Repeat References: Johnny Carson *(Episode 3.3: Bringing Up Baby)*, Raymond Burr *(Episode 4.12: Blind Date)*

EPISODE 5.18: AN ILLEGITIMATE CONCERN

Directed by Terry Hughes. Written by Marc Cherry and Jamie Wooten. Original airdate: February 12, 1990.

Blanche is stunned when a young man claims to be the illegitimate son of her late husband, George. Dorothy and Sophia enter a mother-daughter beauty contest at Shady Pines.

References: Doug Henning, Cher

> **Sophia, dressed as Sonny Bono:** Well Rose, do I look like the mayor of Palm Springs?
>
> **Rose:** Doug Henning is the mayor of Palm Springs?
>
> *Dorothy enters, dressed as Cher.*

Doug Henning (1947–2000) was a Canadian magician and illusionist known for a series of *World of Magic* TV specials in the 1970s and early 1980s, and he dabbled in politics in the 1990s.

Music legend Cher was born Cherilyn Sarkisian in 1946 and rose to fame alongside then-husband Sonny Bono in the 1960s, with hit records like "I Got You Babe." The pair cohosted a variety series in the 1970s while Cher balanced an increasingly successful solo career with her own hits like "Gypsys, Tramps & Thieves," "Half-Breed," and "Dark Lady." Throughout her decades-long career, Cher has weathered various peaks and valleys, successfully tackling music, Broadway, TV, movies, fashion, and pretty much anything else she's tried along the way. A string of hit films in the 1980s culminated with an Oscar win for 1987's *Moonstruck*, while various dips in charting records have been revived by smash hits like 1989's "If I Could Turn Back Time" and 1999's "Believe." More recent efforts have included a Las Vegas concert residency, an appearance in 2018's *Mamma Mia!* film sequel, and an album of ABBA covers.

Reference: "I Got You Babe"

> *Dorothy and Sophia sing the song in costume.*

Written by Sonny Bono, "I Got You Babe" is the 1965 number-one hit and signature song of Sonny and Cher.

Reference: Cheech and Chong

> **Blanche:** You two could be celebrity lookalikes!

Dorothy: Oh Blanche, do you really think so?

Blanche: Absolutely. Now which one's Cheech and which one's Chong?

Cheech and Chong were a comedy duo consisting of Cheech Marin and Tommy Chong, who found success in the 1970s and 1980s with stand-up comedy, recordings, and films based on their hippie personas and a love of cannabis. Their 1978 movie *Up in Smoke* became a cult-classic stoner film and warranted two sequels. Several more films followed before the pair began working on separate projects in the mid-1980s. Following their prime duo years, Chong went on to a role in the sitcom *That '70s Show*, while Marin costarred on *The Golden Girls* spinoff *The Golden Palace* as the hotel's chef.

Reference: Piggly Wiggly

Sophia: The winning mother and daughter are ninety-eight and seventy-seven. If either one of them forgets to take a nitroglycerin even once, Dorothy and I are going to be cutting ribbons at Piggly Wiggly.

Piggly Wiggly is a supermarket chain first opened in 1916.

References: *The Fantasticks*, "Try to Remember"

Dorothy: For the talent section, she was supposed to do a medley from *The Fantasticks*. She started with "Try to Remember," and she couldn't.

The Fantasticks is a 1960 musical by Harvey Schmidt and Tom Jones about two neighbors who trick their children into falling in love by pretending to feud. The original production ran off-Broadway from 1960 to 2002. "Try to Remember" is one of the musical's songs, about nostalgia.

Reference: Andy Rooney

Blanche: You put me through all this, and I could've had Andy Rooney.

Andy Rooney (1919–2011) was a radio and television writer best remembered for his weekly "A Few Minutes with Andy Rooney" segments on the CBS News program *60 Minutes* from 1978 to 2011.

Repeat References: The Seven Dwarfs *(Episode 5.12: Have Yourself a Very Little Christmas)*, 60 Minutes *(Episode 3.7: Strange Bedfellows)*, Morley Safer *(Episode 2.14: The Actor)*, Sonny Bono *(Episode 3.23: Mixed Blessings)*

EPISODE 5.19: 72 HOURS

Directed by Terry Hughes. Written by Richard Vaczy and Tracy Gamble. Original airdate: February 17, 1990.
Rose is afraid that a transfusion she had several years ago contained HIV-infected blood. Dorothy plans a fund-raiser to save the wetlands.

Reference: Trini Lopez

> **Sophia:** If you could buy a celebrity at an auction, I'd be showering every morning with Trini Lopez.

Trini Lopez (1937–2020) was a singer and actor known for hits like "Lemon Tree," "If I Had a Hammer," and "I'm Comin' Home, Cindy."

Reference: William F. Buckley

> **Blanche:** I know what the F. stands for in William F. Buckley.

William F. Buckley (1925–2008) was a conservative author and host who founded the *National Review*, a conservative magazine, in 1955, and hosted nearly 1,500 episodes of the public affairs series *Firing Line* between 1966 and 1999. The "F." stands for Francis.

References: Stonehenge, Druids, Shriners

> **Rose:** Luckily there were some Druid priests who were in town for the opening of Stonehenge Land.... They weren't Druid priests at all, just a bunch of Shriners looking for a good time.

Stonehenge is an English prehistoric monument consisting of a ring of standing stones, believed to have been constructed between 3000 BC and 2000 BC. Druids were the high-ranking class in ancient Celtic cultures, often religious leaders, doctors, politicians, and legal authorities. The Shriners are a Masonic society established in 1870.

Reference: "Anything You Can Do (I Can Do Better)"

> **Sophia:** After I had my prescription filled, I went up to Geriatrics and sang "Anything You Can Do (I Can Do Better)."

"Anything You Can Do (I Can Do Better)" is a tune from the 1946 Broadway musical *Annie Get Your Gun*, composed by Irving Berlin. In the play, the titular Annie Oakley duets with Frank Butler, setting the scene for a climactic sharpshooting contest. The lyrics toss playfully between the two, each proclaiming anything one can do, the other can do better. Ethel Merman originated the Annie Oakley role on Broadway. The song, meanwhile, has been covered multiple times over the years, including a rather memorable joust between Merman and Miss Piggy on *The Muppet Show*.

Reference: Manuel Noriega

> **Dorothy:** They decided to play at the Free Noriega benefit.

Manuel Noriega (1934–2017) was a politician and military officer who was the de facto ruler of Panama from 1983 to 1989. In December 1989, President Bush sent troops to Panama City to arrest Noriega, who fled to asylum at the Vatican Embassy. Troops responded by blasting rock and rap music in an attempt to force a surrender. It worked.

Reference: Maxwell Q. Klinger

> **Rose:** You couldn't trust Klinger on guard duty and you can't trust him now.

Maxwell Q. Klinger was the fictional cross-dressing corporal played by actor Jamie Farr on the television series *M*A*S*H*.

Reference: "The Hokey-Pokey"

> **Dorothy:** What were you doing in my bathroom for two hours?
> **Sophia:** "The Hokey-Pokey." What do you think I was doing?

"The Hokey-Pokey" is a famous children's song and participation dance dating back to the 1800s.

Reference: Shell

> **Sophia:** Hey, I'm making progress. Yesterday, I was using the bathroom down at the Shell station.

Shell Oil Company is one of the largest oil companies in the world. It was founded in Houston, Texas.

References: 4-H, Aldo Ray

> **Dorothy:** In school, I actually joined the math club so I could meet guys.
> **Rose:** I can beat that. I joined the 4-H club to be hip.

Dorothy: The Aldo Ray Fan Club!

Rose: I can beat that, too. No I can't. That's pretty bad.

4-H is a network of nonprofit youth organizations with a distinctive clover logo, which includes four Hs, one in each clover leaf, which stand for head, heart, hands, and health. Founded in the early twentieth century to help youths reach their fullest potential, 4-H in the United States is administered by the USDA's National Institute of Food and Agriculture, with programs conducted through the nation's land-grant university extension services. Though typically considered an agricultural organization, 4-H has modernized in recent times with an increased focus in science and technology programs.

Aldo Ray (1926–1991) was an actor known for roles such as *The Marrying Kind*, *Pat and Mike*, *Let's Do It Again*, and *Battle Cry*.

Repeat References: Jell-O *(Episode 1.20: Adult Education)*, Linda Evans *(Episode 2.6: Big Daddy's Little Lady)*, Jamie Farr *(Episode 2.3: Take Him, He's Mine)*, M*A*S*H *(Episode 3.2: One for the Money)*, Miami Herald *(Episode 4.14: Love Me Tender)*

EPISODE 5.20: TWICE IN A LIFETIME
Directed by Terry Hughes. Written by Robert Bruce and Martin Weiss. Original airdate: February 24, 1990.
Rose must decide whether to rekindle an old romance or continue seeing Miles. Fed up with Dorothy's strict rules, Sophia decides to move out.

Reference: Spike Jones

> **Rose:** I almost married Buzz. We were talking about it when he got a call from the Spike Jones Band.

Spike Jones (1911–1965) was a musician and bandleader popular in the 1940s and 1950s, known for satirical arrangements of popular and classical music.

Reference: *Henry V*

> **Miles:** I was going to take you to see *Henry V*.
>
> **Rose:** It's just as well. I always think by the time they get to number five, those sequels get pretty predictable.

Henry V is a historical play by William Shakespeare, written somewhere around 1599 and telling the story of King Henry V of England.

Reference: Bob Costas

> **Dorothy:** Every time I'd knock on her door late at night, she'd say, "Not now. I'm watching Bob Costas."

Bob Costas was an Emmy Award–winning sportscaster for NBC Sports from 1980 to 2019.

References: Pierre-Auguste Renoir, Georges Seurat, Jackson Pollock

> **Blanche:** Look at this Renoir!
>
> **Maria:** Actually, that's a Seurat. . . . Do you want to see the Jackson Pollock in the john?

Pierre-Auguste Renoir (1841–1919) was a French artist instrumental in the development of Impressionism. Georges Seurat (1859–1891) was a French post-Impressionist artist known for devising the pointillism technique. Jackson Pollock (1912–1956) was a painter considered a major figure in the abstract expressionist movement of the 1940s.

Repeat References: Chiclets *(Episode 3.20: And Ma Makes Three)*, Wolfie's *(Episode 2.1: End of the Curse)*, egg cream *(Episode 5.3: Accurate Conception)*, Rocky IV *(Episode 3.6: Letter to Gorbachev)*, Amos 'n' Andy *(Episode 3.10: The Audit)*, Cher *(Episode 5.18: An Illegitimate Concern)*

EPISODE 5.21: SISTERS AND OTHER STRANGERS

Directed by Terry Hughes. Written by Marc Cherry and Jamie Wooten. Original airdate: March 3, 1990.

Blanche's sister, Charmaine, visits Miami for a book signing, and Blanche is convinced that the novel's plot is taken from her own life. Dorothy is forced to host Stan's visiting cousin from Czechoslovakia, who extols the virtues of communism.

Reference: Czechoslovakia revolution

> **Dorothy:** Rose, the revolution in Czechoslovakia was a peaceful one. Nobody was chased by a pack of dogs.

Known as the Velvet Revolution, the event was a 1989 bloodless revolution in Czechoslovakia, which ended the communist regime after fifty years.

Reference: Sheraton

> **Blanche:** By the time she leaves Miami, she'll be more famous here than I am.
>
> **Dorothy:** Honey, only if they close the Sheraton.

Sheraton is an international hotel chain founded by Ernest Henderson and Robert Moore in 1937.

Reference: Gopher

> **Charmaine:** It was in the will.
>
> **Blanche:** Is this the same will where he promised the summer house to Gopher from *Love Boat*?

Burl "Gopher" Smith was a fictional character on the television series *The Love Boat*, portrayed by Fred Grandy, who later became a US representative from Iowa.

Reference: *Flora, the Red Menace*

> **Blanche:** Where's Magda?
>
> **Dorothy:** You mean Flora, the Red Menace?

Flora, the Red Menace is a 1965 musical by George Abbott and Robert Russell about a woman attempting to find work during the Great Depression who falls in love with a communist. Liza Minnelli originated the role of Flora and won a Tony Award for Best Actress.

Reference: Hickory Farms

> **Dorothy:** She said we are a plastic society with no soul. This was after I bought her beef sticks and spreadable cheese from Hickory Farms.

Hickory Farms is a food gift retailer founded by Richard Ransom in 1951, known for its summer sausage and handcrafted cheese products, among other items.

Reference: Slurpee

> **Rose:** There must be something about this country you like.

Magda: I like Slurpees.

Slurpees are frozen carbonated slush drinks sold at 7-Eleven convenience stores.

References: Joseph McCarthy, Charlie McCarthy

> **Rose:** I remember in the early fifties when McCarthy came to St. Olaf to speak in the town square. I was never so moved by a public speaker. Although some people thought he was a puppet for the Right Wing. No, wait. That was Charlie McCarthy.

Joseph McCarthy (1908–1957) was a Republican senator from Wisconsin who, in the 1950s, began tossing out accusations of communist subversion and that Soviet spies and sympathizers had infiltrated the United States, including many in the film industry who were blacklisted because of the claims. Charlie McCarthy was the famed ventriloquist dummy partner of comedian Edgar Bergen. The character was a top-hat-and-tuxedo-clad mischievous little boy. His popularity eventually eclipsed that of Bergen. In fact, for a time their television variety program was titled *The Charlie McCarthy Show*. Bergen died in 1979, and Charlie is on permanent display at the Smithsonian.

References: Thomas Paine, *Common Sense*

> **Dorothy:** Magda, there are two books that I want you to read. The first one is Thomas Payne's *Common Sense*. I think it'll give you some idea of what freedom is all about. The other is Vanna White's autobiography.

Thomas Paine (1737–1809) was a political activist and American revolutionary who authored *Common Sense*, an influential pamphlet advocating for independence from Great Britain. It was published anonymously in 1776, at the beginning of the American Revolution, and became an important stepping-stone toward independence.

Reference: The Bermuda Triangle

> **Sophia:** We're so close to the Bermuda Triangle, it'd be a shame for her not to see it.

The Bermuda Triangle is an area in the Atlantic Ocean, forming a triangle from points at Florida to Bermuda to Puerto Rico, where several aircraft and ships have mysteriously disappeared.

Reference: "That's Amore"

Sophia sings the song while knitting.

"That's Amore" is a 1953 song by Harry Warren and Jack Brooks and popularized by singer Dean Martin.

Repeat References: *The Love Boat (Episode 2.19: Long Day's Journey into Marinara)*, communism *(Episode 3.6: Letter to Gorbachev)*, Vanna White *(Episode 2.4: It's a Miserable Life)*, Fotomat *(Episode 2.9: Joust Between Friends)*

EPISODE 5.22: CHEATERS
Directed by Terry Hughes. Written by Tom Whedon. Original airdate: March 24, 1990.
Dorothy rekindles a relationship with the formerly married man she dated years ago. Blanche and Sophia become victims of a con game.

References: Charlie Brown, Schroeder, Lucy, Snoopy, penis envy

> **Rose:** I had the strangest dream last night. Charlie Brown was pitching and Schroeder was behind the plate. Lucy and Snoopy were in the outfield, and they wouldn't let me play. When I woke up I was crying. What do you suppose it all means?
>
> **Dorothy:** *Peanuts* envy?

These are all characters from the *Peanuts* comic strip by Charles Schulz. The joke is a play on penis envy, Sigmund Freud's oft-criticized theory of the stage of female psychosexual development in which girls realize they do not have a penis.

Reference: Q-tips

> **Sophia:** Buy genuine Q-tips. If I'm going to put a stick in my ear, I'd like a little cotton at the end.

Q-tips are a brand of cotton swabs consisting of two small wads of cotton on the end of a little rolled-paper stick. Most people use them for cleaning their ears, even though physicians suggest you shouldn't.

Repeat References: *Peanuts (Episode 3.16: Grab That Dough)*, *Jeopardy! (Episode 3.5: Nothing to Fear but Fear Itself)*, Maalox *(Episode 1.8: Break-In)*, Girl Scouts *(Episode 1.19: Second Motherhood)*

EPISODE 5.23: THE MANGIACAVALLO CURSE MAKES A LOUSY WEDDING PRESENT

Directed by Terry Hughes. Written by Phillip Jayson Lasker. Original airdate: March 31, 1990.

The girls attend the wedding of Dorothy's goddaughter. Sophia must confront a man that she put a curse on after he jilted her at the altar decades ago.

Reference: Bryant Gumbel

> **Rose:** Morning, Dorothy.
>
> **Dorothy:** I didn't want to hear it from Bryant Gumbel, and I don't want to hear it from you.

Bryant Gumbel is a broadcast journalist and sportscaster best known for his fifteen-year stint cohosting NBC's *Today* from 1982 to 1997 and for hosting the Peabody Award–winning HBO series *Real Sports with Bryant Gumbel*, which debuted in 1995.

Reference: *Song of Norway*

> **Rose:** We'd end up going home, putting on the cast album of *Song of Norway*, and going crazy on each other.

Song of Norway is a 1970 film based on the operetta of the same name, about the life of composer Edvard Grieg. It starred Toralv Maurstad and Florence Henderson.

Reference: Laurel and Hardy

> **Rose:** I just hope the band doesn't play the St. Olaf wedding march.
>
> **Dorothy:** I think the chances of that are pretty slim.
>
> **Rose:** I don't know. It got awfully popular after Laurel and Hardy started using it as their theme song.

Stan Laurel (1890–1965) and Oliver Hardy (1892–1957) were a popular comedy duo during the Classic Hollywood era and known for films like *The Music Box, Big Business, Sons of the Desert*, and many others. Their popularity has long endured through merchandise, museums, and an appearance in an episode of *Scooby-Doo*.

Reference: The Hippocratic Oath

> **Blanche:** I just hate it when these doctors use the Hippocratic Oath as an excuse for everything.

The Hippocratic Oath is an oath of ethics historically taken by doctors.

Reference: Dizzy Gillespie

> **Rose:** I'm not available, unless of course you like jazz?
> **Doug:** I've got Dizzy Gillespie back at my place.
> **Rose:** Does he like jazz?

Musician Dizzy Gillespie (1917–1993) was a trumpet virtuoso who combined musical skill with showmanship to become a pioneer in modern jazz in the 1940s.

Reference: "Volare"

> **Mangiacavallo:** . . . the band doesn't even know "Volare."

"Volare" is a 1958 song by Domenico Modugno, sung in Italian.

Reference: The Colosseum

> **Sophia:** Checkered tablecloths, the candle in the Chianti bottle, bad paintings of the Colosseum.
> **Mangiacavallo:** You remember.
> **Sophia:** No, but the odds were in my favor.

The Colosseum is an oval amphitheater located in the center of the city of Rome, Italy. Built between AD 70 and AD 80, the Colosseum was used for gladiator contests, public spectacles, executions, and dramatic performances. Its use as an entertainment venue ended in the early medieval era, and it has been substantially impacted by earthquakes. It remains an iconic symbol and one of Rome's most popular tourist destinations.

Repeat References: "The Hokey-Pokey" *(Episode 5.19: 72 Hours)*, *The Exorcist (Episode 2.4: It's a Miserable Life)*

Episode 5.24: All Bets Are Off

Directed by Terry Hughes. Written by Eugene B. Stein. Original airdate: April 28, 1990.

Dorothy's trip to the racetrack revives an old gambling habit. Rose takes up painting. Blanche is insulted by a coworker's rejection.

Reference: George "Goober" Lindsey

> **Blanche:** I have a date with the most cultured, urbane, sophisticated man in the whole world.
>
> **Rose:** You know George "Goober" Lindsey?

George Lindsey (1928–2012) was a comedian and actor best known for playing Goober Pyle on *The Andy Griffith Show* and *Mayberry R.F.D.*, and for a stint on *Hee-Haw*.

Reference: Michael Dukakis

> **Dorothy:** It's nice to know I could still pick a winner.
>
> **Sophia:** This from a woman who has a Dukakis bumper sticker covering up her Mondale bumper sticker.

Michael Dukakis is a former politician who served as governor of Massachusetts from 1975 to 1979 and 1983 to 1991. He also was the Democratic nominee for president in 1988, losing to George H. W. Bush.

Reference: Hialeah

> **Dorothy:** There's a horse that looks good to me at Hialeah today.

Hialeah Park Racing & Casino is a historic horse-racing track and casino in Hialeah Park, Florida, opened in 1922.

Repeat References: Walter Mondale *(Episode 2.21: Dorothy's Prized Pupil)*, Grandma Moses *(Episode 2.8: Vacation)*, The Temptations *(Episode 2.19: Long Day's Journey into Marinara)*, Lamaze *(Episode 5.13: Mary Has a Little Lamb)*, Chips Ahoy! *(Episode 3.12: Charlie's Buddy)*

EPISODES 5.25 AND 5.26: THE PRESIDENT'S COMING! THE PRESIDENT'S COMING!—PARTS 1 AND 2

Directed by Lex Passaris. Written by Marc Sotkin, Gail Parent, Martin Weiss, Robert Bruce, Phillip Jayson Lasker, Tom Whedon, Marc Cherry, and Jamie Wooten. Original airdate: May 5, 1990.
The girls learn that their house is a candidate for a visit from President George H. W. Bush and reminisce while being interviewed by the Secret Service.

Reference: ARCO

Agent Bell: The president wants to stop at one house on his way to dedicate the senior citizens' center.

Sophia: Why can't he use the ARCO station like everyone else?

The Atlantic Richfield Company, or ARCO, is an American oil company that has been providing gasoline for automobiles since 1966. It was one of the largest companies in the world back in *The Golden Girls* days. Buyouts happened over the years, with many stations being rebranded along the way. Today, most ARCO stations are located in the western United States.

References: Underoos, Spider-Man

Sophia: Pussycat, if you're writing to your brother Phil, tell him I said thanks for the Underoos. Spiderman scared the hell out of my doctor.

Underoos is a brand of underwear produced by Fruit of the Loom, featuring popular characters primarily for children. Over the decades, Underoos have featured everyone from Superman to Barbie to He-Man to Harry Potter, among many others. Spider-Man is a fictional superhero in the Marvel Comics universe, created by Stan Lee in 1962. The character is the alter ego of Peter Parker, who gains spider-like superpowers after being bitten by a radioactive spider. He has become an icon over the decades, appearing in multiple comics, television series, merchandise lines, and films, the most recent of which features actor Tom Holland in the role.

Reference: John McEnroe

Dorothy: It's not like I'm some kind of hothead.

Sophia: Please, I'd put you about even with John McEnroe, except McEnroe knows when to stop.

John McEnroe is a volatile tennis player who rose to fame in the 1980s, known as much for his athleticism and skill as for his confrontational behavior that frequently landed him in hot water on the court. He was married to actress Tatum O'Neal from 1986 to 1994 and married rock singer Patty Smyth in 1997.

Reference: Christopher Columbus

Dorothy: I see kids who can't even find India on a map.

Rose: Well to be fair, Dorothy, that stumped Columbus, too.

Christopher Columbus (1451–1506) was a fifteenth-century Italian explorer and navigator whose Atlantic voyages opened the way for European exploration and colonization of the Americas. Columbus has long been considered the discoverer of America in popular culture, despite the fact that a bunch of people were already living there when he showed up and other explorers had reached its shores before him.

Reference: Daniel Ortega

> **Stan:** I just took a bath on those Daniel Ortega buttons that say "Four more years."

Daniel Ortega is a politician who served as leader of Nicaragua from 1979 to 1990, when he lost reelection—hence, this joke. He became president again in 2007.

Reference: The Sierra Club

> **Agent Bell:** What organizations do you belong to? We have to make sure none of them could be considered a threat to the president.
>
> **Dorothy:** Oh, well I'm a member of the Sierra Club.

The Sierra Club is an environmental preservation organization founded by John Muir in 1892.

References: The Oval Office, Herbert Hoover, Hoover vacuum cleaners, the White House

> **Rose:** Is the Oval Office as hard to vacuum as I think it is?
>
> **George Bush:** I don't know. There hasn't been a Hoover in the White House in sixty years.

The Oval Office is the working office space of the president of the United States. Herbert Hoover (1874–1964) was an engineer and businessman who served as president of the United States from 1929 to 1933. Prior to that he was the US secretary of commerce from 1921 to 1928 and director of the US Food Administration from 1917 to 1918. Hoover is a company that produces vacuum cleaners, founded in 1908 by William Henry Hoover. The White House is the official residence and workplace of the US president, located in Washington, DC.

Repeat References: George H. W. Bush *(Episode 3.21: Larceny and Old Lace)*, a thousand points of light *(Episode 4.16: Two Rode Together)*, Benito Mussolini *(Episode 3.7: Strange Bedfellows)*, Daughters of the Confederacy *(Episode 4.19: 'Til Death Do We Volley)*

Season Six: 1990–1991

THE SIXTH SEASON IS AN INTERESTING ONE, IN THAT NOTHING NECESSARILY jumps out to define it like other seasons. Tonally, the show relaxes a little from last season's heavy-handedness on issues, while the writing continues to veer away from the overload of topical references that appeared in the first four years.

If there is a defining arc to the season, it's the exploration of the relationship between Dorothy and Stan, who has apparently divorced the lady he married in season four and, after striking it rich with a baked potato opener, rekindles a romance with Dorothy. The storyline somewhat divided fans and, thankfully, is resolved midseason.

Some of the more timely references we hear this year include nods to *The Simpsons*, the Nintendo Game Boy, and *Teenage Mutant Ninja Turtles*. Perhaps the writers realized a lot of kids were watching the show with their grandmothers—and are probably now reading this book.

EPISODE 6.1: BLANCHE DELIVERS
Directed by Matthew Diamond. Written by Gail Parent and Jim Vallely. Original airdate: September 22, 1990.
Blanche's daughter, Becky, announces her plan to have her baby in a birthing center instead of a hospital. Rose takes figure-skating lessons.

Reference: Rotary

> **Rose:** He was in charge of delivering babies and handing out corn at the Rotary picnics.

Rotary International is a service organization that brings together business leaders and professionals to provide humanitarian service in their communities.

Reference: Laura Ashley

> **Blanche:** I think it would cost less to squat in a Laura Ashley showroom.

Laura Ashley is a British retail chain specializing in furniture and home accessories, founded in 1953 by Bernard and Laura Ashley.

Reference: Skeet shooting

> **Blanche:** Just remember: Pull! Pull! Oh no, that's skeet shooting.

Skeet shooting is a recreational activity in which people attempt to shoot clay targets with a shotgun after they (the targets) have been flung into the air at high speed. When the shooter is ready to begin, they yell, "Pull!" so the person operating the station knows to release the target.

Reference: Bigfoot

> **Sophia:** I call Dorothy Bigfoot. That doesn't mean she has to make tracks all over the Northwest.

Bigfoot is a large, apelike creature in North American folklore who walks on two legs and roams the forests of the United States and Canada.

Repeat References: Milton Berle *(Episode 2.19: Long Day's Journey into Marinara)*, the Great Depression *(Episode 2.6: Big Daddy's Little Lady)*, Lamaze *(Episode 5.13: Mary Has a Little Lamb)*, Mel Gibson *(Episode 3.5: Nothing to Fear but Fear Itself)*, Kim Basinger *(Episode 3.12: Charlie's Buddy)*, Graceland *(Episode 1.18: The Operation)*

EPISODE 6.2: ONCE, IN ST. OLAF
Directed by Matthew Diamond. Written by Harold Apter. Original airdate: September 29, 1990.
Rose meets her biological father at the hospital where Sophia is having hernia surgery.

Reference: Trekkie

> **Rose:** Occupation?
> **Brother Martin:** I'm a monk.
> **Rose:** Oh good. I almost wrote down Trekkie.

Trekkies are fans of the *Star Trek* franchise.

Reference: Wilma Flintstone

> **Brother Martin:** Do I know you? You look awfully familiar.
>
> **Rose:** I get that a lot. People say I look like Wilma Flintstone. Not when she was on the air, more the way she looks today.

The matriarch of the Flintstone family from the animated series *The Flintstones* (see *Episode 4.20: High Anxiety* for more on that).

Reference: Ringling Bros.

> **Rose:** There was a rumor he was a clown with Ringling Bros., but I never believed it. Just seemed too much to hope for.

The Ringling Bros. were seven siblings who transformed a small touring company of performers into one of the world's largest circuses in the late nineteenth century. They eventually merged with another large performing outfit, resulting in the famous Ringling Bros. and Barnum & Bailey Circus, which was active from 1919 to 2017.

References: Errol Flynn, Amelia Earhart, Masters and Johnson

> **Dorothy:** My dad was Errol Flynn and my mother was Amelia Earhart. I wanted Dad all to myself.
>
> **Blanche:** You know who my fantasy parents were?
>
> **Dorothy:** Who, Blanche, Masters and Johnson?

One of the biggest stars of the Golden Age of Hollywood, Errol Flynn (1909–1959) appeared in a string of successful films in the 1930s and 1940s, such as *The Adventures of Robin Hood*, *Captain Blood*, and *Dodge City*. An aviation pioneer and best-selling author, Amelia Earhart was the first female pilot to fly solo across the Atlantic Ocean. She disappeared during an attempted flight around the globe in 1937 and was declared dead in absentia two years later. The pioneering research team of William H. Masters (1915–2001) and Virginia E. Johnson (1925–2013) worked in the nature of human sexual response, disorders, and dysfunctions beginning in the 1950s.

Reference: Bud Abbott

> **Brother Martin:** Then the abbot found out.

305

Rose: Bud Abbott?

William "Bud" Abbott (1897–1974) was a popular comedian, actor, and one half of the legendary duo of Abbott and Costello.

Reference: Lloyd's of London

> **Dr. Tess:** Who is your insurance company?
> **Sophia:** Lloyd's of London. What do I look like? I'm on Medicare.

Lloyd's of London is a British insurance market founded by Edward Lloyd in 1686.

Reference: Volkswagen

> **Sophia:** A few of us gals thought it would be funny to put Gladys's VW on the lawn while she was having her feet sanded.

Volkswagen is a German automobile manufacturer founded in 1937.

Repeat References: Queen Elizabeth II *(Episode 3.25: Mother's Day)*, Medicare *(Episode 3.6: Letter to Gorbachev)*

Episode 6.3: If at Last You Do Succeed
Directed by Matthew Diamond. Written by Robert Spina. Original airdate: October 6, 1990.
Stan strikes it rich with a new novelty item. Rose inadvertently sells to Blanche a valuable stash of St. Olaf war bonds.

Reference: *The Simpsons*

> **Blanche:** I don't want to have to deal with four hundred people in *Simpsons* T-shirts trying to knock twenty-five cents off your "I lost my ass in Vegas" cup.

The Simpsons is an animated sitcom that has aired on the Fox network since 1989. The characters first appeared on *The Tracey Ullman Show* in 1987 before spinning off into their own series, which turned them (especially the character of Bart) into a pop culture phenomenon, with a wealth of merchandise from apparel to toys to a music album filling shelves in the early 1990s.

Reference: Joe Isuzu

> **Dorothy:** Be appalled that Joe Isuzu wasn't played by an Asian actor.

A fictional spokesman for Isuzu cars and trucks in a series of television commercials in the 1980s, Joe Isuzu was depicted as a sleazy, lying car salesman. He was portrayed by actor David Leisure, who played Charley Dietz on *Empty Nest*, as well as Oliver in the original "Empty Nests" crossover pilot episode.

Reference: Game Boy

> **Sophia:** Bring me anything?
>
> **Stan:** Of course. Now, who's my gorgeous gray-haired gal?
>
> **Sophia:** It's me, isn't it, Stan?
>
> **Stan:** You're right.
>
> **Sophia:** Wow, a Game Boy! Very nice!

The Game Boy was an 8-bit handheld video-game console launched by Nintendo in 1989. The portable spinoff of the Nintendo Entertainment System was all the rage upon its release—everyone who was anyone on the playground simply *had* to have one. Subsequent revisions of the Game Boy improved its graphics, added color, and quickly made the original look like a dinosaur. The console was discontinued in 2003.

References: Heering, Ford Fairlane

> **Rose:** She drank some cherry Heering and made love in the backseat of a Fjord Fjairlane. Local car.

Heering is a cherry-flavored liqueur made in Denmark. The Ford Fairlane was an automobile sold by Ford in a full-size model from 1955 to 1961 and as a midsize from 1962 to 1970.

Reference: Hirohito

> **Dorothy:** They loved you, except of course for those Hirohito jokes.
>
> **Stan:** Too soon?

Hirohito (1901–1989) was the emperor of the Empire of Japan from 1926 to 1947 and the state of Japan from 1947 until his death in 1989.

Repeat References: Merv Griffin *(Episode 2.13: The Stan Who Came to Dinner)*, Frank Sinatra *(Episode 1.11: Stan's Return)*

EPISODE 6.4: SNAP OUT OF IT

Directed by Matthew Diamond. Written by Richard Vaczy and Tracy Gamble. Original airdate: October 13, 1990.

Dorothy volunteers for Meals on Wheels and meets a young man who hasn't left his apartment in twenty years. Rose attempts to learn the date of Blanche's real birthday.

Reference: "To the moon, Alice!"

Dorothy: To the moon, Ma!

This is a reference to the line "To the moon, Alice!" It was often uttered by a frustrated Ralph Kramden to his wife, Alice, on the 1950s sitcom *The Honeymooners*, starring Jackie Gleason and Audrey Meadows.

Reference: Meals on Wheels

Sophia: I've been working for this Meals on Wheels program, and I need a driver.

Meals on Wheels originated in the United Kingdom in the 1940s, with versions of the program operating in several countries throughout the world. In the United States, Meals on Wheels America works to address senior isolation and hunger by delivering nutritious meals, along with friendly visits and safety checks, to senior citizens. The organization also provides funding, education, research, and advocacy support.

Reference: Peaceniks

Blanche: I can still see Big Daddy sitting on the porch swing, swilling down home brew, picking off peaceniks with his BB gun.

A peacenik is a member of a pacifist movement.

Reference: Yoda

Blanche: My mistake. I thought since you looked like Yoda you were also wise.

Yoda is a fictional character in the *Star Wars* franchise who first appeared in 1980's *The Empire Strikes Back*. Yoda is a small, green, elderly, and wise alien who trains Luke Skywalker to use the Force.

Reference: "Blowin' in the Wind"

Jimmy sings the song to Dorothy.

"Blowin' in the Wind" is a song written and performed by Bob Dylan, from his 1963 album *The Freewheelin' Bob Dylan*.

References: The Chicago Seven, David Dellinger, Bobby Seale, Tom Hayden

> **Jimmy:** You can name six of the Chicago Seven. I love you.
>
> **Dorothy:** Don't say that. David Dellinger!
>
> [...]
>
> **Dorothy:** Do I have to play hardball? David Dellinger.
>
> **Jimmy:** Don't do this to me.
>
> **Dorothy:** Bobby Seale.
>
> **Jimmy:** It's getting warm in here.
>
> **Dorothy:** Tom Hayden.
>
> **Jimmy:** Oh God, you're good.

The Chicago Seven were a group of defendants charged by the federal government for anti–Vietnam War and countercultural protests at the 1968 Democratic National Convention in Chicago. The defendants were Rennie Davis, David Dellinger, John Froines, Tom Hayden, Abbie Hoffman, Jerry Rubin, and Lee Weiner. An eighth man, Bobby Seale, had his trial severed during proceedings, which means that when Dorothy is rattling off the names of the seven at Jimmy's apartment door and lists Seale, she's not exactly accurate. The story garnered new attention in 2020 with the release of the Netflix film *The Trial of the Chicago 7*, a critical favorite that received a slew of award nominations.

Reference: Kenny Rogers

> **Sophia:** It's like the Good Lord said. You've got to know when to hold them, know when to fold them, know when to walk away.
>
> **Dorothy:** Ma, that's not the Good Lord. That's Kenny Rogers.

Kenny Rogers (1938–2020) was an iconic country music singer known for hits like "Ruby, Don't Take Your Love to Town," "The Gambler" (which is where the lines Sophia says come from), "I Can't Unlove You," and the Dolly

Parton duet "Islands in the Stream." He also dabbled in acting and, in 1991, opened a chain of chicken restaurants called Kenny Rogers Roasters.

Reference: Jackie Mason

> **Sophia:** I'll play the Jackie Mason tapes at half-speed, but I really don't think I'm going to hear anything.

Jackie Mason is a comedian and actor known for his lengthy stand-up career, his work on Broadway, and his roles in films like *Caddyshack II*.

Reference: Pez

> **Blanche:** I must still have some life left in me if I can make Mel Bushman's head snap back like that.
> **Rose:** You mean ol' Pez Head?

Pez is a brand of little block-shaped candy that is inserted into a manual dispenser which is topped with the head of various well-known children's movie, comic, and cartoon characters—Mickey Mouse, Bugs Bunny, Scooby-Doo, Wonder Woman, and so on. The head snaps back to reveal a piece of the candy.

Reference: 8-track tapes

> **Dorothy:** Drive you? Are you kidding? I'll listen to 8-tracks with you.

Predating digital streaming by decades, 8-track tapes were cartridges containing prerecorded music popular from the mid-1960s until the early 1980s. Compact cassette tapes eventually overtook them in popularity, after which 8-tracks were rendered obsolete.

Repeat References: Jimmy Smits *(Episode 5.10: All That Jazz)*, Bobby Vinton *(Episode 3.6: Letter to Gorbachev)*, The Flintstones *(Episode 4.20: High Anxiety)*, Ed Sullivan *(Episode 3.20: And Ma Makes Three)*

Episode 6.5: Wham, Bam, Thank You, Mammy!
Directed by Matthew Diamond. Written by Marc Cherry and Jamie Wooten. Original airdate: October 20, 1990.
Blanche receives a visit from her former nanny, who reveals that she had an affair with Big Daddy. Sophia consults a matchmaker to find Dorothy a date.

Reference: *Playboy*

> **Sophia:** *Playboy* is running a spread on the substitute teachers of Miami.

Playboy is a men's lifestyle and entertainment magazine founded in 1953 by Hugh Hefner, known for its centerfolds of nude and seminude models known as Playmates. Originally a print magazine, it went fully online in 2020.

Reference: San Juan Hill

> **Blanche:** I just can't get over it.
> **Rose:** Over what?
> **Dorothy:** San Juan Hill, Rose.

San Juan Hill was the site of a famous battle of the Spanish-American War, fought on July 1, 1898. Despite heavy casualties, the American forces won the battle.

Reference: *The King and I*

> **Sophia:** You're a substitute teacher. It'll be just like *The King and I*.

The King and I is a 1951 musical by Rodgers and Hammerstein, based on the Margaret Landon novel *Anna and the King of Siam*, about a widowed schoolteacher, Anna Leonowens, hired to teach the children of the King of Siam. The Tony Award–winning original Broadway production starred Yul Brynner and Gertrude Lawrence as the King and Anna. The production has had multiple revivals, as well as a 1956 film version starring Brynner, who won an Academy Award for the role.

Reference: "Tennessee Waltz"

> **Mammy Watkins:** I remember a wedding reception early one June, when the most beautiful bride I'd ever seen danced with her equally handsome father.
> **Blanche:** You were there?
> **Mammy Watkins:** The song was "Tennessee Waltz" and you asked the band to play it twice so you could dance with your daddy as long as possible.

"Tennessee Waltz" is a 1946 country music song written by Redd Stewart and Pee Wee King and recorded by countless artists, including a well-known 1950 Patti Page rendition.

References: "Stardust," *Bonanza*

> **Mammy Watkins:** The music box I gave your father was black enamel and played "Stardust."
>
> **Blanche, hearing the music box:** The theme from *Bonanza*.

"Stardust" is a 1927 Hoagy Carmichael song that has become one of the most recorded songs ever. A US Western television series, *Bonanza* ran on NBC for fourteen seasons, from 1959 to 1973. The show centered on the wealthy Cartwright family of Nevada in the 1860s. Starring Lorne Greene and Michael Landon, the show has aired in reruns for decades and has been named among the greatest TV series of all time. Various revival talks have happened over the years, and a few made-for-TV movies were indeed produced in the 1980s and 1990s, featuring the children of Greene and Landon in starring roles.

Repeat References: Mamie Eisenhower *(Episode 3.2: One for the Money)*, Richard Nixon *(Episode 2.2: Ladies of the Evening)*

EPISODE 6.6: FEELINGS

Directed by Matthew Diamond. Written by Don Seigel and Jerry Perzigian. Original airdate: October 27, 1990.
Dorothy receives threats after flunking the school's star football player. Rose suspects her dentist of sexual assault.

Reference: *The Canterbury Tales*

> **Sophia:** I doubt if *The Canterbury Tales* is going to come up in a huddle.

The Canterbury Tales is a collection of stories written in Middle English by Geoffrey Chaucer between 1387 and 1400. The book has long been a popular choice of reading for high school English classes.

References: *A Tale of Two Cities*, Twin Cities

> **Dorothy:** In his book report on *A Tale of Two Cities*, he said he liked them both but he really prefers Minneapolis, because that's where Prince is from.

A Tale of Two Cities is an 1859 Charles Dickens novel about a doctor released from imprisonment in Paris to live in London with his daughter, whom he's never met. This joke refers to Minnesota's Twin Cities of Minneapolis and St. Paul.

Reference: *Trump: The Art of the Deal*

> **Coach Odlivak:** You let Kevin play this weekend and I'll take you out Saturday night.
>
> **Dorothy:** You haven't read *The Art of the Deal*, have you, Coach?

Trump: The Art of the Deal is a 1987 book credited to Donald Trump and Tony Schwartz. It's part memoir and part business advice manual. Schwartz has since said he regrets writing the book, claims that Trump actually had no hand in its writing, and that it should be recategorized as fiction.

Reference: Raymond Massey

> **Rose:** Do you know who she came out looking like? Raymond Massey!
>
> **Dorothy:** Rose, that's terrible.
>
> **Rose:** That's what I thought when I accused the guy of malpractice and ruined his business. Unfortunately, little did I know.
>
> **Blanche:** Know what, Rose?
>
> **Rose:** That's the look she was going for!

Raymond Massey (1896–1983) was an actor known for roles in radio, film, and television, including *Abe Lincoln in Illinois*, *Arsenic and Old Lace*, and *Dr. Kildare*.

Repeat References: Prince *(Episode 2.22: Diamond in the Rough)*, Sigmund Freud *(Episode 3.24: Mister Terrific)*, Metamucil *(Episode 2.10: Love, Rose)*

EPISODE 6.7: ZBORN AGAIN

Directed by Matthew Diamond. Written by Mitchell Hurwitz. Original airdate: November 3, 1990.

Dorothy rekindles a relationship with Stan. Rose seeks Sophia's help in dealing with an annoying coworker.

Reference: *Ghostbusters*

> **Sophia:** He's been coming on to you like gangbusters, and I don't like it. Not that I've ever actually seen gangbusters. But I did see *Ghostbusters* and I didn't like that either.

Ghostbusters is a 1984 science-fiction comedy starring Bill Murray, Dan Aykroyd, Sigourney Weaver, Harold Ramis, and Annie Potts. The film follows the misadventures of a group of scientists who open a paranormal investigation service to rid New York City of a ghost infestation. *Ghostbusters* was a massive success, spawning endless merchandise, an animated series, an endlessly catchy theme song by Ray Parker Jr., and a 1989 sequel. The movie's cultural impact has only grown over the decades. Director Paul Feig rebooted the franchise with an all-female cast in 2016, and director Jason Reitman (son of the original film's director, Ivan Reitman) helmed a new direct sequel to the original released in 2021.

Reference: David Letterman

> **Sophia:** It's the middle of the night. You want something fresh, turn on Letterman.

David Letterman is a comedian, writer, and host of *Late Night with David Letterman* and the *Late Show with David Letterman* from 1982 to 2015.

Reference: *Teenage Mutant Ninja Turtles*

> **Sophia:** My dart gun was confiscated after the incident with the trick-or-treaters. In my defense, it was dark and I was unaware of this *Ninja Turtle* craze.

Teenage Mutant Ninja Turtles is a popular franchise of comics, cartoons, and films about four anthropomorphic superhero mutant turtles who are martial arts experts and fight crime in New York City. It began as a comic book in the mid-1980s and gained momentum as a subsequent cartoon series that launched a popular toy line and film adaptations.

References: *Marmaduke, Apartment 3-G*

> **Blanche:** I love my comics. Every day, *Marmaduke* and *Apartment 3-G*.
> **Dorothy:** I haven't read *Apartment 3-G* since 1961.
> **Blanche:** Oh, well let me catch you up. It is later the same day . . .

Marmaduke is a comic strip launched in 1954, originally written and illustrated by Brad Anderson, about the Winslow family and their gigantic Great Dane, Marmaduke. *Apartment 3-G* was a soap opera–style comic strip about a trio of career women sharing a Manhattan apartment. The strip ran from 1961 to 2015. The three main characters were supposedly based on a trio of popular actresses from the era of its debut: Lucille Ball, Joan Collins, and Tuesday Weld.

Repeat References: *Nova (Episode 4.19: 'Til Death Do We Volley)*, Studebaker *(Episode 3.25: Mother's Day)*

EPISODE 6.8: HOW DO YOU SOLVE A PROBLEM LIKE SOPHIA?
Directed by Matthew Diamond. Written by Marc Cherry and Jamie Wooten. Original airdate: November 10, 1990.
Sophia announces her plans to become a nun. Blanche gets into an accident while driving Rose's car.

References: Jaguar, Duster

> **Blanche:** I had this really cute guy in a Jag lined up when this dork in a Duster cut in front of me and I nicked him instead.

Jaguar is a luxury vehicle brand introduced in 1935 and manufactured in England. The Dacia Duster was the name used for the ARO 10, a compact sport utility vehicle, in the 1980s and early 1990s.

Reference: Granada

> **Dorothy:** It's a Granada full of nuns.

Granada was a car manufactured by Ford from the mid-1970s until the early 1980s.

Reference: Philatelist

> **Blanche:** When I first saw you I said to myself, philatelist.

A philatelist is a person who loves stamps.

References: Edward G. Robinson, *The Ten Commandments*

> **Sophia:** God, I'm so confused. I don't know where I belong. I'm trying to wrestle with the deep religious questions of the ages, like what

do you really want from me? What is my purpose in life? What was Edward G. Robinson doing in *The Ten Commandments*?

Edward G. Robinson (1893–1973) was an actor known for his roles in *Little Caesar*, *Key Largo*, *Double Indemnity*, and *The Ten Commandments*, which is a 1956 Cecil B. DeMille film starring Charlton Heston, Yul Brynner, and Anne Baxter, depicting the biblical story of the life of Moses.

Reference: John the Baptist

> **Sophia:** They wanted to browse the gift shop. They're having a sale on John the Baptist placemats.

John the Baptist was a Jewish itinerant preacher from the early first century and a prominent figure in Christianity.

Reference: Red Cross

> **Dorothy:** Ma, your life is meaningful. You do nothing but help other people. You do Meals on Wheels, Red Cross, volunteer hospital work.

While the Red Cross movement exists worldwide, each affiliate with its own history, the American Red Cross humanitarian organization was founded in 1881 by Clara Barton. It provides emergency assistance, disaster relief, and disaster preparedness education, as well as conducts blood services that account for more than 30 percent of the donated blood in the United States.

Reference: *The Greatest Story Ever Told*

> **Sophia:** I'll be missing movie night, but so what? After the tenth time, it isn't *The Greatest Story Ever Told*.

The Greatest Story Ever Told is a 1965 film that retells the biblical account of the life of Jesus. It starred Max von Sydow, Dorothy McGuire, and Charlton Heston and scored five Academy Award nominations despite mixed reviews and a weak box office performance.

Repeat References: *Jeopardy! (Episode 3.5: Nothing to Fear but Fear Itself)*, Saint Peter *(Episode 4.7: Sophia's Wedding—Part 2)*, John Forsythe *(Episode 1.5: The Triangle)*, the Lone Ranger *(Episode 1.18: The Operation)*, Tonto *(Episode 2.2: Ladies of the Evening)*, Meals on Wheels *(Episode 6.4: Snap Out of It)*

EPISODE 6.9: MRS. GEORGE DEVEREAUX

Directed by Matthew Diamond. Written by Richard Vaczy and Tracy Gamble. Original airdate: November 17, 1990.

Blanche is shocked to learn that her secret admirer is none other than her supposedly dead husband, George. Dorothy is wooed by celebrities Sonny Bono and Lyle Waggoner.

References: Lyle Waggoner, *Equus*, *Under the Yum Yum Tree*

> **Dorothy:** I went to the dinner theater and I saw Lyle and Sonny in a production of *Equus*. Our six eyes met. Sonny fell into the orchestra pit. Lyle forgot his lines and went into *Under the Yum Yum Tree*.

Lyle Waggoner (1935–2020) was an actor known for his work on *The Carol Burnett Show* and the *Wonder Woman* TV series. *Equus* is a 1973 play by Peter Shaffer about a psychiatrist who attempts to treat a young man with a pathological fascination with horses. The play had a two-year run on Broadway in the 1970s with various revivals over the years, and Richard Burton and Peter Firth starred in a 1977 film adaptation. *Under the Yum Yum Tree* is a 1960 Broadway play by Lawrence Roman, which was adapted into a 1963 comedy film starring Jack Lemmon.

Reference: Greyhound

> **Blanche:** How much trouble can I get into in a public place?
>
> **Dorothy:** How soon we forget the Greyhound terminal incident.

Greyhound is an intercity bus carrier with thousands of locations all over North America. It was founded by Carl Wickman in 1914.

Reference: *The Carol Burnett Show*

> **Lyle:** We did so many restaurant sketches on *The Carol Burnett Show*, I was waxing sentimental.

The Carol Burnett Show is a variety/sketch comedy series starring Carol Burnett, Harvey Korman, Vicki Lawrence, Tim Conway, and Waggoner. Considered one of the greatest series of all time, the show ran for eleven seasons from 1967 to 1978.

Reference: "I'm So Glad We Had This Time Together"

> *Lyle Waggoner sings the song as he exits the restaurant.*

"I'm So Glad We Had This Time Together" was the theme song to *The Carol Burnett Show*, written by Joe Hamilton. At the end of each episode, Burnett would tug her earlobe in a special nod to her grandmother, who raised her; hence, Waggoner's doing the same thing as he sang himself out of the restaurant.

Repeat References: Sonny Bono *(Episode 3.23: Mixed Blessings)*, "I Got You Babe" *(Episode 5.18: An Illegitimate Concern)*

EPISODE 6.10: GIRLS JUST WANNA HAVE FUN . . . BEFORE THEY DIE
Directed by Matthew Diamond. Written by Gail Parent and Jim Vallely. Original airdate: November 24, 1990.
Rose is forced into celibacy due to a St. Olaf tradition, and Sophia debates sleeping with her new boyfriend. Blanche's advice to each of them falters.

Reference: Joan of Arc

> **Sophia:** Last night, I dreamed I was Joan of Arc and he was coming at me with a hose.

Joan of Arc (c. 1412–1431) was a nonmilitary peasant girl who, believing God had chosen her to do so, led the French army to victory over the English in the city of Orléans in the 1400s. She was later tried for witchcraft and heresy and burned at the stake. She's now considered one of history's greatest heroes and saints.

Reference: *The New Lassie*

> **Rose:** I saw it this afternoon on TV when I was watching *The New Lassie*.

The New Lassie is a 1989 reboot of the popular *Lassie* series of the 1950s (see *Episode 4.5: Bang the Drum, Stanley* for more on that). The reboot lasted four seasons.

Repeat References: Kaopectate *(Episode 4.22: Sophia's Choice)*, *The King and I (Episode 6.5: Wham, Bam, Thank You, Mammy!)*, MedicAlert Bracelet *(Episode 4.1: Yes, We Have No Havanas)*

EPISODE 6.11: STAND BY YOUR MAN
Directed by Matthew Diamond. Written by Tom Whedon. Original airdate: December 1, 1990.

Blanche begins dating a man in a wheelchair. Rose hopes to adopt one of Dreyfuss's puppies.

Reference: Nurse Ratched

> **Rose:** You like having [the puppies] over too, don't you, Sophia?
>
> **Sophia:** Yeah, I like them.
>
> **Dorothy:** That's because it temporarily shifts the blame if we find a puddle on the floor.
>
> **Sophia:** Once, Nurse Ratched. Once.

Nurse Ratched is a fictional character and main antagonist from the 1962 Ken Kesey novel and 1975 film adaptation of *One Flew Over the Cuckoo's Nest*. She is portrayed as a heartless tyrant. Actress Louise Fletcher played the role in the film. A Netflix series entitled *Ratched*, based on the same character in a prequel to the novel, debuted in 2020 with Sarah Paulson in the lead role.

Reference: Stephen King

> **Dorothy:** My mother talked me into getting her the new Stephen King.

Stephen King is a well-known author of horror, suspense, and supernatural fiction, among other genres, whose work has been adapted into countless films and TV series. King has published more than sixty novels since he sold his first story in 1967.

Reference: Floyd the Barber

> **Dorothy:** God, here it comes. The honeysuckle mint juleps, three-legged dogs, you and Opie and Floyd at the barbershop. Blanche, get to the point!

Floyd the Barber is Mayberry's mild-mannered barber in *The Andy Griffith Show*, portrayed by actor Howard McNear.

Reference: The Liberty Bell

> **Blanche:** Show me the wonders of Philadelphia. The Liberty Bell, the cream cheese.

The Liberty Bell is a large bell located in Philadelphia, Pennsylvania, that has become a symbol of American freedom. It was commissioned in 1752 and was cracked when it was first rung.

Repeat References: Dreyfuss the dog and Dr. Harry Weston *(Episode 4.4: Yokel Hero)*, Miami Dolphins *(Episode 1.3: Rose the Prude)*, Opie *(Episode 2.17: Bedtime Story)*, Ted Turner *(Episode 4.9: Scared Straight)*

EPISODE 6.12: EBBTIDE'S REVENGE
Directed by Matthew Diamond. Written by Marc Sotkin. Original airdate: December 15, 1990.
Dorothy must give the eulogy at her brother Phil's funeral. Sophia feuds with Phil's wife.

References: *Gigi*, Dorothy Lamour

> **Blanche:** Sophia, people don't say queer anymore, they say gay.
>
> **Sophia:** They say gay if a guy can sing the entire score of *Gigi*. But a six-foot-three, 200-pound married man with kids who likes to dress up like Dorothy Lamour, I think you have to go with queer.

Gigi is a 1958 MGM musical film based on the 1944 Colette novella of the same name. The film starred Leslie Caron and Louis Jourdan as a young Parisian courtesan and the man on whom she sets her sights. Dorothy Lamour (1914–1996) was an actress best known for appearing in the *Road to . . .* movies of the 1940s and 1950s with Bing Crosby and Bob Hope.

Reference: Benny Hill

> **Dorothy:** He looks like he died in a Benny Hill sketch.

Benny Hill (1924–1992) was an English comedian and actor who hosted *The Benny Hill Show*, a comedy variety show that aired in various forms between 1955 and 1989. Hill was a prominent star in British culture throughout his career and did several comedy skits in drag.

Reference: The Brontë sisters

> **Dorothy:** . . . the hundreds of memories I have of just the two of us eating ice cream on the stoop of our building or going through the drawers at Grandma's house or dressing up like the Brontë sisters. How those memories fill me with joy.

Charlotte, Emily, and Anne Brontë were a trio of nineteenth-century English literary sisters. The works of these poets and novelists have risen to classic stature, among them Charlotte's *Jane Eyre*, Emily's *Wuthering Heights*, and Anne's *The Tenant of Wildfell Hall*. Their home in Yorkshire is now a museum that draws thousands of visitors each year.

Episode 6.13: The Bloom Is Off the Rose

Directed by Matthew Diamond. Written by Phillip Jayson Lasker. Original airdate: January 5, 1991.

Rose seeks adventure in her relationship with Miles. Blanche dates a verbally abusive man and ignores Dorothy's warnings about his behavior.

References: Buzz Aldrin, Neil Armstrong

> **Dorothy, working a lunar landing jigsaw puzzle:** Ma, you put Buzz Aldrin's head on Neil Armstrong's body.

Buzz Aldrin and Neil Armstrong (1930–2012) were astronauts who were part of the 1969 *Apollo 11* mission, whose goal was to land on the moon. The mission was a success, and Aldrin and Armstrong were the first two humans to set foot on the moon.

References: Wallace Beery, Adolphe Menjou

> **Sophia:** Boy, he makes Wallace Beery look like Adolphe Menjou.
>
> **Dorothy:** Has been a long time since I've taken you to the movies, hasn't it.

Film and stage actor Wallace Beery (1885–1949), who often played villainous roles, was the highest-paid film actor in the world in the early 1930s. In fact, his contract with MGM at the time stipulated that he would be paid one dollar more than any other actor at the studio. Some of his most notable films include *Min and Bill*, *Treasure Island*, and an Academy Award–winning turn in *The Champ*. Adolphe Menjou (1890–1963), who was often viewed as a well-dressed man about town, was an actor known for roles in both silent films and talkies, including *A Woman in Paris*, *Paths of Glory*, *A Star Is Born*, and *The Front Page*.

Repeat References: Cher *(Episode 5.18: An Illegitimate Concern)*, Paul Newman *(Episode 3.2: One for the Money)*

Episode 6.14: Sister of the Bride

Directed by Matthew Diamond. Written by Marc Cherry and Jamie Wooten. Original airdate: January 12, 1991.
Blanche's brother, Clayton, arrives with news that he is getting married to his boyfriend, Doug. Rose hopes to win a Volunteer of the Year award.

Reference: The Disney Channel

> **Rose:** Hot damn! It's happened, it's finally happened! Oh yes, oh yes, oh yes!
>
> **Dorothy:** I take it we now get the Disney Channel?

The Walt Disney Company's first foray into cable TV, the Disney Channel launched in 1983 as a premium cable channel targeted to kids and families and is now available in nearly one hundred million homes.

Reference: "Moon River"

> **Dorothy:** Now it all makes sense—why the hat check guy serenaded me with "Moon River."

"Moon River" is a song written by Henry Mancini and Johnny Mercer, originally performed by Audrey Hepburn in the 1961 film *Breakfast at Tiffany's*. It won both a Grammy and an Oscar and has been covered hundreds of times by other artists, like Frank Sinatra and Judy Garland.

Repeat References: Bette Davis *(Episode 2.21: Dorothy's Prized Pupil)*, Neiman Marcus *(Episode 1.23: Blind Ambitions)*, *Butch Cassidy and the Sundance Kid (Episode 3.14: Blanche's Little Girl)*

Episode 6.15: Miles to Go

Directed by Matthew Diamond. Written by Don Seigel and Jerry Perzigian. Original airdate: January 19, 1991.
Rose is shocked when Miles announces that he is part of the Witness Relocation Program and is actually Nicholas Carbone from Chicago. Blanche buys an expensive dress with plans to return it after wearing it on a date.

Reference: Scrabble

> **Sophia:** No offense, my little Scrabbleholic, but there's more to life than a double word score.

Scrabble is a board game in which players score points by building words on the game board using letter tiles. It was introduced in 1938.

References: Robert Frost, Jack Frost, David Frost

> **Rose:** It's the one hundred seventeenth anniversary of the birth of Robert Frost.
>
> **Sophia:** I love him, always nipping at your nose.
>
> **Rose:** That's Jack Frost. Robert Frost is the guy who interviewed Nixon on TV. Who's the dumb one now?
>
> **Dorothy:** You're still the reigning champ, Rose. That was David Frost. Robert Frost was a famous American poet.
>
> **Sophia:** And when I was with him, he was always nipping at my nose.

Robert Frost (1874–1963) was a renowned American poet who received a record four Pulitzer Prizes for Poetry and was awarded the Congressional Gold Medal for his poetry in 1960. "Acquainted with the Night" and "Stopping by Woods on a Snowy Evening" are among his most famous works. Jack Frost is the fictional personification of ice, snow, sleet, and just winter in general, known for nipping at people's noses. The character has appeared countless times in song, literature, and film. David Frost (1939–2013) was a British journalist who rose to prominence hosting the satirical news program *That Was the Week That Was* in the 1960s, which he parlayed into success as an interviewer on American television. One of his more-prominent gigs was interviewing former president Richard Nixon in 1977, the first interview Nixon granted after his resignation.

Reference: Witness Protection Program

> **Miles:** The government had to put me in the Witness Protection Program. Gave me a new name, a new job, whole new identity.

The United States Federal Witness Protection Program protects threatened witnesses to crimes before, during, and after trials. The program has protected approximately nineteen thousand witnesses and their family members since it launched in the early 1970s.

Reference: Aesop

> **Dorothy:** And the point, Aesop?

Aesop (c. 620–564 BC) was a Greek fabulist credited with writing *Aesop's Fables.*

Reference: Tony Martin

> **Sophia:** These aren't for Tony Bennett, they're for Tony Martin!

Tony Martin (1913–2012) was a singer and actor known for hits like "Walk Hand in Hand," "Stranger in Paradise," and "I Get Ideas."

Repeat References: Tony Bennett *(Episode 1.7: The Competition)*, Richard Nixon *(Episode 2.2: Ladies of the Evening)*, Poltergeist *(Episode 3.6: Letter to Gorbachev)*, Woodstock *(Episode 1.23: Blind Ambitions)*, The Three Musketeers *(Episode 3.12: Charlie's Buddy)*

EPISODE 6.16: THERE GOES THE BRIDE—PART 1

Directed by Matthew Diamond. Teleplay by Mitchell Hurwitz. Story by Gail Parent, Jim Vallely, and Mitchell Hurwitz. Original airdate: February 2, 1991. Dorothy, who has been secretly dating Stan, announces her intent to remarry him. Rose is stalked by a date's ex-wife.

References: Yahtzee, Battleship, snake eyes

> **Blanche:** Checkmate.
>
> **Sophia:** Checkmate? I thought we were playing Yahtzee. Okay, that's a do-over.
>
> **Blanche:** No, that is not a do-over. You do this every time. Last time you thought it was Checkers. Before that it was Battleship. And twice you yelled out, "Snake eyes!"

Checkers is a strategy board game for two that involves capturing the other player's game pieces by jumping over them. Yahtzee is a dice game introduced in the 1940s whose object is to score points by rolling five dice to make certain combinations. Battleship is a two-player strategic guessing game played on a ruled grid. Each player places their little fleet of ships at various locations on the board and proceeds to guess coordinates, hoping to land a "hit." Landing enough hits will sink a ship, the objective being to destroy the other player's entire fleet first. In gambling, snake eyes is an outcome of rolling the dice and getting one pip on each die.

References: The Westons, Barbara Weston

> **Rose:** Well, that's settled; now let's get a move on!
>
> **Blanche:** Where are you going?
>
> **Rose:** To get the toilet paper for the Westons' house. But remember, we have to be really quiet. Dreyfuss will bark at anything, and Barbara carries a gun.

The central family in *The Golden Girls* spinoff series, *Empty Nest*, the Westons were neighbors of the girls. Barbara Weston was a fun-loving undercover cop and Dr. Harry Weston's middle child. The character was portrayed by actress Kristy McNichol.

Reference: The Terminator

> **Sophia, on the phone:** So, you're Myra. Who am I? Some call me Sophia. Others call me the Terminator.

The Terminator is a 1984 science-fiction film starring Arnold Schwarzenegger as a futuristic cyborg assassin and Linda Hamilton as the woman he's sent back in time to kill.

Reference: Captain Frank Furillo

> **Blanche:** Okay, Furillo, drop your pants. It's time for a little search and seizure!

Captain Frank Furillo is the fictional head of the Hill Street Precinct on the television series *Hill Street Blues*, an NBC police drama series that ran from 1981 to 1987. The character was portrayed by actor Daniel J. Travanti.

References: *Fiddler on the Roof*, Enzo Stuarti

> **Sophia:** Where I'm from, the marriages are arranged by the parents.
>
> **Blanche:** Is that what's bothering you, Sophia? Nobody asked your permission?
>
> **Sophia:** It's the Italian tradition. What do you think *Fiddler on the Roof* was about?
>
> **Blanche:** That's a Jewish musical.
>
> **Sophia:** What do you mean, Jewish? I remember there was Enzo Stuarti, Dom DeLuise.

Blanche shakes her head.

Sophia: I've got to stop seeing these things at dinner theaters.

Fiddler on the Roof is a musical by Jerry Bock, Sheldon Harnick, and Joseph Stein, set in 1905 Russia and focusing on a father of five's attempts to maintain his Jewish culture despite encroaching influences like his daughters' paramours. The original Broadway production opened in 1964, won nine Tony Awards, and spawned several revivals and a successful film adaptation. Enzo Stuarti (1919–2005) was an Italian tenor known for his work in the theater, a string of successful albums, and a series of Ragú spaghetti sauce commercials.

Repeat References: Dreyfuss the dog *(Episode 4.4: Yokel Hero)*, Dom DeLuise *(Episode 2.2: Ladies of the Evening)*, The Godfather *(Episode 2.4: It's a Miserable Life)*

EPISODE 6.17: THERE GOES THE BRIDE—PART 2

Directed by Matthew Diamond. Written by Gail Parent and Jim Vallely. Original airdate: February 9, 1991.

Sophia vows to put a stop to Dorothy and Stan's impending nuptials. Blanche interviews a potential new roommate.

Reference: McDonald's

> **Sophia:** I have an interview at McDonald's today. If I can see over the counter, I'm their new fry girl.

McDonald's is a fast-food giant originally founded as a restaurant in 1940 in San Bernardino, California, by Richard and Maurice McDonald. They turned it into a hamburger stand soon after, and then began franchising. The famed Golden Arches logo appeared in 1953.

Reference: Winnebago

> **Truby:** My husband passed just last summer.
>
> **Rose:** Passed what?
>
> **Dorothy:** A slow-moving Winnebago, Rose.

Winnebago is a manufacturer of motorhomes.

Reference: The Shirelles

> **Dorothy:** My God, Stanley, I feel like one of The Shirelles.

The Shirelles were an R&B and doo-wop group popular in the 1960s, consisting of Shirley Owens, Doris Coley, Addie "Micki" Harris, and Beverly Lee. Their hits included "Will You Love Me Tomorrow" and "Tonight's the Night."

Reference: Marvin Mitchelson

> **Stan:** Dorothy, I want you to meet my best man, Marvin Mitchelson.

Marvin Mitchelson (1928–2004) was a celebrity lawyer whose clients included Robert De Niro, Sylvester Stallone, Zsa Zsa Gabor, and others. He's credited with inventing the term *palimony*—the division of financial assets and property following the end of a live-in relationship between unmarried parties.

Reference: *Winky*

> **Dorothy:** Stanley, whatever happened to openness and honesty and trust? Not to mention the thirty-eight years I spent as your wife, your partner, the mother of your children, the woman who held down two jobs while you were at home staring at a matchbook trying to draw Winky!

Winky was a cartoon deer often used on matchbooks as a recruitment tool for art instruction schools, which attempted to recruit students by urging them to draw the character.

Repeat References: ARCO *(Episodes 5.25: The President's Coming! The President's Coming!—Part 1)*, Shell *(Episode 5.19: 72 Hours)*, Godzilla *(Episode 1.14: That Was No Lady)*

EPISODE 6.18: OLDER AND WISER
Directed by Matthew Diamond. Written by Richard Vaczy and Tracy Gamble. Original airdate: February 16, 1991.
Dorothy gets Sophia a job at a retirement home under false pretenses. Blanche and Rose are hired as models for a local pennysaver publication.

Reference: *Magellan*

> **Rose:** Hi, Dorothy. Cooking?
> **Dorothy:** No, Rose. I'm developing pictures from the *Magellan* space program.

Magellan was a robotic space probe launched by NASA in 1939 to map the surface of Venus.

Reference: Lana Turner

> **Blanche:** I am going to be a model. There I was sitting at the lunch counter and, just like Ms. Lana Turner, I was discovered!

Lana Turner (1921–1995) was an actress and pinup model who was discovered at the age of fifteen while purchasing a soda at a Hollywood malt shop. Among her most notable roles were *Dr. Jekyll and Mr. Hyde*, *Somewhere I'll Find You*, *The Postman Always Rings Twice*, and *Peyton Place*.

References: Pennysaver, *Vogue*

> **Blanche:** Imagine my face gracing the pages of Miami's biggest pennysaver.
> **Dorothy:** Blanche, all this commotion over a pennysaver?
> **Blanche:** Well, I know it isn't exactly *Vogue*, but it is delivered with every daily in Miami.

A pennysaver is a free newspaper circular that advertises items for sale. *Vogue* is a monthly fashion and lifestyle magazine first published in 1892.

Reference: Mike Wallace

> **Dorothy:** Cypress Grove has a great reputation. Did you see the story they did about it on *60 Minutes*?
> **Sophia:** No.
> **Dorothy:** Short piece. It was just Mike Wallace saying, "Sorry I bothered you."

Mike Wallace (1918–2012) was a journalist and TV host best known for his work on the CBS newsmagazine series *60 Minutes*.

Reference: Freddy Krueger

> **Rose:** Let's face it. You have Bette Davis eyes—and Freddy Krueger hands!

Freddy Krueger is a fictional character created by Wes Craven for the *Nightmare on Elm Street* film series who uses his gloved hand with razors to kill victims in their dreams, which also kills them in real life. The role has been played by actor Robert Englund since the first *Elm Street* film in 1984.

Reference: Florsheim

> **Sophia:** You do the best you can with a pair of brown Florsheims, and this is the thanks you get.

Florsheim is a brand of shoes founded in Chicago in 1892 by Milton S. Florsheim.

Reference: Juan Ponce de León

> **Dorothy, reading an ad:** Does your face look like this? Do your hands look like this? You need Ponce de León Anti-Aging Cream.

Juan Ponce de León (1474–1521) was a Spanish explorer who led the first official European expedition to Florida, allegedly in search of the Fountain of Youth. He served as the first governor of Puerto Rico.

Reference: Prohibition

> **Blanche:** That was the night Prohibition started.
>
> **Dorothy:** Blanche, Prohibition started in the twenties.
>
> **Blanche:** Oh, I'm sorry. I meant probation. Big Daddy went on probation.

Prohibition was a nationwide constitutional ban on the production and sale of alcoholic beverages, lasting from 1920 to 1933.

Repeat References: Dr. Scholl *(Episode 1.2: Guess Who's Coming to the Wedding?)*, Dairy Queen *(Episode 1.25: The Way We Met)*, 60 Minutes *(Episode 3.7: Strange Bedfellows)*, The Olympics *(Episode 2.16: And Then There Was One)*, Bette Davis *(Episode 2.21: Dorothy's Prized Pupil)*, Hialeah *(Episode 5.24: All Bets Are Off)*

EPISODE 6.19: MELODRAMA

Directed by Matthew Diamond. Written by Robert Spina. Original airdate: February 16, 1991.

Blanche wants to solidify her relationship with a casual beau, Mel Bushman. Rose tries her hand at news reporting.

Reference: John Bradshaw

> **Dorothy:** We're going to watch one of those John Bradshaw specials on PBS.
>
> **Sophia:** Yeah, we're going to see if we can't get Dorothy's inner child to shut up.

John Bradshaw (1933–2016) was an educator, author, speaker, and host of various PBS educational specials on topics ranging from addiction to spirituality. He wrote several best-selling books and appeared routinely on the talk show circuit in the 1980s and 1990s.

Reference: Will Rogers

> **Rose:** I remember back in St. Olaf . . .
>
> **Dorothy:** Hold it right there, Will Rogers. None of us is in the mood to hear one of those St. Olaf stories.

Will Rogers (1879–1935) was an actor, vaudeville performer, cowboy, and columnist who made more than seventy films, wrote thousands of syndicated newspaper columns, and was well known for his social commentary and homespun humor.

Reference: Claus von Bülow

> **Blanche:** Mel, is that really you?
>
> **Mel:** No, it's Claus von Bülow.

Claus von Bülow (1926–2019) was a lawyer and socialite who, in 1982, was convicted of both the 1979 and 1980 attempted murders of his wife, Sunny, who was left in a persistent vegetative state until her death in 2008. Both convictions were later reversed, and von Bülow was found not guilty at his second trial. The case and its fallout were depicted in the 1985 book and 1990 film *Reversal of Fortune*, starring Jeremy Irons and Glenn Close. Irons won an Academy Award for his portrayal of von Bülow.

Reference: *Jack and Jill* magazine

> **Blanche:** Are you implying I lost my virginity at an early age?
>
> **Sophia:** I'm just saying you're lucky *Jack and Jill* magazine didn't have a gossip column.

Jack and Jill magazine is a bimonthly children's magazine founded in 1938, featuring articles, stories, games, recipes, and other educational activities— but no gossip column.

Reference: *Out of Africa*

> **Mel:** We can rent *Out of Africa.*
>
> **Blanche:** We've rented it five times and never made it through to the end.
>
> **Mel:** I know, but it always works!

Out of Africa is a 1985 epic romance film starring Meryl Streep and Robert Redford, about a woman who moves to Africa to join her husband but develops feelings for another man.

Reference: Deborah Norville

> **Rose:** If Deborah Norville stopped for every serious news story that happened around her, she wouldn't be where she is today.

Deborah Norville is a journalist whose credentials include serving as a correspondent for *CBS News*, cohosting *Today*, and anchoring *Inside Edition*.

Repeat References: PBS *(Episode 3.3: Bringing Up Baby)*, Danny Thomas *(Episode 2.5: Isn't It Romantic?)*, Fred Flintstone *(Episode 4.20: High Anxiety)*, Alan Alda *(Episode 5.16: Clinton Avenue Memoirs)*, Wolfie's *(Episode 2.1: End of the Curse)*

EPISODE 6.20: EVEN GRANDMAS GET THE BLUES
Directed by Robert Berlinger. Written by Gail Parent and Jim Vallely. Original airdate: March 2, 1991.
Blanche is mistaken for her granddaughter's mother by a potential suitor. Sophia prepares for the Festival of the Dancing Virgins.

References: Anton Chekhov, Pavel Chekov, *Star Trek*

> **Dorothy:** I'm going to have students who know that Chekhov is a brilliant Russian playwright, not the guy who was the navigator on the *Enterprise.*
>
> **Rose:** I didn't know the guy from *Star Trek* wrote plays.

Anton Chekhov (1860–1904) was a brilliant Russian playwright and short-story writer whose works included *The Seagull, Uncle Vanya,* and *Three Sisters.* A fictional Russian character in the *Star Trek* TV and film series, Pavel Chekov was portrayed by actor Walter Koenig in the second and third seasons of the original series and the first seven feature films. Anton Yelchin portrayed the character in the 2009 reboot film series. The *Star Trek* media franchise consists of multiple television series, films, books, and merchandise, which began with the 1960s science-fiction television series *Star Trek* and has continued with various incarnations through the present day.

Reference: *The Taming of the Shrew*

> **Blanche:** It so happens our community playhouse is doing *The Taming of the Shrew,* and I am to audition for the role of Kate.

The Taming of the Shrew is a William Shakespeare comedy written somewhere between 1590 and 1592, about the courtship of Petruchio and the headstrong Katherine.

Reference: *Annie*

> **Blanche:** I performed *Annie* for him.
> **Director:** Really? Where?
> **Blanche:** None of your business.

Annie is a Broadway musical based on Harold Gray's *Little Orphan Annie* comic strip. The original production opened in 1977.

Reference: *Breakfast at Tiffany's*

> **Jason:** Did you happen to see *Breakfast at Tiffany's?*
> **Blanche:** Yes.
> **Jason:** Well, I was in the party scene. Audrey Hepburn spilled a drink on me, but they cut it out.

Breakfast at Tiffany's is the title of Truman Capote's 1958 novella in which a writer recalls his days in New York City and his relationship with his unusual neighbor, Holly Golightly. The book loosely inspired a 1961 romantic-comedy film of the same name, directed by Blake Edwards and starring Audrey Hepburn and George Peppard. Hepburn's portrayal of Golightly as an eccentric café society lady has arguably become her most identifiable and iconic role. A makeup-clad, prosthetic-wearing Mickey Rooney as a caricatured version of a Japanese neighbor, however, has rightfully fared less well.

Reference: Walt Whitman

> **Rose:** Oh what a tangled web we weave when first we practice to tell a fib.
>
> **Dorothy:** Walt Whitman here has a point.

Walt Whitman (1819–1892) was a poet and essayist known for the collection *Leaves of Grass*. He didn't actually write the line that Rose paraphrases here. That's from the 1808 poem "Marmion," by Sir Walter Scott, and it's "to deceive," not "to tell a fib."

Reference: The *Spruce Goose*

> **Blanche:** It's so unfair. We're both about the same age, but he can go on making babies the rest of his life. I feel like the *Spruce Goose*. People may visit, play with the controls, but I'll never really fly again.

The *Spruce Goose* was an experimental strategic airlift flying boat intended for use as a transatlantic flight vessel during World War II. It wasn't completed in time to be used during the war, made one brief flight in 1947, and never progressed beyond that one experiment.

Reference: Mensa

> **Dorothy:** There's a meeting at Mensa. That's the organization for people with high IQs like mine.
>
> **Rose:** You know in St. Olaf we had a chapter of Mensa. And across the room was Girlsa. No, wait, those were the bathrooms at St. Olaf's only Italian restaurant.

Mensa is a society founded in 1946 for people with a high IQ. One must score at the ninety-eighth percentile or higher to become a member.

Reference: "They're grrrreat!"

> **Sophia:** Rose, before you bring in the sauce, tell us what ingredient you added.
>
> **Rose:** Well, I don't want to spoil the surprise. I'll give you a hint. They're sugary, and they're grrrreat!

This phrase is a popular slogan of the Frosted Flakes brand of breakfast cereal, uttered by spokes-character Tony the Tiger.

Reference: The Bunny Hop

> **Sophia:** Dorothy, you're going to have to do the dance of the virgins by yourself.
>
> **Dorothy:** Ma!
>
> **Sophia:** You remember—it's like the Bunny Hop, except you keep your legs crossed.

The Bunny Hop is a novelty party dance popularized in the 1950s that is a sort of spin on the conga line concept, only with people hopping back and forth along the way.

Repeat References: Starship *Enterprise (Episode 4.23: Rites of Spring)*, Audrey Hepburn *(Episode 4.23: Rites of Spring)*, Oreos *(Episode 1.16: The Truth Will Out)*, New York Times *(Episode 1.21: The Flu)*, Søren Kierkegaard *(Episode 4.26: We're Outta Here—Part 2)*, Medicare *(Episode 3.6: Letter to Gorbachev)*, Enquirer *(Episode 1.25: The Way We Met)*

EPISODE 6.21: WITNESS
Directed by Zane Buzby. Written by Mitchell Hurwitz. Original airdate: March 9, 1991.
Miles returns to visit Rose, who is now dating a new man. Sophia loses her glasses. Blanche seeks membership in a Southern women's organization.

Reference: Roy Orbison

> *Sophia enters wearing dark sunglasses.*
>
> **Dorothy:** Ladies and gentlemen, Roy Orbison.

Roy Orbison (1936–1988) was a singer-songwriter known for wearing dark sunglasses. His hits included "Only the Lonely (Know the Way I Feel)," "Crying," "Oh, Pretty Woman," and "You Got It."

Reference: "Silly rabbit, Trix are for kids."

> **Miles:** It's me. I was hoping to play a trick on you.
>
> **Sophia:** Silly rabbi, tricks are for kids.

This joke is a play on the famous tagline for Trix breakfast cereal, whose mascot is an anthropomorphic rabbit who always attempted to trick children out of their Trix.

Reference: General Ambrose Burnside

> **Mrs. Ward:** Thank you, Evelyn and Margaret, for that gripping and realistic reenactment of the defeat of General Burnside's troops at Fredericksburg.

General Ambrose Burnside (1824–1881) was a nineteenth-century soldier and politician who served as a Union Army general in the Civil War, as well as governor of Rhode Island and a Rhode Island senator during the 1860s and 1870s. While those were certainly lofty accomplishments, it's for his distinctive facial hair that General Burnside is best remembered. Sideburns are named after him.

Reference: The Harlem Globetrotters

> **Sophia:** Dorothy, I can't see a thing. What's happening now?
>
> **Dorothy:** The Harlem Globetrotters just took the court.

The Harlem Globetrotters are an exhibition basketball team that combines athleticism, theater, and comedy in a popular touring show. The Globetrotters have played thousands of exhibition games all over the world since their founding in 1924. Their signature theme song is a whistled version of "Sweet Georgia Brown."

Reference: *America's Most Wanted*

> **Blanche:** Sophia, you recognize Carl as the Cheeseman?
>
> **Sophia:** You don't? The man's been on *America's Most Wanted* at least six times.

America's Most Wanted is a TV series than ran for twenty-five years on two networks, profiling wanted fugitives through reenactments and resulting in the capture of more than 1,200 fugitives and recovering more than sixty missing children. Hosted by John Walsh, whose own son, Adam, was abducted from a Florida mall and murdered in 1981, the series ran on Fox from 1988 to 2011, and then on Lifetime until 2013.

Repeat References: Barbara Weston *(Episode 6.16: There Goes the Bride—Part 1)*, Witness Protection Program *(Episode 6.15: Miles to Go)*, Captain Kangaroo *(Episode 3.24: Mister Terrific)*, "Hath not a Jew eyes?" *(Episode 4.18: Fiddler on the Ropes)*, Dreyfuss the dog *(Episode 4.4: Yokel Hero)*

EPISODE 6.22: WHAT A DIFFERENCE A DATE MAKES

Directed by Lex Passaris. Written by Marc Cherry and Jamie Wooten. Original airdate: March 23, 1991.

Dorothy is contacted for a date by the man who stood her up for her senior prom. Blanche goes on a diet to continue her annual tradition of fitting into her wedding dress.

References: Sara Lee, *Gulliver's Travels*

Blanche: Blanche Devereaux's going on a diet.

Sophia: Could you hold off until tomorrow? I've got some Sara Lee stock I'd like to unload.

Rose: Wait, can I have those gummy bears?

Blanche: They are good, aren't they?

Rose: Oh, I don't eat them.

Sophia: Then why do you want them?

Rose: To play army. And sometimes I like to line them up around my bed and pretend I'm Gulliver.

Sara Lee is a brand of frozen and packaged foods known for its slogan "Everybody doesn't like something, but nobody doesn't like Sara Lee." *Gulliver's Travels* is an eighteenth-century work of satirical prose by writer Jonathan Swift detailing a series of adventures by Lemuel Gulliver who ends up among people and animals of unusual sizes.

Reference: *The Silence of the Lambs*

Sophia: The last time you went on a diet, you turned into that guy from *Silence of the Lambs*.

The Silence of the Lambs is a 1991 psychological horror film adapted from the 1988 Thomas Harris novel of the same name, about a young FBI trainee who seeks the counsel of an imprisoned cannibalistic serial killer to help her track down another serial killer. The film starred Jodie Foster and Anthony Hopkins and was a massive hit, winning Academy Awards in all the major categories.

Reference: George Kirby

> **Sophia:** Did anyone ever tell you, you look like George Kirby?

George Kirby (1923–1995) was a comedian and actor who appeared on a variety of shows in the 1960s and 1970s, including *The Ed Sullivan Show*, *The Jackie Gleason Show*, and *The Tonight Show Starring Johnny Carson*, among others. He hosted his own variety show in 1972 and was one of the first Black comedians to garner mainstream success at the height of the civil rights era.

Reference: *Gilligan's Island*

> **The Minstrel, singing:** Just sit right back and you'll hear a tale . . .

This song is "The Ballad of Gilligan's Isle," the theme song for the sitcom *Gilligan's Island*, which ran on CBS from 1964 to 1967. The tune was written by series creator Sherwood Schwartz and George Wyle.

References: Mary Ann Mobley, Gary Collins

> **Dorothy:** If my life hasn't turned out perfectly, whose has?
> **Sophia:** Mary Ann Mobley comes to mind. I mean, she gets to sleep with Gary Collins every night.

Mary Ann Mobley (1937–2014) was Miss America 1959, as well as a television personality and actress known for appearances in *Perry Mason, Love, American Style, Fantasy Island, The Love Boat, Falcon Crest*, and other series. In 1967, she married actor and TV host Gary Collins (1938–2012), who appeared in dozens of series and films beginning in the 1960s, and hosted various shows such as *Hour Magazine, The Home Show*, and the Miss America Pageant in the 1980s and 1990s. He won a 1983 Emmy for Outstanding Talk Show Host. A penchant for driving while intoxicated led to several runs-in with the law later in his life.

EPISODE 6.23: LOVE FOR SALE
Directed by Peter D. Beyt. Written by Don Seigel and Jerry Perzigian. Original airdate: April 6, 1991.

The girls prepare for a charity bachelorette auction. Dorothy learns that she and Stan have inherited an apartment building. Sophia's brother, Angelo, arrives in Miami with news that he is broke and has no place to live.

Reference: Eleanor Roosevelt

> **Blanche:** If you can't degrade yourself for a bunch of sick kids, who can you degrade yourself for?
>
> **Sophia:** Listen to this. Eleanor Roosevelt in a garter belt.

Eleanor Roosevelt (1884–1962) was a political figure, diplomat, and activist who served as First Lady of the United States from 1933 to 1945 during the administration of her husband, Franklin D. Roosevelt.

References: Galahad, Richard Widmark

> **Blanche:** Remember last year's auction? That rush of euphoria when the auctioneer calls out "Sold!" and you fall into the arms of your valiant Galahad.
>
> **Dorothy:** My Galahad was a balloon salesman named Sid.
>
> **Blanche:** Who knew that sawed-off little gnome would outbid a navy admiral and a fire chief and that jeweler who was a dead ringer for Mr. Richard Widmark.

Galahad is one of the knights of King Arthur's Round Table in Arthurian legend, known for his gallantry. Richard Widmark (1914–2008) was a film, stage, and screen actor known for such works as *Kiss of Death*, *No Way Out*, *The Tunnel of Love*, *The Alamo*, and *Judgment at Nuremberg*.

Reference: VE Day

> **Angelo:** I haven't been hugged so much since VE Day, which was kind of tricky because, as you know, we lost.

VE Day refers to Victory in Europe Day, May 8, 1945, celebrating the acceptance of Germany's surrender and the end of World War II.

Reference: *Geraldo*

> **Dorothy:** I want to thank you all for holding this event on a night when my hang glider is in the shop, and Congress is in recess, and the lepers are on *Geraldo*.

Geraldo was a daytime tabloid talk show hosted by Geraldo Rivera, which ran in syndication from 1987 to 1998. A 1988 episode of the show, in which the guests included white supremacists and Black activists, led to a brawl that resulted in the host's nose being broken. He later spoofed the incident on a 1992 episode of *Empty Nest*, in which the Westons appeared on *Geraldo*.

Repeat References: Jimmy Carter *(Episode 3.12: Charlie's Buddy)*, hide-and-go-seek *(Episode 3.15: Dorothy's New Friend)*, mariachi band *(Episode 1.25: The Way We Met)*

EPISODES 6.24 AND 6.25: NEVER YELL FIRE IN A CROWDED RETIREMENT HOME—PARTS 1 AND 2
Directed by Matthew Diamond. Part 1 story by Gail Parent and teleplay by Tracy Gamble, Richard Vaczy, Tom Whedon, and Mitchell Hurwitz. Part 2 story by Jim Vallely and teleplay by Richard Vaczy, Tracy Gamble, Don Seigel, and Jerry Perzigian. Original airdate: April 27, 1991.
The deathbed confession of a Shady Pines resident pins the home's 1985 fire on Sophia. With the possibility of a trial looming, the girls reminisce about happier times.

Reference: James Cagney

> **Dorothy:** Before my mother lost it completely, she watched a lot of James Cagney.

James Cagney (1899–1986) was a noted actor who got his start performing in vaudeville as a dancer and comedian who then rose to fame often playing tough guys in such films as *Taxi!*, *Angels with Dirty Faces*, and *White Heat*. Once described by Orson Welles as the greatest actor to appear in front of a camera, he won the Academy Award for Best Actor for 1942's *Yankee Doodle Dandy* and served as the president of the Screen Actors Guild from 1942 to 1944.

Reference: *Awakenings*

> **Detective Parres:** Where were you on the night of September 4, 1985?
>
> **Sophia:** Did you see *Awakenings*? Throw a ball at me. How the hell should I know? I don't even know what color I'm wearing.

Awakenings is a 1990 film starring Robert De Niro and Robin Williams, based on the 1973 memoir by Oliver Sacks. In the film version, a doctor

(Williams) administers a certain drug to catatonic survivors (including De Niro's character) of an epidemic of encephalitis lethargica, or sleeping sickness. They awaken decades later and must adjust to their new world. The film was a critical and commercial success and garnered three Oscar nominations.

Reference: *All's Well That Ends Well*

> **Rose:** All's well that ends well.
>
> **Blanche:** What?
>
> **Rose:** It's the title of a Shakespeare play.

All's Well That Ends Well is a play by William Shakespeare in which a low-ranking woman falls for a high-ranking man who wants nothing to do with her. She sets out to trick him into marrying her anyway and, spoiler alert, is successful. The phrase itself has become a common proverb often attributed to Shakespeare, but it allegedly predates his usage of it in this play.

Reference: "One for My Baby (and One More for the Road)"

> **Sophia:** We were having a couple NyQuil shooters and singing "One for My Baby."

"One for My Baby (and One More for the Road)" is a 1943 song written by Harold Arlen and Johnny Mercer for the film *The Sky's the Limit*, first performed by Fred Astaire and popularized by Frank Sinatra.

Repeat References: NyQuil *(Episode 1.21: The Flu)*

EPISODE 6.26: HENNY PENNY—STRAIGHT, NO CHASER

Directed by Judy Pioli. Written by Tom Whedon. Original airdate: May 4, 1991. The girls are cast as Henny Penny and friends in an elementary school production to encourage reading. Blanche is shocked to learn that a spurned lover has placed a fake obituary in the newspaper claiming that she is dead—and much older than her actual age. Sophia continues a chess-by-mail rivalry.

Reference: Henny Penny

> **Dorothy:** We're doing *Henny Penny*.

Henny Penny is the main character of a European folktale about a paranoid chicken (sometimes called Chicken Little) who believes the world is ending after an acorn falls on her head from a tree. Its origins are fuzzy, but it began to gain momentum in print after the Brothers Grimm got hold of it in the early nineteenth century.

Reference: Humpty Dumpty

> **Dorothy:** Blanche, you could get aroused by Humpty Dumpty.

A fictional character in an English nursery rhyme dating back to the eighteenth century, Humpty Dumpty is an anthropomorphic egg who fell off a wall and couldn't be put back together again.

Reference: PTA

> **Sophia:** Turkey Lurkey was your nickname in high school.
> **Dorothy:** It was not.
> **Sophia:** Really? That's what they called you at the PTA.

PTA stands for parent–teacher association, a common organization at schools made up of teachers, staff members, and parents, with the purpose of facilitating parental involvement at the school.

References: *Show Boat*, "Ol' Man River"

> **Dorothy:** I did once do a production of *Show Boat* in high school and everyone said I was pretty good.
> **Sophia:** No one can sing "Ol' Man River" like my Dorothy.

Show Boat is a 1927 musical based on the Edna Ferber novel of the same name, about the lives of the performers and crew aboard a Mississippi River show boat. "Ol' Man River" is a song from the musical written by Jerome Kern and Oscar Hammerstein II.

References: *Snow White and the Seven Dwarfs*, Napoleon complex

> **Blanche:** I remember when I first read *Snow White and the Seven Dwarfs*. It had a profound influence on me. Seven lonely men living in the woods, needing a woman, all of them with Napoleon complexes, something to prove.

Snow White and the Seven Dwarfs is a 1937 animated Disney film based on the 1812 fairy tale by the Brothers Grimm, about a princess who befriends a group of dwarves while on the run from her wicked stepmother. A Napoleon complex is a theoretical inferiority complex attributed to short people who are overly aggressive or domineering. Its name is a reference to the short stature of the notorious French military leader Napoleon Bonaparte (1769–1821), who conquered much of Europe in his day.

Repeat Reference: *Hamlet (Episode 1.5: The Triangle)*

Season Seven: 1991–1992

The final season.

The last year was a bit of a mixed bag. The show's ratings declined after a timeslot switch and, let's be honest, it was evident that Bea Arthur's interest in the show was winding down. There are several hour-long or two-part episodes, including a couple of themed stunt crossovers with *Empty Nest* and that show's spinoff, *Nurses,* which was new to the Saturday-night lineup.

This season has the fewest cultural references, but there are some great ones, like "La Law," for instance. And all the way to the end, *The Golden Girls* were pop culture name-droppers like no others.

Episode 7.1: Hey, Look Me Over

Directed by Lex Passaris. Written by Mitchell Hurwitz. Original airdate: September 21, 1991.

An old photograph reveals that Blanche once slept with Rose's husband, Charlie. Dorothy worries that Sophia is suffering from hearing loss.

Reference: Gerald Ford

> **Sophia:** As far as we know, I am a citizen. A citizen of the U.S. of A. Home of presidents like Ford, Lincoln. Help me out here, Dorothy.
>
> **Dorothy:** Bush, Ma.
>
> **Sophia, to a bush:** Oh, and Reagan.

Gerald Ford (1913–2006) served as president of the United States from 1974 to 1977, immediately following the resignation of Richard Nixon. Prior to that, he served as vice president under Nixon for less than a year.

Reference: Mothra

> **Sophia:** I thought you said, "I'm Mothra, giant, radioactive insect. Ree! Ree! Ree!"

Mothra is a fictional movie monster depicted as a giant moth, first appearing in the 1961 film *Mothra* and recurring in many Godzilla films.

Reference: Jews for Jesus

> **Sophia:** Every time you get a pamphlet, I get that disease. And not just diseases. I thought for a while I was a Jew for Jesus.

Jews for Jesus is a nonprofit Messianic Jewish Christian organization founded in the 1970s that believes Jesus is the Son of God, which differs from the Judaism belief.

Reference: The Rocketeer

> **Blanche:** Oh my God. Where did you find this [picture]? Oh, I am so embarrassed—my hair, it looks like a helmet!
>
> **Dorothy:** Blanche!
>
> **Blanche:** It's all bunched up and pointy. Honey, you've got to burn this. I look like the Rocketeer.

The Rocketeer is a 1991 Disney film about a stunt pilot who becomes a helmet-clad superhero after discovering a rocket-powered jet pack that enables him to fly.

Reference: *American Gladiators*

> **Rose:** You've landed on your back more than … more than …
>
> **Dorothy:** The American Gladiators.

American Gladiators is a syndicated TV series which ran from 1989 to 1996 and saw amateur athletes compete against one another and the show's "gladiators" in various contests of strength and agility, often winding up on their backs almost as often as Blanche. The gladiators, mostly bodybuilders and former pro athletes, went by nicknames such as Turbo, Nitro, and Ice, and served to thwart the amateur contestants in events such as jousting with big foam sticks. The series proved quite popular, spawning a video game, a soundtrack, a live dinner show, and a kids' version of the show hosted by a pre–*American Idol* Ryan Seacrest in 1994. A revival of the show, hosted by Hulk Hogan and Laila Ali, had a brief run in 2008.

Reference: Xerox

> **Sophia:** There's one thing I do have.
>
> **Dorothy:** Oh, what's that, Ma?
>
> **Sophia:** Two thousand shares of Xerox, which I bought at . . . my health—I've got my health.

Xerox is a corporation founded in 1906 that sells print and digital document products and services, like copying machines.

References: Sunkist Citrus House, Country Bear Jamboree

> **Dorothy:** Here's Blanche in bed with Charlie, but this one is Blanche in bed with a pontoon boat. Here's Blanche in bed with the big orange from the Sunkist building, and here's Blanche in bed with the Country Bear Jamboree!

Sunkist Citrus House was an attraction at Disneyland that operated between 1960 and 1989. The Country Bear Jamboree is a country-western musical revue attraction located in Walt Disney World's Frontierland, featuring a cast of singing bears. The Jamboree debuted in 1971 at Disney World, with similar attractions at Disneyland and Tokyo Disneyland following soon after. The Disneyland version closed in 2001, while the Tokyo one is still in operation. The attraction, long proven a popular draw at the park, consists of a continuous string of country songs sung by the various bears in the cast. In 2002, Disney released a live-action film entitled *The Country Bears* loosely based on the park attraction and starring Christopher Walken. It was a box office bomb.

Reference: *Dying Young*

> **Sophia:** Last night we went to see *Dying Young*. Terrific. I laughed 'til I peed.

A 1991 film based on the novel of the same name by Marti Leimbach, *Dying Young* starred Julia Roberts as the live-in caretaker to a young man (Campbell Scott) battling leukemia. The film received middling to negative reviews.

Reference: Lauren Bacall

> **Sophia:** To me, you've always had the elegance of a young Lauren Bacall.

Lauren Bacall (1924–2014) was a model and actress known for her striking looks who rose to the high ranks of Hollywood with a career that spanned decades, beginning in the 1940s. Her filmography includes such notable entries as *The Big Sleep, How to Marry a Millionaire, The Shootist,* and her Oscar-nominated turn in *The Mirror Has Two Faces.*

Repeat References: Pillsbury Doughboy *(Episode 1.4: Transplant),* Beethoven *(Episode 2.12: The Sisters),* Ronald Reagan *(Episode 3.6: Letter to Gorbachev),* George H. W. Bush *(Episode 3.21: Larceny and Old Lace),* Abraham Lincoln *(Episode 1.2: Guess Who's Coming to the Wedding?),* Disneyland *(Episode 1.14: That Was No Lady)*

EPISODE 7.2: THE CASE OF THE LIBERTINE BELLE
Directed by Lex Passaris. Written by Tom Whedon. Original airdate: September 28, 1991.
The girls participate in a murder-mystery weekend.

Reference: *The Maltese Falcon*

> **Rose:** You got a call last night from something called the Maltese Falcon Club.

The Maltese Falcon is a 1930 detective novel by Dashiell Hammett, featuring his popular character Sam Spade. The book was made into a critically acclaimed 1941 film starring Humphrey Bogart.

References: Sherlock Holmes, Shinola

> **Rose:** Back in Minnesota, I was known as the Sherlock Holmes of St. Olaf.
> **Dorothy:** Figured out which one was Shinola, did you, Rose?
> **Rose:** The hard way.

Arguably the best-known fictional detective ever created, Sherlock Holmes was the creation of British author Sir Arthur Conan Doyle and has appeared in countless works of literature, stage, film, screen, and merchandise since the 1800s. Doyle authored a total of four Sherlock novels and fifty-six short stories, with many others carrying on after him. The character holds a Guinness World Record for being the most portrayed literary human character in history. The list of actors portraying the detective includes Orson Welles, Basil Rathbone, Peter O'Toole, Robert Downey Jr., Benedict Cumberbatch, and Henry Cavill. Shinola is a defunct brand of shoe polish founded in 1877 that entered the American lexicon thanks to the phrase, "You don't know shit from Shinola."

Reference: Ming vases

> **Sophia:** If he has an eye for antiques, you should be a shoe-in.
>
> **Dorothy:** Look who's calling the vase Ming.

Ming vases are fine, sophisticated porcelain pieces dating to fifteenth-century China.

References: Dashiell Hammett, Sam Spade, Raymond Chandler, Philip Marlowe, Monaco Grand Prix, Charlie Chaplin

> **Dorothy:** I have read every word Dashiell Hammett and Raymond Chandler ever wrote. Sam Spade and Philip Marlowe have become a part of me. She had more curves than the Monaco Grand Prix and was twice as dangerous. Her jewelry was mute testimony that Charlie Chaplin wasn't the only tramp who'd hit it big in this town.

Dashiell Hammett (1894–1961) was the author of a series of hard-boiled detective novels and stories, including *The Maltese Falcon*, *The Thin Man*, and *Red Harvest*. His creation, Sam Spade, is one of the most beloved literary detectives in history. Raymond Chandler (1888–1959) was a prominent novelist and screenwriter credited as a founder of hard-boiled detective fiction. His character, Philip Marlowe, is considered a quintessential literary private eye. *Farewell, My Lovely*, *The Little Sister*, and *The Long Goodbye* are among his most prominent works. The Monaco Grand Prix is an annual motor race held each May. Charlie Chaplin (1889–1977) was an English actor, film-maker, and composer who rose to fame during the silent-film era and has become an icon for his screen persona, The Tramp, a bumbling, bowler hat- and mustache-clad vagrant.

Reference: Brer Rabbit

> **Blanche:** I do declare. Your sweet words could charm the morning dew right off the honeysuckle.
>
> **Dorothy:** That's good, Blanche. Now do Brer Rabbit.

Brer Rabbit, or Brother Rabbit, was a trickster character originating in African folklore and popularized through the works of writer Joel Chandler

Harris. Disney adapted the character for the 1946 animated movie *Song of the South*, which has sparked considerable controversy for its handling of race.

Reference: Colonel Mustard

> **Sophia:** It was Colonel Mustard in the library with the candlestick!

Colonel Mustard is a fictional character from the Clue board game, portrayed as a big-game hunter and colonial imperialist. Martin Mull portrayed the character in the 1985 film version of the game.

Reference: Tour de France

> **Rose:** Dorothy, that was a real Tour de France!

The Tour de France is an annual multiple-stage bicycle race primarily held, obviously, in France, while occasionally passing through other countries. It was first held in 1903.

Repeat References: Jay Leno *(Episode 3.5: Nothing to Fear but Fear Itself)*, Johnny Carson *(Episode 3.3: Bringing Up Baby)*

EPISODE 7.3: BEAUTY AND THE BEAST
Directed by Lex Passaris. Written by Marc Cherry and Jamie Wooten. Original airdate: October 5, 1991.
Blanche signs her visiting granddaughter up for a beauty pageant. Dorothy hires a nurse from Shady Pines to care for an injured Sophia.

Reference: "Daisy Bell (Bicycle Built for Two)"

> *Sophia and Nurse DeFarge sing this song together.*

"Daisy Bell (Bicycle Built for Two)" is a song written in 1892 by Harry Dacre and recorded over the years by the likes of Bing Crosby, Nat King Cole, and Alvin and the Chipmunks.

References: *The Nun's Story, Ironside*

> **Rose:** We were going to watch *The Nun's Story*. I've never seen it before.
>
> **Nurse DeFarge:** Oh, she leaves the convent in the end. There it is—*Ironside*.

The Nun's Story is a 1959 drama film, based on the 1956 novel by Kathryn Hulme, starring Audrey Hepburn as a woman who decides to enter a convent but struggles with the obedience required to be a nun. *Ironside* is a TV crime-drama series that aired on NBC from 1967 to 1975, starring Raymond Burr as Robert T. Ironside, a paralyzed San Francisco police consultant.

Reference: "Hasta la vista, baby"

> **Nurse DeFarge:** Dorothy, a man called wanting to know if you were free Saturday night, but I forgot to write down the number. Sorry.
>
> **Dorothy:** Hasta la vista, baby!

"Hasta la vista, baby" is a Spanish farewell phrase uttered by (and forever associated with) Arnold Schwarzenegger's character in the 1991 film *Terminator 2: Judgment Day*.

Reference: "Put On a Happy Face"

> *Blanche performs this song at the beauty pageant.*

"Put On a Happy Face" is a song written by Lee Adams and Charles Strouse, first performed by Dick Van Dyke in the 1960 Broadway musical *Bye Bye Birdie*.

Repeat References: *Peter Pan (Episode 1.9: Blanche and the Younger Man)*

EPISODE 7.4: THAT'S FOR ME TO KNOW
Directed by Lex Passaris. Written by Kevin Abbott. Original airdate: October 12, 1991.
Dorothy discovers an old photo of Sophia in a wedding dress, standing next to a man who isn't her father. Blanche installs a hot tub.

Reference: Rudy Vallée

> **Dorothy:** Look! Rudy Vallée!

Rudy Vallée (1901–1986) was a singer and actor who was one of the first pop stars to be labeled a teen idol.

Reference: Irving Berlin

> **Sophia:** Ah, America. The land of opportunity, where the streets were paved with gold, and a young man named Irving Berlin was writing songs like this. Hit it!

Irving Berlin (1888–1989) is considered one of the greatest American composers and lyricists, with his songs making up a large chunk of "The Great American Songbook," a canon of standards. He wrote 1,500 songs during his six-decade career, including stage and screen classics like "Puttin' on the Ritz," "White Christmas," "Anything You Can Do (I Can Do Better)," and "There's No Business Like Show Business."

Reference: World's Fair

> **Dorothy:** What about this picture of you in a wedding gown with someone who is identified as Guido?
>
> **Sophia:** Uh, World's Fair. At the "Have Your Picture Taken with a Guido" booth.

A World's Fair is a large international exhibition showcasing achievements of nations.

Reference: Spike Lee

> **Blanche:** The moronic Scandinavian nitwit ought to pay it.
>
> **Rose:** She's talking about me, isn't she?
>
> **Dorothy:** No, Rose. She's talking about Spike Lee.

Spike Lee is a renowned producer, director, writer, and actor known for such films as *She's Gotta Have It*, *Do the Right Thing*, *Mo' Better Blues*, and *Malcolm X*.

Repeat Reference: Dreyfuss the dog *(Episode 4.4: Yokel Hero)*

EPISODE 7.5: WHERE'S CHARLIE?
Directed by Lex Passaris. Written by Gail Parent and Jim Vallely. Original airdate: October 19, 1991.
Rose is convinced her deceased husband is sending her signals after she accepts a friendship ring from Miles. Blanche helps her baseball-player boyfriend improve his game.

Reference: Mario Lanza

> **Dorothy:** I'm getting all this stored-up emotion out in a letter.
>
> **Sophia:** Good idea, Pussycat. I'm going to write one to Mario Lanza.

Mario Lanza (1921–1959) was a tenor vocalist and actor known for roles in *That Midnight Kiss*, *The Toast of New Orleans*, and *Because You're Mine*.

References: *Dances with Wolves*, *Bull Durham*, Kevin Costner

> **Sophia:** What was it called? Dances with Bulls?
>
> **Dorothy:** Ma, you're confusing *Bull Durham* with *Dances with Wolves*.
>
> **Sophia:** What's the difference? You get to see Kevin Costner's buns in both of them.

Dances with Wolves is a 1990 Western film produced, directed by, and starring Kevin Costner. The film is based on a 1988 book by Michael Blake about a Civil War lieutenant who travels to the frontier and becomes involved with a Native American tribe. The film, Costner's directorial debut, was a critical and box office hit. *Bull Durham* is a 1988 romantic comedy / sports film about the fans and players of the Durham Bulls, a North Carolina minor-league baseball team. The film starred Costner, Tim Robbins, and Susan Sarandon and was a critical and box office hit, grossing over $50 million in North America. It has been considered among the greatest sports films of all time. An actor, filmmaker, and musician, Costner became one of the biggest stars of the 1980s and 1990s, appearing in a string of successful films like *The Untouchables*, *Field of Dreams*, *JFK*, *Robin Hood: Prince of Thieves*, and *The Bodyguard*.

Reference: Abbott and Costello

> **Miles:** It's a friendship ring, like Abbott might've given to Costello.
>
> **Rose:** So now we're . . . a dead comedy team?

Legendary comedy duo Bud Abbott (1897–1974) and Lou Costello (1906–1959) rose to fame as radio, film, and television stars in the 1940s and 1950s. During World War II, they became the highest-paid entertainers in the world. The pair starred together in dozens of films, including such fare as *Abbott and Costello Meet Frankenstein* and *Abbott and Costello Meet Dr. Jekyll and Mr. Hyde*. Despite a long list of films, shows, and accolades, the pair is perhaps best known for their signature baseball-themed skit, "Who's on first?"

Reference: Mrs. Butterworth

> **Rose:** It's Charlie! He's trying to contact me from beyond the grave. It's a miracle.
>
> **Dorothy:** Look closely, Rose. It's Mrs. Butterworth.

Mrs. Butterworth is a brand of syrups and pancake mixes first introduced in 1961, known for its distinctive bottles in the shape of a matronly, apron-clad woman—an image that came under scrutiny in 2020 when protests over systemic racism led critics to cite it as an example of racial stereotyping.

Reference: "Don't take any wooden nickels"

> **Rose:** Charlie, I want to believe it's you. Tell me something that only the two of us would know.
>
> **Sophia:** Don't take any wooden nickels.
>
> **Rose:** Oh my God, it is you!

"Don't take any wooden nickels" is a phrase typically reminding people not to be naive or allow themselves to be cheated. It dates back to the Depression when wooden tokens resembling coins were used as promotional items but had no actual value.

Reference: Tokyo Rose

> **Dorothy:** Stevie's leaving Blanche for Tokyo, Rose.
>
> **Rose:** Well, I can understand that. She is a big radio personality.

Tokyo Rose was a name given by Allied troops during World War II not to one woman but to all female English-speaking radio broadcasters of Japanese propaganda. After the war, the figure became a symbol of Japanese villainy in various cartoons and films.

Reference: Steve and Eydie

> **Dorothy:** He comes in Steve and goes out Eydie.

Steve and Eydie were a popular singing duo consisting of husband and wife Steve Lawrence and Eydie Gormé (1957–2013), who rose to fame in the 1950s and performed together for decades, until Eydie's death.

EPISODE 7.6: MOTHER LOAD

Directed by Lex Passaris. Written by Don Seigel and Jerry Perzigian. Original airdate: October 26, 1991.

Blanche's relationship with local newscaster Jerry Kennedy is threatened by his overbearing mother. Rose seeks information on Jerry for a roast at the TV studio.

Reference: "The Farmer in the Dell"

> **Rose:** You'll never guess who was just on the phone.

> **Blanche:** The real phone, Rose, or your Farmer in the Dell phone?

"The Farmer in the Dell" is a children's song and game dating back to 1826 Germany. It's been sung in classrooms and on playgrounds ever since.

Reference: "Tastes great, less filling"

> **Dorothy:** Look, Stan, old Stan, new Stan, "tastes great, less filling" Stan
> . . .

"Tastes great, less filling" was a long-running advertising campaign for Miller Lite beer, in which one drinker would comment on the great taste of the beer, while another would note that it is less filling than other beers. This would then escalate into a shouting match between the two, parodying an old Wild West saloon brawl.

Reference: Splash Mountain

> **Sophia:** Wait a minute. This isn't Splash Mountain.

Splash Mountain is a log flume ride that first opened at Disneyland in 1989. There are also Splash Mountains at Tokyo Disneyland and Magic Kingdom.

Repeat References: Walter Cronkite *(Episode 5.10: All That Jazz)*, Captain Kangaroo *(Episode 3.24: Mister Terrific)*, People *(Episode 1.25: The Way We Met)*, Miami Herald *(Episode 4.14: Love Me Tender)*, Sigmund Freud *(Episode 3.24: Mister Terrific)*

EPISODE 7.7: DATELINE: MIAMI

Directed by Peter D. Beyt. Written by Marc Cherry and Jamie Wooten. Original airdate: November 2, 1991.

While Dorothy is out with a prominent doctor, the other girls reminisce about previous dates.

Reference: "Cheek to Cheek"

> **Dorothy:** Heaven, I'm in heaven, and my heart beats so . . .

This is the first line of the 1935 Irving Berlin tune "Cheek to Cheek," from the Fred Astaire / Ginger Rogers film *Top Hat.*

Reference: *Where's Waldo?*

> **Dorothy:** If you need something to keep you occupied tonight, Rose, why don't you take out a good book and see if you can find Waldo.

Waldo is a fictional character in a series of children's puzzle books created by Martin Handford called *Where's Waldo?* The books consist of a series of detailed illustrations depicting lots of people doing a variety of amusing things, with the reader charged with finding Waldo—a bespectacled, thin man with a red-and-white-striped shirt and hat—in the crowd.

Reference: Glinda the Good Witch

> **Waiter:** And who's this? Glinda the Good Witch of the North?

Glinda the Good Witch is a fictional character in L. Frank Baum's *Oz* novels, who first appeared in the 1900 novel *The Wonderful Wizard of Oz.* In the book series, she is one of Oz's four witches, two of whom were good and two wicked, and she ruled over the country's southern lands. In the 1939 musical film adaptation, Glinda is portrayed by actress Billie Burke as Glinda the Good Witch of the North. With her sparkly pink gown and bright red hair, Burke's portrayal is arguably the most iconic version of the character, despite everyone from Lena Horne to Kristin Chenoweth to Miss Piggy playing the role in various adaptations over the decades.

Reference: Elsie the Cow

> **Rose:** What's the matter?
>
> **Arnie:** The cow story. My wife's name was Elsie!

Elsie was a cartoon cow developed as the mascot for Borden Dairy Company in the 1930s.

Reference: Alexander Hamilton

> **Myron:** I'm sorry, Mrs. Petrillo. She's just not my type.
>
> **Sophia:** I see. How about Mr. Hamilton, is he your type?

Alexander Hamilton (c. 1755–1804) was an American statesman considered a Founding Father of the United States who championed a strong federal government and was key in ratifying the US Constitution. He was considered by some to have been an underappreciated, even forgotten, figure in history—that is, until playwright, composer, and actor Lin-Manuel Miranda's *Hamilton: An American Musical* premiered in 2015 and took the world by storm. Hamilton is depicted on the US ten-dollar bill.

Repeat References: Stephen King *(Episode 6.11: Stand by Your Man)*, the Orange Bowl *(Episode 3.4: The Housekeeper)*

EPISODES 7.8 AND 7.9: THE MONKEY SHOW—PARTS 1 AND 2

Directed by Lex Passaris. Written by Mitchell Hurwitz and Marc Sotkin. Original airdate: November 9, 1991.

As a hurricane threatens Miami, Dorothy's sister Gloria arrives and ends up sleeping with Stan. Blanche and Rose hold a telethon to save a local historic lighthouse. This two-part episode was part of NBC's "Hurricane Saturday," featuring crossovers between *The Golden Girls*, *Empty Nest*, and *Nurses*.

References: Jolie, Magda, Zsa Zsa, and Eva Gabor

> **Sophia:** I always thought of us as the Gabors.
>
> **Dorothy:** Well, I'm glad we had this little chat.
>
> **Sophia:** No, hear me out. I'm Jolie, the mother. Your sister Gloria, she's Zsa Zsa. And Eva—well, Eva was of course your brother Phil.
>
> **Dorothy:** I'm not a Gabor?
>
> **Sophia:** You're telling me.

The Gabor sisters were a trio of Hungarian actresses and socialites—Magda (1915–1997), Zsa Zsa (1917–2016), and Eva (1919–1995)—who moved to the United States to launch film careers in the 1940s. Eva was the most successful in her acting career. She hosted her own talk show briefly in the 1950s before rising to fame in the sitcom *Green Acres*. The trio were mainstays not only in New York social circles and tabloids but also in variety and game shows over the decades. Their mother, Jolie (1896–1997), Countess de Szigethy, was also an actress and socialite.

Reference: *The Bonfire of the Vanities*

> **Sophia:** I've seen everything. Twice. Except *Bonfire of the Vanities.* Woof!

The Bonfire of the Vanities is a best-selling 1987 novel by Tom Wolfe, named after the historical 1497 event in Florence, Italy, in which the city's rulers ordered the burning of items that church officials considered sinful (think: books, makeup, and art). The book, however, is about a successful New York City bond trader who finds himself embroiled in a hit-and-run accident that sparks racial and cultural tension. In 1990, the book was made into a much-anticipated film starring Tom Hanks, Bruce Willis, and Melanie Griffith. It was a critical and box office bomb.

Reference: "To Sir, with Love"

> *A man auditions with this song for the lighthouse telethon.*

To Sir, with Love is a 1967 film starring Sidney Poitier about social and racial issues in an inner-city school. The accompanying title song, originally recorded by Lulu, became a number-one hit.

Reference: "I Am Woman"

> **Dorothy:** I am woman, hear me roar.

This is a line from "I Am Woman," a 1972 number-one song by Helen Reddy.

Reference: Carol Weston

> **Dorothy:** Carol, this isn't a good time.
>
> **Carol:** Well, you know me. When is it a good time?

Another character from spinoff series *Empty Nest*, Carol Weston, played by actress and writer Dinah Manoff, is a neurotic divorcée who often found herself at odds with her sister, Barbara, and mooching neighbor, Charley.

Reference: Betsy Wetsy

> **Angelo:** Stan is not a stick. He's not a Betsy Wetsy. He's not a rubber ball. He's a man.

Betsy Wetsy is a drink-and-wet doll that first appeared in the 1930s and gained momentum in the 1940s and 1950s. Betsy would appear to pee after water was poured down her throat. Although the doll was manufactured into the 1980s, that 1950s peak was never recaptured.

Reference: Clark Bar

> **Dorothy:** Would you like a Clark Bar?
> **Stan:** Sure.
> **Dorothy:** Two-fifty.

Clark Bar is a candy bar dating back to 1917, originally owned by the Clark Company and now produced by Necco. Originally priced at five cents, it was popular among World War I soldiers. It consists of a crunchy molasses peanut-butter center coated in milk chocolate, and originally contained a caramel center. The current version is similar to a Butterfinger or Fifth Avenue bar.

Repeat References: Goofy *(Episode 3.22: Rose's Big Adventure)*, Corvette *(Episode 2.7: Family Affair)*

EPISODE 7.10: RO$E LOVE$ MILE$

Directed by Lex Passaris. Written by Don Seigel, Jerry Perzigian, Richard Vaczy, and Tracy Gamble. Original airdate: November 16, 1991.
Rose, fed up with Miles's penny-pinching ways, accepts a date with another man. Dorothy goes out of town, leaving Blanche in charge of a rebellious Sophia.

Reference: AA

> **Rose:** He snuck me into an AA meeting.

AA stands for Alcoholics Anonymous, an international fellowship of men and women who have had a drinking problem and want to do something about it. Known for its twelve-step group of principles to help expel the obsession with drinking, AA meetings are open to anyone hoping to address their drinking problem.

Reference: Garfield

> **Blanche:** Look! Garfield caught a fish!

Garfield is a cartoon cat and star of the Jim Davis comic strip *Garfield*, which debuted in the 1970s. The strip chronicles the life of a fat, orange, lazy, lasagna-loving feline, his owner, Jon Arbuckle, and best frenemy, Odie the dog. The character gained momentum in the 1980s with a popular line of merchandise, TV specials, video games, and a Saturday-morning cartoon series. A pair of live-action / computer-animated films was released in 2004 and 2006 and starred Bill Murray as the voice of Garfield.

Reference: Visa

> **Rose:** She said she cleared it with you.
>
> **Blanche:** She did not clear it with me.
>
> **Rose:** Then giving her my Visa card was a bad thing?

Visa is a financial services corporation founded in 1958, known for its credit cards.

Reference: Sistine Chapel

> **Sophia:** Hey, Mr. Occupato, what are you doing in there, painting the Sistine Chapel?

The Sistine Chapel is a chapel in the official residence of the Pope in Vatican City, famous for the frescoes that decorate its interior, including *The Last Judgment* by Michelangelo.

Reference: Muzak

> **Miles:** God forbid we get into an elevator where there's Muzak.

Muzak is a brand of background music often played in retail stores, elevators, and other public places.

Repeat References: Diet Coke *(Episode 1.3: Rose the Prude)*, Ebenezer Scrooge *(Episode 2.11: 'Twas the Nightmare Before Christmas)*

EPISODE 7.11: ROOM 7

Directed by Peter D. Beyt. Written by Tracy Gamble and Richard Vaczy. Original airdate: November 23, 1991.

Sophia has an out-of-body experience where she receives a visit from her late husband. The girls travel to Atlanta to visit Blanche's family's plantation before it is demolished.

Reference: Boys Town

Blanche: They are tearing down the place where I spent my happiest moments as a child.

Dorothy: Oh, I'm sorry, Blanche. They're tearing down Boys Town?

Boys Town is a nonprofit organization based in Boys Town, Nebraska, dedicated to caring for children and families. It was founded in 1917 by Father Edward J. Flanagan as an orphanage for boys.

Reference: "You dirty rat! You killed my brother!"

Sal says this to Sophia when they meet in Heaven.

This is a popular—and misquoted—line supposedly said by actor James Cagney in the 1932 film *Taxi!* The thing is, it wasn't something he actually said. There is a line calling someone a dirty, yellow-bellied rat, but that's it.

Reference: Bonneville

Sophia: Your Bonneville shakes when you go over sixty-five.

The Bonneville was a model of full-size (and briefly in the 1980s, midsize) cars produced by Pontiac between 1957 and 2005. The popularity of the line waned in later years, and the Bonneville was dropped from Pontiac's lineup after 2005.

Reference: "99 Bottles of Beer"

Rose is singing the final verses of this song as the girls return home.

"99 Bottles of Beer" is an anonymous folk song dating back to the mid-twentieth century in which the singer, often a kid in the backseat of a car on long family road trips, starts with the titular ninety-nine bottles of beer at verse one, takes one down, passes it around, and does so until counting down to zero. Or, in Rose's case, stopping at two just to drive Dorothy crazy.

Repeat Reference: James Cagney *(Episode 6.24: Never Yell Fire in a Crowded Retirement Home—Part 1)*

EPISODE 7.12: FROM HERE TO THE PHARMACY
Directed by Lex Passaris. Written by Gail Parent and Jim Vallely. Original airdate: December 7, 1991.

A soldier returns from the Persian Gulf, seeking to rekindle his relationship with Blanche, who doesn't remember him. Dorothy is angered to learn that Sophia has been hoarding money.

References: *L.A. Law*, Susan Dey

> **Dorothy:** You're using Rose as a lawyer?
>
> **Rose:** I know what I'm doing. Every Thursday, I watch La Law.
>
> **Dorothy:** That's *L.A. Law*.
>
> **Rose:** I wondered why Susan Dey didn't have a French accent.

L.A. Law is a long-running courtroom drama series which ran on NBC from 1986 to 1994. The show was created by Steven Bochco and Terry Louise Fisher and had a large ensemble cast including Richard Dysart, Alan Rachins, Corbin Bernsen, Jill Eikenberry, Harry Hamlin, and Susan Dey. The show won a string of awards throughout its run, including fifteen Emmys. In addition to this show, Dey is also best known for her role as Laurie Partridge on *The Partridge Family*.

Reference: General Norman Schwarzkopf

> **Blanche:** I did keep pretty well up with what went on over there. I saw Schwarzkopf on the Bob Hope special.

General Norman Schwarzkopf (1934–2012) was a US Army general who led coalition forces in the Gulf War.

Reference: *Hard Copy*

> **Sophia:** You try to do right by your kids and you end up the lead story on *Hard Copy*.

Hard Copy is a tabloid news show that ran in syndication from 1989 to 1999, known for aggressive reporting tactics and questionable material.

Reference: The Hopi Tribe

> **Dorothy, regarding Sophia's age:** Hopi Indians are walking around saying, "How does she do it?"

The Hopi Tribe is a Native American tribe located primarily in the Hopi Reservation in Arizona.

Reference: Afro Sheen

Sophia: So Bill, what's on sale?

Bill: Breast pumps.

Sophia: What else?

Bill: Afro Sheen.

Sophia: Moving on.

Bill: Preparation H.

Sophia: Hot damn!

Afro Sheen is a line of unisex hair-care products targeted to African Americans. After going dormant in the 1990s, the brand resurfaced with new products in 2020. The line was founded in the late 1960s by Black business pioneers Joan and George E. Johnson, who took a $250 vacation loan and turned it into a multimillion-dollar organization.

Repeat References: Bob Hope *(Episode 1.9: Blanche and the Younger Man)*, *The Twilight Zone (Episode 2.17: Bedtime Story)*, Haley's M-O *(Episode 3.12: Charlie's Buddy)*, Preparation H *(Episode 2.19: Long Day's Journey into Marinara)*

EPISODE 7.13: THE POPE'S RING
Directed by Lex Passaris. Written by Kevin Abbott. Original airdate: December 14, 1991.
Sophia attends a Papal mass in hopes of getting a blessing for an ill friend. Blanche hires a detective to help Rose determine if Miles is cheating.

Reference: Ziggy

Blanche: Did you get her a Ziggy card?

Ziggy is a fictional diminutive, bald character from the comic strip bearing his name, which was created in 1968 by Tom Wilson.

References: *The Mickey Mouse Club*, Roy Williams

Dorothy: Rose, that is the original *Mickey Mouse Club* sweatshirt that Roy wore.

The Mickey Mouse Club is a children's variety show from Walt Disney Productions, which has aired in various incarnations beginning with a four-year run in 1955. Revivals aired from 1977 to 1979, 1989 to 1996, and 2017 to 2018. Roy Williams (1907–1976) was one of four adult Mouseketeers on the original series.

Reference: Uncle Remus

> **Blanche:** Let me tell you a story of the steamy South, a tale of deception and tragedy.
>
> **Sophia:** Just a second, Uncle Remus.

Uncle Remus is a fictional character who narrated a collection of Black American folktales, published in book form by Joel Chandler Harris in 1881. The tales were written to represent the struggle of Black people in the South, with dialect and framing choices that have led to considerable racial controversy in more recent times.

Reference: Absorbine Jr.

> **Blanche:** It involved a men's club, a vine rope, and a large bottle of Absorbine Jr.

Absorbine Jr. has been providing pain relief for more than one hundred years. The original Absorbine was developed by Wilbur and Mary Ida Young in 1892 as a muscle pain relief ointment for plow-pulling horses. Achy farmers, though, soon realized it helped their own pain and stiffness. Soon enough, along came Absorbine Jr., named after the Youngs' son, Junior, and developed specifically for people. It's been a medicine-cabinet staple ever since.

Reference: Albert Einstein

> **Rose:** For three days, I was another Einstein. Then they pulled out the IV.

Albert Einstein (1879–1955) was a German theoretical physicist and 1921 Nobel Prize winner who developed the theory of relativity and whose work is widely known for its influence on science. His mass-energy equivalence formula, $E = mc^2$, has been called the world's most famous equation, and the generalized term "Einstein" has become largely known to refer to someone of high intelligence.

Repeat References: Snoopy *(Episode 1.11: Stan's Return)*, the Pope *(Episode 2.18: Forgive Me, Father)*, Witness Protection Program *(Episode 6.15: Miles to Go)*, Zsa Zsa Gabor *(Episode 7.8: The Monkey Show—Part 1)*

Episode 7.14: Old Boyfriends

Directed by Peter D. Beyt. Written by Jamie Wooten and Marc Cherry. Original airdate: January 4, 1992.

Sophia begins dating Marvin, who insists on bringing his sister along on their dates. A man claiming to be an old flame of Rose's visits, but Rose can't remember him.

Reference: *Final Exit*

> **Blanche, reading a personals ad:** Elderly white male with broken hip seeks elderly white female. I am into massages, bran muffins, and the book *Final Exit*. Please respond quickly or I'll do it. I swear I will.

Subtitled "The Practicalities of Self-Deliverance and Assisted Suicide for the Dying," *Final Exit* is a 1991 book by Derek Humphry that has been called a suicide manual and shares various means by which terminally ill people could end their own lives.

Reference: Caligula

> **Sophia:** Well, if it isn't Mrs. Caligula.

Caligula (AD 12–41) was emperor of the Roman Empire from the years 37 to 41. Caligula was actually a nickname given to him by his father's soldiers, meaning "little soldier's boot." While few facts remain about Caligula's reign, he is mostly remembered as a cruel, sadistic, and perverted tyrant with an extravagant lifestyle. He was assassinated by group stabbing.

Repeat Reference: Frank Sinatra *(Episode 1.11: Stan's Return)*

Episode 7.15: Goodbye, Mr. Gordon

Directed by Lex Passaris. Written by Gail Parent and Jim Vallely. Original airdate: January 11, 1992.

Dorothy is smitten with a former teacher who enlists her help to write a book review. Rose invites Dorothy and Blanche to appear on a talk show at the television station.

Reference: MIT

> **Blanche:** Once I did have a fling with a calculus teacher.
>
> **Dorothy:** Did you get an A?
>
> **Blanche:** More like a full scholarship to MIT.

MIT is the Massachusetts Institute of Technology, a private research university founded in 1861.

Reference: Sir Lancelot

> **Dorothy:** For forty years, I've had this fantasy that Mr. Gordon would come swooping into my life like Sir Lancelot.

Sir Lancelot is one of the Knights of the Round Table and a close companion of King Arthur in Arthurian legend.

Repeat References: *The Price Is Right (Episode 1.25: The Way We Met)*, Zorro *(Episode 4.11: The Auction)*, Disney *(Episode 1.9: Blanche and the Younger Man)*

EPISODE 7.16: THE COMMITMENTS

Directed by Lex Passaris. Written by Tracy Gamble and Richard Vaczy. Original airdate: January 25, 1992.

Blanche takes Dorothy's place on a blind date after Dorothy wins tickets to see a *Beatlemania* production.

Reference: "Camptown Races"

> **Blanche:** I was singing a little song in my mind. "Camptown Races."

"Camptown Races" is an 1850 minstrel song written by Stephen Foster that's been a part of popular Americana ever since.

Reference: *Beatlemania*

> **Dorothy:** I just won a ticket on the radio to a dinner theater *Beatlemania*.

The word "Beatlemania" refers to the wild fan frenzy surrounding iconic British rock group The Beatles in the 1960s. In 1977, a musical revue show borrowed the term for its title and had a two-year run on Broadway. Billed as a rockumentary, the show was advertised as "not the Beatles, but an incredible simulation." The original *Beatlemania* Broadway production ended in 1979, with various revivals touring the country in later years.

Reference: Shea Stadium

> **Dorothy:** When [The Beatles] came to Shea Stadium, I managed to get a ticket, but one of my kids came down with the flu. It was one of those times where you have to pretend you love your kids more than something you really want to do.

Shea Stadium is a stadium in New York that was home to the New York Mets baseball team from 1964 to 2008.

Reference: Bossa nova

> **Sophia:** I have been known to make princes and kings leave their wives and palaces and dance the bossa nova.

Literally meaning "new trend," bossa nova is a style of Brazilian music fusing samba and jazz that gained momentum in the 1960s. The bossa nova dance, meanwhile, was a fad dance that corresponded to the musical movement.

References: "She Loves You," "hi de ho"

> *Dorothy enters singing "She Loves You."*
>
> **Sophia:** Yeah, yeah yeah? You call that music? Hi de, hi de, ho. Now *that's* music.

"She Loves You" is a 1963 Beatles song written by John Lennon and Paul McCartney. Jazz singer Cab Calloway (1907–1994) popularized the phrase "hi de ho" in songs like "The Hi De Ho Man" and "Minnie the Moocher."

References: George Harrison

> **Dorothy:** Don plays George in *Beatlemania*.
>
> **Don:** And Paul when Ernie's sick.

George Harrison (1943–2001) was a member of The Beatles.

Reference: Yoko Ono

> **Dorothy:** Thanks to me, Don can now perform his own songs. Do you know what that makes me?
>
> **Sophia:** Yoko Zbornak?

Yoko Ono is an artist, activist, singer, and songwriter who was married to John Lennon from 1969 until his death in 1980. Rumors abounded that her relationship with Lennon influenced the disbanding of The Beatles.

References: Ringo Starr, "Help!"

> **Blanche:** They're having a cast party for *Beatlemania* at our house, and the last time I looked, Ringo was hanging over the toilet singing "Help!"

Ringo Starr was a member of The Beatles. "Help!" is a 1965 number-one song by the band for their movie and soundtrack album of the same name. It made *Rolling Stone*'s list of the greatest songs of all time.

Reference: *The Jetsons*

> **Blanche, using a remote-controlled bar:** I wonder how this thing works. Oh, just like *The Jetsons*.

The Jetsons is an animated sitcom produced by Hanna-Barbera Productions which aired in prime time from 1962 to 1963 and in syndication from 1985 to 1987. The show was conceived as a space-age, futuristic counterpart to the popular *Flintstones*. Despite its relatively short time producing new episodes, reruns of *The Jetsons* have aired for decades and produced various animated films, including 1987's *The Jetsons Meet the Flintstones*.

References: "I've Gotta Be Me," "Kung Fu Fighting"

> **Dorothy:** What can you say about a show by an ex fake Beatle that began with "I've Gotta Be Me" and ended with "Everybody Was Kung Fu Fighting"?

"I've Gotta Be Me" is a 1968 tune that first appeared in the Broadway musical *Golden Rainbow* but became a hit when recorded and released by Sammy Davis Jr. the same year. "Kung Fu Fighting" is a 1974 disco song written and performed by Carl Douglas.

Repeat References: The Beatles *(Episode 1.24: Big Daddy)*, Paul McCartney *(Episode 1.2: Guess Who's Coming to the Wedding?)*, Warren Beatty *(Episode 5.15: Triple Play)*

EPISODE 7.17: QUESTIONS AND ANSWERS

Directed by Lex Passaris. Written by Don Seigel and Jerry Perzigian. Original airdate: February 8, 1992.
Dorothy competes for a chance to appear on *Jeopardy!* Rose brings a rescue dog along when volunteering at the hospital.

Reference: Alex Trebek

> **Dorothy:** Alex Trebek and the *Jeopardy!* people are auditioning contestants in Miami.

Alex Trebek (1940–2020) was a TV personality and game show host best known for hosting *Jeopardy!* from 1984 until his death. He also hosted such game shows as *Classic Concentration, High Rollers,* and *To Tell the Truth.* After a much-publicized battle with pancreatic cancer, the beloved host died in November 2020, shortly after publishing his critically acclaimed memoir. His death was followed by an outpouring of love from friends and colleagues.

Reference: The Gulf War

> **Dorothy:** I watch it every night.
> **Blanche:** We know. We missed the entire Gulf War.

Called Operation Desert Shield, then Operation Desert Storm, the Gulf War was fought in 1990 and 1991 between a coalition of forces led by the United States against Iraq in response to the latter's invasion of Kuwait.

Reference: Mahjong

> **Rose:** It's not easy having to spend that much time with people who are old and sick and frail.
> **Sophia:** Oh, that reminds me. I've got mahjong tomorrow.

Mahjong is a rummy-like, tile-based game dating back to seventeenth-century China.

Reference: Mamie Van Doren

> **Blanche:** Hey, that slipper is from the Mamie Van Doren collection!

Mamie Van Doren is an actress, model, and sex symbol best known for the 1957 film *Untamed Youth.*

References: Potsdam Conference, Joseph Stalin

> **Dorothy, dozing off:** Potsdam Conference, July 1945. Present were Truman, Stalin, Trebek . . .

The Potsdam Conference was a post–World War II meeting between world leaders in Potsdam, Germany, to establish order and discuss peace treaty issues. Joseph Stalin (1878–1953) was a dictator who ruled the Soviet Union from the 1920s until his death in 1953. He represented the Soviet Union at the conference.

Reference: Charley Dietz

> **Johnny Gilbert:** Let's bring out today's contestants. First, we have a substitute high school teacher, Dorothy Zbornak. Next, cruise ship purser Charley Dietz.

Charley was a character from *Empty Nest*, portrayed by actor David Leisure. Womanizing Charley epitomized the "wacky neighbor" trope popular in 1980s sitcoms, always dropping by the home of Dr. Harry Weston to mooch food. Note that his name on the *Jeopardy!* screen is spelled "Charlie," which is not the official spelling of the character's name.

References: Loretta Young, *The Farmer's Daughter*

> **Alex Trebek:** Loretta Young played an innocent milkmaid in this Oscar-winning 1947 movie. Charley?
>
> **Charley:** What is *The Farmer's Daughter*? I thought it was a different kind of movie.

The Farmer's Daughter is a 1947 comedy starring Loretta Young (1913–2000), Joseph Cotton, and Ethel Barrymore as a farmgirl-turned-maid, a congressman, and his politically powerful mother, respectively. The film won Young an Academy Award and spawned a 1963 TV series adaptation starring Inger Stevens and William Windom, which ran for three seasons. Young hosted *The Loretta Young Show* from 1953 to 1961.

References: *Old Yeller, The China Syndrome, Madonna: Truth or Dare*

> **Alex Trebek:** *Old Yeller, The China Syndrome, Truth or Dare.* Charley?
>
> **Charley:** What are Miss July's all-time favorite films?

Old Yeller is a 1957 Walt Disney film about a boy and his stray dog, based on the 1956 Fred Gipson novel of the same name. *The China Syndrome* is a 1979 film directed by James Bridges and starring Jane Fonda, Jack Lemmon, and Michael Douglas. The plot involves a TV reporter and cameraman who discover safety cover-ups at a nuclear power plant in Los Angeles. The title stems from the fanciful reference to the result of a nuclear meltdown, where components melt through their containment structures, seep through the earth, and wind up in China. The film was a critical and commercial success upon release, but drew backlash from the nuclear power industry, who called it sheer fiction. *Truth or Dare* is a reference to *Madonna: Truth or Dare*, a documentary film depicting the life of the singer during her 1990 Blonde Ambition World Tour.

Reference: Juicy Fruit

> **Alex Trebek:** Latin term for a colloidal carbohydrate found in certain trees and plants.
>
> **Rose:** What is Juicy Fruit?

Juicy Fruit is an enduring brand of chewing gum introduced in 1893 by the Wrigley Company.

Reference: Ulysses S. Grant

> **Dorothy:** Cary is not the Grant buried in Grant's tomb. Ulysses S. is.

Ulysses S. Grant (1822–1885) was the leader of the Union Army during the American Civil War and president of the United States from 1869 to 1877.

References: Baron Fairfax, Victory at Naseby, Oliver Cromwell

> **Coordinator:** Shared command with Cromwell at Victory at Naseby.
>
> **Dorothy:** Who is Baron Fairfax?

Baron Thomas Fairfax (1693–1781) was a British Civil War general best remembered for victoriously commanding the New Model Army at the Battle of Naseby in 1645. Oliver Cromwell (1599–1658) played an important role under Fairfax in the war and later served as Lord Protector of the Commonwealth of England, Scotland, and Ireland from 1653 to 1658.

References: Henry VIII, Catherine Howard

> **Coordinator:** Fifth wife of Henry VIII.

Dorothy: Who is Catherine Howard?

Henry VIII (1491–1547) was King of England from 1509 until 1547. He is best remembered for his six marriages to Catherine of Aragon, Anne Boleyn, Jane Seymour, Anne of Cleves, Catherine Howard, and Catherine Parr. Howard (c. 1523–1542), his fifth wife, was stripped of her title and beheaded on the grounds of treason for committing adultery.

Reference: Charles Darwin

> **Dorothy:** Hey, Doc, I bet you wish you hadn't wasted all that time on Darwin now.

Charles Darwin (1809–1882) was a British naturalist credited with developing the theory of evolution by natural selection. His 1859 book *On the Origin of Species* discusses the process by which organisms change over time. It's considered one of the most important scientific works ever published.

Repeat References: *Jeopardy! (Episode 3.5: Nothing to Fear but Fear Itself)*, Maybelline *(Episode 1.9: Blanche and the Younger Man)*, Harry S. Truman *(Episode 1.11: Stan's Return)*, Oscars *(Episode 2.2: Ladies of the Evening)*, Cary Grant *(Episode 1.6: On Golden Girls)*, Merv Griffin *(Episode 2.13: The Stan Who Came to Dinner)*, Donald Trump *(Episode 3.21: Larceny and Old Lace)*, Life Savers *(Episode 2.15: Before and After)*

EPISODE 7.18: EBBTIDE VI: THE WRATH OF STAN
Directed by Lex Passaris. Written by Marc Sotkin. Original airdate: February 15, 1992.
Angelo complains of a bug infestation in the apartment building owned by Dorothy and Stan, which ends up getting the two arrested as slumlords. Dorothy and Blanche take Sophia shoe shopping.

Reference: Marion Barry

> **Stan:** How many people get locked up with someone they're attracted to?
>
> **Dorothy:** I don't know. The name Marion Barry comes to mind.

One-time civil rights activist and Democratic politician Marion Barry (1936–2014) rose to prominence as the mayor of Washington, DC, from 1979 to 1991 and again from 1995 to 1999. Why the gap? That's when Barry was caught on tape during an FBI sting operation smoking crack cocaine and ended up serving six months in prison. Barry faced other controversies throughout his career in politics, which continued in varying degrees after his last term as mayor, such as financial woes, racist remarks against Asians, and a lack of support for gay marriage.

Reference: Raul Julia

> **Sophia:** I know a good plastic surgeon. By tomorrow morning, you could be Raul Julia.

Raul Julia (1940–1994) was a Puerto Rican actor who logged a long, impressive list of stage, television, and film credits during his twenty-five-year career, including *Tempest*, *Kiss of the Spider Woman*, and playing Gomez Addams in the 1991 film version of *The Addams Family*.

Reference: Luther Vandross

> **Sophia:** Do you know who I think about going to bed with? . . . Luther Vandross. Ooh baby.

Luther Vandross (1951–2005) was a Grammy Award–winning singer known for such songs as "Here and Now," "Never Too Much," "Give Me the Reason," and many others.

Repeat References: Abraham Lincoln *(Episode 1.2: Guess Who's Coming to the Wedding?)*, Lincoln *(Episode 5.5: Love Under the Big Top)*, Social Security *(Episode 4.18: Fiddler on the Ropes)*, Marvin Mitchelson *(Episode 6.17: There Goes the Bride—Part 2)*

EPISODE 7.19: JOURNEY TO THE CENTER OF ATTENTION
Directed by Lex Passaris. Written by Jamie Wooten and Marc Cherry. Original airdate: February 22, 1992.
Dorothy and Blanche compete for the attention of the patrons at the Rusty Anchor bar. Rose helps Sophia plan her wake.

Reference: *Amazing Discoveries*

> **Blanche:** Dorothy, what are you doing?
> **Dorothy:** Watching *Amazing Discoveries*. Look at that. The thing just shucks the corn right off the cob. Just shucks it off!

Amazing Discoveries is an episodic series of late-night infomercials that aired from the late 1980s through the mid-1990s. Enthusiastically hosted by Mike Levey, the series was seen all over the world and, at his peak, Levey was receiving hundreds of fan letters a week and even appeared as himself on an episode of *Friends*.

References: "Blue Skies," "Always," "What'll I Do?"

> **Ron:** How about some Irving Berlin? "Blue Skies," "Always."
>
> **Dorothy:** Maybe some other time.
>
> **Ron:** "What'll I Do?"
>
> **Dorothy:** D-flat is good for me.

These are all songs written by Irving Berlin. "Blue Skies" is from the 1926 musical *Betsy*. "Always" was written in 1925 as a wedding gift to Berlin's wife, Ellin Mackay. And "What'll I Do?" was written in 1923. It's been recorded by many but mostly associated with Frank Sinatra's 1962 version.

Reference: The Star of David

> **Blanche, tying knots in cherry stems with her tongue:** For my encore, the Star of David!

The Star of David is a hexagram shape that symbolizes modern Judaism.

Reference: "Hard Hearted Hannah, the Vamp of Savannah"

> *Dorothy performs the song at the Rusty Anchor.*

"Hard Hearted Hannah, the Vamp of Savannah" is a 1924 song written by Jack Yellen, Bob Bigelow, and Charles Bates about a Georgian femme fatale who loves to see men suffer. Singer Margaret Young popularized the tune, which has been recorded and performed countless times over the decades by everyone from Peggy Lee to Ray Charles.

Reference: Claude Akins

> **Bartender:** Hey Dorothy, what's your pleasure?
>
> **Dorothy:** Claude Akins on a water bed. Until then, a beer will have to do.

A popular character actor who rose to fame in the 1950s and worked steadily through the 1980s, Claude Akins (1926–1994) appeared in just about everything produced across four decades. Despite his many roles, however, he was perhaps best known as Sheriff Lobo in the 1979–1981 TV series *B.J. and the Bear* and its spinoff series, *The Misadventures of Sheriff Lobo* (shortened to simply *Lobo* for the second of its two-season run). Born in Georgia, Akins grew up in Bedford, Indiana, which hosts an annual memorial golf tournament in his name.

Reference: "I Wanna Be Loved by You"

Blanche performs the song at the Rusty Anchor.

"I Wanna Be Loved by You" is a song written by Herbert Stothart, Harry Ruby, and Bert Kalmar for the 1928 musical *Good Boy* but immortalized by Marilyn Monroe in the 1959 film *Some Like It Hot*.

Reference: "Cry Me a River"

Dorothy: Blanche, why don't we go out there and do a duet?
Blanche: Do you know "Cry Me a River"?
Dorothy: No, I don't.
Blanche: Good. We'll do that.

Not to be confused with the Justin Timberlake tune of the same name, "Cry Me a River" is a popular torch song written by Arthur Hamilton in the 1950s. It was made famous by singer Julie London in 1955 and has been recorded by several hundred artists since.

Repeat References: Irving Berlin *(Episode 7.4: That's for Me to Know)*, Claus von Bülow *(Episode 6.19: Melodrama)*, Jimmy Swaggart *(Episode 3.22: Rose's Big Adventure)*

EPISODES 7.20 AND 7.21: A MIDWINTER NIGHT'S DREAM—PARTS 1 AND 2

Directed by Lex Passaris. Part 1 written by Kevin Abbott. Part 2 written by Tom Whedon. Original airdate: February 29, 1992.

Blanche throws a Leap Day moonlight madness party in NBC's second themed crossover night between *The Golden Girls*, *Empty Nest*, and *Nurses*.

Reference: Jean-Claude Van Damme

> **Rose:** Just when you think she's dead, she gets up again, and you have to give her one of those Van Damme moves to the jaw!

Jean-Claude Van Damme is a Belgian actor and martial artist known for action films like *Bloodsport*, *Cyborg*, and *Kickboxer*.

Reference: *Harold and Maude*

> **Sophia:** I haven't been hit on like this since I stopped hanging out at the midnight show of *Harold and Maude*.

Harold and Maude is a 1971 comedy-drama film about the budding relationship between a death-obsessed young man and the eccentric older woman he befriends. The film starred Bud Cort and Ruth Gordon in the titular roles and was both critically and commercially unsuccessful upon release. It has since become a rather beloved cult classic.

References: Dear Abby, Ann Landers

> **Sophia:** Fools read Dear Abby. Simpletons read Ann Landers. It's a fine line.

Dear Abby is a syndicated newspaper advice column founded in 1956 by Pauline Phillips, under the pen name Abigail Van Buren. A rival column called Ask Ann Landers, which had been around for over a decade already, was taken over around the same time that Dear Abby launched by none other than Phillips's own twin sister, Eppie Lederer.

Reference: *A Midsummer Night's Dream*

> **Dorothy:** Like Puck says in *A Midsummer Night's Dream*, when it comes to love, lord what fools these mortals be.

A Midsummer Night's Dream is a William Shakespeare comedy written in the late 1590s with multiple interconnecting plotlines revolving around the marriage of Theseus and Hippolyta.

Repeat References: Carol Weston *(Episode 7.9: The Monkey Show—Part 2)*, William Shakespeare *(Episode 1.12: The Custody Battle)*, Judas *(Episode 2.12: The Sisters)*, *The Silence of the Lambs (Episode 6.22: What a Difference a Date Makes)*, Barbara Weston *(Episode 6.16: There Goes the Bride—Part 1)*, Dreyfuss the dog (Episode 4.4: Yokel Hero)

Episode 7.22: Rose: Portrait of a Woman

Directed by Lex Passaris. Written by Robert Spina. Original airdate: March 7, 1992.

Rose gives Miles a naughty picture of herself for his birthday. Dorothy is offered an exciting new job from a former student.

Reference: Attila the Hun

> **Randy:** I was ready to bail until they brought in Attila the Sub.
>
> **Dorothy:** I loved that name. I earned that name.

Attila (c. AD 403–453) ruled the Huns, a nomadic tribe from central Asia, from AD 434 to AD 453. Nicknamed the "scourge of God," the barbaric Attila was known for sacking and pillaging Roman cities.

Reference: IBM

> **Dorothy:** Joe Mama's with IBM.

IBM is the International Business Machines Corporation, a multinational tech company founded in 1911 that sells computer hardware and software.

Reference: The Clapper

> **Rose:** Miles and I always make love with the lights off.
>
> **Blanche:** Always?
>
> **Rose:** Always. Well, except for the time we were listening to this concert on radio. When the applause started, his Clapper went crazy. The lights went on, off, on, off, on, off.

Debuting in the mid-1980s, The Clapper is a sound-activated electrical switch that could turn on or off devices that were plugged into it, such as lamps. The gadget was popularized by the slogan "Clap on! Clap Off! The Clapper!"

Reference: Fay Wray

> **Miles:** Hello, Fay Wray! Bring on the plane!

Fay Wray (1907–2004) was an actress best known for the 1933 film *King Kong*.

References: Betty Grable, Rita Hayworth

> **Miles:** Back when I was in the army, inside my locker I kept a picture of Betty Grable, and she was wearing a lot less than you were wearing in my birthday photo. Sweetheart, she was the darling of America.
>
> **Rose:** Miles, she was in her twenties, and she had the most beautiful legs on the planet.
>
> **Miles:** Ah, the second most beautiful.
>
> **Rose:** Oh, Miles.
>
> **Miles:** Rita Hayworth had a set of gams on her!

Pinup girl and actress Betty Grable (1916–1973) was one of the biggest box office stars of the 1930s and 1940s and, at one time, the highest-salaried American woman. Among her most notable works are *The Gay Divorcee, Moon Over Miami, I Wake Up Screaming*, and *How to Marry a Millionaire*. Rita Hayworth (1918–1987) was an actress, dancer, and pinup girl who was also among the biggest stars in the Classic Hollywood era, appearing in more than sixty films including *Gilda, Only Angels Have Wings, Pal Joey*, and *Cover Girl*.

Reference: Jessica Tandy

> **Sophia:** The salesman tried to jerk me around on the price, but once he found out I was Jessica Tandy, I got a deal.

Jessica Tandy (1909–1994) was a stage, television, and film star who received four Tony Awards, an Oscar, a Golden Globe, and an Emmy. Among her most notable projects were the original Broadway production of *A Streetcar Named Desire*, as well as the films *Cocoon, Driving Miss Daisy*, and *Fried Green Tomatoes*.

Repeat References: King Kong *(Episode 5.1: Sick and Tired—Part 1)*, Godzilla *(Episode 1.14: That Was No Lady)*

EPISODE 7.23: HOME AGAIN, ROSE—PART 1
Directed by Peter D. Beyt. Written by Gail Parent. Original airdate: April 25, 1992.
The girls crash a high school reunion, where Rose suffers a heart attack.

Reference: Gideon Bible

Blanche: I have Gideon Bibles for everyone.

Gideon Bibles are little free Bibles distributed by Gideons International, an evangelical Christian organization founded in Wisconsin in 1899. Gideons distribute the free copies in hotels, hospitals, schools and colleges, military bases, prisons, and other locations.

Repeat References: *The Three Musketeers (Episode 3.12: Charlie's Buddy)*, Vaseline *(Episode 1.4: Transplant)*, Bengay *(Episode 1.6: On Golden Girls)*

Episode 7.24: Home Again, Rose—Part 2
Directed by Peter D. Beyt. Written by Jim Vallely. Original airdate: May 2, 1992.
Rose undergoes triple bypass surgery.

Reference: "Macaroni and cheese or cheese and macaroni?"

Dorothy: You have never met this woman's family. They live in a place called St. Olaf. They fight over whether it's macaroni and cheese or cheese and macaroni.

This is from a 1980s advertising campaign for Kraft Macaroni & Cheese, in which young fans of the food suggested calling it Kraft Cheese & Macaroni because of its cheesy goodness.

Reference: "Neither rain nor sleet . . ."

Blanche: Neither rain nor sleet nor dark of night shall keepeth us from our appointed rounds. Amen.

This is a spin on the motto of the US Postal Service.

Reference: "The Marines' Hymn"

Blanche: Oh please, God, hear our prayer, from the halls of Montezuma to the shores of Tripoli.

This line is from "The Marines' Hymn," the official hymn of the US Marine Corps, adopted in 1929.

Reference: Rheingold Beer

Sophia: My beer is Rheingold, the dry beer . . .

Rheingold Beer was a beer produced by New York's Rheingold Brewery from 1883 to 1976. The jingle the girls sing in the episode was its actual radio jingle in the 1960s.

Reference: "Mary Had a Little Lamb"

> **Dorothy:** She turned "Mary Had a Little Lamb" into a musical.

"Mary Had a Little Lamb" is a nursery rhyme dating back to the nineteenth century about a little girl and her beloved pet lamb.

Reference: "Live from New York, it's *Saturday Night!*"

> **Rose:** There's something else I want to tell you. Now lean in close. This is very important. Live from New York, it's *Saturday Night!*

"Live from New York, it's *Saturday Night!*" is the popular line uttered at the end of the cold-open sketch on the long-running NBC series *Saturday Night Live*.

Reference: *America's Funniest Home Videos*

> **Sophia:** I sold that video of you falling into the gorilla pit to *America's Funniest Home Videos*.

Long before viral videos were a thing, people with their clunky cameras were turning around-the-house mishaps and funny pet videos into gold by sending VHS tapes into *America's Funniest Home Videos*, who'd add some witty narration, overlay some music, and let a studio audience vote on a winner for a cash prize. The show launched as a 1989 special and was so successful it was quickly turned into a weekly series. It's been around ever since. Bob Saget hosted through the late 1990s, then John Fugelsang and Daisy Fuentes, then Tom Bergeron, and most recently, Alfonso Ribeiro.

Repeat References: Johnny Carson *(Episode 3.3: Bringing Up Baby)*, Cher *(Episode 5.18: An Illegitimate Concern)*, Henry VIII *(Episode 7.17: Questions and Answers)*

EPISODES 7.25 AND 7.26: ONE FLEW OUT OF THE CUCKOO'S NEST— PARTS 1 AND 2

Directed by Lex Passaris. Part 1 written by Don Seigel and Jerry Perzigian. Part 2 written by Mitchell Hurwitz. Original airdate: May 9, 1992

Dorothy begins dating Blanche's visiting uncle, Lucas. Their courtship leads to a marriage proposal.

Reference: Ingrid Bergman

Sophia: Ingrid Bergman had Paris, my Pussycat has crabs.

Ingrid Bergman (1915–1982) was a Swedish actress with a string of successful films during her five-decade career, including *For Whom the Bell Tolls*, *Gaslight*, *Joan of Arc*, *Murder on the Orient Express*, and, arguably her most famous credit, *Casablanca*, which is where the Paris reference comes from. Bergman won three Academy Awards, two Emmys, a Tony, and four Golden Globes throughout her career.

Reference: Johnny Reb

Sophia: Now listen, Johnny Reb. You march through my front door a total stranger and ask for my daughter's hand in marriage without telling me two words about yourself.

Johnny Reb is a personification of the common soldier of the Confederacy.

Reference: Emerson String Quartet

Dorothy: When you come by tomorrow, why don't you tell Blanche that you took me to hear the Emerson String Quartet?

One of the world's premier chamber music ensembles formed in 1976, the Emerson String Quartet is named in honor of poet and philosopher Ralph Waldo Emerson and has released more than thirty recordings, racking up nine Grammys along the way.

Reference: General Robert E. Lee

Dorothy: You'll feel differently when you come to the hoedown we're throwing on the anniversary of Lee's surrender.

Robert E. Lee (1807–1870) was a general who commanded the Confederate Army during the American Civil War.

Reference: Hop Sing

Dorothy: How classy. A tribute to Hop Sing.

Hop Sing is a fictional cook in the *Bonanza* TV series, portrayed by actor Victor Sen Yung.

Reference: Wimbledon

Sophia: What is this, Wimbledon?

Wimbledon is the oldest and most prestigious tennis tournament in the world, held in London since 1877.

Repeat References: Lana Turner *(Episode 6.18: Older and Wiser)*, Scrabble *(Episode 6.15: Miles to Go)*, Ulysses S. Grant *(Episode 7.17: Questions and Answers)*, Oscar Mayer *(Episode 4.18: Fiddler on the Ropes)*, Metamucil *(Episode 2.10: Love, Rose)*, "The Farmer in the Dell" *(Episode 7.6: Mother Load)*

References Index

Episode Title Index

ABOUT THE AUTHOR

Matt Browning is a lifelong *Golden Girls* fan and aficionado. In 1998 he founded EmptyNestTV.com, which gets thousands of visits per month and has nearly six thousand Facebook and Twitter followers. He lives in South Charleston, West Virginia. Learn more at MattBrowningBooks.com.